To Frank Keegan
with best wishes

with '88.

ALFRED BADER

Adventures of a
Chemist Collector

ALFRED BADER

Adventures of a
Chemist Collector

WEIDENFELD AND NICOLSON
London

For Isabel

First published in Great Britain in 1995 by
George Weidenfeld & Nicolson Limited
Orion House
5 Upper St Martin's Lane
London WC2H 9EA

British Library Cataloguing in Publication Data
A catalogue for this book is available
from the British Library
ISBN 0 297 83461 4

Contents

Introduction

Alfred Bader is a remarkable man. No one can know him or read this autobiography without being impressed by his achievements and moral character: by the extraordinary way he was able to build a widely renowned chemical company through combining strong professional qualifications with personal attention to the needs of his employees, suppliers and customers; by his scholarly approach and discerning judgment in his lifelong appreciation of art, especially that of the Northern Baroque period; by his wit and kindness, and by his warmth and generosity in human relations.

His early years severely tested his capacity to survive and grow as an individual. The economic and political maelstrom that swept Europe prior to World War II disrupted his family relationships and exposed him, as an Austrian Jew, to the terrible persecutions associated with the rise of the Nazis. Sent to refuge in England at the age of 14, he did not fully escape. Soon after the outbreak of War, in response to the general fear, voiced by Churchill, that there might be enemy agents among the Europeans recently arrived in Britain, Alfred was deported to Canada and interned in a harsh camp south of Montreal. He was just 16. But even such gross unfairness in his youth failed to turn him into a bitter person. Instead it apparently released creative energies. (This characteristic was to be revealed clearly again in his later life when he suffered injustice in his abrupt removal from a company he had done so much to create and sustain.)

Perseverance in his studies in the internment camp and a fortuitous contact with Montreal relatives of a family he had met in England helped lead him to Queen's University, where he shone academically and developed broader aspects of his abilities, including his speaking and debating skills. Graduate studies at Harvard demonstrated his competence as a research chemist and opened doors to future contacts helpful in the subsequent development of his international company.

The story of the building of the company is not a dry case study. It is filled with human drama, and the technical descriptions of chemical substances and experiments are not a serious barrier to the non-scientist seeking insights into how he achieved success. (Nevertheless, readers like me may quietly wish they had studied more science.)

There is a sadness about the actions of the company's Board in sev-

7

ering all ties upon his retirement. However, as in his youth, reverses seem to energize him. His activity as an art collector and lecturer has flourished. His generous gifts for the benefit of future students and scholars have been impressive. Indeed, Queen's University has been among his major beneficiaries and, as Principal and Vice-Chancellor at the time of the gift of Herstmonceux Castle in England for an international study centre, I can attest personally to his vision and commitment to assisting others to share in the advantages of an excellent education based on international standards and perspectives.

It is the man himself who captivates one, both in person and here on paper. Grounded in deep religious faith and close family relationships, particularly with his beloved Isabel, Alfred Bader has applied his many talents constructively and with a strong sense of responsibility to helping others. What a wonderful difference his life makes!

David C. Smith
Queen's University
Autumn 1994

1
Childhood

When I was close to 70, in 1991, my wife Isabel and I decided to visit Kyjov in Moravia to try to find some traces of the Bader family, since I knew there were no family members in Vienna, where I was born. My father's family had come from Kyjov, or Gaya as it was then, and although I had been to Czechoslovakia many times as a child and again since the war, I had never tried to trace my roots.

The previous year we had, in fact, visited the castle in Milotice, also in southern Moravia, because until the 19th century it had belonged to the family of my mother, Elisabeth Serényi. Although I had seen pictures of the castle, which has been a museum for the last forty-five years, I had felt no desire to visit it until a cousin, Nicholas Serényi, told me it was well worth seeing. He thought I would be particularly interested in the paintings there, most of them of our ancestors. Isabel has always been closer to her family than I to mine, perhaps because I had known so few relatives, even before the war, so encouraged by her and in the hope of seeing some good paintings, we went to Milotice. The castle, in extensive grounds, is in fairly good condition, and it certainly makes an interesting museum. It contains beautiful frescoes, but the family portraits are third-rate. Why none of Mama's ancestors chose competent portrait painters I cannot imagine, but there were two or three good historical paintings that made the visit worthwhile and the Moravian countryside is certainly beautiful.

As we drove away, we did not notice the signpost: "Kyjov 5 kilometers." Had we done so, we would certainly have gone straight there, but luckily we did set out the following year with the intention of visiting the place, and with the help of a good Czech friend, Vladimir Matous, who was able to make inquiries for us, we found the last Bader in Kyjov. Vera Bader was saved from the gas chambers in Auschwitz because her mother had managed to pull her off the transport that carried her father and brother to their deaths. Now married with a son and grandchildren, Vera was as happy to meet us as we were to meet her. She thought that none of her relatives had survived the war. I could hardly have expected to find her only five kilometers from Milotice. My ancestors had lived in worlds apart. The Baders were middle-class Jews, and the Serényis were devout Catholic aristocrats. I wonder whether they ever met each other, what they would have thought of the marriage of my parents, and what they would think of my life and adventures.

9

I was born in Vienna on April 28, 1924, the son of Alfred and Elisabeth Bader, given the names Alfred Robert, and called Bobby as a child. My father and his sister, Gisela, were the only children of Moritz Ritter von Bader and his wife Hermine, née Freund. I know very little about my grandfather Bader's family, except that they lived in Gaya, where Moritz was born. For a young Jew, he had a most unusual education, studying civil engineering at the Technische Hochschule in Vienna and at the Ecole des Ponts et Chaussées in Paris. On graduation, he joined Ferdinand de Lesseps in the building of the Suez Canal and was later knighted by Emperor Franz Josef for his services as Austrian consul in Ismailia. He died in 1894 from the after effects of malaria contracted either in Egypt or during his extensive travels from Ethiopia to Palestine and Syria. His wife, who was born in Prague of a large middle-class Jewish family, survived him by over thirty years. I can still remember Grossmutter Hermine as a stately old lady living with us in Vienna; she died when I was three years old.

Mama's family was almost unknown to me as a boy. She was the daughter of Count Johann Nepomuk Serényi and Irma, Countess Dessewffy, with family estates in Hungary. The only photographs I have of my grandfather and of one of his brothers are typical of Hungarian noblemen in most uncomfortable uniforms. Another brother, Bela, was Hungarian Minister of Agriculture for many years. I remember Mama taking me to the Stefansdom in Vienna and pointing out the memorial tablet of a direct ancestor, Count Johann Carl Serényi, a field marshal who had defended Vienna against the Turks in 1683. Yet I never lived with Mama and never met a single member of her family while I was a child. When I tried later to find out more about her family, my sister Marion, two years older than I, was little help. She had so disliked what she had been told and had been so very unhappy on the one occasion she had met grandmother Irma that she simply did not want to know about them.

Mama had three brothers. I did meet Miklos, after the war when he and his family came to America, and I have since got to know my cousins, including a number in Hungary. They are all intelligent people, not, I believe, infected by the prejudices of previous generations. I also discovered that one relative on my father's side, Franz Bader, was a distinguished dealer in modern American art in Washington, DC. His family also came from Kyjov and we believe that our grandparents were brothers. I thought it a pity that he had no interest in old masters; I would have loved to become his good customer. He was an excellent photographer. Some of his photographs, taken with a simple camera, have recently been exhibited. I only wish that I had taken more photographs of my family and friends over the years. Sadly Franz died aged 90 in September 1994.

10

My parents met in a sanatorium, where Mama was recuperating from a nervous breakdown after an unhappy marriage that had been annulled. When she fell in love with my father, a Jew, her parents objected violently and tried to have her committed to an asylum, so she and my father eloped in 1912 and were married in London. After the wedding Mama was rejected by her family, although her parents eventually gave her a small allowance.

By all accounts, Mama was a woman of great physical charm, attractive to men. I have been told that she was unfaithful to my father, who has been described as a charming, shiftless gambler, dependent on the kindness of his sister Gisela Reich. As a boy, I was given to understand that he committed suicide two weeks after I was born, but I have since learned that in fact he may have been murdered. Mama was left with almost nothing to support herself and two small children at the height of the extraordinary inflation raging in Austria after the First World War.

My aunt Gisela, who adored my father, tried to persuade Mama to let her adopt both me and my sister Marion. For many years I had so little understanding of, or real interest in, Mama that I never considered the turmoil she must have suffered. What possibility did she have of providing a living for her family? She had been brought up to be a lady but had been cut off from her family, and had no skills whatever with which to earn money. The future must have seemed bleak and frightening. Gisela at the time was a wealthy, childless widow and her offer must have been tempting. Yet Mama refused to give us both up, saying that my sister was not in fact a Bader. True or not, she must have wanted at least to keep her daughter, while seeing an opportunity to give her son a better chance in life. Gisela adopted me officially and, just as she had helped my father financially until his death, she made a financial settlement on his widow, who was always "Mama" to me, while Gisela was Muttili, whom I regarded as "Mother".

The effect of this adoption has been crucial in my life. My sister had a strict Catholic upbringing, against which she reacted strongly because of her experiences in a convent school and her awareness of hypocrisy among many Catholics in Vienna. I was brought up with a love of Judaism. What I learned of the way Mama's parents had treated her made me dislike them. When I was little, I was always disturbed when, on the rare occasions I saw her, Mama made a sign of the cross on my forehead and told me that anyone who could be a Catholic but who chose not to be was sure to go to hell. As I grew older this question of religion really troubled me. There was so much anti-semitic propaganda in the form of hideous pictures and caricatures of Jews. After the Anschluss, showcases all over Vienna displayed horror stories about us. As I read them, there were times when I wondered whether some of them might actually be true. Could Mama be right? Yet I knew a great many Jews. All my friends were Jews and none of them was anything like these monsters. The Nazis around us were the monsters. My life was full of warmth and love from Mother and the good, kind people within the small Bader family of relatives and friends. I believe that my efforts to struggle with this question, to convince myself of the rightness of Judaism for me, has been a cornerstone of my life. It has made me want to learn a lot about Judaism and Christianity. Jews have not often been missionaries, yet perhaps my struggle to understand has made me just that, at least to the women in my life.

Sigmund Reich, Mother's husband, must have been a very astute businessman. He had come to Vienna from Hungary as a poor youngster and ended up as managing director of one of Austria's largest oil companies, the Russian American Oil Company, which now sounds so incongruous. Mother often told me that if only we had not lost the war, the oil fields in Rumania and Persia would have been ours. Sigmund was short, fat and bald, whereas Gisela was tall and beautiful; they must have made an odd couple. Apparently he was an inordinately jealous husband, surely without reason. When he died during a gall-bladder operation in 1922, Mother was ill-equipped for widowhood. She was not particularly well educated, and her husband had taught her nothing at all about his business affairs or his investments. Despite her great wealth, she had no idea how to cope alone.

I have never known anyone who lived in the past as entirely as Mother. She was incredibly proud of my grandfather Bader's accomplishments and, according to her, everyone in the family, including my father, had been angelic. She always wore black after her husband's death, and I never remember her showing the slightest interest in any other man. Her life was firmly fixed in *den guten, alten Zeiten*, the good old days before the war in the time of the monarchy. Every Sunday she and I made a pilgrimage to the cemetery to visit the grave of her parents and my father, all buried together in one plot, and the large mausoleum of her husband nearby. On each visit we said the Kaddish and added small stones to the graves, an old Jewish custom.

Mother had little idea how to bring up children, nor was she a good housekeeper. She had never learned to cook, sew or do anything practical, and while her husband was alive, she had always had servants to do these things. Responsibility for my upbringing was in the hands of two elderly ladies—Mother, who was 50 when she adopted me, and Tante Helene, my grandmother Bader's sister, then in her seventies, whose husband had committed suicide in Berlin after a stock market crash. My memories of Tante Helene are faint, although I recall that she worried me time and again by telling me that no woman would ever marry me if I continued to blow my nose as loudly as I did.

Mother was assisted by Hilda Kozak, a fat, cheerful woman who had been hired as a governess but stayed on to do everything in the house. She was still cooking, cleaning and looking after me long after Mother could afford to pay her. Hilda came from a large Jewish family in Miroslav, a small village in Moravia. Her husband was an Austrian major who had been badly wounded in the First World War. Although a Catholic, he was divorced from his first wife. He did not seem very bright to me, but he must have been a kindly man, for two of Hilda's sisters lived with them in the thirties, and certainly his pension must have been very helpful. I looked on Hilda and her only child, Willy, born in 1929, as part of my family and also got to know and love her brothers and sisters, the Herzogs.

Mother and Hilda spoiled me terribly. They fed me far too much—rolls with more butter than bread and cakes galore—so I was very overweight and hopeless at gym. That was the beginning of my pot belly which has stayed with me all my life. Other children poked fun at me for being so fat and refused to play with me. My shape improved a little at around age 10, partly because of my love for soccer, which I played whenever possible, and partly because of a lack of money, which put butter, cream cakes and sweets beyond my reach.

Mother worried about me constantly. God forbid that I should come home from the Prater, Vienna's amusement park, a few minutes late in the afternoon. She would be on the balcony, wringing her hands and looking anxiously in the direction of the park in case something had happened to me.

We lived in the Praterstrasse, the wide street leading to the Prater. Our first-floor apartment was crammed with paintings, antique furniture and carpets. It had several balconies from which we could watch the many Catholic processions and political parades—including Adolf Hitler's when he came to Vienna in 1938. When I was very small, there was still plenty of money, but by the time I was 9 or 10 I realized that Mother was in serious financial trouble. There was no trustworthy friend to whom she could turn. Her attorney, Leopold Plaschkes, a prominent Viennese politician, advised her to put what little capital remained into mortgages on Viennese coffee houses. The interest rates were high, but the coffee houses failed in the depression and we had to make severe economies. Our lifestyle changed dramatically.

Our villa in Baden, near Vienna, was sold for very little. Few people wanted to buy a villa in the early thirties, not even one with a lovely garden. Antique dealers came to the house but nothing seemed to please them, although they wanted to buy everything for a pittance. Our apartment was divided to save rent, so we lost the bathroom and had to make do with perfunctory cold-water washes. We also lost one bedroom, and I had to sleep with my mother in the salon. This was a beautiful room, originally full of carpets, paintings and pieces of French-style rococo furniture which were gradually sold off one by one.

Mother was always incredibly generous. I remember how embarrassed I was in my first year at school when our teacher in the Volksschule called me to his desk, compared my good clothes to the shabby ones of some of the other children, and told me to tell my mother to send some money to buy them decent outfits. She duly obliged. A few years later, when I was at the Gymnasium, the situation was reversed; it was my clothes that were so well worn. Even when Mother could no longer afford it, her generosity knew no bounds. Beggars would come to the house regularly and groups of musicians would play in the courtyard hoping that listeners would throw them a few Groschen. Mother always kept some change on the windowsill and would often wrap a few coins in newspaper so that they were easy to pick up. There were all sorts of scroungers, all with good causes, but she never turned a single one away, until she literally had nothing left.

I remember little about my first school in the Czerningasse, where Herr Lehrer Strehli was my teacher for all four years, from 1930 until 1934. Apart from the episode with the clothes, there is only one thing that really stands out in my memory. In my fourth year, Herr Strehli discovered that I had a mental flaw. I could not follow more than three letters at a time if a word was spelled out to me, and I had the same difficulty with numbers. I still have trouble when a word is spelled out, but fortunately I can remember thousands of paintings and their locations, and I remember the melting points of even more compounds. Herr Strehli, however, wondered whether I should go to a school for retarded children. Mother was all the more concerned because, just the week before, Kurt Stavenhagen, a distant relative on the Freund side, had expressed a similar thought. The Austrian photographic company, Voigtlander, was offering a box camera for 10 Austrian Schillings, and Uncle Kurt had given me that princely sum to buy a camera for my tenth birthday. Instead, I used the money to buy an old master drawing, which I have since given to the Minneapolis Institute of Art. When Uncle Kurt heard what I had done, he suggested that Mother take me to a child psychologist, who talked to me, admired the drawing and then reassured her that buying a drawing instead of a camera was a matter of taste and that I would learn to live with my mental flaw, which was unrelated to intelligence.

Uncle Kurt was determined that I have a camera, and on his next visit brought me one, complete with film. When I took my pictures for development, I was asked whether I wanted positives or negatives. My obvious question was, "Which is cheaper?" "Why, negatives of course." So I opted for negatives and got ghostly, celluloid nothings. That experience put me off photography for many years, although I was careful not to relate these experiences when visiting Eastman Kodak years later.

In 1934 I entered the Sperlgymnasium, a high school not far from my home, where I remained until July 1938 when I was forced to leave, as Jewish students were forbidden to stay at school beyond the age of 14. There were about thirty students in each class, most of us Jews. The teachers ranged from incompetent to superb. The worst was Herr Professor Prem, who "taught" mathematics and was also our Klassenlehrer. He was our first teacher every morning, had to take attendance and supervise academic details. I blame him for my incompetence in math. In the summer of 1949, I visited him and asked him whether he remembered me; I had, after all, been in his class from 8 o'clock to 9 in the morning of every school day for four years. He shook his head—how could he possibly remember one of the many students he had taught?

Herr Professor Sedlmayer was a different kind of teacher altogether. He brought German poetry and prose to life, and I owe it to him that my written German is still almost perfect. To use the dative instead of the accusative in an essay was cause for a *nichtgenügend*, a failing grade, but Sedlmayer was not just strict, he also made it clear that he really wanted us to do well. Knowing that, we all tried. Everybody cheated with Professor Prem. Only one of us would do the homework, the others just copied it. Nobody ever cheated in Professor Sedlmayer's class, and we all considered it a great honor to be asked to read our essays aloud. Later I learned that he had been a member of the Nazi party, although that never seemed to influence his fair treatment of his Jewish students. After the war he retired to Wiener Neustadt, a small town near Vienna. He remembered me clearly when I visited him in 1949, and told me sadly that he had expected something quite different under National Socialism.

At first there were four of us in the Gymnasium who did everything together, until Harry Gozlan, a Sephardic Jew, whose father dealt in sponges from North Africa, died of leukemia when he was only 12 and then we were just three. Hansi Hoefler, Felix Landau and I spent most of our free time together between 1934 and 1938. Years later I met them again. By this time Hansi had become a toolmaker in Chicago, and Felix a dealer in modern art in Los Angeles. I discovered that we had little in common except our childhood memories.

School ended at 1 pm and after a hasty lunch we would dash off to play soccer in the Prater. This was against the law, but that never bothered us unless two policemen teamed up to catch us. Whenever only one policeman appeared, we would just run away and resume our game when he was out of sight. I was only caught once and Mother had to pick me up at the police station. I felt miserable.

My favorite soccer teams were Austria and Hakoah, the Jewish team that had surprisingly won the Austrian championship once, the year I

15

was born. The great disappointment of 1934 was the defeat of the Austrian Wunderteam by England, 4-3 on December 7, after a run of some forty wins. I have not seen a soccer game in years, but I can still remember that team; Hiden in the goal, Rainer and Schmaus the backs, Sindelar, *der Papierene*, the center forward, and Vogel on the outside were my heroes. I would love to have been a good soccer player, but I was too slow and clumsy, although years later I was good enough to play right back on the Queen's University team in Canada.

Besides soccer, we played two games inspired by it. One, played mainly during breaks in the Sperlgymnasium, was called *Knieball*, or knee-ball. Two opposing players, or sometimes teams, faced each other. The ball was a tightly wadded brown paper bag. One player would bounce it off his knee and then try to shoot it into the other's goal. As we grew more adept, we tried to keep it in the air with our feet, as a juggler would with his hands, before the final shot. I remember my last game on our last day in the Sperlgymnasium—Hansi Hoefler's and my way of celebrating our very last day in school.

The other game, called *Knopfball*, or button ball, was played at home, mainly on winter evenings. All you needed was a large table and two teams of eleven buttons each, as well as a small shirt button as a ball. The goalie was one very large button, the other ten usually smaller flat buttons that could be moved easily on the table to shoot the "ball" into the goal. We raided the button boxes of our mothers and female relatives to find just the right assortment.

Some of my spare time was taken up with reading. My mother loved Victorian novels, her favorite being *The Channings* by Mrs Henry Wood, which she read in German. It was the first long novel I read and enjoyed. When I was about 10, I discovered the adventure stories of Karl May—some sixty of them which I read from cover to cover two or three times. The first six dealt with a German explorer and his Arab guide, Hadschi Halef Omar Ben Hadschi Abul Abbas Ibn Hadschi Dawuhd al Gossarah, who got in and out of all sorts of scrapes in the Middle East. Then there were the Wild West stories of Winnetou and old Shatterhand, and best of all was the story of the ongoing enmity between a German and a French family from Napoleonic times to the Franco-Prussian War of 1870. Years later I learned to my amazement that Karl May had never even visited the Middle East, but had written many of these exciting stories while in prison for Socialist agitation. What an imagination!

When I was 6 or 7, Emil Bader, my *Vormund* or legal guardian, a distant cousin and editor of the *Wiener Tagesblatt*, gave me a stamp album with some stamps. From then on I was hooked on collecting. As I grew older and money became tighter and tighter, paradoxically I became more and more involved. Karl May's adventure stories were replaced by the Michl stamp catalog, which I studied for many hours in the hope of becoming a knowledgeable dealer.

Until I was 10, our holidays were identical. On August 2 we left Vienna for Grado, an Adriatic resort between Venice and Trieste, where we stayed for three weeks. The journey itself was fun. It started early in the morning with the first of my two taxi rides of the year, to the Südbahnhof, and grew more and more interesting as the train climbed higher and higher in the Alps. By the time we arrived in Grado late at night, I was dead tired. Grado itself was a bore because the four of us, Mother, Hilda, Willy and I spent all our time on the beach, and Mother carefully timed my stay in the water: one minute the first day, two the second and so on. Mosquitoes at night made falling asleep difficult and the only redeeming features of the hotel were the ice cubes in the drinking water and real toilet paper—luxuries unknown in our apartment in Vienna. There we used newspaper, which was harder, although more instructive if read before use.

My real holiday began on August 22 when we travelled from Grado to Neuberg an der Mürz, a town in Styria where my grandparents Bader had taken Mother and my father in the 1880s. We always stayed in the Hotel Post, right on the ice-cold River Mürz. There was no bathing, but there were some lovely walks up into the mountains on either side of the river, fields full of cyclamen to delight the eye and wild strawberries to be discovered and eaten, as well as lovely views when we reached the mountain tops. Many years later I took my wife Danny and our sons and then my wife Isabel and our good friends, the Löw-Beers and the Rosners, to Neuberg, where I relived the pleasures of my childhood. Unfortunately Mother told me on our holiday in 1934 that we would probably not be returning the following year because the trip was too expensive. I still remember lying in an Alpine field for a long time that September afternoon, watching the clouds and wondering where they and I were going.

In fact, the next few summers were far more fun. Hilda took Willy and me to visit her family home in Miroslav, half way between the Moravian capital, Brno, and Znojmo on the Austrian border. Two of Hilda's brothers, Hans and Robert Herzog, still lived at home with their mother. They had a wonderfully exciting business, or at least so it seemed to me. They used to travel from village to village on a set weekly schedule, visiting butchers to buy the skins of slaughtered animals and supplying leather to all the village shoemakers. Robert allowed me to go with him in his open truck while Hans, the elder brother, stayed at home. I know far more villages in that area than anywhere else in the world. I helped load and unload the hides, salt them and store them in the spacious cellar of the Herzog home. Of course the place had a strong smell—others might have found it revolting, but to me it was the scent of hard work. Twice a year, a tanner from Nikolsburg called to buy the

17

entire stock after vigorous bargaining which lasted most of the day. Payment was partly in cash and partly in leather to be sold.

It was not all work, although I found it so exciting that I would not have minded if we had collected skins every day. There were day trips to the fabulous Mazocha caves and to the castle in Brno. We also made some two-day journeys to Prague where we roamed through the Jewish quarter, looked at the cemetery and the Altneuschul, the synagogue dating back to the Middle Ages, and I managed to buy some drawings, usually for 5 Czech crowns each. I had the choice of spending 5 crowns on a drawing or on ten ice cream cones, and I usually bought the drawings, many of which I still have.

Another of Hilda's brothers, Dr Arnold Herzog, was an eminent medical man. I remember how proudly Hilda spoke about his research. He and his family died in Buchenwald in the last days of the war. Their youngest sister, Nellie, a beautiful girl, was the mistress of a Nazi officer who had promised to shield her but did nothing. Hilda's son, Willy, survived the war, protected by the church, in which he was very active.

Robert and Hans were sincere and idealistic Communists. They assured me that once the Communists took over, Mother would have all she needed, as would all widows and orphans. When the Nazis invaded Czechoslovakia, Robert and Hans escaped to Britain where they joined the Czech Legion. They returned to Miroslav in 1945, but when the Communist Party assumed power three years later, Robert, a very outspoken fellow, protested that Communism in practice differed from the idealism preached. He was promptly convicted of anti-state activities and given six months' hard labor in a mine. Hans and his family emigrated to Israel, but Robert stayed in Miroslav. He and his wife, Edith, a survivor of Auschwitz, were the last Jews in what was once a thriving Jewish community.

Although a professed Communist, Robert taught me a great deal about business. He had a superb rapport with his customers, the cobblers in the Moravian villages, and I found the days of bargaining with the tanner from Nikolsburg a thrilling experience that has proved invaluable to me in my own business dealings.

If my business education started with Robert Herzog, my religious education began much closer to home. Between the wars there were 200,000—300,000 Jews living in Vienna, a large number of them in the Leopoldstadt, Vienna's second district, which for this reason was then often called the *Matzesinsel*, the island of matzah or unleavened bread. Many were recent arrivals from former provinces of the Austro-Hungarian Empire, mainly Galicia and Bukovina. My mother was convinced of the rightness of Judaism, lit candles on Friday evenings, never ate pork, taught me to say the Shema before falling asleep and the Kaddish at the cemetery. She had not however had a good Jewish education. Luckily, in the apartment above us, was a family of orthodox Hungarian Jews, the Mayers, who had a strong influence on my religious life. David Mayer, a well-to-do textile manufacturer, and his wife had three children, Gustav, Piry and Lilly. Lilly, the younger daughter, was the first girl I ever thought of as beautiful. The Mayers were wonderful neighbors and invited me for dinner many Friday evenings and both evenings of the Seder at Passover.

To me, the Sederim were the high points of the year. I usually went to the Mayers' apartment well before David Mayer, his son Gusti and some of their guests arrived from the services of the Schiffschule, the orthodox Hungarian synagogue they attended. Everything in the house was festive, especially the large tables with candelabra, flowers, the Seder plate and the cups for wine, with the largest cup set aside for Elijah the prophet. I was only worried in case I might make a mistake in the *Ma Nishtana*, the four questions traditionally asked by the youngest. David Mayer sang the entire Hagadah, the singing interspersed with long discussions about religious points and interpretations between Gusti, home from Yeshiva, his father and the guests, who included erudite, orthodox strangers whom Mr Mayer had just met in the Schiffschule. "Let all who are hungry come and eat" had real meaning in the Mayer household. Halfway through the Seder, the meal was served—and what a meal it was! Mrs Mayer's specialty was shadroe in jelly, the like of which I have never tasted anywhere else. This was followed by soup with matzah balls that melted in the mouth, delicious chicken with all the trimmings, tea and cake. The Seder ended just before midnight. Paradise could not have been better. Sadly, Mother never came with me although I am sure that the Mayers invited her. She knew the Shema, the Kaddish and the blessing over candles, but she could not read Hebrew, apart from which, she once explained to me, she would have felt out of place, because they were so orthodox.

The Mayers helped to shape my religious life. Although I did not go to the Schiffschule, studied very little Hebrew in the Gymnasium, attended services in a large conservative synagogue only irregularly and gave little thought to religion, I so admired the Mayers that they must have become role models for me. I have been to many Sederim since, some of them very orthodox, but have found none as moving as those at the Mayer household. In the 1950s and 1960s, I invited all my Sunday School students who did not have a Seder at home to come to our Seder, which we tried to model after that of the Mayers. Many of my students have since told me how they remember the Seder in our home. The influence of the Mayers has passed on to another generation.

Mother and Hilda were my family. I saw little of Mama and my sister Marion when I was small, although they did visit us. In 1930 Mama married Josef Newman, a nasty character who, I later learned from my

19

sister, treated Mama horribly. He was a member of the Austrian Nazi party when membership was illegal. After the Anschluss, he became an *Arisierer*, a man who worked in Jewish-owned companies until he had learned the business and then threw out the Jewish owners. He tried to rape my beautiful sister Marion, who dreamed of becoming an actress, and despite his Nazi prominence, was jailed for several months. Little did I realize how lucky I was to have escaped ever living in that household.

In my early teens, the Newmans lived in Hitzing, on the other side of Vienna, and Mama sometimes gave me 70 Groschen for the tram tickets to visit her. I would walk for two hours one way to save the fare. In the winter I would spend 5 Groschen for a hot baked potato at one of the open air stands—more to warm my hands by shifting it from one pocket to the other than to fill my stomach. I never considered the cost of the shoe leather. The first thing that happened on each visit was an invitation to take a bath, by then a great luxury in my life. Only later did it dawn on me that the reason for the invitation may have been that I was dirty and smelly. When I was very little, before I started school, we had a bathtub and, every Thursday evening, Hilda would lift me into a hot bath and we would celebrate the event by having a delicious frankfurter. By the time of my visits to Hitzing, we had of course lost our bathroom, so hot baths were a distant memory. It didn't seem to matter; Hilda was far too busy to do a good job cleaning and I grew up seeing bed bugs every time I moved the mattress.

During my last year in Vienna Mother tried to earn a few Schillings by making bunches of imitation flowers from plastic pieces supplied to her by a store. I often tried to help her and have hated plastic flowers ever since. Twenty years earlier she had been a multi-millionairess, now she was grateful to receive the 30 Groschen for every bunch that sold. What a sad occupation for a woman of such grace and kindness who had always been so generous!

Between July and December 1938, when I was no longer allowed to go to school, I had time on my hands and became even more seriously involved in philately. I wandered from dealer to dealer, and scanned the newspapers for collections for sale, hoping to earn a little money, most of which I used to buy basic foods. I made friends with Dr Ferdinand Wallner, a well-known Viennese stamp dealer, the world expert on old Greek stamps. He helped me enormously by giving me stamps on consignment, buying from me and teaching me about fakes. My involvement grew and years later, in Hove, then at Queen's, at Harvard and in my first few years in Milwaukee, I was still buying and selling stamps. Almost 60 years later, as I wander from art dealer to art dealer in London, I realize that this is not very different from my dealing in 1938, except that paintings are much more fun and the stakes are higher. In

Vienna, I also had my personal collection of Austrian stamps, of which I was very proud, and I still wear two hats, buying paintings both for my own collection and for sale.

From the time of Hitler's rise to power in Germany, Mother often discussed events there with our relatives and friends. How could this horror happen—and in Germany of all places, the bastion of culture? Yet when Hitler marched into Vienna on his birthday, April 20, 1938, and half of Vienna's population greeted him with tears of joy in their eyes, "*Der Führer kommt*", Mother was shattered. Would she consider leaving Austria for Palestine, Britain, any country that would accept us? The answer was always a firm no; she was an Austrian patriot, truly a *Lokalpatriot*, a woman born in Vienna who loved the city.

After the Kristallnacht, the Nazi attack on synagogues throughout greater Germany in November 1938, the British government allocated 10,000 visas to allow Jewish children between the ages of 12 and 16 to enter Britain. Mother applied for me to go, but still refused to consider leaving Austria herself.

In the first week of December we were informed that I was to be included in the first Kindertransport leaving on Saturday evening, December 10. Mother had a distant relative on the Freund side, Mrs Bessy Emanuel, who lived in England, and she wrote to her asking her to help me. In fact Bessy and her husband Moritz helped hundreds of Jewish refugees, and she arranged for Mrs Wolff, an elderly lady, to pay a guinea a week for my room and board. I had no idea of this when I left Vienna.

Each child was allowed to take one small suitcase, but practically no German money. Mother gave me one American dollar, which she had once received from a friend. I visited Dr Wallner to discuss which stamps might be most valuable in England, and traded some of my Austrian stamps for those of greater interest to British collectors. I hid my personal stamp collection in my case, hoping it would not be confiscated by the Germans. In the last few days I said goodbye to friends, and spent as much time as I could with Mother.

At 9 pm that Saturday we were on Vienna's Westbahnhof for a tearful goodbye—Mother, Mama, Hilda and I, surrounded by hundreds of children with their parents and relatives. We hugged each other for the last time. I hurried into a carriage, found a seat by the window, and leaned out to wave as the train pulled quickly out of the station. I looked back until I could no longer make out the group of three people I had left behind. Hilda died of cancer during the war; Mother was forced to leave her apartment and go to a Jewish old people's home, then in June 1941 was taken to Theresienstadt, the Nazi concentration camp near Prague, where she died five months later; Mama died after a stroke in 1948. It was just as well that, as I said goodbye to them that evening at the station, I had no idea that I would never see them again.

There was no one I knew in the carriage. I had long been unhappy to be called Bobby, because there were two large dogs living near us with that name, and there were hundreds of "Count Bobby" jokes going the rounds at that time in Vienna. As I settled down to sleep, I determined that I would use my first name, Alfred, in the future. When I awoke in the morning we were travelling through central Germany. There were occasional stops, and finally we realized that we were following the Rhine. Early on Sunday evening we reached the German/Dutch border, where German customs officials went through the train. Fortunately their inspection was very cursory. The train moved into The Netherlands where we were welcomed by a delegation of Jewish women with flowers, chocolate and candy. At last we were out of Germany. At Hoek van Holland we boarded a ship that arrived in Harwich, England, on Monday morning.

From there we were taken to Dovercourt, a holiday camp near Lowestoft, where we slept in pleasant, but unheated, cabins, clearly unsuitable for December weather. After a few days, we were moved to a nearby school, which was empty during the Christmas holidays. There it was discovered that several of us had caught measles, so we were taken to the Lowestoft Isolation Hospital. I remember little about that week except the awful daily tapioca pudding, which looked like oysters and tasted like nothing, but how pleasant it was to have a young, red-headed nurse make my bed and tuck me into it. This was my first fleeting contact with a girl, except for my sister, who didn't count, and Lilly Mayer whom I had admired at a distance.

From the hospital, I was sent to a rooming house in Westcliff-on-Sea, near Southend, joining other boys who had been in the Lowestoft holiday camp. Our hope was that we would soon be adopted by an English family and be able to work or continue our education. Finally on February 4, about twenty of us were taken to Woburn House in London and told that families had been found and we would be collected that very day. We sat waiting for the door to open and to be called out to meet the person or persons who had agreed to look after us. The wait was agonizing. I had a dreadful cold and could hardly sit still. Hour after hour went by until I was the only one left. Was nobody going to claim me? At last, at 5.30, a rough male voice called out: "Come with me, boy." I was taken by bus to Victoria Station and then by train to Brighton. I had never seen a double-decker bus before and was scared to climb up the steps. I could only stammer, over and over again, the words: "I have a very great cold." Mr Sidney Scharff's roughness was all on the outside, but how was I to know that? I relaxed slightly when his wife, Ethel, welcomed me into their home at 85 Holland Road, Hove. My room was tiny. Sitting on my bed, I could touch all four walls, but the house was full of Ethel's kindness and soon became my home. I learned later that Sidney sold printing of all kinds in London. On a good week, he might clear £2. Ethel supplemented their income by taking in boarders, and they were glad of the guinea a week which Mrs Wolff paid for me.

On the evening I arrived, Ethel gave me the first of many lessons. When she offered me a cup of tea, she asked whether I took sugar. Mother had instructed me many times: "Whenever you are offered anything, you must say 'No, thank you.' Only if your hostess persists may you say, 'Yes, please.'" Clearly Mother and Ethel had not gone to the same school, so when I said, "No, thank you," Ethel took no for an answer and never asked me again. For the next fourteen months, I had to drink tea without sugar, although I much prefer it sweet.

The Scharffs had two daughters. Sonia, the elder, a kind, thoughtful person, was a schoolteacher. Diana, who was about 17, was attending secretarial school and still lived at home. The family also gave room and board to two brothers, Otto and Herbert Marx, Jewish refugees from Westphalia, brought over by their uncle, William Brown, a director at Lyons. I always hoped to meet Herbert after the war, but I understand that he emigrated to Palestine and died there at a young age. I liked Otto less. He later changed his name to Frederick Marsh and eventually joined the army, and then Lyons and advanced rapidly in both. Later, he became a successful entrepreneur and business advisor.

The whole house was held together by the kindness and competence of Ethel Scharff. Sidney came home dead tired in the evenings and spent much of his free time working for the Jewish community. Every Saturday we went to the Middle Street synagogue in Brighton. I certainly admired its minister and Sunday School teacher, the Rev I N Fabricant. I really enjoyed studying Hebrew, and I still treasure a copy of Hertz's Genesis inscribed by the Rev Fabricant "For good work in Hebrew." Nearly 50 years later, in 1989, it gave me much pleasure to put my arms around him when he came to Falmer the day I received my honorary DUniv from the University of Sussex.

One or two Sundays a month I made duty visits to Mrs Sarah Wolff, who paid my board at the Scharffs. She was very deaf and I had to shout into an ear trumpet that looked like a large funnel. She urged me many times to become a rabbi—what a failure I would have been!—and told me in boring detail about her son and six granddaughters in Montreal. What interest could I possibly have in strangers living on the other side of the world?

I was very apprehensive on February 14, 1939, when I started at the East Hove Senior School for Boys on Connaught Road near the gasworks. It was a council school which boys left at 14 to become shop assistants at 25 shillings a week if they were lucky. Yet I really enjoyed

23

it and learned a lot, not academically, but about the British. What an eye-opener! The students were just as badly behaved as the boys in the Sperlgymnasium, but there was absolutely no cheating, and if a teacher asked who had done something, the culprit owned up to it immediately, even though he knew a caning would follow. Any student behaving like that in Vienna would have been considered insane. My respect for the British is based more on my education in that school than on anything else.

The French teacher, Mme Fuller in 3a, was an elderly, very short-sighted English lady with a poor French accent. I had never had French lessons at school, although when I was 4 or 5 Mother had engaged a French teacher for me. My French is very halting, but my accent is good, certainly better than Mme Fuller's. More often than not, the class's attention was riveted on a particularly wild boy masturbating at the back of the class. Mme Fuller was short-sighted; we were not.

In September, I was put into Form 4 with Mr Dimberline as the form master. I have forgotten what subject he taught, but remember his effective tirades against chewing gum and the ungentlemanly practice of putting hands into trouser pockets longer than necessary to extract something, and his lectures about washing carefully behind the ears.

My first honor anywhere was to become a school prefect charged with regulating traffic up and down the stairs during breaks. I had one friend, Tony Alce, a shy lad with bright red hair, who talked to me a lot about stamps during our breaks and on the long class walks over the Downs. I had no pocket money and was jealous of the Marx boys who each had half a crown a week, a princely sum. So I sold stamps to the students. Some I had brought with me from Vienna, others I bought in the Brighton Lanes. I was terrified when I was summoned to attend court on Tuesday, May 14, 1940, accused of earning money contrary to my visa regulations. Many years later, Tony Alce told me that Mr Spowart, a stamp dealer in Queen's Road, Brighton, had told him that he had informed the police of my activities, suggesting that I was a dangerous enemy alien. He must have thought I was serious competition.

I believe the teachers thought well of me, and somehow Mrs Bessy Emanuel managed to have me accepted at Brighton Technical College in January. Perhaps I was helped by the recommendation of Mr George Ralph, the Hove school headmaster. I still have a copy. ". . . in spite of natural handicaps [i.e. I was not British], he . . . made remarkable progress . . . He is very honest and trustworthy . . . I am sure he will make further progress in any type of secondary school." My conduct must have improved in England.

I remember very little about Brighton Technical College, except that I thoroughly enjoyed the drafting, the machine shop and the chemistry, all more challenging work than at the school in Hove, and I no longer had a problem with lack of pocket money. The college was too far for me to go home for lunch, so Mrs Scharff gave me 9d every day to buy lunch. I discovered that the Lyons near the college sold beans and tomato ketchup on toast for 5-1/2d so I was able to save 3-1/2d a day, which came to 1s 5-1/2d a week.

My sixteenth birthday was a very unhappy day. No one in Hove remembered the occasion. But next day, there was a wonderfully long letter from Mother, who wrote to me regularly, even from the old people's home. Her letters always reassured me that she was well and expressed her fears that something terrible might happen to me. I must be sure to listen to my elders, not go swimming too long, avoid this and that. If only I had been in a position to look after her. There is an old Hebrew saying *Secher Zadik livrocho*—"the memory of the righteous is a blessing." I have never forgotten her kindness, nor the horrible way she was treated. Perhaps my railing at injustices of all kinds is prompted by the injustices she suffered.

Sunday, May 12, exactly two weeks after my birthday, was memorable for two events. At 11 am, during the break in Hebrew school at the Middle Street synagogue, I asked a girl for the first date in my life and she accepted. Ten minutes later, two detectives picked me up, drove me home to collect some clothes and a toothbrush and took me to a detention center on the Brighton racecourse. Churchill had become alarmed about the activities of fifth columnists during the invasion of Holland, Belgium and France. How many were there among the thousands of refugees in Britain? "Collar the lot"—all between the ages of 16 and 65. I had just turned 16, and my childhood was over.

2

Internment

The detectives who picked me up were polite and firm: "We are sorry, but under the emergency regulations we have to arrest you." Since I knew that I was to appear in court on May 14 to explain my dealing in stamps, I wondered if this was related, but when I joined the hundreds of other men on Brighton racecourse I realized that it was something quite different.

From Brighton we were taken to a large internment camp in Huyton near Liverpool, where we slept in tents. Food was scarce and poor, and we were surrounded by barbed wire. It rained a lot, the ground got very muddy and our shoes were soon very dirty. Clearly the occupation of choice, at least for a penniless boy of 16, was to polish shoes, which I did for twopence a pair. Of course it wasn't all gravy, because I had to acquire shoe polish, rags and two brushes.

There were quite a few orthodox Jews in the camp, and they kept the Sabbath strictly. Their lives would have been easier if there had been an "*eruv*", a fence around their habitation. They could have carried books, for instance, from tent to tent. Without an *eruv*, carrying was forbidden on the Sabbath. But there was a fence, the barbed wire. If only they owned it, they would have the perfect *eruv*. The leaders of the orthodox group asked the British colonel in charge whether they might purchase the fence. He must have been astounded. Although they explained the reason for their request, he must have feared a trick that would allow them to escape, and refused to sell.

During our time in Huyton there were all sorts of rumors that unmarried "enemy aliens" were to be shipped out of Britain. I believe that some of the unmarried Nazis in the camp tried to exchange papers with married men so that they could remain, because they expected the Germans would soon invade and that they would be liberated.

In June many of us were transported to the Isle of Man, where two barbed-wire camps had been set up around a number of hotels at Douglas and Ramsey. I was put into The Bay, a Victorian hotel right on Ramsey beach. The promenade was not muddy, so shoes did not need shining, but clothes needed washing, and there was a large old-fashioned laundry where a few of us offered to wash clothes for a very modest charge.

In early July some of us received notice that we would be leaving. On the day of our departure I noticed a British lieutenant handing out cigarettes to men he knew. I learned later that he was Lieutenant Ralph Layton, who had gone to Germany in 1938 and 1939 to identify young Jews without foreign relatives. He sponsored several hundred men whom he brought to the Kitchener camp in Kent, where they were awaiting visas to other countries. There were 272 of them among the internees in Ramsey. As we boarded a ship, Layton was in tears, shaking hands with these men, and handing them gifts of thousands of cigarettes—what a man!

We had no idea where we were going. It was only much later that the story of this whole episode was revealed. Fearing an imminent invasion, the British government had decided to ship a number of internees to Canada and Australia, who had agreed to help Britain by receiving prisoners of war. The *Arandora Star* was torpedoed, with the loss of hundreds of lives. The *Ettrick*, on which conditions were horrible, most of its prisoners getting dysentery, was the first ship to reach Canada. I was lucky to sail on the *Sobieski*, which also carried real German prisoners of war—"POWs First Class" as they were called. We were designated "POWs Second Class". Labelling us POWs instead of just enemy aliens assured our admission into camps in Canada.

Conditions on the *Sobieski* were bearable. Most of the older men slept in cabins, but the younger fellows slept on the floor of the bar. Some of the men from the Kitchener camp looked after me, and a strapping cattle dealer, Lachmann, kindly offered me his arm as a pillow every night. It was from him that I learned about Lieutenant Layton and the men from the Kitchener camp, among whom there were forty-nine orthodox Jews.

At first the *Sobieski* was part of a large convoy, but after a few days our ship developed engine trouble and we were left behind—a sitting duck. We were of course afraid, but perhaps the Germans knew that we had Nazis on board, and we were not attacked. The engines were repaired and in due course we sailed into an unknown port, which we learned later was St Johns, Newfoundland. As we continued along a wide river, the geography experts among us concluded that it was the St Lawrence. We disembarked at Quebec City on July 15, jeered by the population, who called us all Nazis. The authorities had decided to keep the 272 Kitchener camp men together, and I was allowed to go along with them. We were told to leave our suitcases on the dock—they would be sent on later—and we travelled by train to the bank of the Richelieu River where a ferry took us across to a fort on the Ile aux Noix.

Fort Lennox had been built before the war of 1812 to defend Canada from American attack. Apparently it had remained unoccupied ever since. Dust was inches deep all over, bats flew out as we entered, the bunks had no mattresses and one of the 20-gallon pails serving as a latrine leaked. As we lined up to enter the camp early in the evening, we were given numbers—I was No 156—and ordered to state name and age. Since I was the youngest, the camp commandant, Major Kippen, called me over and said he was surprised that a 16-year old had parachuted into England. When I told him that I had not parachuted but was a Jewish refugee, he replied that he didn't believe me. "Do not pretend to be a Jew," he said, "I do not like Jews either."

The stone barracks served as our sleeping quarters, kitchen and recreation areas, and we quickly built latrines outside, to improve hygiene. Many of the fellows had been farmers and cattle dealers and some were skilled in carpentry, construction, and cooking. The camp was surrounded by barbed wire, with armed soldiers manning the towers. We elected Martin Fischer, an able fellow of about 30, as our camp leader, and tried to organize life as best we could. Food was good and plentiful, but the fifty orthodox Jews—of whom I was one—refused to eat meat or to work on the Sabbath. At first the officers did not believe we were Jewish. Years later I saw a letter that Major Kippen had written to the Canadian Jewish Congress, asking for a member of the "Jewish clergy" to come to the camp to see whether we really were Jews! An elderly bearded rabbi, Hirsch Cohen, arrived from Montreal, and it took him no time at all to realize who we were. He came in August 1940, just days before the 9th of Ab when Jews commemorate the destruction of the Temple by fasting and not shaving. The officers had taken a dim view of prisoners who refused to shave and had some shaved forcibly. That was no problem for me—I had no beard as yet—but some of the men told Rabbi Cohen about this and other rather horrible experiences. Our luggage had come from Quebec City some days after our arrival, but most of it had been cut open and the contents stolen. Major Kippen gave us slips of paper acknowledging the thefts, but the luggage had been handled by different groups of soldiers and it was difficult to allocate blame. Luckily one of the fellows had carried a small Torah scroll by hand into the camp so not everything important had been lost. The officers had told us that we must do compulsory labor six days a week for 20 cents a day, except "on the Lord's Day as recognized by Canadian legislation". Some of the orthodox who were willing to work on Sunday but refused to work on the Sabbath were put into solitary confinement. Rabbi Cohen sat down on the grass, just inside the barbed wire gate and wept like a boy.

We had a very low opinion of the officers "guarding" us. We considered them insensitive characters who had been totally unprepared for our arrival and had no idea what to do with us. The sergeant major was a brute, and the veteran guards who replaced the first contingent once it was discovered that we were harmless were a sorry lot. In our camp paper *The Lennoxer Tageblatt*, we wrote a spoof on the requirements to be a guard: no more than two teeth, little hair, syphilis preferred.

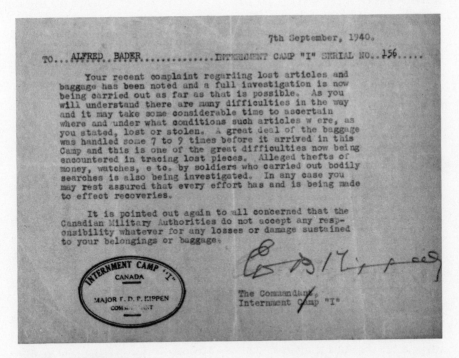

7th September, 1940.

TO... ALFRED. BADER............... INTERNMENT CAMP "I" SERIAL NO..156.....

Your recent complaint regarding lost articles and baggage has been noted and a full investigation is now being carried out as far as that is possible. As you will understand there are many difficulties in the way and it may take some considerable time to ascertain where and under what conditions such articles w ere, as you stated, lost or stolen. A great deal of the baggage was handled some 7 to 9 times before it arrived in this Camp and this is one of the great difficulties now being encountered in tracing lost pieces. Alleged thefts of money, watches, e tc. by soldiers who carried out bodily searches is also being investigated. In any case you may rest assured that every effort has and is being made to effect recoveries.

It is pointed out again to all concerned that the Canadian Military Authorities do not accept any responsibility whatever for any losses or damage sustained to your belongings or baggage.

The Commandant, Internment Camp "I"

Theft acknowledged.

The one *Mensch* was Bruno, a French Canadian sergeant. He was helpful with everything. He brought us wood to build an ark for the Torah, tools for carpentry, and cigarettes for the smokers among us. Many of the fellows doubtless had experience with girls and alcohol, but these were little missed. Cigarettes were different. Many of those distributed by Lieutenant Layton in Ramsey had been stolen with the rest of our belongings, and now the smokers took to following guards, hoping they would throw their butts through the barbed wire into the camp. Sergeant Bruno was the only one who tried to help in every way he could.

Unfortunately he really took a liking to me. We arose at 6.45 am, to be ready for roll call at 8 o'clock after prayers and breakfast, but around 6.00 am, while Julius Kastner in the lower bunk was still fast asleep, Bruno would appear at my bedside and start playing with my penis. He wanted me to go outside the camp with him and walk around the island in the afternoon.

What was I to do? Mother had told me absolutely nothing about sexual matters, nothing about girls and certainly nothing about men. What little I knew was all second- and third-hand, mainly from students in the Sperlgymnasium. I was confused. The sergeant had a wife and six children—he had shown me photographs—and he was such a good person

29

in every other way. I told him I was scared to go outside the barbed wire, that surely it was forbidden. "I can get a permit," he replied, and in self-defense I asked him to get a permit also for my good friend Max Mahler, a young cattle dealer who had been one of the fellows who had urged me to join the group. Clearly Bruno did not want extra company and, to my great relief, did not pursue the matter.

Early that autumn he told us that he was being transferred to another camp, one with POWs First Class. There was a tumultuous goodbye. Many of the prisoners were in tears, but not I. Several of my friends asked me how I could be so heartless and not even look sad at the departure of our best friend, our only friend. They could not know how relieved I was to see him leave. We learned later that he was imprisoned for helping some Germans to escape. If any of us had wanted to escape, it would not have been very difficult because our camp was just a few miles from the American border. To steal a boat and row to the American side of Lake Champlain would not have been impossible, but none of us tried. Some real prisoners of war did escape to the United States, neutral at the time, and returned to Germany.

Since then I have thought about homosexuality and cannot understand the unbending attitude of many people. I have been friends with quite a few homosexuals, particularly art historians. Many of them are kind, caring, intelligent people. What difference does their sexual preference make, except perhaps to alleviate over-population, the world's greatest problem? The Bible condemns sodomy, but surely it cannot condemn homosexuality if it is caused genetically. It took Popes several centuries to admit that the earth was not flat, and only a strong rabbi like Gershom ben Judah could change the laws concerning polygamy. It will take a strong Pope and an equally strong Chief Rabbi in Israel to declare that homosexuality is "God given" and hence not a sin. What is a "sin" is to mislead straight youngsters, and after Sergeant Bruno not one of my homosexual friends ever made advances to me.

The first weeks in the camp were particularly hard because we had no news, no papers or radio. Occasionally the wind blew some scraps of newspapers into the camp which we squirreled away and read carefully. One day in August, by a strange chance, I saw a page from the *Montreal Gazette*. It contained an obituary of Mrs Irene Wolff, daughter-in-law of Mrs Sarah Wolff of Hove, England. This was my Mrs Sarah Wolff! Irene Wolff was survived also by her husband, Martin, and their six daughters. The family lived in Montreal. Of course I wrote to Martin Wolff at once, but my first letters were stopped by the censors.

At first we were all put to work under heavy guard, some in forestry, some farming, or making camouflage nets, all for 20 cents a day. Slowly but gradually, conditions in the camp improved, particularly after Rabbi Cohen's visit. By the autumn more prisoners arrived from other camps, and we were permitted to start a camp school, headed by an able engineer from Siemens in Berlin. As students we worked only half days, keeping the camp clean, unpaid of course. The International Student Service supplied us with textbooks.

Throughout 1940, the officers continued their pressure on orthodox Jews who refused to work on the Sabbath. They posted a copy of a letter that Lieutenant Colonel H Stetham, the acting head of internment operations, sent in November to Camp B in New Brunswick, where most of the orthodox Jews were interned. He wrote strongly about the Jews' lack of cooperation. "Strictly speaking, under existing Canadian legislation, including the Lord's Day Act, it would be quite in order to state that the internees will carry out compulsory labour six days a week and the only day which shall be observed as a day of rest will be the Lord's Day as recognized by Canadian legislation." A list of recalcitrant Jews was to be compiled and forwarded to Stetham's office, ". . . in order that same may be noted in connection with any question that may arise in the future, regarding permission to reside in Canada or to emigrate to other countries other than Palestine." Stetham also threatened that "if any large proportion of the camp population . . . are antagonistic to authority . . . or if they adopt an undesirable attitude, it may be necessary to take away some of the privileges . . ." By November however we were allowed mail, newspapers and a radio, which we enjoyed particularly on Saturday afternoons. Hearing Fidelio, conducted by Bruno Walter with Alexander Kipnis as Rocco and Flagstad in the title role was a delight even to me who had been bored when Mother took me to the opera in the early thirties. Later we even saw movies!

I now know that an influential figure in the Canadian Immigration Service, Frederick Charles Blair, who had successfully kept Jewish immigration into Canada to a trickle, had for a year frustrated any chance we may have had of being released into the community. At the end of 1940 however came the news that we could volunteer to return to England, either to join the Pioneer Corps of the British Army or to work in war industry. Quite a few of the internees applied to return, and I wrote to Mother in Vienna and to Mrs Scharff in Hove for their advice. Neither wanted to decide for me, so I stayed. Major Kippen was replaced as camp commandant, promoted to colonel and given the DSO for his services in guarding Canada against these dangerous POWs Second Class. Major Racey, his successor, was a much more friendly, laid-back fellow. After the war he became an insurance salesman and wrote to each of us to remind us that he had taken good care of us in the camp and wanted to continue looking after us with insurance.

Another turning point was Ralph Layton's visit in February 1941. He had been promoted to major since we had seen him in Ramsey, and his appearance among us was tremendously encouraging. Although other men had joined us and a very few had left, there were still many among us whom he had personally selected in Germany. He made it clear that our status as internees was a dreadful mistake, and we knew that he was doing his best to improve our conditions.

During the next few months a number of internees returned to Britain, and in June 1941 all the orthodox Jews from the camp in New Brunswick joined us on the Ile aux Noix. By that time life had become quite pleasant.

I studied six to eight hours a day, but also went swimming and played soccer. In July 1940 we had been issued prisoner-of-war clothing, rough blue shirts with a big red circle on the back, to facilitate shooting us should we try to escape. Now we were given pieces of blue cloth to sew over the circle, and the camp's designation was changed from prisoner-of-war, first to internment and then to refugee camp. The barbed wire disappeared. Major Racey discovered the joy of having a good German cook in the officers mess and of having his officers and their families painted by a competent artist who used the pseudonym Van Pinto. Major Racey supplied Heymann, aka Van Pinto, with artists materials, so that he was able also to paint some of the prisoners, for one dollar each. I bought my first oil painting from him, inscribed it "*Meiner Teuersten Mutter zu Chanukah 5702*" and sent it to a family friend in New York City to forward to Mother. Unfortunately communication between the US and Nazi Germany broke off after Pearl Harbor, and Mother never received the painting which Rabbi Carlebach returned to me later.

Late in 1940 I became a close friend of a very able young man, Heinrich "Heinz" Wohlauer, who had come with two sisters from Berlin to Birmingham, in England. He returned in February 1941 to take up a 60-hour a week job in a war industry. Heinz was exactly five years older than I and was the very first friend with whom I could discuss everything. I missed him terribly and was elated when I received his birthday greetings from Birmingham in April, ". . . and I shall think of the lone island in a river in Canada where my friends are, and just are celebrating the birthday of one of them, the one whom I liked most. Alfred, become a good and honest man! There are so few about now and the world is in need of them." Sadly, I lost touch with Heinz. I looked for the name Wohlauer in many directories and learned too late that he had changed his name to Henry Warner and died in 1991.

In June 1941 the International Student Service arranged for sixty-four of us to take the McGill matriculation exams in Fort Lennox. A total of 201 Canadian students took the same exams at other examination centers and the *Montreal Gazette* reported the results in July. Ninety-eight Canadians had passed, three with over 800 marks, and eleven over 700. We were able to compare our own scores. Five of us had over 800,

My grandmother, Hermine Bader (née Freund), with Marion and me.

My grandfather, Moritz Ritter von Bader.

Below My grandmother, Irma Serényi (née Countess Dessewffy).

Left My grandfather, Johann Nepomuk, Count Serényi.

Mother, Gisela Reich (née Bader). Painting by Tom von Dreger, 1917.

Mama, at about 16, with her three brothers (left to right), Ladislaus, Johann and Nikolaus.

Mama, at about 30.

Mama, at about 60.

My father.

With Mama and Marion, *c.*1927.

With Marion, *c.*1927.

At the age of 6.

At the age of 8, with Willy Kozak.

David Mayer.

Our salon, 1930.

The Praterstrasse, c.1934.
x – our apartment, the Mayers' above that.
xx – where Josef Loschmidt taught, c.1860.

In Vienna, May 1938.

Ethel, Sidney and Diana Scharff in Hove.

Behind barbed wire on the Ile aux Noix.

Painted in the internment camp.

Studying chemistry in the camp school.

Hillel Foundation executive,
1944–5; Willie Low, top left.

Student branch of the Chemical Institute of
Canada, 1944–5, with Harry Daggett on my right
and Professor Norman Jones, seated.

Graduation, 1945.

With the Wolffs in Westmount.

With Martin Wolff and his first grandson, J J Elkin.

At the Sefardi Synagogue annual ball in 1946 with Rosetta Elkin, Rachel, Esther and Annette.

twenty-five over 700; I had 726 and was very happy. Good teachers and the absence of distractions in the camp really worked for us. We heard that the McGill authorities wondered whether we had been invigilated properly, and when we entered for Senior Matriculation in September they insisted that we sat the examinations in Montreal. Our results were much the same as in June. This first trip from Fort Lennox was great fun. A bus took us to Camp S on St Helen's Island in the St Lawrence River, part of Greater Montreal. After the exam, the Jewish community invited us to a reception and a wonderful dinner at the Montefiore Club, where I met Martin Wolff for the first time. Two veteran guards accompanied us on the ride to the club. They had known for a long time that we would not try to escape, so they left us and asked to be picked up three hours later at the corner of St Catherine and St Lawrence in Montreal's red-light district. They were drunk when we collected them, but the bus ride from there to St Helen's Island was short and uneventful. Within a few weeks Martin Wolff succeeded in gaining my release by sponsoring me.

Looking back on the fifteen months in Fort Lennox, I realize that it was a great time in my life. Of course we were treated badly at first because the Canadians had been given no information about us, but what was that compared with the concentration camps of Europe? Not a single man died in the camp and those who wanted a great education received it.

November 2, 1941 was a red-letter day. It was the day of my release. Before leaving, I had to sign a form renouncing all claims against H M Canadian government—a small price to pay for freedom. I wonder how much longer any of us would have had to wait if we had mentioned the slashed suitcases and stolen belongings. I was also cautioned not to tell anyone where I had been, otherwise I would be sent back to the camp, and I had to report weekly to the local office of the RCMP.

My new home was that of Martin Wolff and his daughters at 442 Argyle Avenue in Westmount, a suburb of Montreal. How I wished that I had listened more carefully to old Mrs Sarah Wolff's descriptions of her family! It took me years to piece the whole story together, but I gathered eventually that young Sarah Andrade, the daughter of a well-known Sephardi clan in England, had married Julius Wolff from Frankfurt, seventeen years her senior. It was an arranged marriage, as was customary, and unfortunately Sarah came to dislike Germany and everything German. Their sons, Joseph and Martin, and a daughter, Rachel, were born in Frankfurt, but Sarah brought them back to England shortly after her husband died. Martin spent four years at Clifton College in Bristol, and after fighting with the British army in the Boer War, emigrated to Canada in 1906. He wanted to become a medical doctor, but his mother forced him to study civil engineering, hoping that he could work with his older brother. However, he was allowed to select his own bride, although his mother hurried out to Canada to inspect his choice. Fortunately she approved of the bride and her parents, and in 1909 Martin married Irene Joseph, the direct descendant of Aaron Hart, who had arrived with General Amherst's army in 1760 and was the first Jew to settle in Canada. The Harts, the Josephs and Martin Wolff were religious Sephardi Jews, and Martin served as treasurer of the Spanish and Portuguese synagogue in Montreal.

Martin Wolff became the first father figure in my life. In Vienna, there had been no man in the family. In Hove, Mrs Scharff, rather than her husband, had been the head of the house. Martin was a conservative in the best sense of the word, an introvert, hard-working, totally honest, basically a shy man. The subject of sex was never mentioned. When eventually I had girlfriends, they were simply friends.

It was quite a new experience for me to be in a house where there were girls. Martin had asked all his daughters whether they would be willing to take me in as a younger brother, and all had agreed. The five sisters (a sixth had died recently) were as different from one another as sisters could be. I had met Sarah and Annette previously at their grandmother's in Hove. Both were working in London at the time. Sarah, the eldest, had studied dietetics at McGill. She was quiet, thoughtful, shy, and struck me as the type who was bound to remain a spinster, but after returning to Canada in 1946 she met Philip Orkin, a slim young Canadian PhD, very intelligent, with an impish sense of humor. They fell in love, got married and have lived happily ever since. They are a fun couple. Phil became an ichthyologist at Aberdeen University in Scotland, and when he retired they moved to London to be nearer their sons. Isabel and I are happy to stay with them whenever we are there.

Annette was as different from Sarah as could be. As easily angered as Sarah was calm, she became very enthusiastic about whatever she was involved in and considered it of great importance. I was fascinated when she told me she had been a link between Roosevelt and Churchill during the war, until I realized that she had been a telephone operator. Annette loved men, particularly naval officers, and this disturbed her father greatly.

Rachel kept house for her father after he was widowed, and married only late in life. She was a quiet, caring person who was there whenever she was needed. Rosetta, who had gone to Queen's University, was already married to Victor Elkin and had a son, JJ. I admired her intelligence, sense of humor and grace and later got to know all her children quite well. Esther, the youngest of the sisters, was away from home, studying nursing.

I was terribly shy during those first two weeks before I left for college. The house at 442 Argyle was small but comfortable, and Mr Wolff's financial means were so limited that one room was let to a schoolteacher. On the day I arrived, he gave me $5 in pocket money, but unfortunately did not tell me how long it was to last.

He was a keen stamp collector, who appreciated the expertise I had acquired in Vienna. Whenever I returned to Montreal, we spent evenings working on his collection, strong in the British Empire and especially in Canadian stamps. We both enjoyed this time together, for although he was so English and formal, he was warm and very kind, and I believe that in some way I took the place of the son he never had. I always called him Mr Wolff, and it was only when I went to Harvard that he signed his last letters "Daddy Wolff".

On Friday evenings there was a service in Hebrew at home. Unlike me, all the family had fine voices and it was a pleasure to hear the distinctive Sephardi chants, so different from the tunes of the orthodox German and Eastern European Jews who had come to Fort Lennox from Camp B. On Saturday mornings the whole family walked to the Spanish and Portuguese synagogue on Stanley Street, and the meal following the service was the highlight of the week, concluded by the singing of the grace after meals and followed by an afternoon nap. At four o'clock the family received friends for high tea, very pleasant and very English.

As in Vienna, the most enjoyable holiday of the year was Passover, but the Sederim were very different. At the Mayers there had been a great deal of singing and discussion; in Westmount, there was also a lot of singing, although with Sephardi tunes, but little discussion, and everything was formal, even our dress. I was happy with these different traditions and disagreed with Mr Wolff only about his thinking that Sephardi Jews were much better than eastern European Jews, and that Yiddish was a slang not to be tolerated in polite society. In the Middle Ages, some of the greatest scholars were indeed Sephardim, but since the end of the 15th century the scholarship of eastern European Jews has been superior.

On the Ile aux Noix I had studied a good deal of Hebrew, many Biblical commentaries and even part of a tractate in the Talmud. My Bar Mitzvah in Vienna in a conservative temple on a Saturday afternoon had consisted of reciting the two short blessings before and after the reading of the Torah. Was that a "kosher" Bar Mitzvah, the rabbis in the camp had asked? So I had studied for a second Bar Mitzvah, in April 1941, reading the whole long portion dealing mainly with the distinction between clean and unclean animals. Despite being unable to chant properly because I cannot keep a tune, the reading had gone well. Every Friday evening and Saturday afternoon in the camp I had studied the weekly Torah portions, which helped me become a good Sunday School teacher years later. I know that Mr Wolff really appreciated my Jewish knowledge and, in his shy way, he treated me like a son.

My first priority when I was taken into this wonderful family however was to continue my education. The school term was already well advanced, so on November 3 I applied for admission to McGill but was refused at once. The following week the University of Toronto turned me down. Then Mr Wolff suggested I try Queen's. He wrote to the registrar and a civil engineering friend, Professor Low, and I was accepted. I was a free man, I had been welcomed into a Canadian family and had been accepted by a prestigious Canadian university; I was determined to do my best.

3

Queen's University

My first days at Queen's were scary. I had been warned that I must never tell anyone where I had been, but how could I expect not to be asked that question? However, when I arrived on Thursday, November 15, 1941, and was greeted by Jean Royce, the Registrar, a kindly, firm lady who introduced me to Professor Art Jackson, the Secretary of the Faculty of Science, neither questioned me about my past. With my fellow students, the situation was more difficult. By mid-November most of the freshmen already knew one another, but I was a curiosity. Appearing so late in the term and with a strong German accent, I was naturally asked where I was from. This was an ongoing worry to me. Yet there was an advantage to my late arrival: I was not subject to the freshman initiation which I considered pretty horrible when I saw what happened the next year.

Professor Jackson showed me the campus layout, then told me to go into the chemistry building to claim a locker and get equipment for the lab work. Mr Heiland, the stockroom manager, gave me my first scare at Queen's: "Have you paid your fees yet?" he asked. When I said I had, he just roared with laughter: "Why, this is highway robbery. You can't come here in mid-November and expect to pass. Go back, boy. Get your money back and then come next September." Since neither Jean Royce nor Art Jackson struck me as highway robbers, I stayed, but with trepidation.

Bennie Scott, a medical student and a friend of Rosetta, took me under his wing. He introduced me to people and helped me find a pleasant room near the campus, $3 a week for bed and breakfast. Every day except Friday, I had lunch at the student union, 35 cents a meal, and once a week I bought bread, cheese and apples for supper. Friday evenings were very special. Mr and Mrs Isaac Cohen, who lived just a block from the campus, invited me to their Sabbath dinners, sumptuous chicken with all the trimmings. So I saved the 35 cents for lunch that day. Years later, their house was acquired by Queen's and torn down to build the John Deutsch Center, and whenever I enter that building, I still think of those wonderful dinners.

The academic work was difficult and very different from that in the camp. I am totally unmechanical and very clumsy, yet I had chosen engineering because I thought it was expected of me. My paternal grandfather had been a civil engineer and so was Martin Wolff. I had done well in chemistry in my matriculation exams, and Queen's had a course in engineering chemistry with the emphasis on chemistry, but all first-year students in engineering had to take the same eleven courses, and only one was in chemistry. How I envied the students working for their BAs—only five courses! But what could I do with a BA? The course I found most difficult was engineering drawing, taught by Professor Jackson. As he took me into the large room with many drafting tables, he explained that all the students were busy drawing plans of a Model T engine block. This was my first assignment. Model T? Engine block? I had never heard of either and had, in fact, never looked closely at a car. Yet Art Jackson and the students were immensely helpful, and I passed the course with an A. To me it was a miracle. The following September I proudly related to Mr Heiland that I had passed with nine As and two Bs, and he admitted grudgingly that miracles did still happen. But the greatest miracle was that I won a Roberta McCulloch Scholarship in engineering English, worth $30. I still have Jean Royce's two-sentence letter, now yellowed and faded. I looked at that letter many times that summer and wondered just who Roberta McCulloch was and said to myself that, if ever I could, I would also establish such scholarships.

My first summer in freedom was boring, but at least I had a job, at 45 cents an hour inspecting soldering of radios at RCA Victor, near our home in Westmount. I worried about small things. Why was I making so little? I disliked what I was doing, but I did a good job and could not understand why I was not given a 5 cents raise after two months of hard work.

Little did I know what a horrible time my mother was experiencing, forced to leave the apartment and go to a Jewish old-age home in Vienna. I still have her very last postcard, written from the home in the Malzgasse on June 5, 1942. It is much like all her notes, full of care and worry about me, never a complaint about herself. Later that month she and Aunt Helene were in the first transport from Vienna to Theresienstadt, arriving there on June 21. Mother was prisoner No. 821. Helene, aged 84, died there in September, and my mother, aged 68, died on November 23, 1942. "The memory of the righteous is a blessing." I have been truly blessed by her goodness.

Life at Queen's changed dramatically in my second year because the recently founded Science '44 student co-op invited me to join. At the time I did not know why I was asked; now I believe that Professor Jackson suggested me. The members of the co-op lived near the campus in Collins House, which had been donated to the university by A E Collins, a Queen's graduate and vice president at Inco. The students paid $8 a week, shared the housework and all expenses, and in the spring received a refund of a dollar or two per week. Clearly this was much better than living by myself. Most of the members of the co-op were a year ahead of me at Queen's, engineers in Science '44, but my roommate, Harry Daggett, was in engineering chemistry in my year, Science '45. Harry was a tall, thin, rather dour fellow, a religious Baptist who totally abstained from liquor and girls. He was very interested in re-writing the co-op's constitution and keeping the minutes of its meetings, and of other organizations he served as secretary. I often wondered what his parents were like. His father was mayor of Prince Rupert in northern British Columbia, but Harry seldom talked about them. I liked him very much. He was kind but very shy. We were both hard workers, but conversation between us was rather difficult even after we had shared the same room for a couple of years. I was very relieved when I finally plucked up enough courage in my third year to tell him about my life in the internment camp. He in no way held this against me. On the contrary, he told me that he was relieved to know the reason for my saying so little about my past. By then the weekly requirement that I visit the local office of the RCMP had become a formality—just a quick wave to the officer, his smile, and I was gone. I no longer feared that I would be put back into the camp if I talked about it. Also by then about a dozen other internees had been admitted to Queen's and all of us were doing well.

Harry's end was very sad. He went to Brown University for his PhD in electrochemistry. While there, one of his professors persuaded him to try alcohol. On graduation, he returned to British Columbia to an assistant professorship at UBC. I learned later that he killed a child while driving under the influence, and then committed suicide. If only we had talked more, perhaps even got drunk together! Life is full of "what ifs."

I do not think I was a good member of the co-op. I certainly didn't enjoy snow shovelling or peeling potatoes, yet most of the members were patient with me and I admired their savvy. They all knew what a Model T engine block was, and so much more. Harry may have known nothing about girls, but most of the other fellows did, and some were even engaged!

In Vienna, I had not talked to any girls except my sister. In Hove I observed the Scharffs' younger daughter, Diana, several years my senior, and asked a girl in Hebrew School for my first date. Her name was Phyllis Cooper, who had been evacuated from London to Brighton the previous year. Unfortunately I could not keep the date at the West Pier because that very morning I was picked up by the police and interned. At Queen's I dated a number of girls, one of whom, a pretty girl from Ottawa, Helen Ewers, took me seriously. We spent many evenings together. She taught me a little about dancing and somewhat more about bridge, her favorite pastime. Although she was an Anglican, she became very interested in Judaism. I really liked her, but I just was not ready for marriage. She planned everything, right down to the names of our three sons. Worst of all, she seemed so wealthy: the only child of an accountant in Ottawa who owned his own home! I had nothing. As she became more serious, I got more and more scared.

After my second year at Queen's I had the good fortune to find a great summer job, as lab technician with the Murphy Paint Company in Montreal, not far from home in Westmount, at the fabulous salary of $130 a month. It was such interesting work, formulating paints and lacquers, with such a genial and helpful boss, the chief chemist, James Rankin. I was in heaven when Jim asked me to return the following summer, at $160 a month, and for my first full time job on graduation at $250 a month, the highest salary paid to any Queen's Science '45 graduate.

My summer savings and various scholarships and prizes covered my expenses; not of course by strict accounting, because during the holidays I lived at home with the Wolff family at no cost. But dating was expensive. A Friday evening dance at Grant Hall cost $1.25, and with two milk shakes afterwards, there went $2. So I found myself a little short of cash in my third year, and combed the university calendar to look for prizes or scholarships that might be available in mid-year. I found the Andrina McCollough Scholarship in Public Speaking, worth $50. How silly could I get? Public speaking—and me with a thick German accent! Still, $50 was $50, and so I tried and won. Dr William McNeill, one of the judges in the competition and the vice principal of the university, took me aside and urged me to join the debating society—something engineers never did. Still, I joined and won that year's debating cup. There was no inter-university debating in wartime, but three years later, while working for my MSc, I joined the debating society again, won the cup and then also the inter-university debating championship. I have enjoyed public speaking and debating ever since.

In my fourth year, I was elected president of the Queen's Hillel Foundation, and we worked hard to buy a house for the society, very close to the campus. $11,000 seemed a lot to raise, and we were proud when we succeeded. My association with Hillel made me think about the problems Jews faced in universities.

The only difficulty facing orthodox Jewish students at Queen's was that each year they failed exams held on a Saturday. They would wait until they were held again the next autumn. One such student, Willie Low, who had come from the Ile aux Noix and later became a well-known physicist and founder of the Jerusalem Institute of Technology, went to Jean Royce and said, "Look at my record. Each year I have all As and one F. I will be able to explain why. But will Queen's?" Miss Royce asked Willie just one question, "Can I have your word that you will not discuss the exam with anyone if we allow you to take it later?" From then on Willie got all As.

What a different reaction from that of Colonel Stetham, who had objected so strongly to orthodox Jews not working on the Sabbath in the camp. Curiously, Colonel Stetham retired to Kingston, found out that some of us were attending Queen's and wrote a scathing letter to the Kingston *Whig Standard*, inquiring why Queen's admitted "enemy aliens." Jean Royce called me into her office and assured me that the university's view would not change. Stetham died in Kingston in 1943, unmourned by me.

While I experienced no anti-semitism at Queen's, a protracted discussion went on at the university's Board of Trustees meetings regarding the increasing number of Jewish students. Before the war, two or three per cent of the students were Jews, by 1944 this had risen to ten per cent. They came mainly from Montreal where McGill enforced a *numerus clausus*. Jews had to have higher marks than Christians to be admitted, so Jews who were refused by McGill sought admittance to Queen's. Should Queen's limit the number of Jews? Much later I learned about these discussions at the Board meetings between 1942 and 1945, and I found them fascinating. Principal Wallace worked hard to delay a decision, with a practical rather than a moral rationale: should one discriminate in wartime? The obvious question—should one ever discriminate?—must have been asked in private, but was not recorded in the minutes, but one of the practical consequences of non-discrimination was the admittance of the first Jews from the internment camp to a Canadian university. Our two years in the camp, education without distraction, followed by four years at Queen's was a great beginning for a successful life. Many of us have done remarkably well. Carl Amberg became dean at Carleton University; Arno Cahn director of research at Lever Brothers; Klaus Schaye, vice president of Grace; and Kurt Rothschild started his own very successful electrical engineering company in Toronto.

This story of non-discrimination has an amazing sequel. In 1980 Dr Robert Bater, the principal of the Queen's Theological College, proposed that all Christian prayers be removed from Queen's convocations, lest non-Christians be offended. Predictably there was an uproar, much directed violently against Bater. I wrote to him at the time:

"I can just hear those who are against your suggestion saying, more or less strongly: this is a Christian (or Protestant or Presbyterian) university; let those who don't like it go elsewhere. And of course, historically they have a point: Queen's was founded as a Scottish, Presbyterian university, and there was a time when every principal was a minister of the Church and every member of its Board of Trustees was a minister, or at least a Presbyterian. I seem to remember that our current charter, I believe of 1912, still calls for Queen's to be a Christian university. But obviously times have changed: we live in a pluralistic society, and there are at Queen's today many students who are not Christian. And you should weigh—as obviously you have done—whether the hurt caused by Christian prayers at university functions is in consonance with true Christianity, as you understand it.

". . .What is important to me is that you, a Presbyterian theologian, are making that suggestion out of a spirit of true love: you do not want to do anything that might hurt someone unnecessarily. That is in the best Queen's tradition as I know it."

Actually, I doubt that many non-Christians were ever really offended by the Lord's Prayer. I really enjoy it, and whenever I hear "Our Father which art in heaven, Hallowed be Thy name . . .", I translate it into Hebrew and feel at home. Matthew 7, 9-13 is a universal prayer and traditional Judaism at its best. What mattered most to me in this discussion was that the principal of the Queen's Theological College would be so considerate. Only at Queen's.

Eventually the university senate voted against Dr Bater's proposal, 22:11, but a year later reconsidered and voted to delete the Lord's Prayer. Since then I have thought a good deal about a letter written to me by Kurt Rothschild, an old, orthodox Jewish friend. We were in the camp and at Queen's together, and since then Kurt has worked immensely hard to help Jewish causes in Canada and Israel. He wrote:

"The question of Christian prayer or religious instruction in public schools and universities is not an easy one. Most certainly, I appreciate and applaud the courageous and humanitarian stand of Robert Bater.

"On the other hand, I am greatly bothered by the entire problem of State and Religion. No doubt, the Church—whether Catholic or Protestant—has brought great unhappiness to our People over the centuries and yet, a world without churches is no better place. The claim that religion is exclusively the private domain of an individual— not deserving encouragement and support from Government—is self-defeating. We are creating a secular, materialistic, permissive society, which has not enhanced the general feeling of brotherhood and mutual understanding that we look for.

"I sometimes feel therefore that Christian prayer in a Christian land is not quite as detrimental as people think, and I have felt uncomfortable with some of the extreme positions taken by American Jewish

Congress in their battles on the issues of State and Religion.

"The open society of the West is devouring and alienating our Jewish youth at a clip as fast as the Holocaust. I do not mean to welcome the antisemitic expressions in Christian prayer books and from Christian pulpits; nor do I welcome hypocrisy—whether it be in Church, or in Synagogue. But I do look with great uneasiness at a world that is freeing itself from the shackles of Divinity.

"The quest for a better world is studded with many thorns."

Ever since childhood, I have taken a keen interest in Christianity. Perhaps it was a defense mechanism at first. In Vienna, the word "Christian" became abhorrent to me, whether connected with the Christian Socialists or this or that Christian school or athletic club, for it meant that I, a Jew, was excluded. But only study could convince me that the Christians were wrong. The Church preached brotherly love, but that seemed pure hypocrisy since it did nothing whatever to help Hitler's victims. Joseph Klausner's *Jesus of Nazareth* and *From Jesus to Paul* taught me about early Christianity. Queen's taught me that there are two kinds of Christians, those to whom Christianity is just an empty shell and those to whom love, respect and care for neighbors are reality.

The principal, the registrar and the professors treated me with care and respect; one family, that of Professor Norman and Grace Miller, treated me with love. Norman was a distinguished teacher of mathematics, a graduate of Queen's and Harvard to whom teaching at high school and undergraduate levels seemed more important than research. Grace was also an able mathematician, yet mathematics never dominated the conversation in their home. I have no idea why I was invited there so often. Norman was not one of my teachers, but he and his family treated me most kindly. Principal Bater's thoughtfulness confirmed that indeed there were Christians who wanted to live justly. All this consideration for me cancelled my hatred of Christians. Years later, Principal David Smith and his wife, Mary, a minister, again proved that the Millers and Principal Bater were not isolated examples.

My graduation from Queen's with the medal in chemistry coincided with the end of the war in Europe, a time of great euphoria, particularly in Canada where everything pointed to a great future. My work for the Murphy Paint Company was most enjoyable, formulating lacquers and enamels for industry. During the war there had been many shortages and customers had had to take what they could get. Once the war was over, I read about the new vinyl polymers that had been developed in the United States. Their formulation was easy and the supply was soon plentiful. Our customers were amazed at the low temperature and short baking schedules, and our salesmen, largely on commission, were ecstatic. What a pleasure it was to visit customers, inquire what they would really like in a baking enamel, brushing aside their grumble, "What I would like and what I can get are two different things." I listened carefully to their requirements and enjoyed formulating a vinyl finish close to their hopes and bringing them a 5-gallon sample the next day. Business boomed, but paradoxically Harry Thorp, the president and principal stockholder of the company, called me into his office the following spring and told me that he thought I should leave the company temporarily to further my studies. "You only have a BSc in chemistry," he said. "Think what you could do with a PhD." Clearly Mr Thorp knew the paint business, but little about academic research.

In my last year in engineering chemistry at Queen's, I had undertaken a "research project", studying the isomerization of linoleic acid using UV spectra, and really enjoyed the work and the caring guidance of my mentor, R N Jones. I had however been away from "real" chemistry for over a year and could hardly apply to a PhD program and hope to succeed. So I decided first to brush up on my chemistry, getting an MSc in organic chemistry at Queen's, and then to find a great graduate school. Mr Thorp offered to help me financially, $600 towards my MSc, $1000 towards my PhD—but he wanted me to come back to Murphy Paint when I had my PhD. I had stayed in touch with Queen's, taking a BA in history extramurally, and was accepted for an MSc, the highest degree then offered there in chemistry. A young assistant professor, Arthur Ferguson McKay, fresh out of graduate school of the University of Toronto, offered me a fellowship, $100 a month, enabling me to save Harry Thorp's gift for later.

A F McKay was a singular chap. In his late twenties, tall and handsome, he was a workaholic who loved experimental chemistry. I was his first and only student at the time and shared his lab on the ground floor of Gordon Hall. He had just received his PhD from Professor George F Wright, one of the two academics in North America with the worst reputation for slave-driving their students. The other was Henry Gilman at Iowa State who was Wright's teacher. Gilman was a gentleman in manners. Wright looked like a gentleman, small and dapper, but often used language he had learned in the Merchant Navy. It was said that Wright had driven some chemistry students into theology. Art told me that just after he was married, he asked Wright whether he could take Christmas Day off. "What the hell," Wright replied, "next thing you will want is New Year's Day off. So you just got married, eh, now I know why you are f—ing up everything around here." His years with Wright had turned Art's hair prematurely silver grey.

Art was a great teacher in laboratory technique, always ready to show me everything he knew. He put me onto two problems, one in chemistry related to the explosive RDX; the other was experimentally a much more difficult problem, the preparation of all the possible stereoisomers of the tetrahydroxystearic acids obtainable from linoleic acid.

Mr Heiland had scared me a little in November 1941. Art McKay scared me much more five years later. As I tried to walk into our lab on my return from a brief Christmas holiday, he barred my way, shouting, "You Goddamned SOB, you crook, you cheat!" What had I done? The easiest part of my work had been to condense nitroguanidine with 1,2-propanediamine to make a 5-membered ring compound. The desired compound was nicely crystalline, the yield good, the analysis correct. During the holiday, Art had tried to repeat my work and had obtained a totally different compound. The melting points were different, the mixed melting point was depressed and Art's compound also analyzed correctly. So Art assumed that I had just made up my results and found an isomeric compound somewhere to account for the correct analysis which he himself had commissioned. He was furious with me, but I argued that to hunt around finding such an isomeric compound would have involved much more work than just making it, and I had given him several grams. I was truly scared. He assured me that I would never find another school that would accept a crook. My defense must have sounded reasonably plausible however because he finally agreed to let me repeat my work while he watched my every move. I produced my same compound, different from his. He was truly baffled and asked me to watch him. He came up with his compound. We had both taken our nitroguanidine from the same bottle but had used two different bottles, both from Eastman Kodak, labelled 1,2-propanediamine. In those days, before infra-red spectra, it took us hours to figure out what had happened. Through the identification of solid derivatives, we finally discovered that Art's bottle had been mislabelled; it really contained 1,3-propanediamine, and his isomeric compound had a 6-membered ring. Years later, when our employees filled many thousands of bottles with many different compounds, mix-ups also happened at Aldrich, and thinking back to those scary hours in December 1946, I always tried my best to prevent such mistakes.

Unhappy experiences can have their silver linings. In this case we had found another new compound, and Art learned a great deal about me that day. From then on he worked closely and happily with me on my MSc project in fatty acid chemistry. We accomplished our goal. Art was an excellent, patient experimentalist. In fact he was a much better experimentalist than a theoretical chemist, and when he published our joint work,[1] the stereochemistry reported was wrong. Yet again there was a silver lining. The mistake was corrected by one of the world's experts in the oxidation of fatty acids, Daniel Swern, who became my good friend—and one of Aldrich's first stockholders. I learned many experimental details from Art and what was more important, the joy of succeeding in the lab. Without that year at Queen's, I could not have succeeded as I did at Harvard and later at PPG. Also, I learned how to make MNNG, which was the first product offered by Aldrich. Art was the first to make it,[2] and it nearly killed him. When he treated MNNG with alkali, it gave off a gas which he at first thought was nitrogen. In fact, it was the deadly diazomethane.[3]

Art worked immensely hard, ten or twelve hours a day, and once or twice a month would try to unwind on a Saturday afternoon by going to a pub and getting drunk. He often asked me to go along so that I could take him home in a taxi. His wife, a strict Christian Scientist, frowned on drinking and would simply leave for a day or two with their three little children.

Art's subsequent history was not a happy one. Shortly after I left Queen's he was accused of sexual harassment and was asked to leave. He then worked at the Defence Research Board of Canada in Ottawa for several years, and later accepted the position of director of research and vice president of Monsanto Canada. When I started Aldrich in 1951, I gave him one of the first hundred shares of Aldrich stock as a small token of my appreciation for all his help in the past. Our original capital was $500, so that one share was then worth $5—a tiny thank you. Some three years later we met at an ACS meeting in Chicago, and Art told me that he had been fleeced in a downtown bar while he was drunk. "What is that share of Aldrich worth today?" he asked. Sales had grown nicely, to $15,000 that year, and the book value of the share was $90. Art declined my offer of a loan, but asked me to buy back his share. Eventually his drinking problem led to his dismissal from Monsanto and also from his next research job, and I lost track of him. I often think of him and wish that I could tell him how much I appreciated his teaching.

REFERENCES:
1. *J.ORG.CHEM.*, *13*, 75 (1948)
2. *JACS*, *68*, 3028 (1946)
3. *ibid*, *70*, 1974 (1948)

4

Harvard

I wanted to get my PhD at the best school that would admit me and applied to Harvard, the University of Zurich and the ETH. All three accepted me, but only Harvard offered me a fellowship. So I went there in September 1947, to get my doctorate with one of the country's best-known chemists, Louis F Fieser. Professor Fieser had done fine work in the chemistry of polycyclic aromatics, steroids and naphthoquinones. He had helped develop Napalm, was a brilliant lecturer and still did a lot of experimental work himself. In collaboration with his wife, Mary (*née* Peters), he wrote some of the best-known textbooks, including a classic basic text in organic chemistry, the first comprehensive book on steroids and an annual guide to new reagents, *Reagents for Organic Synthesis*, on which Mary still continues working.

My first PhD problem.

On my first morning at Harvard he showed me my lab, Converse 205, the one closest to his office, and outlined my PhD problem on a piece of yellow paper. Fieser had worked for years with naphthoquinones and had perfected a practical way to make the best known of these, vitamin K. He and his students had made many hundreds, because some of them had been found to be promising antimalarials.

Fieser's interest in quinones was of long standing, beginning with his PhD work under J B Conant. Mary Peters' MSc thesis at Bryn Mawr College, completed under his direction, was also in quinone chemistry. From 1926 Fieser's interest was heightened through his collaboration with a very singular chemist, Samuel C Hooker, who had started working on a naturally occurring naphthoquinone, lapachol, in 1889. Hooker left this research in 1896, became a key executive in a sugar company and returned to basic research only after his retirement from industry. He was a giant of a man with two loves, magic and chemical research. In his home in Brooklyn, he built a magic theater and his own research lab, fitted to his great size, where he returned to lapachol when he found that practically nothing had been done in the field since his own initial work. He discovered a reaction, called the Hooker oxidation, truly fit for a magician. Lapachol is a 3-hydroxy-2-alkenylnaphthoquinone which is easily hydrogenated to a 3-hydroxy-2-alkylnaphthoquinone. When they are oxidized with permanganate, each "magically" loses one methylene group. The reaction is general. Thus, for instance, if the side chain is octadecyl, C18, the Hooker oxidation converts the side chain to heptadecyl, C17, another oxidation, and C16 is produced, and so on. A most singular oxidation—an excision of a methylene. Towards the end of his life, Hooker entrusted Fieser to continue his work on lapachol and related compounds, and Fieser obtained ample funding from the government when the antimalarial activity of some of Dr Hooker's quinones was discovered.

Fieser's chemistry was *terra incognita* to me. He explained that 3-hydroxynaphthoquinones give blood-red solutions in alkali. But the solution of one, 2-cyclohexyl-3-hydroxynaphthoquinone, turned from red to yellow in a few hours. "Find out what happens," Fieser told me. I shared the lab with another first year Fieser graduate student, Raylene Adams, also working on a naphthoquinone problem, and for the first few weeks Fieser saw us regularly while I was making a large batch of the quinone to be studied. Then he left us alone for a long time.

PhD students at Harvard had to pass four qualifying exams, which I managed easily, take a couple of simple courses, submit an acceptable thesis, and pass eight cumulative exams. These examinations were given monthly and were marked on a curve; only half the students passed, usually the more experienced ones. I failed the first eight. Perhaps my poor showing the first year was due to my romantic involvement with my lab partner, Raylene, a Californian from Pomona College and the University of California in Berkeley. She had a photographic memory, knew a lot of chemistry, was intelligent, attractive and right there in Converse 205. I invited her home to Westmount for the Christmas holiday, to the distress of the Wolff family, unhappy about my dating a Christian. Her family's distress must have been greater still, for they persuaded her to leave Harvard after her first year and get her PhD in Berkeley.

Early in my first year I learned that Mama was very sick. I explained this to Fieser and asked him whether I might take three weeks off to visit her as I had not seen her since 1938. I had passed my qualifying exams, the lab work was going well, and I could get a friend to cover my work as a teaching fellow, but Fieser denied my request—"Go next summer," he said, but Mama died on April 2, 1948.

My work in the lab went very well because it was so easy to handle nicely crystalline, distinctively colored compounds, compared to the fatty acids in Art McKay's lab. I was proud to be able to teach other students what Art had taught me. In Converse 205 I set up a permanent diazomethane generator with plenty of MNNG made by Chemistry 20 undergraduates. To help crystallization I gathered hundreds of different crystals from the Converse sub-basement and sprinkled them into a big box. I was never sure whether syrups really crystallized faster there, but many students thought they did. When Fieser heard about this "black box", he also placed some syrups in it and said jokingly, "Alfred, you could crystallize a hamburger."

In my second year, Jack Tinker took Raylene's place in Converse 205. Jack and his wife, Mary, more or less adopted me, fed me many good meals and amused me by their wonderful, laid-back sense of humor. Jack was never quite certain whether he wanted to be a professional bassoonist or a chemist, and was good at both. He eventually became a computer information specialist with Eastman Kodak in Rochester.

My second year at Harvard was really so enjoyable that I even began looking forward to the cumulative examinations which I had dreaded after failing all eight in the first year. Fortunately I passed the next six. There is nothing like success to make one look forward to more. The academics at Harvard took turns to set these exams, and I thought that I had done particularly well in the one set by Dr Bernard Witkop, a German who had come to work with Fieser and then with R B Woodward, but I got a failing grade, just below the line. Checking through my little blue exam book I realized that Dr Witkop had overlooked two correct answers right in the middle of the book! With the marks for those answers, I would have passed. Of course I showed the book to Witkop and—blow me down—he asked me whether I had left the two pages blank during the exam and filled them in later. I was angry, although I knew where he came from: Germany. In Vienna, perhaps even more than in Germany, that was the sort of trick students would have played; but I had not. Reluctantly, Witkop gave me a passing grade, but he added insult to injury by decreeing that, in future, students must draw a line across all pages left empty in exam notebooks.

Years later when Witkop had a senior position at the National Institutes of Health, he worked closely with Aldrich's director of research, John Biel, and I got to know him much better personally. He was a very able medicinal chemist, a cultured man and a great politician. Neither of us referred to that incident. Perhaps he had forgotten, but I could not.

Although I saw very little of Fieser because he travelled a lot, lecturing and consulting, there were many others to help with my chemical problem. Gilbert Stork had just come to Harvard as an assistant professor. Two of my best friends, Gene van Tamelen and Leon Mandell, were his students, and Gilbert was very easy to talk to. So was Bob Woodward, particularly since I was willing to chat to him late in the evening. Both helped me with my problem, which was to provide the solution to just how that "magical" Hooker oxidation cut out one methylene group. The man who helped most was Martin Ettlinger, who had already received his PhD with Louis Fieser on a naphthoquinone problem, and who was now a member of that very select group of Harvard scholars, the Society of Fellows. He was paid a generous stipend, given a lab and could do whatever he wanted.

Martin was the only child of two able scientists in Austin, Texas—his father a mathematician, his mother a biochemist. Martin was a child prodigy who had taken his MSc in mathematics and his PhD in organic chemistry while very young. Perhaps because he suffered from deep depressions, he had few friends, but he took me under his wing, both then and later. Yet when I asked him questions that he considered stupid, he just walked away. He was one of the brightest chemists I ever knew and in the early fifties I bet his father $100 that Martin would win the Nobel Prize in chemistry within twenty years. I did not count on Martin's long spells of depression, and lost the bet. He spent some time at the Rice Institute where he was denied tenure and then many years in the chemistry department of the University of Copenhagen where he did excellent work in natural product chemistry. Excellent, but not enough for the Nobel Prize. We have visited him occasionally in Copenhagen where Danish students smiled at this brilliant giant who spoke Danish with a strong Texas accent. His first marriage to a social worker from Alabama was childless and ended in divorce. He later married a younger Danish botanist. When I saw them last, they had two young children, and Martin seemed much happier. He helped me greatly at Harvard, then at the Pittsburgh Plate Glass Company and above all in my early years with Aldrich.

In the spring of 1949, Fieser inquired how my research project was going, and I replied that I thought I had solved it. "Good," he said, "give a seminar," which I did and which he liked. So my thesis was ready to be written up and published.[1] Most Fieser students were afraid of Mary Fieser's criticism of their English; she was an excellent writer who demanded at least competence from her husband's students. I received no criticism from her, although I did have a rather unnerving experience. Fieser—we were never on a first-name basis—asked me to make a derivative related to my work, a compound Mary Fieser had made earlier. This was a monoacetate of a di-tertiary-diol. Although I tried several times, I only got the diacetate, never the compound she reported. When I took counsel with her, she agreed that her monoacetate was hard to make. "Set up twenty batches, each of one gram of the diol, and let the solutions sit in various places in your lab; some will give you the monoacetate." Indeed, three out of twenty did, although that experimental difficulty had not been reported in their paper. The paper in fact was correct but incomplete, but a much earlier paper, based on her master's thesis at Bryn Mawr,[2] was definitely in error. It described the addition of diphenyldiazomethane to naphthoquinone followed by pyrolysis to yield a highly colored product, to which they had assigned an impossible structure, with a double bond at the bridgehead. The well-known Bredt's Rule states that such structures cannot exist.

With my PhD practically finished, I decided to go to Europe. I returned in seventh heaven: I had found the right woman and wanted to leave Harvard quickly, begin my industrial work and get married. Fieser suggested that I make one more quinone, to test the generality of the rearrangement that led to the change in color of the alkaline solution, and of course I had to get my thesis written, typed and accepted. The earliest I could leave was December 1949, and I would receive my PhD in March 1950. That left plenty of time for other experiments, and I suggested to Martin that I repeat the work Mary Peters had done for her thesis and see what really happened. Experimentally, all went exactly as described in the paper, but her product was really a mixture of two compounds, easily separated by column chromatography, of course with structures different from the one they proposed. I asked Fieser whether I could give a seminar on that work. One of my fellow students was M B Rubin, and many years later he introduced me before a lecture at the Haifa Technion with the words: "Dr Bader is the most undiplomatic chemist I have ever met." Me, undiplomatic? He reminded me of that seminar, and said that the Fiesers had sat at the back of the room, visibly angry at my audacity in correcting Mary's thesis. It had not occurred to me that they might be angry; I had thought it was preferable for one of Fieser's students to correct the work, rather than a stranger.

In the autumn of 1949, the University of New Brunswick offered me

51

a junior teaching position which I would have liked to accept. Perhaps I should have stayed at Harvard a third year—many students took three or even four years to get a PhD—but I wanted to start my own family and that seemed more important to me at the time than learning a good deal more chemistry. The offer of an academic position in Canada was enticing. I had no legal obligations to return to Murphy Paint but felt a moral obligation, so I wrote to the president, Harry Thorp, to ask his advice. He replied that the company's sharply increased sales to which I had contributed, had attracted the attention of the Pittsburgh Plate Glass Company, which had purchased Murphy Paint. All research would be done in Milwaukee not Montreal. He urged me to forget about Frederickton and go to Milwaukee.

I said goodbye to my many chemist friends at Harvard and to my wonderful landlady, Mrs Nickerson, who had given me bed and breakfast for $6 a week for two years and much care without charge—and set off for Milwaukee via Westmount and Kirkland Lake, where I went to meet Isabel's parents.

REFERENCES:
1. *JACS*, 73, 681 (1951)
2. *ibid*, 53, 4080 (1931)

5
First Years in Milwaukee

I arrived in Milwaukee on January 15, 1950. Dr Howard Gerhart, the director of research for PPG, had found a comfortable room for me, near downtown, in the apartment of an elderly widow, Blanche Hogue. She really enjoyed the give and take of politics, pointed with pride to the chair in which Senator Taft had once sat, and was a proud member of the Wisconsin Republican Delegation. I did not tell her that I preferred Truman to Dewey, and was amused when she once confessed that although she was a Republican in life, when alone in the voting booth she sometimes voted Democratic.

I have liked Milwaukee since the day I arrived. It is a clean city with many beautiful parks and a shoreline, sandy in parts, along Lake Michigan. You can go swimming if you like cold water, which I do not.

Most of the Milwaukeeans I knew were hard workers. Frank Zeidler was the city's model mayor from 1948 to 1960. One of only two Socialist mayors in the country, he was industrious, intelligent, totally honest, without any show, riding to City Hall every morning on his bicycle. I heard that his predecessor, his brother Carl, who died in the Navy during the war, was even better, but I wondered how that could be. Having come from Boston and Montreal, I found the honesty in government astounding. One of the first stories I read in the *Milwaukee Sentinel* described an alderman accused of receiving a 10% discount on a car he purchased from a dealer who wanted a favor. Many aldermen in the east would have laughed in the dealer's face: "You want a favor? Give me a car, and a good one."

From my first days in Milwaukee, chemistry, the Bible and art have been the interconnected motifs in my life. On my first Saturday in the city, I took a bus to the Jewish Reform Temple, Emanuel, inquired whether they had an opening for a Sunday School teacher, and was taken on probation for two weeks and then permanently for the next thirty-two years. I really enjoyed teaching. At first I taught grades 5 to 7 on Saturday and Sunday mornings and the "Junior Congregation," high school students, on Sunday evenings. Eventually I settled down to teaching only 5th and 6th grades, the same students for two years. In the 5th grade I taught the Torah, the five books of Moses, and in the 6th, the books of Ruth, Amos and Jonah as well as selections from the other books. On three Sundays in the year, we discussed Christianity. I really tried to get to know the students, invited them to Hanukkah and Purim parties at home, and of course to our Passover Sederim, hoping that they enjoyed learning as much as I enjoyed teaching. In my last years as a teacher, I had quite a few students whose parents I had taught, and one of the most enjoyable honors I ever received was to be named his most influential teacher by a distinguished graduate of the University of Wisconsin, Jim Abrams, the well-known Hollywood film producer. I remember Jim as a small, shy and very able student. I doubt if my teaching made him a better film producer, but I hope I helped him to become a really good person.

Soon after my arrival I met and came to appreciate and love Rabbi David Shapiro. How can one describe a truly great person? The physical facts are simple, the spiritual are close to impossible to describe.

Born in Philadelphia in 1909 of a long line of rabbis, some of great fame like Ezekiel Landau, the 18th century rabbi of Prague, David Shapiro graduated from the Hebrew Theological College in Chicago, held rabbinical positions in Savannah, Erie and Indianapolis, and came to Congregation Anshe Sfard in Milwaukee in 1948.

The congregation had been organized in the 1890s by a group of Russian immigrants who followed the Sefardi ritual. By that time Jews had been in the city for about fifty years, but they were mostly German, with a sprinkling of Austrians, Bohemians and Moravians who had settled in Milwaukee's downtown and near east side. The earlier settlers looked down on the new arrivals from eastern Europe who founded their own congregations—the Russian Schul, Anshe Sfard, the Polish Schul, and the Hungarian Schul, in what is now Milwaukee's inner city. When Rabbi Shapiro arrived, his synagogue, built in 1928, was at the corner of 12th Street and Garfield Avenue, a few blocks from several other orthodox synagogues.

Within a few years, he was recognized as the "rabbi of rabbis" in Milwaukee for his vast erudition, his personal kindness, his involvement in many civic efforts, and his scholarly books. When I joined his congregation in 1950, he had been there for only two years and was still almost unknown. Furthermore, the congregation was deeply divided: some members wanted the synagogue to become "conservative", with men and women praying together rather than divided as in orthodox synagogues. Rabbi Shapiro felt comfortable teaching at the Reform Jewish Temples, at the University of Wisconsin, even at the Sacred Heart School of Theology, a Catholic seminary, but he wanted his synagogue, his spiritual home, to remain orthodox. The officers of the congregation became very impatient with him, reduced his salary to $50 a week and argued, at times almost violently, at the meetings of the board of directors. The finances were in shambles. Nowadays a congregation sends out statements for membership dues, the treasurer keeps books and the executives are aware of the synagogue's financial health. At Anshe Sfard in the early 1950s, each congregant paid for his family's synagogue seats in cash, just before the High Holy Days. There was an appeal for money on the Day of Atonement and most of the pledges were collected, again in cash, during the days following. One year, shortly after the Day of Atonement, the officers with the cash just left. But so did most of the arguments. The remaining directors, of whom I was now one, struggled on, and in time were joined by some of Milwaukee's ablest and most dedicated Jews, including my best friend Marvin Klitsner, Max Karl, the founder of MGIC, one of America's most innovative insurance companies, and Art Levin, a successful real estate developer. When I first joined the board, much of the discussion at the meetings was in Yiddish, for which my German was a substitute, but after the departure of the dissidents, the emphasis, now mainly in English, was on how to improve the congregation, not on how to make it conservative or dismiss the rabbi.

Gradually Rabbi Shapiro became widely appreciated and loved, not only in Milwaukee. He gave wonderful sermons—wonderful, provided you listened carefully—and he was willing to talk about anything and everything connected with Judaism, but not about himself. Ask him a personal question, and he would draw into his shell, except when it related to his minor love, the violin. Why is it that so many great violinists are Jews? I do not know, and neither did Rabbi Shapiro, but he said that had he not become a rabbi, he would have liked to be a violinist. "I play now, but I play very badly," he said, but he was one of the greatest teachers of Judaism I have known. We were grateful he had chosen the rabbinate.

In the early fifties, the Shapiros invited me to their Passover Sederim, with much singing and long discussions, reminiscent of the Sederim at the Mayers in Vienna. Their home then was in Milwaukee's inner city, near the synagogue, but in time it became clear that both home and synagogue had to move, and as the congregation's financial health improved, the board's discussions turned more and more to the question of where to relocate. Hindsight is always 20:20, and we should have moved to Milwaukee's east side, but in fact we moved to the northwest, the location of other orthodox synagogues, and built a modest structure in 1958, which the congregation sold some thirty years later. Now it has merged with a younger orthodox congregation on the northeast side of Milwaukee.

Very sad was the rabbi's severe stroke in the mid-eighties; God works in mysterious ways. The rabbi never complained, could understand everything, but could respond only by shaking his head. He and his wife decided to move to Jerusalem to be near their elder daughter Iolet and her family. He died there in 1989. What would many Milwaukeeans have been like without his outstanding leadership and guidance?

Certainly different, undoubtedly worse. He drew some of the greatest modern Jewish thinkers to study with him whenever they came to the Midwest. One of the reasons why Milwaukee has a strong and significant Jewish population is Rabbi Shapiro's influence.

We met Jane and Marvin Klitsner through their daughters, Frances and Betsy, who were in my class at Temple Emanuel. In August 1955 we were with them at a Jewish summer retreat where Abraham Joshua Heschel, one of America's great Jewish teachers, spent the Sabbath with us. Rabbi Heschel was an inspiring speaker. His sincerity was compelling, his enthusiasm contagious. I still recall vividly the Friday evening talk in which he spoke of man's building cathedrals and temples to God—temples in space. God, he said, had built a temple for man, but this was a temple in time—the Sabbath—a temple for eternity.

The next day Heschel, who looked and spoke like a prophet, explained the essence of prophetic teaching. It was not to make us be good to save us from punishment, rather to make us sick at evil. When Ahab says to Elijah, "Have you found me, oh my enemy?" we are not concerned at what will happen to Ahab, just sick at what Jezebel and Ahab did to Naboth. And when Nathan says to David, "You are the man," we do not worry about David's punishment, but are sickened that David treated Uriah, his loyal general, so cruelly. I am certain that my revulsion at evil was sharpened by Heschel's teaching.

At the time, the Klitsners were members of Temple Emanuel, the reform congregation, but they were so moved by Heschel that they talked to him at length, eager to know how they could come closer to the essence of Judaism. Heschel's reply was simple: "You have a great scholar, a saintly man in Milwaukee, Rabbi David Shapiro; study with him." That advice changed our lives as well as those of the Klitsners and all our children. Marvin and Jane became orthodox Jews, moved close to Rabbi Shapiro's synagogue and eventually, when Marvin retired, moved to Jerusalem to be near their three children and nineteen grandchildren.

Marvin was born in the small town of Augusta, Wisconsin, the second of five children. His parents moved to Milwaukee, where Marvin spent most of his growing years. During the depression, they went to Lancaster, a small town in southwestern rural Wisconsin, where his father started over again with a general store. It was there that Marvin completed high school. He then went to the University of Wisconsin in Madison, receiving his bachelor's degree and then his LLb from the law school from which he graduated with the highest marks any law student had ever received there. After serving in the Navy from 1942 to 1946, mainly on the USS *San Diego*, an anti-aircraft cruiser, he returned to Milwaukee to join the oldest and most prestigious Wisconsin law firm, Miller, Mack & Fairchild (now Foley and Lardner). Marvin is a brilliant lawyer, a clear thinker and an impassioned advocate, able to move judges and juries. Most important, he is a truly good person.

Another lifelong friend I made in Milwaukee is a remarkable bookseller, Michael Hatcher. We first met in an antique store in 1952 when Michael was 11. I watched this young lad studying various objects with great interest and clearly with considerable knowledge, and was immediately taken with him. We got to know each other by chatting at antique stores and auctions and have worked together with books, paintings and antiques for many years.

Michael is almost totally self-educated and is fascinating to talk to. In the early sixties he worked briefly at Aldrich. He was slow, reliable and totally honest, but he was not cut out for regular hours. He is wonderful at buying old books, loves studying them into the night, but is often reluctant to sell them. Fortunately his habits as a night owl are no problem when he looks after our house for us when we are travelling. His honesty and reliability are what count. We sleep more peacefully knowing he is back home looking after things.

But back to PPG. Howard Gerhart, then 40, was a boyish-looking chemist, with a PhD from Northwestern University. I particularly admired his enthusiasm. Most of the chemists on his team were working on surface coatings and on the "hardening" of drying oils through treatment with cyclopentadiene— the term cookbook chemistry came to my mind. I had been forced on them because Harry Thorp had "invested" in my future, but they did not know what to do with me. Several chemists expressed surprise, not in an unpleasant manner, that the company had hired me at all, since there was an unwritten rule not to hire Jews and blacks, and there were no Jews or blacks among the hundreds of employees.

My immediate supervisor was Henry Vogel, a pleasant fellow who had received his PhD in "oil chemistry", doing something with soybean (or was it linseed) oil at the University of Wisconsin in Madison. His boss, Stewart Gloyer, had received the same degree, in similar chemistry from the same school. Neither they nor my next supervisor, Roger Christenson, same school, same chemistry, knew much about what I considered real chemistry, but after handing me the first problem, they left me very much alone.

That problem was the study of an unusual observation they had made. Soybean oil contains all sorts of interesting products in small quantities, some steroids, some tocopherols, vitamin E. Without these impurities, soybean oil makes a better paint medium. So the team had studied purification by countercurrent extraction, trying many different solvents, and had finally settled on furfural. While testing methyl and ethyl acetoacetate, they had obtained some very odd products. What were they?

All esters can be transesterified in the presence of catalysts. Surprisingly, ß-keto esters like methyl and ethyl acetoacetate can be transesterified without catalysts—an interesting though neither an earth-shaking discovery nor one of great value to a paint company. But for me it led to two papers in the *Journal of the American Chemical Society*[1,2] and the pleasure of hearing Gilbert Stork's positive comments. I was happy with this work, and luckily, Howard had invited a "real" chemist, Charles Hurd, one of his professors at Northwestern University, to consult. I really looked forward to his monthly visits, and we became life-long friends. It was such a pleasure to be the Charles Hurd lecturer at Northwestern years later and to relate many facets of that friendship.

When I realized after a few months that the team had only one chemical problem for me to solve, I had to think hard of other problems to propose, problems with interesting chemistry and of potential value to PPG.

Phenol was cheap, pennies a pound, and so were dienes such as butadiene, isoprene and PPG's favorite, cyclopentadiene. If only one could react these dienes with phenol to give unsaturated phenols, they might be exciting new monomers. Many chemists had tried these reactions and had always failed. First, I wanted to study the one simple, unsaturated phenol that had been reported in the literature as being easily made, o-vinylphenol.[3] Unfortunately, neither I nor anyone else could repeat that preparation; it was a hoax. So I studied the reaction of the simplest phenol with the simplest diene, phenol with butadiene,[4] and I was overjoyed when I found that I could control the reaction conditions to yield the pure monomers, ortho- and para-2-butenylphenol. Isoprene and cyclopentadiene reacted similarly.[5] So here we had three sets of monomers, each a mixture of ortho and para isomers, which could be produced quite cheaply, and Roger Christenson took them and made tin-can coatings from them. The company was happy because the work led to many US and foreign patents, and so was I, particularly after I was permitted to publish the work.

The key lay in the control of the catalyst, and I was particularly happy to find that I could predict which other catalysts would work, once I had found one that worked in any given system.[4] Also, each diene gave unconjugated unsaturated phenols. Naturally I conjugated each pure isomer.[6] It was not world-class chemistry, but it was fun.

The supply of research chemicals still depended almost entirely on Eastman Kodak which did not give good service, and so I asked Howard whether I might start a tiny division to offer new products. He just shook his head and said, " no, it would not fly." Since I am a workaholic and needed more to do, my friend Jack Eisendrath and I started a company, Aldrich, working evenings and weekends to offer research chemicals.

I had stayed in close contact with Martin Ettlinger, who helped with all the chemical problems and with the much more complicated chemistry leading to the correct structures of the compounds first described in Mary Peters' MSc thesis. Every so often I got weary working with the smelly alkenylphenols, and it was a change to spend a little time, in the evenings, working with those nicely crystalline, colored compounds which I had separated at Harvard. When I sent Martin the first draft of our manuscript,[7] he objected to my beginning our paper, "In the elegant work of Fieser and Peters . . ." "To be elegant," he said, "it should at least be correct."

Of course the work with dienes was much more practical. If phenols react with dienes, why not anilines? That study[8,9] led to a new method to make indoles. Alkenylphenols smelled; the indoles structurally related to skatole, skunks' revenge, stank. I had not yet learned to drive but now found it so much easier to find a seat at the back of the bus.

Economically the most rewarding chemistry came almost accidentally. One day, I think in 1952, a Quaker Oats salesman visited us at PPG and told us that levulinic acid would become commercially available. Levulinic acid is a ketone and an acid. The simplest ketone is acetone which had been reacted with phenol to give bisphenol-A, an important monomer made in large quantities. Obviously I could take levulinic acid, make the bisphenol and see what I could do with the product, bisphenolic acid—which had not been made before. I started the work the day we received a sample of levulinic acid, wrote a patent application and submitted a note to the *Journal of the American Chemical Society*.[10] I was astounded when Howard talked to me shortly after that note appeared in print. Johnson Wax in Racine had inquired whether PPG had filed a patent application, and if so they wanted to buy the rights. "What should we ask?" Howard inquired. The answer was simple. The work had taken a few days, so $10,000 would have been ample payment, but if they wanted the patent really badly, why not ask for a million? So that is what PPG asked, and received.

The Quaker Oats salesman had travelled from his office in Chicago to Johnson Wax in Racine, then to PPG in Milwaukee and then to 3M in Minneapolis. Every chemist hearing about the commercial availability of levulinic acid decided to make the bisphenol. What a bit of luck that I had begun the work the day I received the sample. Our patent attorney told me later that 3M fought our patent application as if it infringed on their Scotch Tape patents. But my work was clearly described and dated in my company notebook, and PPG received and assigned the patent to Johnson Wax (US Patent 2,933,520). Russ Eberly, the PPG patent attorney, sent me the patent along with a note saying, ". . . it would have been more appropriate for us to send you a copy with a gold border."

I never fully understood why Johnson Wax was so interested. The company was basic in neither phenol nor levulinic acid, but one of their chemists had made some interesting resins from the diphenolic acid and Johnson Wax actually built a plant to produce the bisphenolic acid on a large scale. The economics, however, were clearly against the enterprise and they eventually sold the process and closed the plant.

One result of the sale of this patent was that my many notebooks were scrutinized carefully by several of the company's patent attorneys in Pittsburgh. Personally, I was happy: I had repaid Harry Thorp's "investment" with interest. My starting salary at PPG in January 1950 was $400 a month, the lowest received by any Harvard PhD. My laboratory was atrocious. I was on the second floor of a firetrap of a wooden building put up as a temporary structure during World War I. Yet I enjoyed my work, which was appreciated by the company, and by 1954 my salary had doubled. Also, I had been able to start Aldrich, had married and had made many friends.

Early in 1954 Howard told us that PPG was going to move the paint division's research labs from Milwaukee to Springdale, near Pittsburgh. He told Charles Hurd that he did not really care whether any of the chemists moved, apart from me. This was good for my ego, but I did not want to relocate. I really liked Milwaukee, and so I gave notice. Howard thought I was crazy. "You are a very good chemist, but you are not a businessman and Aldrich will go bankrupt. But don't worry, we will always have a job for you, and in the meantime please consult for us," which I was happy to do.

REFERENCES:
1. *JACS*, 73, 4195 (1951)
2. *ibid*, 74, 3992 (1952)
3. *ibid*, 53, 806, 3390 (1931); 77, 4155 (1955)
4. *ibid*, 79, 6164 (1957)
5. *ibid*, 75, 5967, (1953); 80, 3073 (1958)
6. *ibid*, 78, 1709 (1956)
7. *ibid*, 75, 730 (1953)
8. *ibid*, 80, 437 (1958)
9. *ibid*, 83, 3319 (1961)
10. *ibid*, 76, 4465 (1954)

6

Isabel and Danny

Isabel and I met on the SS *Franconia* which sailed from Quebec City to Liverpool on July 9, 1949. It was my first trip to Europe, and I was looking forward to visiting family and friends who had survived the war, first in England and then on the Continent. There were some 900 passengers on the ship, and I did not meet Isabel until Wednesday the 14th. By the following day we knew that we cared for each other, and when we docked at Liverpool on Friday, we arranged to meet in London. Wartime price controls were still in effect, and no meal could cost more than 5 shillings, so I could afford to take Isabel to dine and dance at the Trocadero in Piccadilly a good many evenings, and I asked her to marry me the following Friday.

During those nine days I thought of only two problems, one important, one trivial. How to bridge our difference in religion was the major issue. The minor one was whether our greatly differing eating speeds would make life difficult, for I eat quickly and Isabel eats very slowly; indeed she takes at least twenty minutes longer over a meal than I do. An hour a day is 365 hours a year; I worked out that, if we lived together for thirty years, I would spend an additional 456 days—well over a year—just eating. I concluded that Isabel was worth it.

Many years later, the son of a friend at Merck, Bob Philips, a student at MIT, asked me where I had found such a wonderful woman, and I explained that it had taken me nine days to propose. "Nine days," he said in amazement, "it would have taken me two days!" I, too, might have taken just two days, if only our backgrounds had been similar.

Isabel is the second daughter of a deeply religious Protestant family in Kirkland Lake in northern Ontario, rough gold-mining country. Her father, Herbert Overton, was a cabinet maker who had emigrated to Canada from England in 1906 and made a modest living in the carpentry shop of a goldmine. Her mother, Stella Sirr, came from a large family in New Liskeard; she had left school at the age of 13 to help her mother look after her six younger brothers and sisters. Herbert and Stella's lives centered on their church. Herbert was often a lay preacher, and they both sang in the choir. They moved from church to church, looking for one where they could feel really comfortable—spending a few years with the Jehovah's Witnesses and many years in the Anglican church before ending up in the United Church of Canada. Herbert studied the Bible throughout his life, and left some mystical writings about the time of the coming of the Messiah. In another age, of another people, he would have been a Kabbalist.

Life in Kirkland Lake must have been exceedingly difficult for Isabel's parents. It was a rough community, consisting mainly of immigrants from Europe, miners who had neither sympathy nor understanding for the other-worldliness of the Overtons. The price of gold was pegged at $35 an ounce, and the effects of the depression were devastating. Sir Harry Oakes was able to move millions from the "golden mile" of Kirkland Lake to Bermuda, but there was little for the workers in the mines. Isabel has told me how happy she was one day when she found a dime under a davenport pillow; it enabled her mother to buy vegetables for the next meal.

Herbert was a man of firm principles. In the First World War he was a conscientious objector—at a time when this was not only unfashionable, but a danger to a man's freedom. He was born in 1882 and so luckily just missed conscription. Higher education, which neither he nor Stella had enjoyed, was important to them, and two of their three children went to university. Isabel won an Ontario scholarship to Victoria College in Toronto, while Clifford, the youngest, studied chemistry at Queen's.

Despite her upbringing in such a tough mining town and four years at the University of Toronto, Isabel had led an immensely sheltered life. How all the fellows at the university could have overlooked a woman of such inner and outer beauty, such goodness and intelligence, was beyond my understanding. Drinking, smoking and sex were certainly out, but fortunately I cared nothing for the first two and not enough for the third for it to matter. I remember later that summer, after my hands had once again been repulsed in a gentle necking session, I asked Isabel what must surely have been the most stupid question I have ever asked her, "Are you frigid?" In fact, as I discovered thirty-three years later, she is a most wonderfully sensuous, giving woman. But I am rushing ahead too fast.

Then as now, Isabel was a beautiful woman. She did not have the chocolate-box beauty of a Hollywood star, which has always frightened and repelled me, but a quiet beauty—with gentle eyes, accentuated by lovely freckles and long, soft hair. I felt so at home with those freckles—and cannot imagine why some people try to remove them. She has always had an almost stately figure, beautiful legs, and above all, an inner beauty reflecting true goodness. There has never been a day spent with Isabel when I have not felt good being with her. Of course at the time, in London, I did not realize how intelligent she is. A man deeply in love does not subject a girl to an IQ test, nor did she tell me that she had been an Ontario scholar. Many years later I visited Jean Macdonald, one of Isabel's schoolfriends, a missionary in Tokyo, who had shared a room with her in Victoria College. I asked Jean, quite innocently, whether

Isabel had been a good student. Jean was amazed at the question—Isabel had been one of the best students in the college. "Isabel succeeds at everything she tries," Jean added. True, almost always.

During the nine days before I proposed to Isabel in Green Park and in the months that followed, my mind was in turmoil, and so was Isabel's. She was speechless when I proposed, and afterwards our thoughts and talk were never far from religion and how to reconcile our differences. I very much wanted a family, but a Jewish family, and our children could not be Jewish unless their mother was a Jewess. Neither Isabel nor her father (I learned much later) were orthodox Christians, and did not believe that Jesus was God or was born of a virgin and rose in the resurrection. Many Jews, including myself, believe that Jesus was a very great teacher whose teachings were greatly misunderstood by his disciples, and I urged Isabel to read Joseph Klausner's works on Jesus and Paul. How far apart were we really?

After a few days in London and Brighton visiting the Scharffs, I went to the Continent, Austria, Czechoslovakia, Switzerland and France. My mind was constantly with Isabel and so I cut short my trip, hoping to meet her earlier than arranged. Unfortunately, I did not know her travel plans, except that she was likely to be visiting some of her father's family near Birmingham.

My sister Marion, whom I hardly knew, had fallen in love with an Englishman, and they were getting married that August in Burton-on-Trent. A glance at a map showed that Burton was not far from Birmingham, so why not go to Burton, combining a good reason, the wedding, with the real reason—looking for Isabel? Cyril Edge, my new brother-in-law, told me that there was one cathedral in the Midlands that I just had to see, Lichfield, not far from Burton. I much prefer looking at paintings to cathedrals, but I let myself be persuaded, and looked at this fine building without great interest, until I saw the one woman who had been on my mind so constantly, also looking at Lichfield Cathedral. Statistically, what are the chances of a man looking for a woman in the Midlands and finding her? So much in my life has been "by chance." My Jewish ancestors had a word for it—*Beschert*.

Isabel and a college friend, Ruth Hunt, had come to England together, planning to look for a one-year teaching post, and then return to Canada. Ruth had found a job, Isabel was still looking. I was scheduled to return to Harvard in mid-September, and so we decided to spend the remaining time together—a week or so in Sussex looking for a teaching job, and also visiting Brighton, so that I could introduce Isabel to the Scharffs and Mrs Emanuel, and a final week at the Edinburgh Festival.

We bought railway run-around tickets and decided to stay in Lewes, because it seemed so central, at a bed-and-breakfast place with adjoining rooms that cost all of 7s 6d each per night. We went for many long walks in and around Lewes, talking and talking. How little attention I paid to anything but Isabel was brought home to me forcefully many years later when we visited Lewes again, and I realized how hilly a place it is. I had thought of my week with Isabel in Lewes many times, but I had so concentrated on talking to her that the terrain had made no impression whatever.

We took leisurely trips to Brighton and Hastings, visiting Bexhill-on-Sea, a sleepy seaside resort, where St Francis School, a private school for girls, had a vacancy to teach English and history. Isabel was offered the position. I paid little attention to Bexhill, because it was to be just an interlude, one year in her life. Little did I know . . .

Our week in Edinburgh was a great deal busier, but all was over-shadowed by the letter she gave me as I left for Liverpool. I have kept all of Isabel's 408 letters, neatly numbered and some starred; this is number 8 with three stars:

"How long have I dreamt of meeting someone like you? I guess I can't tell really. I have never been happier than when I'm with you. Forgive me Alf if I sometimes look sad when I'm with you—it's not sadness, it's a sort of inward contentedness, comfortableness, at-homeness—if you see what I mean. It seems silly that it would affect my looks so, but I don't just sit there looking sad to annoy you. It's a part of me you'll probably have to get used to unless I can change it. Please don't let it affect you adversely. I hope tomorrow you won't be too tense and worried Alf. I can't tell what the future will bring—no one can. If I feel as I do now in ten months time, I'll be sure to see you again. How can I forget these last two months when they are the happiest ones I've spent. You may be justified in your worries Alf, but I don't think so. Somehow I can't realize that you won't be in London when I go back, or at Bexhill when I'm truly in need of love and under-standing. I guess I'll come to with a bang one of these days, and these past days and weeks will seem like a fantasy.

"I'll see you tomorrow Alf. It will be the last day for ever so long. I pray that I can make you happy on this day, that I can calm your fears and be only yours for these few hours. My thoughts will be with you on your trip. In the hectic first days of my teaching I'll wish so very much that I could be with you to find peace from the agony of teach-ing for the first time. May I not fail in this effort. I could never look anyone in the face again. I guess my pride's as great as yours."

The envelope of letter number 1 is now in shreds and has had to be mended with Scotch Tape. Some of the next letters, sent to Vienna, are philatelic curiosities, because they were censored and bear postage-due stamps—Isabel was unaware that postage to the Continent was higher then. After seventy-nine letters, she wrote to say that she did not think our marriage would work, and she would not write again. In many of the intervening years I read Isabel's first eighty letters on her birthday, November 1, and letter 8 was the hardest to read and understand. Had she been playing games with me all along? Was she now happily married to a WASP in Walsall, with six children, occasionally laughing at the fool Jew who had fallen so head over heels in love with her? Reading her letters was a bit of a masochistic exercise, and I was so wrong in what I thought.

This is a good place to try to describe Isabel's personality, of course with hindsight, after being married to her now for some years. I do not think she has changed a great deal: today, in her sixties, she is far more enthusiastic and willing to help than many adolescents we know. Intelligent, kind, clean, hard-working and enthusiastic are the adjectives that best describe her. Also, she is quite easily upset, and has a rather nervous disposition, perhaps partly inherited, and partly acquired during her hectic life in Bexhill. Sometimes she can be quite pessimistic, and perhaps that contributed to her turning me away in 1950. She is also outspoken and does not suffer fools gladly; she is never devious and you know exactly where she stands. I cannot bear to think what my life would be like without her. She loves gardening, music and the theater, all acquired from her parents, has become an expert on costumes, and is most talented linguistically, speaking Spanish, German and French. She is very interested in the Bible—an interest acquired from her father—and in old master paintings, perhaps out of an eagerness to help me.

I met Danny—Helen Ann Daniels—in the spring of 1950. We were introduced by Barbara Breslauer, the daughter of the directress of the Sunday School where I taught, who had gone with her to Downer College in Milwaukee.

In the following months, I dated a few girls—more for company than anything else—and of course compared each girl, unfavorably, with Isabel. Danny came closest. She was shy, pretty and had a background very similar to Isabel's: a religious, Protestant home in Aberdeen, a small town in South Dakota. Like Isabel, she had studied Spanish, and loved music and flowers. Danny loved and identified with her father, a patient, quiet, truly lovable man, a druggist in Aberdeen. Her mother was a rather domineering woman, very active in the Christian Science Church, apparently oblivious to the incongruity of her husband's profession. Danny was very interested in comparative religion, became sincerely interested in Judaism, and converted in an orthodox ceremony supervised by Rabbi David Shapiro long before I proposed to her. I really cared for her and what set her apart from Isabel was that she wanted to marry me and have a Jewish home and family.

I proposed to her on her birthday, May 20, 1952, and we were married that July. On the first evening of our honeymoon she said to me, "Alfred, I didn't really think that you would ever marry me; you care so much for that girl in England." Indeed on our first dates I had spoken mainly of Isabel, and I remember one summer evening in 1951 when Danny broke out in tears, inquiring, "Why do you keep thinking always of a woman who has pushed you away?"

By 1952 I had been alone, without a family, for half my life, and I dearly wanted a wife and children, a Jewish home. On our honeymoon we made the mistake of going to Edinburgh—among many cities of Britain and the Continent—and we walked where I had last seen Isabel in September 1949. I became physically sick, and Danny knew why, but she remained patiently with me.

This was not a good beginning for a marriage and yet, as marriages go, between 1952 and 1975, it was better than most. This was largely due to Danny's love, patience and hard work.

We were married by Rabbi Shapiro in his home—after a curious difficulty. By orthodox law, Danny, having converted, was a Jewess. But was I a Jew? I had been circumcised when I was adopted at the age of two weeks, but I knew of no one who could vouch that this had been according to Halachah, or Jewish law. The mother's religion determines that of the child, and my mother was a devout Catholic before she married my father, and after he died. I had become active in Milwaukee's Jewish community and Rabbi Shapiro did not want to subject me to gossip, and so sent me to a ritual bath in Chicago, for conversion there.

I have never been able to call myself orthodox, conservative or reform with any kind of conviction, although I am a committed Jew. I taught Sunday School for over thirty years at Temple Emanuel, a reform temple, only because I enjoy teaching and the temple was close to my home. Luckily, none of the reform rabbis ever questioned my views on reform Judaism and I was careful never to tell my students that I felt Reform Judaism was rather watered down, colorless and uninspiring. While Danny and Isabel, our boys and I have attended an orthodox synagogue on Sabbaths and holy days, we are certainly not orthodox, and we used to drive to Rabbi Shapiro's synagogue, some seven miles away. We are probably closest to Conservative Judaism, but have not felt at home in Milwaukee's conservative synagogues. The Mayers in Vienna instilled in me a love for Jewish tradition, which has been strengthened by the sincerity of the orthodoxy in the Wolff family in Montreal and the great wisdom and kindness of Rabbi David Shapiro. In 1987 Isabel and I joined a small orthodox congregation very close to us, and it gives us great pleasure to be able to walk there on Sabbaths.

Why am I a Jew? Chosenness sounds elitist, almost incongruous in the modern world, and yet I am convinced that Jews have been chosen to be teachers of morality. How else can it be that such a large proportion of teachers of morality, from Moses through Amos and Isaiah to Jesus, were Jews—a people tiny in number? True Judaism is the Judaism of the prophets, perhaps best and most simply described in the anger of Amos. It is neither the blind fanaticism of the ultraorthodox, nor the bland unitarianism of the reform. While a student at Harvard, I picked up a tiny book by Martin Buber in a used book sale for 10 cents: *Drei Reden über das Judentum*; this book, along with Benno Jakob's *Genesis*, has taught me more than the hundreds of other books on Judaism I have read.

What would Amos say today? I think that he would be aghast mostly at morality in Israel. For 2000 years our people prayed three times daily "Return us to Jerusalem" and it happened in our lifetime—a miracle if there ever was one. The early Zionists were tremendously dedicated, idealistic people, bent on establishing a just society. Today there is much that is beautiful in Israel, but also much that is ugly. There is such materialism, petty politics, dishonesty in government and business, such arrogance, religiously within Judaism and against Arabs. We had a dream and it has turned into a nightmare. Will modern-day prophets be able to rectify this? Probably not in our lifetime.

After our honeymoon in Europe, Danny became a lab technician at PPG, and eventually a full time employee at Aldrich. Even after our boys, David and Daniel, were born in 1958 and 1961, she continued to work part-time at Aldrich, mainly handling the many importations of chemicals from abroad. Life could not have been very easy for her, running the house, looking after the children, helping at Aldrich, entertaining our many guests. I was travelling a good deal—to Europe to see suppliers in the summer, to visit customers in the United States in the spring and autumn—usually leaving Danny at home. She never complained.

Late in 1975, twenty-three years after my marriage to Danny, I had repeated frightening nightmares about Isabel's father whom I had met in Kirkland Lake only once when I visited her parents in January 1950, just before coming to Milwaukee. In these dreams this gaunt old man whom I had not seen for twenty-five years chided me, "Why are you not with Isabel?" In my first eighty letters from Isabel, she had indicated in increasingly strong terms that we could not marry. I needed a Jewish wife and she could not be that. When my many letters and notes to her went unanswered, I suspected that she had found another man and was now smiling about that interlude in her life with a Jew.

I did not know where Isabel was, and so I wrote to the Queen's University alumni office to inquire about the address of her brother, who informed me that she was still in Bexhill, that sleepy place in Sussex where I had taken her in 1949. She was still unmarried! During a Friday evening at Oberlin in February 1975, after a sad visit with the widow of an old art historian friend, Wolfgang Stechow, I wrote to Isabel—my first letter to her in many years—and then carried the letter with me until Sunday, wondering whether to mail it. I posted it that snowy Sunday afternoon in Cleveland, and it changed my life and that of many other people. Isabel replied, and on my next trip to Europe, in April, I called her from Germany and arranged to visit her in Bexhill. That very week her father died, at age 93. He knew that I had contacted Isabel. That first visit, and many subsequent ones, were very strange. She had given me directions to a costume museum just a short way up the hill from the railway station. Of course I had hoped that she would meet me at the station, but she could not, and I walked up the hill in trepidation. There, in the small museum, was Isabel, so little changed, with Harry and Christine Portch, the couple she had lived with since 1950. Supper and discussion afterwards were very odd. Isabel was clearly very nervous, and at 10 pm Harry said sharply, "That's enough, I'll take you back to your hotel." Luckily I had the wit to ask Isabel to go for a walk with me the next morning. Alone with me on Sunday morning, she was in tears most of the time—especially when I picked some forget-me-nots in the garden and purchased a card for her, depicting that beautiful blue girl by Verspronck in the Rijksmuseum. She had never cared for another man, and for years had hoped that I might return to her. Her love for me had been stronger, more singular than mine for her! She had spent twenty-five years with no husband, no children—just working hard, teaching at the Bexhill Grammar School, starting a drama school named Thalia and a costume museum with Christine and Harry. I asked if she would join me for lunch, but she said no. How about dinner, but the answer was the same. "You are a happily married man with two children," she told me. "Go away."

Returning to Milwaukee, I called Stella Overton, Isabel's 80-year-old mother, still living in the tiny family home I had visited in Kirkland Lake in 1950. I arranged to visit her in June, amd we talked late into the night. Isabel was flying over to see her mother in August and I resolved to go back to Kirkland Lake while she was there. I telephoned Isabel before I left, and she implored me not to come, but I ignored her request. We spent two days together. The first day, Saturday, Isabel hardly talked and ate practically nothing. Sunday was easier; the heat broke and we went for a long walk to the edge of town, where we were caught by a sudden downpour. Isabel's mother and her sister Marion left us alone and we talked, just holding hands, till my bus left for Toronto late that evening.

I had told Isabel that I would be in England in the autumn, and planned to visit her in Bexhill on her birthday, November 1st. She said she would be there, but then wrote to me: "Don't come, I won't see you." When I arrived, she had left town, and on a further visit in the summer of 1976, she had again left.

I cannot describe the effect that woman had on me then, as she had in 1949, and years later still does. I was not prepared to give up, and strengthened my resolve by visiting her mother, meeting her brother in Vancouver and talking to an old friend of hers in Tokyo. Finally, in April 1977, she agreed to spend a day with me and got permission for me to join her on a school outing to Rochester Castle. I had an anxious wait outside the hotel till Isabel picked me up at 9.00 am. I wonder what her students thought of that middle-aged man with their teacher—looking very sad, sometimes in tears—who was not exactly known for the male company she kept!

From then on communication between us improved, and for the next five years we exchanged many letters and met at Christmas in Kirkland Lake and Ottawa and during my visits to England.

Of course all this made life more and more difficult for Danny. I had shared everything with her. At first, I had not thought of a divorce— Danny was a loving wife and mother—but she realized that I came back from my visits to Isabel like a man entranced, and I did not realize fully what this must have done to her. Years later, David said to me, "Dad, mother would have gone to the end of the world for you." Late in 1981 Danny told me that she felt that life could not go on as it had; she wanted a divorce. Our sons were flabbergasted, and so were our friends. The mechanics of the divorce were simple and the only slight material argument we had was who would keep our dog, Charlie. Each of us had about the same number of Sigma-Aldrich shares, our main assets, and our best friend, Marvin Klitsner, agreed to represent both of us. When the judge inquired how Marvin could do this fairly, Marvin could explain that there was no argument whatever—and the only material cost of the divorce was the legal out-of-pocket expense of $150. The emotional cost, particularly to Danny, was tremendous. She had met Isabel during a visit to Bexhill in the summer of 1980, but could not bring herself to speak to her in Milwaukee. Isabel would very much have liked to become Danny's friend.

Danny had six fulfilling years after our divorce, with many friends, interesting work at the Milwaukee Jewish Home and getting a master's degree in social work. I saw her often and tried to help with her financial records, the acquisition of art and being with her and David and Daniel when we were all in Milwaukee. Our friends' reaction to our divorce varied greatly. Some did not speak to me at all; some like Muriel Emanuel, Ralph's wife—not without some justification—thought I was deluded and able to oversimplify everything; some, like the Klitsners, tried hard to remain friends with us both. The man most hurt and shaken was Rabbi Shapiro, who had guided and married Danny and me, and his grief was obvious during the Jewish divorce proceedings. Sadly, he never really had a chance to get to know Isabel well because of his stroke in 1984.

7

Aldrich

The notion that I might have a niche in the fine chemical business first came to me in 1949 while a graduate student at Harvard. In those days when you needed a research organic, you looked into one catalog, Eastman Kodak's. If it was in there, you bought it; if not, you made it. The starting material required for the last product necessary to complete my research was 2-isopropylphenol. The Eastman catalog listed it, and I ordered 500 g. Six weeks later, when it had still not come, I went to see Warren Stockwood, the storeroom supervisor, to ask for advice. He handed me a sheet of Harvard Chemistry Department stationery and told me to write to them. "See what happens," he said.

I received a form postcard—I wish I had kept it because today I'd have it framed. It simply said that my order had been received and would I please not add to the paperwork; Eastman would ship the material when they had it. At that point I said to myself, "My gosh, if that's how the fine chemical business is operated in the United States, maybe I have a place in it."

When the director of research of PPG in Milwaukee told me that the company would not be interested in starting a fine chemical division because no one could compete with Kodak, I agreed that he might be right about Kodak as a whole, but that it might be possible to compete with their fine chemicals division. It offered only about 4000 products, and research chemists would be interested in many more products if they were available. So a friend of mine, Jack Eisendrath, a Milwaukee attorney, and I started a company to offer research chemicals. We incorporated on August 17, 1951, with the minimum required capital of $500, each of us putting in $250. We tossed up for the name; I lost the toss. Jack was engaged to a charming girl, Betty Aldrich, and the company was named the Aldrich Chemical Company. At first all the paperwork, storage, weighing, labeling, packaging, and invoicing was done in Jack's office; later we rented a garage on Farwell Avenue on Milwaukee's east side for $25 a month. Our first product was methylnitrosonitroguanidine (MNNG) that I had learned to make while working for my MSc with Dr McKay at Queen's. He had moved to Monsanto Canada, and we contracted with Monsanto and also with a small company in Milwaukee to make this product for us. MNNG is an excellent precursor for diazomethane. It is a stable crystalline solid that melts at a temperature of 118°C, and its great advantage over other precursors is that it yields diazomethane with aqueous rather than ethanolic alkali, as is the case with other precursors. I had told Fieser about this compound, and he had every student in Chemistry 20, the first organic chemistry course, make one batch. I then took all these batches, crystallized them once from methanol to get rid of all the cigarette butts and bobby pins, and the chemistry department then had a sufficient supply of MNNG to last for the entire year. We had a permanent diazomethane still in my lab so that anyone needing diazomethane could use it. What we did not know at the time was that MNNG is one of the most powerful mutagenic agents known.

The first Aldrich catalog was a mimeographed sheet that we sent to some 2000 research chemists around the country. Our mailing list consisted of the senior authors of organic papers in the *Journal of the American Chemical Society* and the *Journal of Organic Chemistry*.

Gradually we added other compounds not listed by Kodak. Catalog number 2 was again a single mimeographed sheet, but unfortunately I do not have a copy of it. Some thirty years later we made an unsuccessful appeal to chemists, offering a fine English landscape for that single sheet. Sales in the first year were $1705, and as we took no salaries at the time, we actually showed a $20 profit. In the second year sales climbed to $5400 and reached $15,000 by the third year. Not bad for part-time work.

Of course, Aldrich had no capital, and neither Jack nor I was in a position to put any money into the company. When I decided not to move with PPG, we went to a friend, a Milwaukee businessman, William Kesselman, and persuaded him to buy a third of the company for $25,000. The agreement was that he would put in $5000 immediately and then $1000 a month for the next twenty months. To conserve capital, my salary was to drop from the $800 a month I had been making at PPG to $500 a month, and I was not to cash the salary checks for the first six months. Bill had the option at any time to withdraw his capital in exchange for his stock. After seven months, in 1955, he came to me and said, "Look, Aldrich has been growing nicely, sales are up practically every month, but still, I do not think that the company will ever be worth $75,000 to justify a $25,000 investment for one third, so I want out; please return my money."

In such decisions, people usually have good reasons and real reasons, and these are often quite different. When I pressed him for his real reason, he said, "Well, I was so disappointed in you. You will recall that some weeks ago you had a friend of yours, Martin Ettlinger, visit you, and you paid him a consulting fee of $100 without asking my consent." Martin helped enormously with the publication of papers, with helpful suggestions, and with many chemical matters, and when he visited us, that small honorarium seemed entirely justifiable. Our investor, of

TELEPHONE BROADWAY 2-1600

Aldrich CHEMICAL COMPANY

161 WEST WISCONSIN AVENUE
MILWAUKEE 3, WISCONSIN

N-methyl-N-nitroso-N'-nitroguanidine for the preparation of Diazomethane

is now being distributed for the first time anywhere by the Aldrich

Chemical Company.

Diazomethane is an invaluable reagent for the methylation of
carboxylic acids, phenols and enols, for the preparation of
heterocyclic compounds and in the Arndt-Eistert reaction.
It has hitherto been prepared through intermediates which are
unstable and strong skin irritants.

Diazomethane can now be prepared most simply by the action of
alkali on methyl nitroso nitroguanidine. (cf. McKay JACS 70,
1974 (1948); McKay et al, Can. J. Res., 28, 683 (1950);
Organic Chemistry, Fieser and Fieser, 2nd. Ed. 178.

Methyl nitroso nitroguanidine is a crystalline compound, m.p.
118°C. which has been kept in brown bottles at room temperature for over a year without decomposition. The addition of
this crystalline compound to a cold 50% aqueous potassium
hydroxide solution covered with ether yields diazomethane in
70-90% yield. Numerous experiments have shown that when this
ethereal diazomethane solution is distilled and added to an
ethereal solution of a pure carboxylic acid, then evaporation
of the resulting solution leaves the analytically pure methyl
ester of the acid.

N-methyl-N-nitroso-N'-nitroguanidine Prices:

10 gms.	$ 5.00
25 gms.	10.00
100 gms.	25.00

We shall be pleased to receive your introductory order.

ALDRICH CHEMICAL COMPANY

Aldrich's first catalog, 1951.

course, was on our board of directors and there was tight control of expenses. For instance, the only action of the last board meeting before his departure was to allow me to buy another badly needed second-hand desk at a cost not to exceed $35! Still, a consulting payment to Martin of only $100 seemed so well-deserved that it had not occurred to me to ask for board approval.

We were now in a difficult position. Bill had put $12,000 into the company and was entitled to receive that back over the next couple of years. Jack had helped a great deal in the early days, but his law practice reduced his input very considerably, whereas I was working twelve

IOWA STATE COLLEGE
OF AGRICULTURE AND MECHANIC ARTS
AMES, IOWA
May 14, 1953

DEPARTMENT OF CHEMISTRY
CHARLES A. GOETZ, HEAD

Aldrich Chemical Company
161 West Wisconsin Avenue
Milwaukee 3, Wisconsin

Dear Sirs:

    May I know whether you have for sale any 3-hydroxypyridine.
If not, may I know whether you make up special compounds like
this.

            Very truly yours,

            Henry Gilman

HG:ls

AIRMAIL.

Dear Professor Gilman,

*Thank you for your inquiry for 3-hydroxypyridine.
We do not have any in stock, but our heterocyclics chemist
is looking into its preparation, and we shall send you a
quotation shortly.*

*   Yours sincerely,*

*   JNE.*

Enclosures: all three catalogues.

*One of our first inquiries, May 1953. The request was from Professor
Henry Gilman for 3-hydroxypyridine (H5700-9). Aldrich then had one
chemist, Alfred Bader, and if someone wanted a heterocyclic, the answer
was that our "heterocyclics chemist" would look at it; if someone wanted a steroid, our "steroid chemist" would look at it, and so forth. Those
"chemists" were all one and the same!*

to fourteen hours a day. Moreover, every move, including minor purchases, required mutual agreement, making progress and decisions difficult. With the withdrawal of the only real capital, everything had to be
generated by our own efforts. Under the circumstances, a 50:50 interest
between Jack and me did not strike me as fair, so I consulted Harry

Kovenock, another attorney known for his uprightness and legal wisdom. He worked out three alternatives for me to submit to Jack: first was that I sell him my 50% for $3000 and use the money to start the Bader Chemical Company; second was that Jack sell his 50% to me for $10,000, to be paid over two or three years; and third was that he sell me 20% for $6000, so that I would have 70%. Jack did not like any of these alternatives and became very angry. He tried to find another chemist to run Aldrich, but eventually sold out completely for $15,000, payable over three years. I am really sorry that he has not spoken to me since.

When I left PPG, Aldrich moved from the garage to a 1000 sq ft laboratory near Capitol Drive in Milwaukee. By this time the debts were substantial: $12,000 to our former investor and $15,000 to Jack. Sales, however, skyrocketed to $39,000 that fourth year, and luckily we received our first really large order. Du Pont had written to a number of companies asking for quotations for 500 lb of suberic acid. I had never made suberic acid, but the preparation seemed straightforward and the starting material, 1,6-hexanediol, was available very inexpensively from Union Carbide. I had no idea how to figure costs of production but felt that we could not go wrong if we got the order at $38 per lb. Believe it or not, we got the order for delivery by the end of the year. That $19,000 really helped.

There was still much work to be done to complete the papers on the diene reactions. Although all the work with dienes was begun at PPG and all the patents were applied for from there, I was happy to submit the papers from PPG and Aldrich—great and free advertising for a tiny company with one chemist!

The greatest problem every entrepreneur faces is how to find really good employees. Our first was Lorraine Leitner, a secretary hired by Jack Eisendrath; moody and competent, she stayed with us until her retirement in 1978. When I left PPG, George Skeff, a very able lab technician, came with me and did everything that was needed, even driving me to US Customs, as I had not yet learned how to drive. His initial salary was $250 per month. Mine was twice that, but he could cash his salary check, I could not. Then two young ladies joined us in quick succession. Beverly Horick is still with Aldrich, now in purchasing. Of the early employees, Beverly was most interested in the growth of the company. She decided to collect all the documents and became the unofficial company historian. I had grave doubts about hiring Stella Ward, but only during her interview. She was working in a laundry in Milwaukee's inner city at $1 per hour. We were offering $1.10. In the early years of Aldrich, Danny and I invited prospective employees for supper at home. Understandably, she came to our apartment all dressed up, of course not knowing how I hate to wear ties in my office or anywhere else. But she was intelligent, quick witted, a pleasure to talk to, and was willing to work wherever she was needed. When I put my arms around her during her Aldrich retirement party in 1992, I thought how gracefully she had aged, and then listened to one of her grandsons, a strapping black fellow, who marvelled at his grandma who had worked with one company for thirty-seven years; he was only 25 and had already held five jobs!

After we received our first US government research contract, an inspector visited us to ascertain that we hired fairly. After talking to our employees for a couple of hours, he came to my office and asked in a heavy Southern drawl, "Dr Bader, do you perchance discriminate against white Protestants?" I was staggered, and all I could say was, "But we must have some." It just so happened that most, perhaps all, our secretaries at that time were Catholics. I did not know or care what their religion was. Yes, we did try to hire blacks, for an obvious reason: blacks are the only people in the country whose ancestors were forced to come here as slaves, and they have been ill-treated ever since.

I made mistakes: I was too tight-fisted in the first twenty years, checking and double-checking too much, and many good employees left for better pay elsewhere; but we had the best health insurance and profit-sharing plans possible, and we were one big family. In the fifties we had "record month dinners", four or five a year, and when we had so many employees that ordinary restaurants could not seat us, we changed to a "record year dinner", complete with dance band, and—more recently—5 to 35 year awards and speeches. At one of the last speeches I gave, I paraphrased a character in the comics, saying, "Working at Aldrich may sometimes seem to you like wetting the pants of your dark suit; nobody notices, but it gives you a warm feeling." David Harvey, my successor, told me that that was the worst speech I had ever made. David has many good qualities; a sense of humor is not among them. In 1955 we also started a monthly sales chart that got longer and longer; by 1984 it was 55 ft long. It could not have grown like that without our caring employees.

With one minor exception, no union ever threatened us, and we never had a strike. In the fifties, I received some very good advice on labor relations from a friend, Saul Cooper, a lawyer working for a local union. Whenever an employee asked for anything that seemed unreasonable to me, I asked Saul what a union could reasonably demand, and then followed his advice. Sadly, Saul died when still a young man, but as I got to know Marvin Klitsner better and better, I realized that I would do well to follow his advice. Once we even sought the help of a Catholic priest: our first employee, Lorraine, who had joined us as a part-time secretary, was a strict Catholic who thought that taking letters dealing with Jewish charities was against her religion. I urged her to discuss this with her priest, and she then stayed with us without further religious reservations until her retirement.

To survive in the early years, we had to make every penny count. Our employees understood why I was so careful of even the smallest expense. We did everything together from opening envelopes in the morning to filling bottles during the day and taking the shipments to the post office in the afternoon. We were the Aldrich Family even as we grew to hundreds. We never borrowed money, although this was suggested to me as the way to grow more quickly. Our growth came through the quality and reliability of our products and the service we offered, and I made sure our employees knew that these were dependent on the dedication of every one of them.

Then in 1970, the Oil, Chemical & Atomic Workers Union, a division of the AFL-CIO, wanted to organize the forty-six lowest paid Aldrich employees, our people in packaging and shipping. They made some preposterous claims—for instance, that management played golf on Friday afternoons while our workers slaved! I held one long meeting in which I asked our employees what a union could give them that they did not have already, except that they had no union dues to pay and we had never had a strike. The vote that December went 39:7 against the union, and the day after the election, six of the seven left the company. I presume they had joined to unionize our people.

I felt very uncomfortable with that episode. In many companies, particularly in the past, unions were essential to protect workers' rights. Here in Milwaukee, we have had the spectacle of top executives earning salaries in excess of $1,000,000 while laying off thousands of employees: "down-sizing" their operations was the ugly term. Whose fault was it, management's or the workers'? I promised our people that if ever we had a recession as deep as in the thirties, our first move would be to cut management's salaries, then a reduction in working hours; but nobody would be laid off for lack of work, and nobody ever was. At the time of our merger with Sigma, I was asked how many I thought we could lay off—"rationalization of effort" it was called. The merger, I said, would make us grow so much faster that we would need more people, not fewer. If layoffs were planned, they could forget about the deal! Maybe I am a romantic simpleton without a business-school education, but I really meant it when I told our people that I wanted them to love the company as much as our customers did. But love and care cannot be a one-way street, and I certainly wanted our people to know that I cared.

It became clear to me very early on that we could not succeed if we sold only what I knew how to make; we must combine production with resale, particularly of imports. I knew western Europe fairly well, spoke German fluently and French haltingly, so I decided to spend a month or two every year travelling in Europe, visiting small and medium-sized chemical companies, inquiring what we might purchase from them. Of course, I knew what was in our own catalog, and I always carried a Kodak catalog with me to check whether the chemicals offered were listed there. If they were, I declined—how could we compete with Kodak?—but if they were not, I bought $100 or $200 worth to ship to Milwaukee and add to our catalog.

A few years later, an interesting experience changed this policy. Professor John Sheehan of MIT, an old friend, contacted me and urged me to offer a new peptide reagent that he had developed, dicyclohexylcarbodiimide, which Kodak did not have. The preparation is not particularly easy as it involves a mercuric oxide oxidation and the material is a strong eye and skin irritant, but we listed it, and sales did very nicely. Then one day I glanced through a new Kodak catalog and noticed to my great chagrin that they were now offering DCC at a few pennies per bottle less than ours. I figured that that was the end for that product; no one would buy DCC from Aldrich. But I was mistaken: sales kept going up. Then I realized that we could compete, and from then on we listed whatever useful products we could buy or make, regardless of anyone else.

By then, Marvin Klitsner and I had become the best of friends, and he was the moving spirit in the growth of Aldrich. For years before he became a director in 1961, he advised me on everything we did. When I was introduced as the founder of Aldrich and later as one of the founders of Sigma-Aldrich, my thoughts invariably turned to Marvin: yes, indeed, I was a founder, but without Marvin, Aldrich would have remained one of those medium-sized fine chemical companies existing around the world, successful, but without distinction.

We started the Bader-Klitsner Foundation, which has helped Jewish causes in Milwaukee and Israel, and B & K Enterprises, which owns Alfred Bader Fine Arts; Marvin joined me on the board of directors of Rabbi Shapiro's synagogue, and in founding the Hillel Academy, Milwaukee's Jewish day school.

Readers will have realized by now that I tend to be a bit of a *Spitzbub*; not—I hope—dishonest, but streetwise, educated in the jungle of Vienna in the depression. I enjoy a fight, and Marvin kept Aldrich and me out of many lawsuits. The few in which we engaged had his full support.

Despite my being so pugnacious, I was sued in Milwaukee only once under circumstances that still make me cringe. Perhaps the details can serve as a lesson to some people, particularly hospital administrators.

Following minor surgery at Mount Sinai Hospital in 1959, I contracted a urinary infection because a hospital orderly, who was paralyzed in one hand, tried vainly for over half an hour to catheterize me, a procedure that took the doctor less than a minute when he was finally called. I was very reassured when one of Milwaukee's ablest internists, Burton Waisbren, was called in as a consultant, because just two years earlier he had been most helpful when I contracted jaundice following a gall bladder operation at Columbia Hospital.

Dr Waisbren charged $35 for the first consultation. Aldrich's Blue Cross policy stated specifically that Blue Cross would pay any reasonable fee for consultation services to the extent of one consultation. Yet surprisingly, Blue Cross paid only $25 and adamantly refused to pay more. I would not have been surprised if Dr Waisbren had sued Blue Cross for the $10, but he decided to sue me in Milwaukee's small claims court, despite twelve letters from me to Waisbren, his attorney, Blue Cross and the administrator of Mount Sinai Hospital, explaining the circumstances. Of course I considered suing Mount Sinai for malpractice, but as my mother would have said, *es passt sich nicht*—it's not right to sue a hospital, and so I refrained.

I asked Marvin what should be done, and he said that if the amount involved were $10,000 instead of $10, the procedure would be to interplead Blue Cross and say precisely what I thought, that either the bill was reasonable and Blue Cross should pay, or it was unreasonable and consequently I should not pay. The whole thing was over a ridiculously small sum, but I was really angry at Blue Cross, and if no one ever stands up to powerful institutions, such pettiness will continue.

There were many people waiting for their cases to be heard in the small claims court, and I remember the sudden silence when the case of Dr Burton Waisbren against Dr Alfred Bader was called. Foley & Lardner appeared on my behalf, another lawyer on behalf of Blue Cross, and attorney Sol Goodsitt on behalf of Dr Waisbren. The judge exclaimed: "Three lawyers on a $10 claim! I want to see counsel in my chambers." I have never seen a man quite so red in the face as Sol Goodsitt when he left the judge's chamber. I learned what occurred there when the judge, in effect, knocked the heads of Blue Cross's attorney and Sol Goodsitt together and required them to split the $10.

This story has two interesting sequels. A few years later Dr Waisbren asked Aldrich to make a product specially for his research, and of course we did—at a reasonable price! And in 1975 Dr Waisbren sent me a check for "$25 for the alleged overcharge plus interest", explaining that it had come to his attention that I was still disturbed and had "not seen fit to contribute to Mount Sinai." Dr Waisbren's last paragraph showed so clearly how we were talking past each other:

"As a physician I can assure you that should another of my colleagues ask me to see you in consultation when and if you develop a severe infection in some hospital, I would do so, but next time I can assure you also that I will let you set the fee as to how much your life is worth."

I had not thought that he overcharged me at all, just that my insurance policy covered his fee. Blue Cross and Mount Sinai were to blame. If the hospital's administrator had ever heard of that vital commandment, "You shall not stand idly by the blood of your neighbor," he had forgotten it. Of course I returned Dr Waisbren's check, repeating the story for the thirteenth time, and I just hope that I will never again have to be in Mount Sinai Hospital.

Perhaps it was a coincidence, but we had no further arguments with Blue Cross. This was just one more consequence of Marvin's guidance.

Of course my main efforts centered on finding new products for Aldrich, not fighting windmills, and most new products came from Europe.

My annual trip always began in England, and one of my first calls was to Ralph Emanuel's office in the Leather Market near London Bridge. At first this was just a friendship visit because Ralph was the younger son of Bessy and Moritz Emanuel who had helped me settle in Hove in 1939. Ralph, who soon became a firm friend, had inherited his father's leather business when he was 18, and he was a good businessman who understood British business practices. By 1955 I realized that Aldrich should be selling outside the United States. We would need a British agent, and I asked Ralph to keep his eyes open for a suitable person. I wondered if he might consider the job himself. He had a large warehouse and plenty of space, but he was not at first tempted. His own business was going well, and the importing and reshipping of our tiny bottles was probably a nuisance for him, but he was willing to help out by clearing the occasional parcel through customs and shipping it on.

In time I was able to persuade him despite the misgivings of his brother, Alfred, an able accountant, who wondered what problems Ralph might be running into. Our British branch, Ralph N Emanuel Ltd, began in 1959 with Ralph's wife, Muriel, acting as honorary bookkeeper and his brother as the outside accountant. Although sales the first year were less than $1000, Ralph became fascinated. He asked for 100 of our thin catalogs, offering small quantities at low prices, and distributed them to potential buyers.

The company grew nicely. Ralph and Muriel invited me to make their home my base whenever I went to Europe. We soon had to hire full-time staff and twice moved to larger premises. By 1973 there were almost thirty employees in the British company and Derek Allen, a director, hired by Ralph, located a fine site in Gillingham, Dorset. This small town offered cheap land, a good potential workforce and an excellent rail connection with London, but it was far from Ralph's home. Through a friend, he found David Harvey, who became responsible for all our European operations. Ralph remained a director of the British as well as the American parent company and was always available to give advice, which was often invaluable.

The company at first was half-owned by Ralph and Muriel, and half by trusts for my sons. In 1969, trusts for Ralph's children acquired the second 50% and then exchanged all the stock for stock in Aldrich.

When Ralph's attorney looked over the details of this exchange, he asked Ralph whether he had "a special relationship" with me. My relationship with Ralph was indeed special, but probably not in the way the attorney meant. Ralph was a good and intelligent man who could be critical when he felt criticism was needed and who was a wise friend.

Ralph N Emanuel Ltd, later renamed Aldrich Chemical Company Ltd, succeeded so well that it became Britain's largest supplier of research chemicals. It is now Gillingham's largest employer and owns over 100 acres, suitable for future expansion. At the time of Aldrich's merger with Sigma, Ralph became a Sigma-Aldrich director.

Ralph is a truly caring employer. I know of no other boss who was left part of his estate by an employee who had enjoyed working for him, but that actually happened to Ralph!

Finding new suppliers and many new products was a continuous day-to-day effort, helped by the many friends I made around the world. This was our bread and butter. But in 1955 we became involved in a much more exciting area—medicinal chemistry, through Dr I Herbert Scheinberg, a friend of Martin Ettlinger. An MD, then at Albert Einstein College of Medicine in New York, Herbert was working with patients suffering from Wilson's disease. This is a rare and usually fatal disease of patients who accumulate copper in the liver. Herbert showed me the liver of a patient who had died of the disease; it appeared to be a solid chunk of copper. He also showed me a map of eastern Europe, where the patients and their parents and grandparents had originated; almost all were Jews from Lithuania, Poland and Russia. When he gave these patients a daily gram of a simple amino acid, penicillamine, the copper in their livers became chelated and was excreted, enabling them to live normal lives. Without penicillamine they died. Merck had been supplying penicillamine, but there were so few patients with Wilson's disease that they stopped production. Herbert asked whether Aldrich could supply it? What a challenge! I made a small quantity, but in our 1000 sq ft laboratory we certainly could not make the kilo lots needed. I was able however to persuade Peboc, an English company, to make it. This story had three interesting sequels. Reports appeared that penicillamine with colloidal gold also helped to combat rheumatism, so Merck resumed production. Further research into Wilson's disease revealed that, although rare, it was very widespread—even some Japanese suffer from it, and Herbert's predominantly eastern European patients were not a representative sample. Unfortunately, some patients eventually became allergic to penicillamine, and in 1980 Herbert inquired whether we could supply an alternate copper-chelating agent, triethylenetetramine.

By then we had good production facilities in Milwaukee, and we offered kilo lots, with a note to Herbert:

". . . looking back over 29 years in business, I don't recall a single example which has given me as much personal satisfaction as has providing you with penicillamine back in the 50's, because I know that it was truly saving lives.

"I am so happy now to have the opportunity to help provide an alternative for those suffering with Wilson's disease who are allergic to penicillamine."

Penicillamine was the first of many "orphan drugs" made by Aldrich. By 1958 we had about a dozen people, and we had outgrown the rented laboratory. We then purchased a three-story building in Milwaukee's inner city. It had been used by a shoe company and a cosmetics maker, and at first the 27,000 sq ft building looked cavernously empty. We had heard that the Milwaukee County Expressway Commission was planning to build an east-west expressway nearby, the so-called Park Freeway, but the commission assured us that our building was not in its path. We were growing at a tremendous rate, and by 1960 the building was so chock full that we had to buy a second, much larger one just a block away, the former home of the Badger Meter Company, with 70,000 sq ft. Again before buying, we checked with the Expressway Commission, and we were again assured we were safe. Our requirements for space were satisfied, at least for a decade or two, in two well-built factory buildings, or so we thought until in July 1962, Ken Fry advised us that the expressway plans had changed: all our buildings would be taken! When? No one knew. Fry was the commission's Director of Economic Development, but over the next years we had cause to think of many more appropriate titles. Aldrich had grown wonderfully well, with sales of $1,000,000 in 1962, up from $5400 a decade earlier, and we had cheerfully located in Milwaukee's oldest and most run-down section. Now we operated in total uncertainty until three years later, when the County held a public hearing where we were told that acquisition of the properties would begin in 1966 and would take two to three years to complete. We had to start looking for another location. By 1969 all buildings surrounding ours had been pulled down, and ours stood out on an otherwise level landscape. What a nightmare turned to reality! The County gave us an immensely hard time, not just with the uncertainty of timing but with appraisals. The first appraisal became outdated and had to be redone. The second became invalid because the appraiser had left the American Appraisal Company.

Bureaucrats and politicians kept mouthing platitudes about wanting to help growing companies. What bull! We had doubled our sales between 1962 and 1965 to $2,000,000, and we were employing over 100 people, but no one did anything to help us. The final appraisal in 1970 was an insult to our intelligence. It valued the buildings only and not the extensive laboratories we had built. It took another three years and legal action before that matter was settled.

Then came the final blow. When the whole area resembled the moon landscape, plans changed once again. The Park Freeway was cancelled. It never was built. Milwaukee's government is, I believe, honest, but honesty does not equate with intelligence.

The delays and mismanagement of this affair were costly to everyone. Early in 1966 we were offered a fine site downtown, a sturdy, eight-story L-shaped building near Marquette University, completely surrounded by existing expressways. It belonged to General Electric, which valued it so highly that the Expressway Commission decided to build around it rather than acquire it, although it had to buy GE's air rights. Then GE decided that access to the building was too difficult and offered it for sale. But how could Aldrich consider buying it without knowing when the Commission would purchase our inner-city buildings? Finally Marvin and I cut this Gordian knot by buying it ourselves and giving Aldrich an option to buy it at our cost. The commissioners grumbled when they learned that we had paid only $300,000, $2 per sq ft, because GE's unwillingness to sell to the Expressway Commission had added millions to their cost. What an expense to taxpayers and—in Aldrich's case—to us because the Commission could not or would not give us definite answers.

We later acquired many other large properties, one building across the street for offices, and others mainly for storage and distribution. Storing millions of bottles and shipping more than 95% of all orders on the day they are received takes a lot of space, and luckily industrial buildings in Milwaukee are very inexpensive. Despite the troubles we have had, Milwaukee has been a fine city in which to run a company. Industrial property is cheap, taxes have been relatively low and we have had few environmental problems.

Most of our sales were for catalog items, and right from the beginning I paid special attention to our catalogs and publications. At first, they had to be simple and inexpensive, just a list of compounds, as in the Kodak catalog. But within a few years we added empirical formulae and structures, and many physical constants and literature references followed. Today the catalog resembles, and in fact is, a handbook of chemicals.

The credit for the idea of using an old master painting on the cover belongs to Bernie Edelstein, the company secretary. I was worried that such a painting would seem out of place on a scientific catalog and was against it, but the vote at the next meeting of the board of directors was 3:2. *The Quill Cutter* by Paulus de Lesire, a Rembrandt student, seemed suitable and was the first to be used—on our 1967/68 edition. We offered reproductions of the cover (plate 1), thinking that perhaps only forty or fifty chemists would respond. In fact they ordered them in their thousands, often with hilarious comments. To quote just one, from Stanford University:

"The Art Appreciation Group of Dr. Djerassi's lab would like to have a copy of your Squill-Pitter, Pull-Squitter, Kill-Qutter, Cull-Squirter . . . the chap who hasn't heard about ball-points on your new catalog cover."

From then on, the choice of painting became a biennial challenge; covers should be alchemical, beautiful or both. I am glad that this tradition has continued even after my dismissal.

In the early sixties we offered our new products between catalogs on simple file cards, which were sent to our best customers. Then a thought occurred to us: why not mail a regular publication three or four times a year, publishing selected scientific papers, repeating our full-page advertisements in chemical journals and offering our new products? Of the first issue of the *Aldrichimica Acta* in 1968 only 10,000 were printed, but by the eighties over 200,000 copies went out worldwide, and chemists lined up at conferences to have their names added to the mailing list.

We put a great deal of effort into our full-page advertisements, which appeared regularly on the back covers of many chemical journals. One almost got us into a fight with the American Chemical Society and another with the German *Berichte*. Aldrich was the first company to advertise regularly on the back covers of the *Journal of Organic Chemistry*, and we had agreed in writing with the ACS, the publisher of *JOC*, that we would have all the back covers as long as we wanted them. Other companies soon realized what was clear to me: a back-cover advert is worth far more than ads anywhere else, and in time our competitors also wanted the back covers. When *JOC* changed from twelve to twenty-six issues a year, they advised us that we could retain twelve covers while the other fourteen would be shared by two competitors. Of course I remonstrated: "all issues" meant all, not just twelve, and Aldrich had spent many thousands of dollars leading readers to the back covers. Luckily the ACS understood and Aldrich has had all the back covers of the *JOC* ever since. Our argument with the *Berichte* was funnier and less serious. One ad, listing many benzimidazoles, was headed by two rabbits in a happy cuddle with the legend "One good thing leads to another." A disgusted reader inquired, "How can you allow such a

The advertisement of Fig. 1, of five years ago, states one of our most important aims: the sale of fine organic chemicals used to support fundamental research. That we have saved chemists throughout the world millions of man hours of labor by supplying chemicals not available elsewhere, is obvious. But Aldrich is today the only major supplier of organic laboratory chemicals whose major—in fact, whose only—business is in organic chemicals, and we have plowed a good share of our earnings back into fundamental research. Five years ago we had made only the modest beginning referred to in the ad. Today we have a Research Department headed by one of the country's foremost medicinal chemists, with some fourteen chemists turning out novel structural classes of chemicals of great significance to both organic and medicinal chemists.

Our dream is coming true.

PROCEEDINGS   FEBRUARY 1963

...of things to come!

Oil on copper, 5" × 5"   Hofstede de Groot No. 240
THE SCHOLAR BY CANDLELIGHT

One of our chemists collects Dutch paintings and managed to pick up a small, early Rembrandt in Vienna some years ago.

Discussing this painting with us, he admitted that he would prefer a late Rembrandt portrait, and yet he almost got us to share his enthusiasm for this small piece of copper. Done in Leiden when Rembrandt was in his early twenties, it clearly foreshadows the great things to come: "The Supper at Emmaus," in the Musée Jacquemart André in Paris; and the "Self-portrait Before the Easel," in Boston, painted only a year or two later.

Perhaps what struck us so forcefully about these comments was their likeness to our own dreams for Aldrich: a modest beginning—a new synthesis of indoles, our work on unsaturated phenols, on o,p'-DDD and cyclohexenones—foreshadowing the things to come: the sale of fine organic chemicals used to support fundamental research.

Figure 1

Our dream for Aldrich.

vulgar ad on the cover of our *Berichte*?" and we were asked to be more careful.

Our decision to include scientific papers was a challenge. Would we be offered really excellent papers for the *Acta*? At first some good friends contributed, Everette May for instance, one of the world experts on analgesics at the NIH, and Jim Fergason, one of the great entrepreneurs in liquid crystal technology. I included a few papers on matters close to my heart, "Prague Revisited", on alchemical paintings and one of my dreams for the company.

ABC referred both to Alfred Bader Chemicals and to Art, Bible and Chemistry in my life. We put some of our best paintings on the *Acta* covers, and I sometimes mixed art history with philosophy and Bible stories in my commentaries about our covers.

In 1977 the *Aldrichimica Acta* reprinted a hilarious article from the ICI safety news-letter—a spoof describing the discovery of a new firefighting agent called "Wonderful And Total Extinguishing Resource", WATER for short. Strong opposition to this new substance was reported. Immerse your head in a bucket of WATER and "it would prove fatal in as little as 3 minutes." "It had been reported that WATER was a constituent of beer. Did this mean that firemen would be intoxicated by the fumes?" ". . . it caused clothes to shrink. If it did this to cotton what would it do to men?" But one has to be careful not to laugh too loudly. We received some scathing letters as a result of printing the article. A chemist from a school in Texas assured us that we would not receive another order from his institution. When we checked, we found that he had ordered only one product the previous year, value $6.80.

We need not have worried about receiving enough papers. The prizes we established with the American Chemical Society, the Royal Society of Chemistry and the Chemical Institute of Canada requested the winners to send us their award papers. Authors realized that the *Acta*'s presentation of their papers was excellent and the distribution greater than that of any chemical journal. Also, the papers were abstracted by *Chemical Abstracts* and we provided free reprints. Barry Sharpless, one of America's most inventive chemists, told me that he received more requests for reprints of his *Acta* article than for any paper he had ever published. Not all the authors were well-established chemists. In San Francisco we met Steven Gill, a young fellow with great enthusiasm about chemiluminescence. What he lacked in academic credentials he made up for through practical experience, and his paper was a gem. Of course Clint Lane, who came to us from Herb Brown's lab, wrote many fine papers on hydroboration, as did Chris Hewitt and Mike Silvester at Bristol Organics on fluoroaromatics. Many of our full page ads in the *Acta* were mini-review articles.

Our first "dedicated" *Acta*, in 1977, honored Bob Woodward on his sixtieth birthday, and David Dolphin's article written partly seriously and partly tongue-in-cheek is one of the funniest biographical essays I have ever read. Other dedications to truly great chemists followed: Gilbert Stork, that wonderful teacher at Columbia for his sixtieth birthday; Herbert Brown, the father of Aldrich-Boranes for his seventy-fifth; Ralph Raphael, Cambridge University's great father-figure for his

MNNG- CANCER RESEARCH TOOL, MUTAGEN, ANTIMALARIAL

No compound has excited our imagination as much as has N-methyl-N'-nitro-N-nitrosoguanidine (MNNG), the first compound ever offered by Aldrich. At first we sold it only as a precursor for diazomethane (1) for which our "Diazald"® is much less expensive and safer. The first biological activity discovered was the action against leukaemia L1210 in mice (2). Many analogues were evaluated, but MNNG proved to be among the most potent (3). Mutants of *Escherichia coli* S, selected for increasing resistance to MNNG, were also resistant to analogues with alkyl groups other than methyl (4). MNNG rather than its breakdown products was shown to act as a mutagen in bacteria (5). The inhibition of *E. coli* was shown to be reversed nonspecifi-

Looking For VITAMIN C?

On a winter Monday afternoon in 1839, Professor P. J. Robiquet ceremoniously presented the Académie des Sciences in Paris with a sample of sinigrin (potassium myronate), which had just been isolated by Bussy (1) from black mustard seed and thus became one of the early pure organic chemicals from plants. Yet it took 88 years till a reliable procedure (2) was described for the isolation, and 117 years before the correct structure I of sinigrin was proposed and established. (3)

$$CH_2 - CH = CH_2$$
$$C - S - C_6H_{11}O_5$$
$$N - O - SO_3^- K^+$$

How To Find A Great Herbicide

Alfred Bader

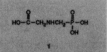

In the spring of 1984, we at Aldrich were surprised by the visit of two teams of lawyers and chemical experts who came to question us about the best-selling herbicide ever. Round-up® herbicide which contains N-(phosphonomethyl)glycine (1) as its active ingredient was patented by Monsanto in 1974 and 1983 (U.S. Patents 3,799,758 and 4,405,531), but the Stauffer Chemical Company had developed a related herbicide having the trademark Touchdown® and questioned the validity of Monsanto's patents.

We had offered the compound at Aldrich through our *Library of Rare Chemicals*, and had listed it in both the 1967 library catalog and the 1972 Catalog/Handbook — hence, the day-long interrogation by the two teams of lawyers and their experts. How had we obtained the compound, when and why, and what had we done with it?

(A) Sharpless Chemistry

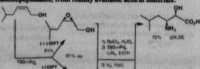

In 1980, Professor Barry Sharpless and Dr. Tsutomu Katsuki introduced the titanium alkoxide/tartrate-catalyzed epoxidation of prochiral allylic alcohols as a versatile and highly enantioselective method for the preparation of homochiral 2,3-epoxy alcohols.¹ The numerous publications which appeared within a few years following this initial report attest to its usefulness for the syntheses of biologically important organic compounds (*e.g.*, leucotrienes,² pheromones,³ terpenes,⁴ anthracyclines,⁵ and carbohydrates⁶). The utility of the Sharpless Asymmetric Epoxidation is limited only by the development of new applications for the derived homochiral 2,3-epoxy alcohols. Thus, to extend the scope of the reaction, Sharpless and co-workers have since investigated the selectivity of nucleophilic ring-opening reactions of these substrates.⁷ The following

Application of the Sharpless Asymmetric Epoxidation/RuO₄ oxidation in conjunction with the titanium isopropoxide-induced ring opening of the derived glycidic acids has afforded selectively *all four stereoisomers* of the unusual N-terminal amino acid of amastatin, a tripeptide competitive inhibitor of aminopepsidases, from readily available achiral materials.¹¹

Extracts from our advertisements—mini reviews.

5-Thio-D-Glucose: How Do Enzymes Work?

John W. Frost
Department of Chemistry
Harvard University
Cambridge, Massachusetts 02138

5-Thio-D-glucose (1) can be a key to the enzymatic synthesis of a myriad of products, each of which would constitute a unique enzymic mechanistic probe.

Monomeric carbohydrates in aqueous solution can exist as pyranoses, furanoses, acyclic carbonyls, or acyclic hydrates. Generally enzymes will bind only one of the forms available to a substrate although this may not be the form subsequently processed by the enzyme. Since the rate of ring

Scheme I - Glycolysis

5-thio-D-glucose (1) → hexokinase → 5-thio-D-glucose 6-phosphate (2) → isomerase → 5-thiofructose 6-phosphate (3)

Scheme II - Pentose Phosphate Shunt

Inspired by Gilbert Stork

Selected Synthetic Transformations {1971-1981}

In his long and distinguished career, Professor Gilbert Stork has pioneered some of the most creative synthetic methods to appear in the chemical literature.[1] Aldrich salutes Professor Stork on his 35th anniversary! Below are some highlights of important synthetic methodologies developed by Professor Stork and his group during the last decade.

A recent paper introducing the regiospecific and stereoselective reductive alkylation of enediones (i.e., 7→8) demonstrates several other important Stork synthetic techniques, namely, formation of the kinetic enolate of 4, the α-silyl vinyl ketone annulation reaction (4+5→6→7), and the isoxazole annulation reaction (7→8→9). Reagent 5 is prepared from vinyltrimethylsilane.[1]

TPAP: a mild catalytic oxidant

Professor Steven Ley, Dr. Bill Griffith and their colleagues at Imperial College, London, recently developed a novel reagent for the oxidation of alcohols to carbonyl compounds which promises to be a highly useful addition to the synthetic chemist's repertoire.[1]

The reagent, **tetrapropylammonium perruthenate** (TPAP, 1), used in catalytic quantities together with *4-methylmorpholine N-oxide* (NMO), oxidizes primary alcohols to aldehydes and secon-

$$MeCH_2CH_2-\overset{\overset{\displaystyle CH_2CH_2Me}{|}}{\underset{\underset{\displaystyle CH_2CH_2Me}{|}}{N}}-CH_2CH_2Me \quad RuO_4^-$$

1

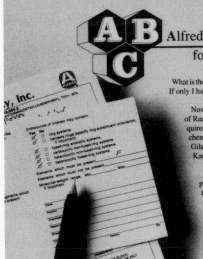

Alfred Bader Library of Rare Chemicals
for your screening and research needs

What is the first thing that comes to a researcher's mind when he finds a lead? If only I had twenty or thirty related compounds, analogs, to test that lead!

Now he can have just that at a nominal cost. The Alfred Bader Library of Rare Chemicals (ABC) contains some 50,000 research samples acquired from all over the world — many from some of the world's ablest chemists —Professors R.B. Woodward, Tadeus Reichstein, Henry Gilman, L.F. Fieser, Melvin Newman, Oskar Jeger, George Wittig, Karl Dimroth, Ralph A. Raphael, to mention just a few.

All of our compounds are searchable by structure, and the computer printouts can be yours, free of charge. Suppose, for instance, that you have found some activity in a fluoroaniline — write us, and you will receive a computer printout of 110 fluoroanilines, both those listed in our Catalog/Handbook and those in our ABC Library.

Each ABC sample costs $30.00 although the amounts differ. How much you receive depends upon how much we have. When we have 25 or 50 grams, the sample size is 5 grams; but when we

87

sixty-fifth; John Roberts, Cal Tech's inspired teacher for his seventieth; and Albert Eschenmoser, one of a great succession of brilliant chemists at the ETH for his sixty-fifth birthday. In 1984 we published *Selections from the Aldrichimica Acta*, containing the best papers published from 1967 to 1982, and using the painting that had graced the Woodward *Acta* on its cover. Many chemists had thrown their early *Acta* copies away and appreciated this beautiful and inexpensive volume.

I am as proud of the *Acta* as I am of the Aldrich catalog/handbook and happy that my many friends at Aldrich continue this tradition.

Gradually we also became more involved in custom syntheses, particularly for pharmaceutical companies. Among these, Upjohn was by far our best customer in the early days, and many of its chemists became my good friends. For years I thought Upjohn might purchase Aldrich. I found out later that a number of the chemists there thought so too, but others in management counseled against it because we were, in their view, just a "one-man company".

In 1962 executives from J T Baker visited us and were blunt in expressing their wishes. They wanted to buy Aldrich for $1.5 million, either in cash or in Richardson-Merrell stock. We had, they explained, two alternatives. We could sell and become part of the great J T Baker organization, or not sell, in which case Baker would compete with us in the fine organic chemical business. They had such wonderful distribution that they were sure they would quickly capture our entire market. Because $1.5 million is a lot of money, we thought about this carefully before saying no. Baker went into the fine organic chemical business, but in a rather odd way. They bought several thousand products from the Swiss company, Fluka, which gave them such a modest discount that in fact they could not really compete with us. Some years later they went out of this business, and when they offered us their stock of several thousand products, we declined.

By 1962 some able chemists had joined us. Dr John Biel, director of laboratories at the Lakeside Laboratories in Milwaukee for a number of years, became our director of research. That year we were joined by Bernie Edelstein, a chemist from the University of Wisconsin, who graduated from the University of Michigan Law School and became the company secretary. By 1965 we had fifteen chemists, including seven PhDs, working on various research contracts, mainly for pharmaceutical companies and the government.

Many of our chemist friends were keen to buy Aldrich stock. We felt that we had such a good record of steadily growing sales and revenue that it was time to go public in 1965—not on any grand scale but simply by offering 100,000 of the total 600,000 shares to a select list of chemists and friends who had often expressed an interest. We went to a small Milwaukee stockbroker, the Marshall Company, and asked what

PROSPECTUS

100,000 Shares

ALDRICH CHEMICAL COMPANY, INC.

Common Stock

$1 Par Value

The shares of Common Stock offered hereby are outstanding shares presently owned by the Selling Shareholders whose names and holdings are stated herein under "Selling Stockholders." The Company is not selling any of these shares and will not receive any of the proceeds.

The Selling Stockholders entered into an agreement appointing The Marshall Company, Inc., 111 East Wisconsin Avenue, Milwaukee, Wisconsin, as their exclusive agent to obtain subscription agreements for the shares being offered. Since The Marshall Company, Inc. is not obligated to acquire any of the shares being offered, there is no assurance that any or all of the shares will be sold. For further information on the agreement with The Marshall Company, Inc., see section on "Offering Arrangement" herein.

Prior to this offering, there was no public market for the Common Stock offered hereby.

THESE SECURITIES HAVE NOT BEEN APPROVED OR DISAPPROVED BY THE SECURITIES AND EXCHANGE COMMISSION NOR HAS THE COMMISSION PASSED UPON THE ACCURACY OR ADEQUACY OF THIS PROSPECTUS. ANY REPRESENTATION TO THE CONTRARY IS A CRIMINAL OFFENSE.

	Price to Public	Underwriting Discounts and Commissions	Proceeds to Selling Shareholders(1)
Per Share	$10.00	$.17	$9.83
Total	$1,000,000.00	$17,000.00	$983,000.00

(1) Before deducting expenses estimated at $10,000.00, payable by the Selling Shareholders.

Until March 31, 1966 all dealers effecting transactions in the registered Securities, whether or not _____ iver a prospectus. This is in addition to the _____ g as Underwriters and with respect to their

December 30, 1965.

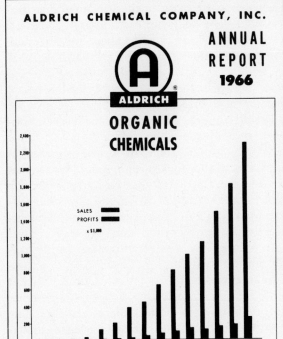

ALDRICH CHEMICAL COMPANY, INC.

ANNUAL REPORT 1966

ORGANIC CHEMICALS

SALES
PROFITS
x $1,000

Aldrich's first stock offering and annual report, 1965-6.

the minimum commission would be for selling the stock at $10 a share on what they called a best efforts basis. The minimum permitted by the SEC was 17 cents, and so my family and I offered 100,000 shares at $10 a share. We had considerable difficulty with the Wisconsin regulatory agency, which protested that $10 a share for a company whose earnings were only 30 cents a share was very high, but since it was a best-efforts basis only, we finally did receive permission. What we did not realize was that when people called the Marshall Company to inquire about Aldrich stock, the stockbrokers discouraged them, suggesting that if they wanted to speculate, better stocks could be had for $10 a share—and probably better commissions for the brokers. As a result, we sold few shares in Milwaukee and only about 16,000 around the country to about 200 chemists and friends who knew us well. After the offering closed, the market generally dropped, and the executives of Marshall, who really did not understand our business, began to sell the stock short, feeling that the $10 a share had been too high. They did not understand, at least at first, that all our new stockholders had known the company for some years and had faith in it. In fact, during the first year following the offering, only forty-five shares changed hands, those owned by an investment club in Ann Arbor which folded. Marshall merrily kept selling stock short—4000 shares—until they realized some months later that they could not deliver. They then came to me in some panic and pointed out that they had helped by selling the stock and asked if I would please help them now. Their offering of $14 a share had not elicited any sales, and I got them out of their misery by selling them 4000 shares at that price.

During the next year, William Schield, a stockbroker at Robert W Baird, a more substantial Milwaukee brokerage house, got to know me well personally and became intrigued by the company. He persuaded Baird to offer 120,000 shares of Aldrich stock at $23 a share (including a commission of $1.45 for Baird), again a sale by my family and me, not the company. This sale did well, and the stock has never sold below that $23. The original shares have now been split into 24 Sigma-Aldrich shares, which in the last years traded between $59 and $30 per share.

We were interested, concerned and at times amused by the stock market, but we never feared it. Our one fear was accidents. Our first serious one was an explosion of an acetylene in a one-gallon autoclave which carried the autoclave head right through the roof, over the building and onto the street, which fortunately was empty at the time. I marvelled at the coolness of George Skeff, the autoclave operator. George still comes to the dinner parties with our old-timers from Aldrich. His face, like mine, is furrowed, but I hope not because of that acetylene, benzylpropargylamine.

The second serious accident was a fire that started in a walk-in freezer in January 1969 in our 30th Street plant. One of our best selling products was MCPBA, safer to store if refrigerated—so we thought. Unfortunately the cooler malfunctioned and it may have been warmer inside the cooler than outside. Anyway, the peroxybenzoic acid caught fire, and it spread and consumed the entire adjoining inventory, from A to C. Everything from D to Z was saved. The fire started right after work, and I remember how scared I was when Al Galvan, our maintenance man, rushed into my office to tell me. Except for a minor wrist cut to a fireman, no one was hurt. Inventory can be replaced, and it was easy to tell customers when we could ship: decacyclene from stock, cystine in four to six weeks.

We had one more serious fire, in 1986, which started in our St Paul Avenue Laboratories when a chemist let a rotary evaporator run dry. Damage to equipment was extensive, but no one was hurt and there was a fire wall between the laboratories and the inventory.

Far more serious was an accident in 1990 at our Aldrich-Boranes plant, unrelated to chemicals. Maintenance men had miswired some high-pressure boiler connections and the boiler explosion killed two of the men. It was a case of human error. One had to feel almost as sorry for the supervisor responsible as for the families of the dead men. Nightmares come in many forms, and among the worst is a chemical accident with lives lost.

Throughout the history of Aldrich, we had excellent relations with our customers. The one surprising, if temporary, exception was G D Searle, one of America's major pharmaceutical companies.

For some years Aldrich was the American agent for chemical intermediates supplied by Sandoz in Basel. In November 1978 Searle ordered 13,500 kilos of a pharmaceutical building block, DIPC, to be supplied by Sandoz over a period of nine months in 1979. The first four shipments were satisfactory and then, out of the blue, Searle cancelled the last five giving the reason that they did not need any more material. The real reason may have been that they had found a less expensive supplier. We could not budge the Searle purchasing people, and so I wrote to each of the 160 chemists at Searle, explaining why we were stopping all shipments of research chemicals to the company. I also wrote to Donald Rumsfeld, the president of Searle, who replied promptly that the matter would be looked into. Many Searle chemists called in frustration, but when several months went by with no word from purchasing, we filed a simple suit in circuit court in Milwaukee. Fortunately there was a reorganization in Searle's purchasing before the case came to court and the order was reinstated, to our relief and Sandoz's satisfaction.

By the late 1960s, it was clear to me that the greatest growth in chemical research lay in biochemistry, and we were not biochemists. Organic chemistry seemed to have peaked with Woodward's synthesis of strychnine; Sharpless's chiral epoxidation and Brown's hydroboration were not yet with us. So we started a small biochemical department, with a modest but eye-catching catalog, and began considering a merger with a biochemical company. In Europe, large companies like Boehringer-Mannheim might have considered buying Aldrich, but that would not have been a true merger. In the United States there were three important companies. Calbiochem had just been purchased by Hoechst, and in my experience a large company usually ruins the entrepreneurial spirit of a smaller one, although that spirit is really the reason for the acquisition. J T Baker would have ruined the spirit of Aldrich; Hoechst the spirit of Calbiochem. The second, Nutritional Biochemicals, had been bought by a curious company, ICN, which struck me as being a conglomerate acquiring companies here, there, and everywhere. For some years, one of their men called me regularly to inquire when we would join their "family of companies", and I just laughed and declined.

The third company, Sigma in St Louis, was the ablest and most interesting of the lot, presided over by the towering figure of Dan Broida. Dan was one of the most interesting men I have ever known. On graduation as a chemical engineer, he was employed by Midwest Consultants, a small company owned by two brothers, Aaron Fischer and Bernard Fishlowitz, in St Louis. Midwest Consultants was the forerunner of the Sigma Chemical Company, set up first to make saccharin and then biochemicals. Dan, Aaron, Bernard, and their families each owned about a third of Sigma, at first just a small storefront operation.

Dan was intelligent, handsome, immensely hard-working, totally honest, opinionated, and disdainful of most PhDs, calling all and sundry "idiots" if they disagreed with him. You could never win an argument with Dan, but the love and care of his well-balanced and charming wife, Roma, made him bearable.

Dan built Sigma into a singular company where service, purity of products, and lowest price in the marketplace were absolute essentials. Employees could not leave at the end of the day until the last order was shipped. The company did not advertise, but their service and product quality were second to none. Dan truly believed that any biochemist who was foolish enough to buy from a competitor deserved what he received.

Sigma placed greater emphasis on production than Aldrich. If a product sold well, Sigma would make it. Dan regarded suppliers as a necessary evil, and treated them (including Aldrich) disdainfully. Products were often rejected for good reasons, but Dan never explained why, in case the suppliers improved their products and sold them to competitors! Aldrich, on the other hand, worked hard to establish good relations with suppliers, and many of them became our good friends. By working with reliable suppliers, we were able to concentrate our efforts on new products, and when requirements for these became so large that we could no longer handle them, we could go to a company with the right equipment. I am sure that our relationship with suppliers was a real eye-opener to Sigma on our merger, as was their insistence on same-day service to Aldrich.

Aldrich also had good relations with competitors, many of whom—like Fluka and Kodak—were also our suppliers and customers. In contrast, Dan refused to sell to Sigma's competitors and attacked them in the introduction to the Sigma catalog.

I approached Sigma in 1967 to suggest a merger between them, then still family-owned, and Aldrich, now a public company. I was quickly rebuffed. They went public through Goldman Sachs in 1972. Of a total of about 3,000,000 shares, 700,000 were sold at $22 each. This offering did not do well and the stock price dipped to $11 per share in 1973, partly because of some undeserved bad publicity. That was when I first became a Sigma stockholder. Dan's manner caused many scientists to leave over the years, and Bernard Fishlowitz, who was competent and very people-oriented, died in 1968. Sigma was so thin in top management that when we resumed talks in 1974, the directors became interested. Only Dan objected vigorously.

Scientifically, the merger made excellent sense. By 1975 Sigma was the leading supplier of biochemicals, Aldrich of organics. Technical competence in both areas had become important to both companies as the two fields became more interrelated. None of our organic competitors had a substantial share in the biochemical market, and none of Sigma's competitors knew as much organic chemistry as we did. To Sigma stockholders, it was a sensible deal because it gave Sigma organic know-how, which was valuable in the development of many biochemical products, and the potential for a new, balanced management—a balance difficult to achieve with Dan alone at the helm. To Aldrich stockholders, it opened up the biochemical field.

The valuation of Sigma and Aldrich stock was fairly simple: neither of us had debt, and Sigma had long been about twice the size of Aldrich in sales and profits. Each had very conservative accounting policies and there was no question—so often present in merger negotiations—that either had overstated its earnings.

We merged in August 1975, Aldrich shareholders receiving one third and Sigma two thirds of the new Sigma-Aldrich Corporation stock. Dan became chairman of the board and I president of the merged company. Neither one of us was designated chief executive officer, CEO, the all important position in American companies. There has never been a time when any of us have had reason to regret the merger on economic terms, although it made our personal lives, certainly Dan's and mine, much more difficult. Our customers of course benefited from the better service they received after the merger. This was the end of Aldrich as an independent company.

Chemists have often asked me whether it would be possible to start a chemical company today as I did in 1951, and I am not sure. I have encouraged and helped many to start their own companies, urging them to begin by specializing in their fields of expertise, and Aldrich often became their first and best customer, but government restrictions are much tighter today, and are often enforced by bureaucrats with little practical experience. This is clearly illustrated by a cautionary tale from Sigma. I have referred to the value of their shares dropping following bad publicity, and these are the circumstances.

Being one of the few companies selling controlled drugs, Sigma had to act most carefully. Each order was checked and double-checked and the drugs were kept under lock and key. In 1973, before our merger, an inspector visited Sigma, where one of the drugs he checked was mescaline, the hallucinogen, which Sigma imported. Each time a legal order for mescaline was received, the bottle was brought out and the quantity weighed. The inspector checked all the orders, and everything was fine. Then he checked the inventory. A kilo had been purchased, 940 one-gram units had been sold, which should have left 60 g, but there were only 30 g in the bottle. This was a 50% discrepancy and the minimum fine was $10,000! Sigma's lawyer counselled paying. Sometimes high legal expenses preclude defense against bureaucratic stupidity. Unfortunately for Sigma, the incident received publicity.

The reason for the 30 g discrepancy is in fact clear. When you weigh one gram individually, you are likely to give just a little bit more so as not to short-change your customer. Had it come out exactly, Sigma might have worried that it had undershipped some orders. After all, 30 g represents about 30 mg, 3% more, for each of the 940 bottles weighed. Now, of course, Sigma takes the incoming kilo, fills about 970 one-gram bottles, documents the tiny loss and avoids a fine.

Few fine chemical companies handle drugs, none more carefully than Sigma, but almost every chemical company deals with products that might be drug intermediates. This is one major problem for small companies. Another, which every company faces, is pollution control where, again, bureaucrats often over-react.

Fortunately for society, analytical methods have improved tremendously during my lifetime and today we can determine the presence of dangerous chemicals in tiny amounts. But often the media are uneducated. Not long ago, *The Milwaukee Journal*, a competent newspaper, had bold headlines on the front page, alleging that 2 ppb of benzene had been found in the water of a well near a chemical company in Port Washington. Two ppb—I wonder what the editor would say if someone pointed out to him that gasoline contains 2% benzene, and 2% is

10,000,000 times as much as 2 ppb! Our analytical methods have become better and better and before long we will be able to show that everything is everywhere, at least in minute amounts. Like 2 ppb.

We were lucky that no one checked the safety in our first laboratories, nor how we shipped our products. Pollution was not a problem in our first years simply because we produced so little, less than university laboratories, but every small company starting now would be hedged about by regulations and would be checked much more carefully.

By merging with Sigma we ceased being a small company, and together had the expertise to handle most technical problems.

8

Collecting Chemicals

I am an inveterate collector. It may be a sickness, and it began with stamps at 8, drawings at 10, paintings at 20, and rare chemicals at 30. I became involved in the last by chance. In fact, the collection began life as the "Violin Chemicals".

In the middle 1950s Joe Karabinos, an excellent chemist in Joliet, Illinois, had a laboratory in his basement where he made all sorts of interesting compounds. On one of my visits I inquired, "Could we purchase these and list them in our catalog?" "The ones I can scale up easily, yes, the others, no," was his reply. Joe and his wife Ann became our good friends; they were delightful people, very musical, and had the only home I have ever been to where there were two harps in the living room. I offered Joe the position of my right-hand man, but he had to decline. With a large family, he could not live on $12,000 a year. My own salary was in fact less than that at the time. A year or so later Joe visited us at home and very much liked an antique violin by Rocca which I had bought in Vienna a few years earlier. Then the idea struck me—might he trade the violin for his collection of those chemicals he would not scale up? Our "Violin Chemicals" had begun.

Joe accepted a senior research position with Olin in New Haven, where he made a great many compounds of herbicidal interest. When Olin laid him off along with many other chemists, he started his own company, Carbolabs, which became a good supplier to Aldrich. Sadly, he died of a brain tumor, and Ann found an excellent Purdue graduate, Phil Pivawer, to run the company. Phil collected over 2000 of Joe's samples to add to our Library at Aldrich, and we still look forward to his annual visits to discuss Carbolabs' new products.

Eventually this collection of rare chemicals was called the Alfred Bader Chemicals Library, because I became so interested in rescuing research samples that otherwise might have been lost. Hundreds of thousands of such compounds have been thrown out—sometimes through ignorance of their importance, sometimes just to make space, and more recently because of perceived potential hazards. Bureaucrats fear the unknown, and it is easier to have samples incinerated than to consider what value they could have for generations of future researchers.

Saving these research samples for the Library has been great fun. Just to handle the bottles containing chemicals made during the working life of a great chemist is like walking through time. Often they bear the labels of students who in turn have become well known; what a great way to study the history of chemistry.

In the early seventies I visited Professor and Mrs Fieser at Harvard to discuss the possibility of purchasing their collection of quinones for the Library. They agreed to sell, and knowing Mrs Fieser's love of cats, I turned to her and said, "I would also like to give you a fine painting of cats." Her reply really surprised me. "Well," she said, "perhaps you aren't such a bad fellow after all." When I inquired what she meant, she said, "You can't imagine how angry I was with you when you published that advertisement on our *Experiments in Organic Chemistry*. I was so angry with you that I then told Louis never to help you again."

I recalled the occasion when Professor Fieser had told me of that decision. In the very early days of Aldrich, he had suggested many new products, but during my first visit after this particular ad appeared, he told me that he could not help any more. We were competing with Kodak, and if he helped me, he would have to help them. When I pointed out that Kodak had hundreds of chemists whereas Aldrich had only one, he said it did not matter, he just would not help me. I had no idea that this was on instructions from Mrs Fieser.

When she explained why she had been angry, I explained that I had used Professor Fieser's 1955 edition and that the author of that edition was Louis F Fieser. She agreed, but said that a footnote to the chapter on reagents indicated that it had been written by Mary Fieser, and I had not pointed that out.

How easy it is to hurt someone without knowing—in this case quite inadvertently. If Mrs Fieser had spoken to me in 1956 I would gladly have corrected my oversight, and Aldrich and the chemical community would have continued to benefit from the Fiesers' help.

I knew the collection of naphthoquinones well; in fact I had made some of them. Yet we ran into an unexpected problem. In 1980 Dr Ed Glazer at Pfizer complained that a quinone from our Library was mislabelled. The terminal substituent was decalinyl instead of cyclohexyl. I had to reply:

"We have been selling chemicals for 29 years and this is the first time that I have to blame a mislabelling on mice. Professor Fieser's entire collection of quinones was stored in the basement of Converse which had a flood in the 60's. As a result, mice got to the moist bottle labels and chewed up parts of some and all of others. The mice were quite undeterred by Professor Fieser's great care in instructing his students how to label; in fact, they may have found the lacquer over the labels quite delectable . . . what we thought to be cyclohexyl is really decalinyl."

The ad that hurt Mary Fieser, JOC 1956.

I had not taken enough care with these small samples, and I said to myself, "To err is human; to forgive myself is not my policy."

I had a problem with the painting of cats as well as with the chemicals. Good paintings of cats are much harder to find than those of dogs, and it took me until 1977 to find a fine work of three cats by de Neuville to send to Mrs Fieser. Unfortunately, she became upset once again and returned the painting angrily. Luckily, this time, it did not take many years before I found out the reason for her anger, and was able to explain quickly just what had happened.

Back in the forties, Professor Fieser had developed excellent molecular models and persuaded a company near Harvard, Data Packaging, to manufacture and sell them very inexpensively, so inexpensively that they eventually discontinued the line. Fieser was hurt by this and shortly before his death asked me to try to persuade Data Packaging to make them again. By guaranteeing to purchase 2000 sets initially and 3000 sets annually thereafter, I was able to persuade them to do this, but exclusively for Aldrich. However, I knew that Mrs Fieser wanted a publisher of her books to offer the models with the books as a package, and I agreed that Data Packaging could sell directly to that publisher. When she learned that chemists could not order the models alone from Data Packaging, she reacted sharply, telling us we could not use the Fieser name, nor sell her books, and she returned the painting. When I explained all the facts to her and Professor E J Corey, who also wanted the Fieser models to be available, both understood and agreed, and I returned the painting to her. All's well that ends well. Communication between people is so important. If only Mrs Fieser had written to me as sharply when she was unhappy with our Fieser reagents ad in 1956, I could have cleared up that problem at once. It was not long before Data Packaging again discontinued the models, but Aldrich found a manufacturer in England who became an excellent supplier of the models and other equipment.

One of the largest collections we ever acquired was Professor Henry Gilman's in Ames, Iowa. Gilman was a brilliant scientist, one of the pioneers in organometallic chemistry. A major figure in American chemistry, he worked tirelessly and had the reputation of being a hard taskmaster. I had never met him, but he had suggested one of the most important compounds ever offered by Aldrich—our bestselling chemical, 3-hydroxypyridine. When I was invited to lecture at Iowa State University in the mid-1980s, I looked forward to learning more about this professor who had been such a key figure in the growth of Aldrich. A brief visit to Professor David Hoffman, chairman of the chemistry department, gave me an opportunity I had not expected. Professor Hoffman told us of the trouble they were having in disposing of Gilman's samples. He took us to the large room where they were kept— unfortunately the single lightbulb had burned out—and asked our advice. New regulations made it impossible for them to leave them where they were, and a disposal company wanted $8000 to remove the

99

thousands of bottles. Would we offer to remove them for less than that? Sometimes in life one has to take a chance, and so I offered $10,000 for the collection, virtually sight unseen, and arranged to have a truck go to Ames to pick it up. Our most serious error was to send too small a truck; we had to make a second trip. Of the 20,000 or so bottles, we had to throw out about half because, while valuable in Gilman's day, the compounds were now listed in the Aldrich catalog, and the cost of analysis of small samples was too high. Some 6000 had to be discarded because labels had fallen off or the compounds had decomposed, but that still left about 3000, which we offered through an attractive, yellow catalog.

This story has an amusing sequel. One evening we were chatting at home with Sarah and Herb Brown—he the Nobel Laureate, she the quintessential Jewish mother—and when I mentioned Gilman, Herb said, "A very hardworking man. Do you know there are only four American chemists who have published over 1000 papers, Henry Gilman, Isaac Kolthoff, Carl Djerassi and I, and all but Gilman are Jews?" I could not help thinking, "So what?" The number of papers alone does not indicate great quality. Bob Woodward published very few papers, but what papers! Or Loschmidt, one tiny book—but what a book!

But then on my next visit to the University of Sussex, Professor Eaborn told me that he had been asked to write Gilman's obituary. Gilman had been a Fellow of the Royal Society, but was it true that his father had been a rabbi? I was very surprised. Naturally Jews are proud of the accomplishments of other Jews, and while you do not go around asking whether someone is Jewish, you generally find out. Certainly neither Herb Brown nor I had ever heard that Gilman was a Jew. Back in Milwaukee I called Professor Hoffman in Ames who assured me that Gilman was not a Jew; he had attended Gilman's Episcopalian funeral. Just to make sure, he gave me the phone numbers of Gilman's son and grandson, a likeable artist still living in the Gilman home. The son was very brief. "No, I don't know where such stories come from." The grandson was less definite, but going through his grandfather's papers he had come across the name of a cousin, a lawyer in Boston, and he gave me his telephone number. When I asked the lawyer whether he knew of his Uncle Henry in Ames, he said that his grandfather was Henry's father. And had he been a rabbi? "My grandfather, *olov hashalom*, may he rest in peace, a rabbi—no, he was a tailor who came to Boston from Lithuania and was very active in the trade union movement." A Jew yes, a rabbi no. Presumably Henry Gilman, who studied at Harvard, had encountered the usual difficulties that confronted Jews trying to make their way in the world. He had met and loved a devoted Episcopalian, and had stepped out of the Jewish world. But I have to smile about Herb's comment on the authors of 1000 publications.

Only once did a collection—one of our best—involve us in a hassle. It worried me greatly for a few days. Bob Woodward was very interested in our Library, and we both hoped that his own wonderful collection of samples would come to us one day. After his untimely death in 1979, I discussed Bob's samples with Professor von Doering, as well as Dr Donald Ciappenelli, the lab manager at Harvard, who told me, to my surprise, that the Harvard lawyers had decided that the samples belonged to the estate, not to Harvard. It was suggested that the samples remain at Harvard while still needed by Woodward students, after which, I should negotiate their purchase with Bob's daughter, Crystal Woodward, an artist who lived in France.

Early in January 1981, it was indicated to me that the time was ripe, and Crystal would be visiting Cambridge that month. I arranged to meet her, but the day before the meeting I received a call from Dr Ciappenelli. On reconsideration, the Harvard attorneys had decided that the samples really belonged to Harvard after all. How could we tell Crystal without hurting her feelings, he wondered? My answer was simple: "Let me buy from Harvard the rights that are Harvard's and from Crystal the rights that are the estate's." Each negotiation took only a few minutes, and seemed satisfactory to everyone. Crystal wanted historically important samples—such as a bottle of synthetic quinine, which I later sent her. Ciappenelli wanted Harvard to retain clearly marked boxes relating to Vitamin B_{12}, needed by Professor Eschenmoser, erythromycin for Professor Kishi and some bottles required by Professor Dolphin.

The discussions took place on a Friday morning, and in the afternoon Dr Steven Benner, one of Bob Woodward's most brilliant students and later professor at the ETH, spent several hours with me and Barry Young, Aldrich's Eastern sales manager, packing the several hundred larger bottles and 261 cigar boxes full of tiny bottles into Barry's car. Barry had come to Cambridge so that Harvard would not be burdened with the packing and shipping, and Steven, checking each bottle and box, assured us that we were not accidentally taking samples still needed at Harvard. Finally Barry drove off to our Eastern warehouse where the collection would be packed for shipment to Milwaukee, and I took a plane to Washington for an ACS committee meeting.

Then all hell broke loose, or so it seemed. That weekend we received anguished phone calls from Dr Ciappenelli, from Warren Stockwood, my old friend who had given me the idea of starting Aldrich, and from Professor Jeremy Knowles, the department chairman. All said essentially the same thing: the students were in an uproar. How could Harvard have let the samples go, and why the hurry? "We must go back to square one," they said, "to last Thursday. You must return all the samples." But we could not do that. As I wrote to Jeremy, if we returned the samples, somewhere along the line someone was bound to say, "Bader had no business taking the samples, and that is so close to stealing that the difference will become fuzzy."

In my mind the settlement of that argument has become a model. If both parties clearly understand what the other needs, settlement is at hand. The students wanted free access to the samples; we wanted to avoid false accusation of impropriety. We offered to keep the samples untouched until the last Woodward student had graduated, and to deliver any samples needed, without charge. The students agreed. I thought of the episode as a tempest in a teapot; Jeremy corrected this to a storm in a teacup, a smaller perturbation. Actually, there was only one request for samples, from Professor Ray Bonnett at Queen Mary College in London, who needed many porphyrins and related compounds for a comprehensive paper on chlorophyll. I delivered the samples by hand and picked them up some years later. Ray cautioned me to be careful: among the samples was enough tetraodotoxin, the fugus poison, to kill me and several thousand others.

After the last Woodward student graduated, three of Aldrich's best chemists worked diligently to prepare a catalog with structures and the names of Woodward's associates, and of course the catalog was in blue, Bob's favorite color. Had the samples remained at Harvard, many would have been lost, none would have been so accessible, and what about the tetraodotoxin?

Often in life, one good thing leads to another. When I delivered the porphyrins to Queen Mary College, I also met Professor David Kirk who, since 1954, had built a library much like ours at Aldrich, but limited to steroids—over 4000! What a resource! He too made small quantities available to researchers around the world at a nominal charge only, and hoped that eventually his collection would be taken over by the UK Medical Research Council. I introduced Professor Kirk to the chemists at Sigma who were working on a library of steroid spectra. He supplied them with a great many samples to add to their spectra collection, and the ABC Library supplied him with the steroids not in his reference collection. It was a very happy collaboration, but on a later visit I learned that Kirk had become terribly discouraged. The MRC had decided that it would not take over his collection. I do not know whether that decision was made because of lack of funds or because someone thought that research interest in steroids was waning. Research is indeed a "fashion business". Focusing on cortisone and "the pill", both steroids, thousands of chemists worked with steroids in the forties and fifties, and again when steroid hydroxylation by fermentation was discovered, making possible the syntheses of many new steroids. Interest may now be lower, yet with the discovery of a safe abortion pill, also a steroid, it will rise again.

Thousands of man *years* had gone into the making of these samples;

they had to be saved, and I suggested that Sigma-Aldrich purchase them. Kirk had an able associate, Anna Loisidou, skilled in the intricate nomenclature of steroids, and several of his associates were already working at Sigma in Poole, Dorset, having joined us when Kirk's research funds had been reduced a year or so earlier. It made sense to move his entire collection and all our steroids to Poole, including many from Professor Reichstein in Basel, particularly since Anna was willing to move there. I was saddened and gladdened by a fax I received from Poole in November 1992. Professor Kirk had died of a massive heart attack in October but the steroid collection was in place there. I know from my long discussions with Kirk how happy he was that his life's work would be continued.

Many of the most pleasurable encounters in our quest for library samples came to us through chance meetings. Two young eastern European chemists offered us some compounds already listed by us. We arranged to meet in Budapest and were very happy that the chemicals supplied were of good purity. Knowing how much American dollars would mean to them, I paid $300 up front to help their travel expenses, but unfortunately they underestimated the ability of Hungarian thieves: their money was stolen. We were later disappointed, too, because subsequent deliveries were totally unsatisfactory. We could not rely on them. I explained how important it was to have reliable suppliers, particularly once we had listed a product in our catalog, which went to a million chemists around the world. Then I had the idea: why not set up a system to collect research samples for the Library? These could be offered on a one-time basis, and further supplies were unnecessary. They thought the idea seemed workable, and set about the business with such enthusiasm and ability that through their continuing efforts thousands of interesting samples have come to us.

The success stories of some of these ABC Library compounds are wonderfully heartening. You never know when a particular sample will help someone. I often said to myself: "If only I had been collecting samples in Strasbourg in the last century, DDT would have been discovered much earlier"—although I am not sure this would have been a good thing! I was never happier than when Fred Vinick at Pfizer told me that one of our quinuclidines, actually made at Aldrich but placed in the Library because of lack of general interest, led to a most exciting lead. Or when Quentin Soper, one of Lilly's most productive chemists, invited me to an almost royal reception at Lilly's agricultural research labs in Greenfield. I was puzzled. Why were they making such a fuss? "Haven't you heard about BEAM?" "No," I said, "I don't know much about bourbons, I prefer Southern Comfort." Quentin explained that BEAM was not a whiskey, but a fungicide that sometimes as much as doubles rice production in the Far East. Its lead had come from a Library compound. When I checked, I found that it was from a group of samples acquired from an old friend, Dr A de Cat working at Gevaert, the photographic company in Belgium, who had made them to test as antifogging agents in photographic films. They had failed as far as that use was concerned, but you just never know.

What is certain is that it will not be possible to put together a collection like this in the next century. Chemists work with smaller and smaller samples; the Woodward compounds from the 40s were often in gram quantities, from the 70s there are just milligrams.

9

Searching for Suppliers

In the early days of the company, I concentrated on visiting European suppliers, usually not the large companies with their own operations in the United States, but the relatively small chemical manufacturers that had no marketing presence here. Knowing exactly what was in the Aldrich catalog, I took only the Kodak catalog, and then asked each company what products they produced. Until the mid-sixties, I had no interest in purchasing anything offered by Kodak; John Sheehan's recommendation that we offer DCC and the subsequent events changed all that.

Among the first visits were two that had a profound effect on Aldrich. One was to Fluka, which I first visited in August 1952 when it was operating from an inn in St Gallen, Switzerland following a disastrous fire in its Buchs laboratories. I purchased our first compounds from Dr Ernst Vogel, the managing director, and I still have that first invoice for five compounds, including ethyl diazoacetate, tetranitromethane and ethanedithiol, all to be shipped by parcel post. Today it would be impossible to ship them through the mails, but they arrived safely. Many purchase orders to Fluka followed. One was for a large group of pyridine aldehydes and their derivatives, but when I discovered that these were all made by an excellent company, Dr F Raschig in Ludwigshafen, we placed further orders directly with the producer.

Over the years I got to know Ernst Vogel quite well. He had received his PhD from Leopold Ruzicka at the ETH and after graduation became active in this tiny company, Fluka, and was soon its managing director. Ernst and his wife Beatrice worked closely together—she on the catalog and he on production and purchasing of chemicals. He suffered severely from depression. He was a deeply religious Catholic and a mystic, and we would sometimes be talking about the availability and pricing of a chemical when his mind would wander and he would inquire whether I did not think that a certain passage in the book of Daniel clearly foretold the date of the coming of the Messiah. One of our most delightful days together was when the Vogels took me to a monastery in Dissentiss, in the mountains south of Buchs. They were good friends of the monks, and the visit opened my eyes. These men were real people, interested in the Bible as I was, intelligent and well spoken, not the stereotype monks I had expected.

Vogel had the habit of trying to persuade small manufacturers to offer

```
Aldrich Chemical Co.,Inc.
Dr. Bader                          Aug. 19th, 1952.
Milwaukee 3, Wis.
161 W. Wisconsin Ave.


                                Fluka AG
                                Chemische Fabrik
                                St. Gallen


                O R D E R

                                               sFrs.

    20  x  10  gr    Diazoaceticester            70.--
    20  x  10  "     Tetranitromethan            80.--
     2  x 100  "     Ethanedithiol              150.--
          1   Kg    Benzolsulfinicacid Na-salt   65.--
         10   gr    Cyclopentadecanone           40.--

                                               405.--


    à cto. bezahlt  Fr. 300.-- ( Dreihundert )
    St.Gallen, den 19. August 52.

                    FLUKA A.G.
                    Chem. Fabrik St. Gallen
```

Our first invoice from Fluka, 1952.

all their products exclusively to Fluka, but I wanted to buy directly from the manufacturers. Initially, Fluka had a better looking catalog than Aldrich, and packaged its products beautifully—more like the packaging of perfumes than of chemicals. I suggested to Ernst many times that it would be a good idea for Fluka and Aldrich to merge, but he would not hear of it. He never told me that he only had a small share of the company, that most was owned by a tough Swiss, Dr Albert Schmidheini, who would not have been interested in merging with a small American chemical company.

J T Baker, who had tried to buy Aldrich in 1962, made a serious effort to purchase Fluka in 1967. Howard Hartough, vice president at Richardson-Merrell, the pharmaceutical company that owned Baker, went over to negotiate. Three of the four major Swiss pharmaceutical companies—Ciba, Geigy and Hoffmann La Roche—became alarmed about the possibility of an American pharmaceutical company owning Fluka, their major supplier of research products, and quickly made an offer of 8,800,000 Swiss francs. This was slightly lower than the American offer, but without the conditions imposed by Hartough. The

poker game is related delightfully in a book about Fluka, privately printed in 1985. The owners accepted the Swiss offer and, from 1968 to
1989, Fluka belonged to these big Swiss companies, Roche, and Ciba
which merged with Geigy. The new owners invested heavily. Sales mul-
tiplied more than sixfold, but the number of products and—more importantly—the earnings were stagnant. In 1980 Dr Walter Graf was chosen
to succeed Dr Vogel, who planned to retire in 1984. Graf was to head
the scientific division, Paul Kühnis, an excellent salesman and long-term
employee, was to continue as commercial director, and a committee of
four, including Graf and Kühnis, formed the management committee.
Sadly, Graf and Vogel could not work together, and Beatrice and Ernst
left Fluka, feeling that they had been driven out.

Walter Graf may have sensed that Ciba-Geigy and Roche were not
happy with Fluka and left in 1988 to join Lonza. Shortly afterwards, on
a Tuesday morning at a Sigma-Aldrich board meeting in St Louis, we
received a phone call from Roche. It had been decided to sell Fluka; the
first company to offer 80,000,000 Swiss francs would get it. David
Harvey flew to Switzerland, negotiated with skill and persistence and on
June 23, 1989, Sigma-Aldrich purchased Fluka for 66,000,000 francs.
Sadly, Ernst Vogel died days before the announcement of the sale.

We had hoped that Paul Kühnis would become the new managing
director, but he and two other top managers left, clearly hurt by the sale.
Only Robert Küng, the computer manager, stayed. Fortunately, Aldrich
understood the business and Fluka continues and prospers.

Isabel and I still visit Beatrice Vogel whenever we go to Buchs and
reminisce about old times. Their only son, Ernst Jr, got his PhD from
Albert Eschenmoser at the ETH and is a very able chemist, but the management of Fluka did not want a young Vogel, just as Sigma did not
want Richard Broida, Dan Broida's son, who would have liked to work
at Sigma.

Another visit by me in 1952 had an even greater impact on Aldrich.
The Heidenheimer Chemisches Laboratorium in Heidenheim, a small
town between Stuttgart and Ulm, was operated by two very different
men. The chemist, Dr Ernst Reif, had fled Thuringia when the Russians
took over. He was a brilliant experimentalist, very personable and easy
to talk to. His partner, Gerhard Keppler, was a rather dour businessman,
trained as a banker, who had spent some years as a prisoner of war in
Siberia. Gerhard had a prodigious memory; although he knew no chemistry, he could tell you the starting materials of every chemical his company made, who supplied them and what they cost. It was uncanny.
Ernst and Gerhard welcomed me with open arms and showed me their
entire handwritten card file of the chemicals they could make. I immediately ordered every product not listed by Kodak. Before long, Aldrich
was their best customer and they our best supplier. Every year I spent

most of a Sunday talking chemistry with Ernst, discussing all the compounds that he thought he could make, and then ordering them. By the time of my next visit the following summer, 80-90% of these chemicals had been shipped and we would be ready for a new session to select many more compounds. One of their major products was a coronary vasodilator, erythrityl tetranitrate, made by the nitration of erythritol. This was dangerous chemistry, and tragically there was a serious explosion just after the management had decided to bar the windows because there had been some petty thefts in the laboratory. Several workers died, because they could not escape. Ernst was tried, convicted and put on probation. All this greatly affected his outlook, and may have caused the onset of multiple sclerosis, from which he died some years later.

Aldrich became more and more involved with HCL, loaned it substantial sums of money and worried about the possible bankruptcy of its best supplier. In time, the company was recapitalized, renamed EGA Chemie and moved from Heidenheim to a nearby village, Steinheim am Albuch. The name EGA came from the first names of the principals, Ernst Reif, Gerhard Keppler, Alfred Bader. At that point, Aldrich owned 80% of EGA and Ernst and Gerhard the balance. Eventually Aldrich acquired the entire company and finally changed the name from EGA to Aldrich Chemie.

In 1963 we were fortunate to find a very able organic chemist, Dr Alfred Griesinger, straight out of graduate school at the University of Tübingen, and he became one of EGA's managing directors. Travelling with Alfred, particularly visiting our German suppliers, was such pleasure. His knowledge of German chemists was extensive, and whenever there was a supply problem—which was often—one phone call from Milwaukee to Alfred was the beginning of the solution. He has many interests outside his work, including art, and we really enjoy our annual Sunday afternoon and evening visit with him and his wife, Erika, to discuss paintings with Prof Sumowski in Stuttgart.

Prior to my trips to Europe, I always looked through the commercial chemical magazines for the names of as many small or medium-sized companies as I could possibly include in my itinerary. A great many of these were in Germany, and although I had no language problem, many of the trips in the 1950s were difficult. No one had heard of the Aldrich Chemical Company at that time, and yet the visits were productive despite the times when, tired and frustrated, I felt that I had accomplished very little. Fortunately some were particularly fruitful. In Ludwigshafen, for instance, I visited Raschig, whose director of research, Dr Wilhelm Mathes, became my good friend. He had developed an elegant method—still the best method today—for making pyridine aldehydes, and I purchased every product he made and advertised their availability in the United States. Nearby were two other suppliers,

Weyl, owned by a much larger chemical company, Rütgerswerke, and Zellstoff Waldhof. Each supplied us with a great many products, so year after year my routine was pretty much the same. I would arrive late in the afternoon in Mannheim, spend the evening with Dr and Mrs Mathes, chatting about their exciting chemistry, purchase the Raschig products in the morning, and then visit the other two companies in the afternoon.

Another really interesting supplier was a relatively small company, Chemische Werke Lahr, at the edge of the Black Forest. Its chemical director was a very excitable, intense chemist, Dr Hans Joachim Renner, who had come from East Germany and built up the chemical facilities, concentrating on high-pressure hydrogenation. We also became good friends, and I was always interested to discuss what new products could be made with his unique equipment. I was, however, rather uncomfortable during my visits because he insisted on putting me up in a luxurious hotel. Clearly he enjoyed playing host, but the lavish wining and dining was not my style.

Sadly, many years later, the management of Chemische Werke Lahr conspired with Libya to build factories producing poisons, and I fear that Hans Joachim must have been involved in the negotiations; when the plot was unmasked he tried to commit suicide and was found close to death in the woods. By the time we visited him in a sanatorium, he was improved, but no longer the great lover of life whom we had known.

Long before then, we had approached him with an exceedingly difficult problem, one of many he helped us to solve. In the 1960s both Union Carbide and Shell had dabbled with the production of 1,2,6-hexanetriol, which both companies had hoped could compete with glycerine as a versatile solvent. They eventually gave up production. I had regular meetings with my friend Ed Newton who kept me informed about drum quantities of discontinued chemicals that Aldrich could buy from his company, Union Carbide. One was hexanetriol, of which we were able to purchase a few drums at 50 cents per lb. When we developed a market, we went back to the company and persuaded them to make 200,000 lbs especially for us at about $2 per lb. With that material, we were able to pursue the market, but when we tried to purchase larger quantities, we were told that the equipment had been dismantled and they were unwilling to make more at any price.

Since the production of hexanetriol involves hydrogenation, I sought Hans Joachim's help. We needed many tons, and his equipment simply was not large enough, but he undertook to try to find a large company to make it for us. He introduced us to Degussa in Frankfurt, who were most interested since they had a plant in Antwerp capable of producing multi-ton quantities.

Our most important customer for hexanetriol was Syntex, who needed it as a solvent for a fluoro-steroid already on the market. They were willing to take 10 tons per year for ten years. In 1976 their great interest allowed us to sign a four-year contract with Degussa to supply 50 tons annually. All went well for the first three years. Degussa delivered and Syntex accepted the quantities contracted. Syntex then told us that they had greatly overestimated the quantities needed and wanted to know what it would take to cancel their contract for the last 70 tons. A few days later, Degussa advised us that they were losing money at the contract price of DM22.50 per kilo and wanted to know whether they could cancel further deliveries! We quickly agreed that Syntex would pay us $450,000, and we also settled amicably with Degussa, so all was fine. The only disadvantage was that in the next year's accounting we had to make comparisons with the previous year "with and without" the HT profit. Actually, that was not the end of the saga. The availability of the product brought us other customers, and we were later able to interest Degussa in making it again, albeit at a higher price. Both Union Carbide and Shell had miscalculated the cost of producing hexanetriol, but the experience we gained showed us how much can be done when you have a good position in an interesting bulk product.

Schuchardt in Munich was the oldest of all the fine chemical companies in the world, and was our main competitor in Germany in the 1950s. It was run by Dr Weil, a dour old man whose family had started the company in the eastern part of Germany in the 19th century. We bought many compounds from them, particularly in the early 1960s. Schuchardt was eventually sold to E Merck of Darmstadt, a large company whose main business is pharmaceutical. They also offered a large line of common laboratory chemicals, and through Schuchardt were hoping to diversify into the more esoteric fine chemical market. Yet they slashed the number of compounds offered from 10,000 to 3000. This was a great help to us because it showed Aldrich which were their 3000 bestselling chemicals. We then concentrated on offering those that we did not already list. What few contacts Aldrich had with E Merck were friendly, but distant. The company has tried to get into the American market but I do not think they have been very successful.

I was particularly intrigued by two companies in the Ruhrgebiet, the VfT in Duisburg Meiderich and another division of the Rütgerswerke, in Castrop Rauxel. These two companies competed with each other, extracting all sorts of exciting products by coal-tar distillation. They took out not only compounds such as the dimethylnaphthalenes, which occur in large quantities, but also many polycyclic hydrocarbons and nitrogen-containing bases, which occur only in tiny quantities. Their products were wonderful additions to our catalog. Sadly for us, however-er, the two companies merged some time in the seventies, and stopped isolating most of the interesting products. I remember Dr George Grigoleit, one of their ablest chemists, saying to me shortly before his retirement, "Alfred, we have worked together for some thirty years. I have a gift for you. We have a little over 100 kilos of chrysene which we will never isolate again. If you would like it, it's yours at DM40 per kilo." I snapped it up, but for years I had to answer the same question from our auditors—Aldrich only sells about a kilo of chrysene a year— why we had over 100 kilos in stock without writing it down? I have never really studied economics, but it seems to me that if you have a totally stable compound of which you can sell a kilo for more than you had to pay for the 100 kilos in the first place, there is no need for a write-down. I just wish we had more such compounds.

We worked with many small companies. Of these, one of the best was also the smallest, that of a "lone operator", Walter Griesmeir, in Schwabmünchen near Augsburg. Walter is the direct descendant of Januarius Zick, one of Germany's best rococo painters. He understands more about high-pressure hydrogenation than anyone I know, Hans Joachim Renner included, and he built a well-equipped high-pressure laboratory where he made all sorts of out-of-the-way compounds on quite a small scale. He was also a consultant to larger companies like Firmenich in Geneva, but I sensed that his greatest enjoyment came from making compounds himself that hardly anyone else could make. To him, chemistry was more an art than a science.

Eventually, my itinerary became tailored to the rail schedules. I always bought a Eurail Pass and, as I sleep well on trains, I often took an inexpensive second-class couchette, travelling overnight. I liked to visit chemical companies in Switzerland during the week of the auction of paintings at the Galerie Fischer in Lucerne. I could preview the sale early in the week, visit a number of chemical suppliers and be back in Lucerne on Friday afternoon just in time to bid for paintings that interested me. I knew I could catch a night train to Florence, where I could then spend Saturday discussing paintings with Professor Middeldorf, before travelling overnight to Vienna or Hamburg and on to Copenhagen.

Some of my best friends are chemists who began as Aldrich suppliers. Among the oldest are Niels Clauson-Kaas and Henning Kaaber in Denmark. They first visited us in Milwaukee in the early 1960s and delighted our children by standing on their heads, something I certainly could not do. Since then, we have visited them many times in their plant in Farum and usually stayed overnight with Niels in Copenhagen. Niels, now in his seventies, is one of Denmark's finest practical chemists, a chemical engineer by training with an honorary doctorate in chemistry, recognizing his major contributions in furan and pyridine chemistry. During their first visit they explained that Niels had developed a practical method for making 3-hydroxypyridine from furfuryl alcohol, and had offered the method exclusively to Cilag Chemie, a Swiss manufacturer of various pyridines, who was not very interested. By coincidence, one of our first ever inquiries (see p.73) had come to Aldrich from Professor Henry Gilman, one of America's most famous chemists, who had asked whether we could supply 3-hydroxypyridine, and John Biel had subsequently developed a number of important drugs for Lakeside Laboratories which were based on 3-hydroxypyridine. Naturally I was immediately interested and signed a contract, which was exclusive to Aldrich provided we took a certain tonnage every year. Niels and Henning insisted that the contract be conditional also on my remaining associated with Aldrich. Years later, after I stepped down as chairman but before I was dismissed, I urged Henning and Niels to remove that condition, but they declined, saying that they wanted to find out how the company would function without me.

Although 3-hydroxypyridine was not the only product we got from Niels Clauson-Kaas and Wolff & Kaaber, it was by far the most important. It also caused us some difficulties with Cilag Chemie, who soon realized how much 3-HP we were selling, and who now regretted not having signed with the Danish chemists. At that time, we represented Cilag exclusively in the United States, and were steadily increasing their sales through certain bulk products such as quinuclidinol and trichloroethanol. Sales had climbed to several million francs annually, many times the turnover with which we had started. Cilag had been purchased in 1959 by Johnson & Johnson, who did not much interfere however with the management in Switzerland. Cilag's sales manager was aggrieved by our 3-HP contract and also felt they could do a better job selling directly in the United States. They cancelled our exclusive contract, but I was not surprised that their over-all sales in the United States declined sharply in the years following.

Another European company bought by Johnson & Johnson was Janssen Pharmaceutica in Belgium. Their research was far superior to Cilag's, and J & J instructed Cilag to close down their R & D. I purchased their 4000 research samples for our Library of Rare Chemicals. One of the products in that collection later became the bestselling herbicide in the world, ROUNDUP, developed by Monsanto, but because Aldrich was offering the compound through its Library, Monsanto could not get a product-of-matter patent. Imagine our surprise when one day several attorneys, from Monsanto and Stauffer, visited Aldrich to find out how we had acquired the compound. It was such an amusing story that we published an advertisement about it[1] (see p.86). Dr Henri Martin, who had made it as a chelating agent, left Cilag to become Ciba's head of agricultural research, but never tested it for its herbicidal activity.

On my first trips through Europe, I did not visit any chemical companies in Austria. In the mid-1950s, however, Dr Pickholz, an Austrian chemist then working at Peboc in London, told me of his old friends Dr Robert Tauber and Dr Paul Löw-Beer at Loba, a chemical company in Vienna. I visited Loba the following year and have been to Vienna every year since.

Dr Tauber is a most singular man. A Jew, educated in Vienna, he spent the war years in Shanghai. He started by delivering bottled kerosene on a tricycle. Then he supervised the production of ether. He explained that the Chinese had a very simple safety plan. They were so certain there would be fires that they produced the ether in shanties. Whenever there was a fire, the shanty burned down, and no great harm was done. His last position in China was chief chemist of the China Soap Company, part of Unilever. Tauber returned to Vienna after the war and teamed up with another most interesting chemist and businessman, Dr Paul Löw-Beer. I found Robert a delightful person with a great many stories to tell, and an encyclopedic knowledge of what chemicals could be obtained and where. If he had any fault, it was that he loved to keep everything in his own hands. Because of this, it was quite a few years before he introduced me to Paul, the owner of the company, who has since become one of my very best friends.

The Löw-Beer family was well known in Czechoslovakia for the production of textiles and cement. The family also had a textile mill on an island, Fischamend, close to the airport in Vienna. After the war, they could not recover the factories in Czechoslovakia, but did regain the factory on the island, and bought a plant in Vienna itself.

Paul did not think it practical to restart as a textile company, but converted the Viennese factory to the production of naphthenic acids and naphthenates, of the first liquid soap offered in Austria and of rustproofing compounds which became very popular throughout central Europe. In the 1980s he sold that business to Mobil.

The textile factory at Fischamend, which had some buildings dating back to the 17th century, was converted into a chemical company making analytical reagents and dyestuffs and also dealing in chemicals and packaging common chemicals for shipment behind the Iron Curtain.

Over the years Aldrich became a good customer of Loba, who introduced us to Chemapol in Prague and purchased many chemicals for us from Czech and other eastern European sources. Outsiders might have thought of Loba and Aldrich as competing with each other, but this was not the case.

Paul's wife, Ala, a Russian born and educated MD, worked in the Viennese social system, in women's prisons and helping disadvantaged children. Ala and Paul are truly caring, and Paul is one of the best "bosses" I have known anywhere. We now stay with the Löw-Beers whenever we visit Vienna and look forward to what has become a traditional dinner with our friends from Loba. I have stayed in particularly close touch with Robert Tauber's successor, Dr Robert Rosner, because of his interest in the history of Austrian chemistry.

Over the years, Paul inquired gently whether it might not make sense for Sigma-Aldrich to purchase Loba. However, it was thought, probably correctly, that Loba did not produce many products that we could not make ourselves in Germany, and to have manufacturing in yet another country would cause problems.

In the late eighties and early nineties, MTM, a very curious British company, began purchasing other small British companies, including Lancaster Synthesis, a competitor of Aldrich. Then they bought a number of firms in the United States, and in 1989 purchased Loba for about $3,000,000. MTM tried to pay in stock whenever possible, but when it was not, as with Loba, they paid in cash.

After an acquisition they often sold more stock on the market, and I suspected that MTM was a house of cards relying on acquisitions and curious accounting to show substantial profits in order to sell more stock. Eventually, their auditors realized what was happening. The moving spirit at MTM was Richard Lines who sold millions of his own shares in the £2-3 range, just before the stock collapsed, to trade at a few pennies per share.

The old management of Paul Löw-Beer and Robert Rosner retired after the purchase by MTM, and the new management was able to effect a buyout for less than MTM had paid. Most of MTM's chemical operations, both in Britain and the US, were recently sold to a large English company, British Tar Products.

Suppliers have been vital to Aldrich. Knowing them personally, understanding them and working with them fueled our growth. Of course there were many headaches, but also such pleasures and the beginnings of such great friendships.

REFERENCE:
1. *Aldrichimica Acta*, *21*, 15 (1988)

10

Friends and Competitors

We purchased a great many chemicals on the Continent, but Britain was just as important to us, and I could always look forward to another few busy weeks across the Channel. I found a very interesting contrast, particularly between German and British companies. Whenever I called a German company to inquire how early I could visit, the answer invariably was 7.30 or 8.00 am. In Britain, it was more likely to be about 10 am, but admittedly the British worked later in the afternoon.

My first close chemist friend in England was a delightful man, Michael F Carroll, chief chemist of a small company, A Boake Roberts, making perfumery chemicals in London's East End. Michael did not have a PhD, but had an enormous amount of practical knowledge, and he and his wife were happy, unpretentious, helpful people. At our first meeting in 1952, he told me about the pure products his company offered. This was a bonanza. Aldrich's next catalog, number 3, the first one we actually printed, jumped from twelve products to over 100.

Michael was certain that diketene reacted with ketones, acetone for instance, to form stable adducts. This struck me as astounding because Union Carbide had made diketene from acetone for many years, and if the two formed an adduct, I assumed that Union Carbide would know. Michael gave me a small sample, and I was able to establish its structure. When I submitted the manuscript for a communication to my old friend, Marshal Gates, the editor of *JACS*, he at first rejected it because he too believed that this reaction must be known. Publication of the communication[1] and a subsequent full paper[2] in fact led to a lot of interest in the diketene-acetone adduct. Many tons are now made by Kodak, Lonza, and Wacker. In my laboratory at PPG, I kept a 5-gallon can of diketene, assuring that it always stayed acidic by adding a few drops of acetic acid from time to time. Today, people have become quite scared of diketene, and the acetone adduct is used widely as a substitute.

As so often, one good thing leads to another. I had become a good friend of Herbert Gutowski while he was a student at Harvard University, working with a home-made instrument on NMR spectra. He was professor at the University of Illinois when I suggested that the structure of diketene could be determined unambiguously and very easily by NMR. I believe that our paper[3] was one of the first instances of NMR being used to determine the structure of a compound.

Michael Carroll told me about another home-made instrument, a gas chromatograph in his laboratory that could be used to determine the purity of liquids, until then much more difficult than determining the purities of crystalline materials. Michael was the first to show me what could be done with GC, which has really revolutionized analytical chemistry. I have often wondered how many companies would appreciate a self-effacing chemist with Michael's wonderful techniques.

Unfortunately, as happened with so many good small companies, A Boake Roberts was merged into one larger perfumery company, Bush Boake Allen, which in turn was swallowed up by Tenneco. Michael retired in the 1950s and passed away soon afterwards. As I look at his photograph in my office, I often wish I could still spend an evening with him on every trip to England, discussing his many practical discoveries.

My friendship with Dr Herbert Bondy was even more productive. Herbert had worked with the Nobel Laureate Staudinger, but lost his position as Privatdozent in Freiburg when the Nazis came to power. After some years at university in Paris and in industry in Holland, he went to England in 1940. Coalite, a company near Chesterfield in Derbyshire, had developed an excellent process to heat coal to relatively low temperatures, remove the distillate and market COALITE, the smokeless fuel, all over the world. In 1943 they offered Herbert a job at £4 a week to see whether he could isolate some chemicals from the distillate, which until that time could be sold only for its heating value. I visited Herbert once or twice every year, and before long my time with him fell into a routine. I arrived in Chesterfield late in the afternoon, and spent the evening and part of the following day with him, discussing new compounds that he and his chemists had been able to isolate; I then ordered whatever compounds they were willing to sell me. Years later, Roland Moore, another of the chemists who had become my friend, told me that in the middle and late fifties he and the other chemists would go around the laboratories to hide the bottles with the compounds of which they had only isolated relatively small quantities. They were afraid in case this fellow Bader ordered ten or even 100 lbs, which they would be unable to supply. Some of the compounds isolated by Herbert and first purchased by Aldrich did indeed become very large tonnage items.

The first was 2,6-xylenol. General Electric ordered first 100 g, then a kilo, then 10 kilos. One day I received a phone call from Jack Welch, the chemist working with this material, who wondered whether we could supply tonnage lots. I told him about Coalite, and we flew over with a GE executive, Ruben Gutoff. I vividly remember the bargaining that took place during our visit to Coalite's headquarters. GE wanted to purchase the then astounding quantity of 250,000 lbs to be used for a new polymer that Jack Welch had developed. Mr Gutoff acted in a most arrogant manner, and I was amused when Coalite's chairman, Francis

Waring, told me after the meeting that he had become so angry with Gutoff that he had upped the price at which they would have been willing to offer that quantity by 6d per lb. As Aldrich was getting a 5% commission from Coalite, this was fine with me. The rest is history. 2,6-Xylenol became so important to GE that it developed its own synthetic method. The polymer developed by Jack Welch, NORYL, has become one of the world's bestselling polymers, and Welch is now CEO of General Electric. I understand that Ruben Gutoff became a senior vice president at GE, but then left the company.

One interesting compound involved Aldrich in two deals. Coalite was very good at chlorinating phenols, but could not fish all the xylenols out of their low-temperature coal tar. We also bought xylenols from the Rütgerswerke in Castrop Rauxel which we shipped to Coalite for chlorination there. A derivative of a chlorinated 3,4-xylenol became of great interest to Upjohn as the starting material for a promising herbicide. We introduced Upjohn to Coalite and arranged for the 3,4-xylenol to be shipped from Germany to England. Upjohn wanted to assure themselves of multi-ton supplies, and so Herbert Bondy demanded and received substantial up-front capital to install the equipment to make this chlorinated xylenol. However, the derivative turned out to be too toxic for them to market, but it was a good try, and we sold substantial quantities of both the xylenol and the chlorinated product.

Another really interesting product from Coalite, 3,5-di-tert-butylphenol, led one eminent chemist, Ernest Eliel, to become quite angry with us. I had found that under some conditions I could react phenol with isobutylene to give the 3,5-isomer, but I could not reproduce the results consistently. When I mentioned this to Herbert Bondy, he told me that Roland Moore had no trouble with the process, and from then on we purchased it from Coalite. Ernest Eliel, then professor at Notre Dame, questioned the identity of Aldrich's compound, and I do not think he really believed me when I assured him it was correct. When he then converted our phenol to the di-tert-butylbenzene, and found that it was the meta-isomer, he became even angrier because it proved the correctness of our structure. Why, he asked, had we not published the procedure? But how could I have done so when I could not repeat my work consistently, and when Coalite's method was still confidential? Eventually Coalite built a plant to make large quantities, used as a starting material for a new insecticide developed by Boots. Unfortunately this insecticide failed in the final field trials in Australia.

Another really interesting compound on which Herbert and I collaborated was 2-methylresorcinol. This had never before been fished out of coal tar, and Herbert gave me a small bottle in the mid-fifties and asked me to confirm its structure. He had isolated it quite easily from the aqueous liquor condensate. Previously, 2-MR had been made only from 2,6-

dimethylaniline in an elaborate process, and in my experience all 1,2,3-trisubstituted benzenes with different substituents were interesting. I urged him to isolate further quantities and placed the first purchase order for 100 lbs at 11 shillings per lb.

The importation of this product involved us in an intriguing—and to me enjoyable—hassle with US Customs. The chemists at Customs pointed out that they had a book listing all the compounds ever isolated from coal tar. The book was important to them, because at that time all such compounds were duty-free. But the book did not list 2-MR.

In those days, the owner of a company could challenge Customs in Customs Court, appearing in person, without the aid of an attorney. I did so, and when the case came to trial, I produced Herbert Bondy's affidavit and his paper, which was published in the *Journal of the Chemical Society* in 1958, for the first time describing the isolation of 2-MR. The book published by the US Bureau of Mines was dated 1954. I simply pointed out to the judge that a coal tar chemical is a chemical isolated from coal tar, and not just one included in an outdated publication. It was a relatively easy case to win and I realized that I had enjoyed the challenge.

The case involving 2-MR was straightforward, as was another case about the importation of a 6-membered ring compound called Hagemann's ester. The chemist at US Customs jumped to the conclusion that every 6-membered ring compound must be derived from a benzenoid compound, and so was subject to 25% duty. I pointed out that 6-membered rings could also be made by ring closure, as was done at EGA, making Hagemann's ester from ethyl acetoacetate. I won that case as I did all but one of the many cases brought before the Customs Court.

Mind you, not all cases were as easy. The most complicated dealt with compounds where the decision could really have gone either way. The most important from a financial aspect involved trichloroethanol. Eli Lilly had ordered many tons through us from Cilag Chemie. If trichloroethanol was an aliphatic alcohol, then the duty was 5%; if it was a chlorohydrin, the duty was 7.5%. Technically, on paper, trichloroethanol appears to be a chlorohydrin, but it certainly does not react as such. US Customs had asked a professor of organic chemistry, Stuart Fenton from the University of Minnesota, to be its expert witness, and I had asked Lilly to send the production manager, Dr Brown, who used the substance. Stuart Fenton and I had both attended Queen's, graduating in engineering chemistry in the same year. Stuart apologized for having to testify against us, explaining that when Customs had asked him to be an expert witness, he had not known that he would be opposing me. I am sure of course that his friendship did not in any way influence his testimony. The judge, James Watson, was black, as indeed was Dr Brown, and I was concerned that the judge might think that we had called a black witness in order to influence the court. I asked Marvin Klitsner about this, and he said that we must make it clear in developing Dr Brown's qualifications that he had been called because of his expertise with this particular product. I may not have been wrong to be concerned because during the recess, the judge asked to see Dr Brown in his chambers. Later we learned what had occurred. The judge had asked him, "Why would they call you?" Brown had explained that Aldrich had asked Lilly for the expert most familiar with the product and he was that expert. The judge responded, "I'm glad that is the only reason." We really had the better case, and we won.

Another case was equally technical, but less clear. Years earlier, we had started to import a number of natural products, all mold metabolites called cytochalasins. The important question, again before Judge Watson, was whether or not cytochalasins were alkaloids. If so, then the duty was considerably lower than for amines. The case pitted two very able experts, Professor Edwin Vedejs of the University of Wisconsin in Madison against Professor James Cook of the UW-Milwaukee. Professor Vedejs had worked on the synthesis of the cytochalasins and Professor Cook had worked with many alkaloids. Most chemists in the field would not consider cytochalasins to be alkaloids, but by the definition of the Customs Code we believed that they were. We had to show that cytochalasins were alkaloids and "natural substances". The government's attorney stressed that a synthetic medium had to be used to grow the fungus, arguing that cytochalasins could not therefore be regarded as natural substances. We were concerned, of course, whether a judge who was not a chemist would understand the intricacies of the argument. Clearly he did, for in his decision he said that the use of the synthetic medium to grow the fungus "has no more bearing on the naturalness of the cytochalasin B than a synthetic diet for cows would have on the naturalness of the milk." What a fine way of putting it! We were relieved to win that case.

Many years later, an attorney in the East told me that he had come across my name many times because it was cited so often in legal literature. No wonder I was able to tell Queen's University in 1986 that I was happy to receive an honorary LLD because I enjoy fights when I know, or think I know, I am right. We were certainly relieved to win the coal tar case and to be able to import 2-MR for a few years free of duty. We set to work and developed three interesting uses for it. One was to make trimethylpsoralen, a drug used to treat albinos, which we made for Paul B Elder, a small pharmaceutical company in Ohio. A few hundred pounds of 2-MR were enough to satisfy their demand. A second application was in Ozalid-type chemicals. The third, and most important, was as a starting material for a non-carcinogenic hair-dye. In that application, we worked with a relatively small Brooklyn dyestuff manufacturer, J Lowenstein, whose chief chemist, Irwin Schwartz, already knew us very well. For years we had sold Lowenstein large quantities of 4-nitro-o-phenylenediamine for use as a hair-dye starting material, but the FDA had begun to question the safety of the products. Irv Schwartz then looked for substitutes and worked with us, using 2-MR. He knew we imported it from Coalite and he spoke to them from time to time about continuing supplies. However, he always respected that we had brought 2-MR to his attention, and we in turn tried to protect Lowenstein when many of their customers tried to buy direct from us.

By the early 1970s, we were buying a ton or two of 2-MR from Coalite per year, but it was insufficient for them to keep the isolation going. I urged them not to give it up and guaranteed a minimum purchase of 2 tons per year to assure continuing supplies. Fortunately, Lowenstein's needs grew. As long as Coalite had a management that knew of my substantial efforts over the years to increase the demand for 2-MR, we were protected by the company and were able to purchase about 80% of what they were able to isolate. This grew to 6 to 8 tons per year, and when even that was insufficient, I urged them to check their method of isolation because I suspected—correctly, as it turned out—that they were isolating only 30-50% of the material actually contained in their condensate.

As the demand increased, so did Coalite's price, from the original 11 shillings per lb to £19 per kilo. Then, however, came the retirement of Bob Marshall, the last of the old directors who had worked so closely with Herbert Bondy. Herbert had died of a heart attack in 1972, and men like Roland Moore who had known me since the 1950s, the last chemists working on coal tar distillation, were asked to leave the company.

After Herbert's death, Coalite hired one director of research after another, none of whom had Herbert's vision of what could be done. Then Anglo United, a small company headed by a very aggressive entrepreneur, David McErlain, made an unfriendly takeover offer. Although Anglo United was much the smaller company, in the heyday of the eighties McErlain was able to borrow several hundred million pounds and succeeded in purchasing Coalite. He put in an entirely new management who questioned why Coalite should be selling 2-MR to Aldrich when they could be selling direct to the hair-dye manufacturers. They were not interested in the history of the product or who had built up the 2-MR business. The bottom line was what mattered. They raised the price from one day to the next—£19 per kilo to £50 per kilo. In time, this may lead to some other company synthesizing 2-MR and competing.

McErlain had planned to sell a number of Coalite's subsidiaries to repay the banks, but the British economy soured, and his task became more difficult. The creditors insisted on a restructuring of Anglo United

Ordering lab-quantity organics from Kodak may not have been fast enough for you. Or it could have been complicated. And we may not have been able to give you all the personal attention and service you deserve.

So we have a solution: Don't order from us (except for larger than lab quantities—which we can still supply quite admirably).

Contact one of the dealers shown on the next page for EASTMAN Organic Chemicals.

Advertisement from Kodak and Aldrich's reply, 1976.

"Please Bother Us."

One of the most pleasurable aspects of my work is talking to our customers. I spend several days a month going from lab to lab at universities, and meeting with our industrial customers to ascertain that the quality of our service is good and the purity of our chemicals excellent, and to get suggestions from fellow chemists about new products we could add to our Catalog/Handbook.

Occasionally I may even get a complaint—hardly ever about purity, but sometimes about delays in deliveries. We list over 8,000 organic compounds in our Catalog/Handbook. Well over 95% of these are in stock, ready for immediate delivery. A few products are back ordered, and we make a great effort to reduce their number.

Nothing is as important to me as having our customers know that we think of them as individuals, not as names on a printout or numbers on a list. It would be unthinkable to send our customers to intermediary dealers who cannot possibly give as good service or know as much about our products as we do. At Aldrich, we want no barriers between us and our customers. Order from Aldrich directly, and if you have any questions, ask us. We want to be bothered.

I hope Aldrich will never become so large that we cannot be "bothered" by our customers. We care immensely and sincerely, and if you should ever wish to discuss a problem directly with me, please call me at (414) 273-3850. Chances are that, if I'm in Milwaukee, I will answer the phone myself. It is important to me that we preserve our tradition of service and quality. So please, bother us.

Dr. Alfred Bader, President, Aldrich Chemical Company, Inc.

Aldrich Chemical Company, Inc.

940 West Saint Paul Avenue, Milwaukee, Wisconsin 53233 · Telephone (414) 273-3850

and forced McErlain out. It will be interesting to see what happens to Anglo United and Coalite now.

In 1963 our old friend, Dr Siegfried Pickholz, who had moved from Peboc to Ward Blankensop, drew to our attention what he thought was a really exciting compound. Siegfried had already supplied several compounds and I always listened to his advice. Aldrich listed this new suggestion as A7992-2, 9-amino-1,2,3,4-tetrahydroacridine hydrochloride hydrate, now known as THA or Tacrine. Siegfried explained that he did not know for what purpose it could best be used, but suggested that it could well be important in enzyme and brain chemistry, and he was willing to sell us a kilo and tell us how to make it. We listed it for years, selling a few hundred grams annually. Then Dr W K Summers, a medical researcher in California, thought that acridines might be important in the treatment of Alzheimer's disease and asked us for a computer printout of all acridines supplied by Aldrich. He ordered small quantities of each, including A7992-2, 100 g, then a kilo, and then even larger quantities for use in a new drug application. Again, the rest is history. THA was, I believe, the first drug licensed by the FDA in the treatment of Alzheimer's disease and is now marketed by Warner-Lambert. It is not effective in all cases, nor does it cure the disease, but is does ameliorate the condition for a good many sufferers. It is known that acetylcholine levels in the brains of Alzheimer's patients are low and that Tacrine boosts that level through a mechanism recently explained by scientists at the Weizmann Institute. One of Helen Bader's great goals was to help Alzheimer's patients, and the Helen Bader Foundation continues her work. Little did we know how important that suggestion of Dr Pickholz would be. Again, my ancestors would have said *Beschert*—God works in mysterious ways.

Our relationship with our real competitors varied greatly. In the United States, Kodak, which had a virtual monopoly, paid no attention to Aldrich in the 1950s and little after that. In 1976 Kodak published a singular, full-page advertisement urging its customers not to buy from Kodak, but to order from its dealers. Once I stopped laughing, I responded with one of our best ads ever. How could a dealer know as much as the chemists who had made or at least analyzed a product? If a customer called Aldrich and needed help, we could immediately give a great deal of technical information, physical constants, literature references, even how to dispose of the compound. Dealers could not.

The next time I visited Rochester I decided to go to Kodak to shake the hand of the man who had written their ad, but learned that he was no longer with them. Jim Fuess, Kodak's manager, welcomed me and gave me six original watercolors which they had used in some of their best advertisements. They showed various laboratories in disarray, an explosion here, a flood there—always with the same caption: "It is easier to get it from Kodak." How I envied them those great ads. Jim explained that Kodak was a large company, run by committees, which had looked into the response to these ads and had discovered that they were able to react positively to just one out of a hundred suggestions they had generated. The ads had therefore been discontinued, and since he knew of my love for art, he wanted me to have the watercolors.

No wonder the fine chemicals division of Kodak kept declining and finally had to be sold, but I suppose that if I had a multi-billion dollar business in cameras and films, I might not worry too much about a small chemical division. What a wonderful competitor!

J T Baker, which wanted to acquire Aldrich and later Fluka, has almost disappeared from the fine chemical scene. Yet another company, MCB in New Jersey and a suburb of Cincinnati, competed strenuously with Kodak in the fifties, but declined and was eventually purchased by Will Ross Company in Milwaukee, which in turn was purchased by E Merck of Germany, which has done little with it.

I remember the president of MCB, Tom Layton, inviting me to visit him in Cincinnati and then, during a sumptuous lunch at his club, laughing at me about our full-page, back-cover advertisements for individual reagents. "Not one in a hundred customers can possibly be interested in these reagents, and you are doing it all wrong," he told me. "What you should advertise is the purity and speedy delivery of your compounds." I disagreed because our advertisements showed that we were at the cutting edge of research and had good chemists with us.

Through my contacts with MCB, I met Dr Floyd Green, one of the country's experts in biological stains and dyes. After the war, Floyd had worked with Arthur Coleman (the "C" in MCB), a pioneer in biological stains. He had spent twenty-seven years with the company, but despite his long tenure was not really appreciated and left in 1973 to start Aristo Custom Chemicals in Cincinnati. During a visit early in 1977, I learned that Floyd was in hospital after having a pacemaker implanted. I visited him, and telephoned him a few weeks later at Aristo to inquire how he was doing. His response was surprising: "You must be calling because you heard that I am about to sell to a company in the East." I had not heard, but if Floyd was going to sell Aristo, he should consider joining Aldrich, particularly as we were now with Sigma, who were very interested in biological stains. So we invited Floyd to Milwaukee where Marvin Klitsner looked at the offer Floyd was considering and prepared a much better one. He accepted, moved to Milwaukee in the fall of 1977, and became an Aldrich vice president in charge of our Floyd Green stain and dye division. Sales grew substantially year by year and, as anticipated, helped in particular the sales of Sigma Diagnostics.

In 1979 I received an anguished letter from the director of the division of the US Environmental Protection Agency (EPA), which tests drinking water. Basic fuchsin, the dye essential to test for the presence of feces in water, was in very short supply, and Dr Joseph Cotruvo wrote that he wished "to express my concern about what appears to be a shortage" and about "determining what precipitated the shortage and whether there is reason to believe another shortage is likely." It was the EPA that had caused the shortage! Basic fuchsin had previously been made by two large American companies, which had discontinued its production and that of many other low-volume dyes because of regulatory pressures. This dye was economically unimportant, so why hassle with the government? I replied that the Floyd Green division of Aldrich realized that there was a need for the dye and was beginning to produce it. We would fill the void and continue production "unless the EPA goes after us also."

Then came one of those lucky breaks that made us appreciate our good rapport with our competitors. Fisher Scientific, a customer and competitor of our stain and dye division, had obtained many small drums of basic fuchsin, but the dye was old and needed purification. Floyd agreed to purify it, provided we could keep 100 kilos at Fisher's cost of $20 per kilo. We analyzed the drums routinely and found to our amazement that some contained pararosaniline, a far scarcer and much more expensive dye needed as a bacterial flagella stain. Sigma was offering this at over $2000 per kilo, but had been unable to obtain any for a long time and had back orders for over $50,000. Floyd asked us what to do. Some of us felt that we should keep the pararosaniline and return only purified basic fuchsin; Fisher had bought the material as basic fuchsin, would receive basic fuchsin and would never know the difference. I am certain that Floyd was happier to follow my advice: call Fisher, explain that some of the material was pararosaniline, and offer to separate the two, provided that Aldrich was permitted to keep half the pararosaniline at Fisher's cost of $20 per kilo. Fisher agreed, Aldrich was able to help Dr Cotruvo and the EPA, and Sigma filled all its back orders for pararosaniline.

Our relationship with Aldrich's major British competitor was closer but much less friendly. L Light & Co was owned by a very knowledgeable chemist, Dr Henry De Laszlo, the son of the well-known Hungarian painter who had come to England and become a distinguished society painter. Henry De Laszlo travelled all over the world visiting suppliers, just as I was doing. Often he would make a visit immediately following mine, in which case he would inquire what I had bought, and try to buy the same materials, if possible at a lower price. I remember his coming to Milwaukee in 1955, visiting our laboratory on Booth Street, and then that evening making a most unusual offer. He told me that he had some money in a Swiss bank account and would give me $10,000 from that account, in cash, if I then sold him 50% of Aldrich for $1! "Just think,"

he said, "how much you and I could do if we could work together."
Henry was charming, and we had many interests in common, but this
suggestion was unethical and I would not have been comfortable col-
laborating with him. He was terribly angry with me when I declined.

In some ways we might have enjoyed working together. He knew a
great deal about products that could be isolated from plants, and he also
had a superb collection of Chinese antiques, but he was certainly not a
man I felt I could trust. He had a hard time building up the management
of L Light, and over the years many of his associates left to start other
companies. Towards the end of his life he was forced to merge with a
company from the East End of London run by an excellent organic
chemist, Philip Koch, who knew a lot about fluoro-aromatic chemistry.
Light merged with Koch to form the Koch-Light laboratories. Dr De
Laszlo died in a car accident, and for some years Dr Koch tried to run
Koch-Light almost singlehandedly. Clearly he had the same difficulties in
attracting really good people, and he lacked Dr De Laszlo's international experience and flair. Eventually Koch-Light went into bankruptcy and
the market was pretty much taken over by Aldrich's English company in
Gillingham, Dorset.

As Aldrich became more and more proficient in marketing organic
chemicals, we looked into related areas. We purchased Diaprep, a small
company in Atlanta, very proficient in making deuterated solvents. It
was owned by three professors who employed two chemists, Bob Askins
in Atlanta and Dr Tom Wickersham in Houston, to make their compounds. It was a well-run operation, but the three academic owners had
other interests, and sold the company to Aldrich in exchange for Aldrich
stock. We moved Bob Askins and Tom Wickersham to Milwaukee, the
production of deuterated solvents expanded very nicely indeed, and I
think that Aldrich is today the largest manufacturer of these solvents.

The starting material for all deuterated compounds is heavy water,
which Aldrich was able to purchase from the US Atomic Energy
Commission. At first the price was about $30 per lb. They raised it to
about $50 and then to over $90 before they stopped selling heavy water
altogether. The material was also available from Russia, a very unreli-
able source, from Norway, safe but distant, and also from the Canadian
Atomic Energy Commission in Chalk River, Ontario. We contracted to
purchase ton lots from Chalk River and were rather annoyed that the
Canadians, too, increased their prices substantially year after year. They
had a curious clause in their purchase contract that if payment was not
received within thirty days, there was a rather large penalty. Canadian
mails can be very slow, and one day we received an invoice for a big
shipment seventeen days after it had been mailed. We called Chalk River
to ask for the details of their account so that we could wire-transfer the
funds. They told us not to worry, but simply to mail the check that day.

We did so, and then were penalized some $2000 because the check arrived three days late. Our director of purchasing, Lee Curry, complained and was told that we need not pay the penalty, but in that case we need not order from them again!

Naturally we were really angry, and during my next visit to Canada I complained about this situation to many Canadian chemists. A friend at the National Research Council in Ottawa, Dr Ian Smith, suggested that I order heavy water from Ontario Hydro. I had not even known that they made heavy water, and when I next visited Queen's I asked the principal, Dr Watts, whether anyone at Queen's was familiar with the company. Luckily one of the Queen's professors had been an executive at Ontario Hydro, and he guided me to the right people. In fact, Ontario Hydro had 8000 tons, an unbelievably large quantity, and they were not only interested but happy to sign a long-term contract to supply Aldrich with very pure heavy water. They had not known that there was a market in the fine chemical business, and the manager, Michael Arnold, a delightful person, probably captured most of Chalk River's customers. Year after year, Chalk River later invited us to resume purchases, and of course we declined politely, but with great pleasure.

Diaprep and Aldrich made most of the deuterated solvents we sold, but we also bought from ARMAR, owned by my friend Dr Armando Geiger, who had been production manager at a large Swiss company, Uetikon, which had sold deuterated compounds to Fluka and E Merck.

Another area we thought would be interesting to explore was chromatography. Early on we purchased a 40% interest in Camag, a company in Switzerland, which made chromatography equipment. In the United States the best supplier of materials needed in chromatography is Supelco, which was acquired by Rohm & Haas some years ago and was bought by Sigma-Aldrich in May 1993. I regarded this an excellent purchase because the Sigma, Aldrich and Fluka catalogs would greatly assist Supelco to sell its products. However, I was truly taken aback when I learned that, within days of Supelco's being taken over, more than eighty of its employees were asked to leave. When Sigma merged with Aldrich, I was careful to make certain that no employee was laid off, but sadly that spirit of caring is a thing of the past.

During the 1960s it became clear to me that Aldrich should produce more and perhaps expand its production through acquisition. In the Bronx, there was a small producer of chemicals, Hexagon, publicly owned, with a thin market for its stock. When one of its founders died, Aldrich purchased 20% of the stock from his widow, 80,000 shares, at $2 per share. I thought that through such friendly ownership, we would get to know the company well and perhaps, in time, be able to acquire more or all of the stock. However, the more I got to know about Hexagon the less I liked it, not because the executives and chemists were unfriendly, but because it operated in New York City. In forty-one years with Aldrich in Milwaukee, not once did I come across a single case of dishonesty by a city official. This was certainly not the case in the Bronx, and we did not want to operate in such a climate.

Some years after we had purchased the 20% interest in Hexagon, Murray Prester, its president, told me that J T Baker was considering buying Hexagon and asked at what price we would be willing to sell our stock. I told Murray that we would be delighted to sell it at $3 per share, and in fact even that was negotiable.

Imagine my surprise when I received a telephone call one day from Dieter Zander in New York, a chemical company executive whom I had known for some years. Dieter told me that Boehringer Ingelheim, a large, privately-owned pharmaceutical company in Germany, had decided that they wanted a production presence in the United States and were making an offer for Hexagon of $6.25 per share. For a moment I was speechless, and all I could mutter was, "Is that the best you can do?" Of course we accepted, but wondered whether Boehringer Ingelheim knew something about Hexagon that we did not. That was not the case, for they, too, discovered that operating a chemical company in New York City was practically impossible, and eventually sold Hexagon to some of its executives at a substantial loss, I presume.

Although we worked mainly with a few large European companies, most of my efforts were with small companies owned by a single chemist. Most of them shared a problem that made me wary. They were good chemists and often excellent entrepreneurs, but they had a very hard time finding younger chemists to work with them who could in due course become their successors.

The first such man I met was a delightful person, Max Gergel, who ran the Columbia Organic Chemical Company in South Carolina. Max knows a great deal about aliphatic halogen compounds, speaks and writes well, and perhaps has more friends than anyone else among chemists in the United States. He started Columbia Organics in the late 1940s.

My first collaboration with Max was quite important when we received the contract from du Pont in 1955 to supply 500 lbs of suberic acid. I knew how to make it from 1,6-hexanediol, available for less than a dollar per lb from Union Carbide, but Aldrich certainly did not have the equipment in its small laboratory at this time to make 500 lbs of anything. So I supplied Max with the hexanediol and had Columbia Organic convert it to suberic acid. I have never forgotten that help from Max, and we purchased many products from Columbia Organic.

Some years ago, Max handed over Columbia to his son-in-law, but the company got into environmental problems and went into bankruptcy. Max published two humorous books in the eighties, describing the early days of his company. Unfortunately he used his great salesman's flair for exaggeration to write about pollution by Columbia, and his two books have been used against him in lawsuits, which have troubled him a great deal. When hearing about such problems, I say to myself: there but for the grace of God go I. Aldrich produced so little in the fifties and sixties, when pollution of the environment was not a national concern, that we had no such problems. Columbia however made all sorts of halides, such as methyl iodide and alkyl bromides and chlorides, on a moderately large scale, and simply dumped the by-products, a common practice.

Another small company with which we became involved quite closely had the unlikely name Kaplop Laboratories, in Detroit. It was owned by an excellent chemist, Bill Lotherington, quite a wild character, whose father had been involved in the distribution of Canadian liquor in the Detroit area during prohibition. Bill and I became friends, and I was always struck, when invited to his home, at how immaculately clean it was kept by his deeply religious Methodist wife. Here was Bill, making chemicals in a filthy laboratory, cussing all day long, and then going home to a beautifully clean place, a totally changed man in the evening. His two main products were oxalyl chloride and resorcinol disulfide. He made the former in 50-liter batches, mixing anhydrous oxalic acid with phosphorus pentachloride, pouring a little phosphorus oxychloride to mix the two solids, and then stepping back in case the reaction got out of hand. He made the disulfide, an important Ozalid-type material, from resorcinol and carbon disulfide, liberating copious quantities of hydrogen sulfide.

At one point, Aldrich actually owned a substantial interest in Kaplop Laboratories, but sold it when we realized the physical problems involved. Bill had a right hand man, Bob Gillmann, who took over the operation of the Kaplop Laboratories when the Lotheringtons decided to move to California. We discovered that Gillmann was making and selling resorcinol disulfide on the side, using the Kaplop facilities and selling the product to Kaplop's customers. We sued and recovered $38,000.

We found a much happier collaboration at Bristol Organics in Gloucestershire. I visited Elizabeth and Michael Buxton, the owners, year after year, purchasing all the fluoro-aromatics made by them in small laboratories right in their own home. Their products were very interesting. Michael was a fine chemist, but deliveries were pretty terrible. It was clear they were thinking of selling the business, but Aldrich was reluctant to purchase so small an operation. We were also buying fluoro-aromatics—but different compounds—from Yarsley, a small company in Surrey, then owned by the British Institute of Physics. I had become a good friend of their manager, Dr Jim Jappy, a very able Scot,

CHEMISTS

With Martin Ettlinger, Converse 205, Harvard, 1948.

Jack and Mary Tinker, Harvard, 1949.

Charles Hurd, 1971.

With Arthur F McKay and Daniel Swern, Chicago, 1954.

With Bernie Landau, Leon Mandell and Ira Kukin, Harvard, 1948.

My sister Marion, 1947.

Her wedding in Burton-on-Trent, 1949.

With Isabel and Ruth Hunt in Edinburgh, September 1949.

Isabel.

Danny at her graduation.

Danny at her favorite pastime.

Our wedding in Rabbi Shapiro's study, July 1952.

Seder with students, March 1956.

Danny with David and Daniel.

Danny with David.

Our third building,
1967.

Our first building,
1958.

Our baseball players, 1975. Left to right: Phyllis
Kratzer, Stella Ward, Mary Barnes, Barbara
Feustel, Pat Fredrich, Kris Korthoff, Doris
Lamontagne.

Our first four employees,
Lorraine, George, Stella, Beverly, 1978.

Marvin Klitsner.

Ralph Emanuel.

With Rabbi and Mrs David Shapiro.

CHEMIST FRIENDS IN EUROPE

Michael Carroll.

Ernst Vogel.

Ernst Reif.

Niels Clauson-Kaas.

ALDRICH EXECUTIVES

Bernard Edelstein, 1978.

Ike Klundt, 1978.

Hank Koppel, 1993.

Bob Gorzek and Jai Nagarkatti at Bob's farewell.

Clint Lane, 1994.

Floyd Green, Milwaukee, 1978.

and had suggested that Yarsley might be interested in purchasing Bristol Organics. However, the British Institute of Physics was not interested in investing more money in chemical production.

One day, I received a telephone call from one of our men in Gillingham, telling me that Michael was thinking of selling Bristol Organics to Philip Koch. I telephoned Michael at once and suggested that he consider selling to Aldrich. They accepted our better offer, a very modest £40,000, and Elizabeth and Michael stayed with us until their retirement in 1991. I am certain that they would have been unhappier owned by Koch-Light and then involved in Koch-Light's bankruptcy. Aldrich really expanded their production, and today sells well over $1,000,000 worth of fluoro-aromatics. Only small quantities are still made in Gloucestershire and larger quantities are produced in Aldrich's various facilities in Wisconsin, at Aldrich Chemie, and Sigma Poole.

Some time later the British Institute of Physics sold Yarsley to Shell, which moved the operation to the Midlands. I believe that large companies almost invariably do poorly running a small chemical operation driven by entrepreneurial spirit, and Shell and Yarsley was no exception. They kept Yarsley for only a couple of years and then sold it to yet another large company, BNFL Fluorochemicals Ltd. Dr Jappy and his associates left, went back to Surrey and started their own imaginative and growing company, JRD Fluorochemicals Ltd. I believe that, with Dr Jappy's ability and enterprise, the company will succeed as it could not have done under either the British Institute of Physics or Shell.

BNFL, British Nuclear Fuels, is an interesting government-owned company that has been producing elementary fluorine since the early 1950s. Fluorine is one of the most dangerous and most reactive elements, yet was needed in large quantities for the production of uranium hexafluoride for nuclear fuels. BNFL made fluorine safely and efficiently, but what is it to do now that nuclear applications are declining? Who has ever heard of a government operation wanting to get smaller? In 1992 BNFL decided to set up BNFL Fluorochemicals and went on a shopping spree. First it purchased Fluorochem, not a manufacturer, just a distributor, of several thousand fluorine compounds, all acquired from other companies like Aldrich and Yarsley. I was asked many times whether Aldrich should not buy Fluorochem for around £1,000,000, but what was there to buy other than a list of suppliers and customers? Next, BNFL bought the assets of Yarsley from Shell, without the excellent chemists. Then they purchased part of the old Imperial Smelting and Flutec business from Rhone Poulenc. Dr Buxton, of Bristol Organics, had come from Imperial Smelting, from whom I had bought fluoro-aromatics for many years. They were successful producers, but had been neglected by Rhône Poulenc. Flutec liquids are fully saturated perfluorocarbons containing only carbon and fluorine, with many specialized applications. Will BNFL do better with them than Rhône Poulenc did? In the meantime, BNFL Fluorochemicals is trying to coordinate all this and to work closely with Russian producers of fluoro-aromatics, actually sending its own truck to Russia to avoid the uncertainties of Russian transport. Much will depend on the entrepreneurial spirit of the manager of BNFL Fluorochemicals. At first, it is bound to lose money, but the parent company loses so much more that it may not seem important. If it succeeds, all the better for the British taxpayer.

I believe that private industry, companies like Bristol Organics and JRD, will do better than a government-owned company. Production and marketing of chemicals is not easy; having friends among your suppliers and competitors helps.

REFERENCES:
1. *JACS*, 74, 6305 (1952)
2. *ibid*, 75, 5400 (1953)
3. *ibid*, 78, 2385 (1956)

11

Joint Ventures

While Aldrich worked with many companies around the world as their customer and supplier and also invested in a few, we had joint ventures with only two companies.

The first involved the formation of Alfa to market inorganic chemicals.

Very late one autumn afternoon in 1962, my secretary told me that a man from Metal Hydrides wanted to see me. He had no appointment. I assumed he was a salesman and, as we bought almost nothing from Metal Hydrides, I was tempted to say I could not see him, but I took pride in being available and so asked the man to come in. He was not a salesman, but Milton Lauenstein who had recently become president of MHI.

The company had had an interesting and checkered history. Incorporated in Massachusetts in 1937 with capital from Ventures Limited, a Canadian holding company that also controlled Falconbridge Nickel, MHI had tried to capitalize on the technology of its president, Dr Peter Alexander. Since his graduate work at MIT, Alexander had been interested in the applications of nascent hydrogen and in metal hydride reducing agents, and the company marketed metal hydrides such as sodium and calcium hydrides and the particularly important reducing agents, lithium aluminum hydride (LAH) and sodium borohydride. In 1952 the company decided to go public, with Ventures Ltd retaining virtual control until a further public offering in 1968.

In the 1950s sodium borohydride became the company's most important product. It is stable, water soluble and performs many of the same reductions as LAH, but safely, in aqueous solution. The US Navy became MHI's biggest customer for sodium borohydride and helped build the safe and efficient plant in Danvers, Massachusetts. In 1950 MHI licensed the patents from the inventors, Drs Brown, Finholt and Schlesinger, and sales rose because the Navy was considering the use of diborane, made from sodium borohydride, as a rocket fuel. But by 1962, when that interest had petered out, the company was losing money, and the 36-year-old Milton Lauenstein was brought in to rejuvenate the faltering operation.

Milton was a most personable man, with a BSc in chemical engineering from Purdue, an MBA from Chicago and management experience with several companies such as Bell & Howell, where he was director of long range planning. He was also an accomplished realistic painter.

He had come to Milwaukee that day to discuss the possibility of some kind of collaboration with Aldrich. For some time we had been thinking about going into inorganics, and since we did not have a single inorganic chemist, this looked like a good opportunity. I invited Milt for dinner, spent the evening with him, and within a few weeks we had arrived at the decision to form ALFA Inorganics, AL from Aldrich, FA from Falconbridge Nickel, the major stockholder of MHI. We each put in $5000 as initial capital and owned 50% of the capital stock. MHI and Aldrich were to offer their services to Alfa at their out-of-pocket costs, and Alfa was to be located in Beverly, Massachusetts, in MHI's headquarters. All this was straightforward. The only question, which plagued us for many years, was how to define an inorganic chemical. The initial agreement read, "Inorganic chemicals . . . shall include all compounds having no organic component except those in which the organic component is of a secondary or incidental nature. An organic component is defined . . . as carbon in a form other than a carbide or carbonate. Alfa will offer for sale only inorganic compounds except that it may offer specific organic compounds with the prior consent of Aldrich."

To head Alfa, Milt found a good inorganic chemist, Steward Stafford, a Harvard 1961 PhD, and Aldrich successfully taught him how to sell research chemicals through Alfa's catalogs.

In 1965 Milt changed the name MHI to Ventron. At Aldrich we were just preparing our initial public stock offering. Milton suggested that $10 a share was too high and that we should merge with Ventron instead. Ventron had grown nicely, particularly by developing new uses for sodium borohydride, and also by acquiring all sorts of small companies in totally unrelated fields, from magnets to silicon chips, mercurials and scientific instruments. Despite Milt's background in business administration, I did not see how such a hodgepodge could be managed. I felt very uneasy about Ventron's future and certainly did not want to merge. Indeed, within ten years Ventron had discontinued five of the businesses, and its largest acquisition, Cahn Instruments, was losing money. Only sodium borohydride sales and Alfa were doing really well. I felt that Milt relied too much on business-school textbooks and on Andrew Kahr, a financial *Wunderkind*. Andrew had graduated from Harvard at 19, received his PhD from MIT at 21, and after consulting for Ventron became its financial vice president. He worked from his home and knew how to price everything from research chemicals to companies.

Alfa was much closer to Ventron than to Aldrich, and not just geographically. Milt and I served on Alfa's board, with Steward Stafford and Professors Dieter Seyferth of MIT and Eugene Rochow of Harvard, two very able academic chemists. Two matters caused considerable disagreement, the desirability of analyzing each compound offered by Alfa and

132

their choice of compounds. Most of Aldrich's and Alfa's products were purchased. Aldrich insisted on in-house analysis of every product; Dr Stafford thought this unnecessary when the product came from a reliable source. Mix-ups did happen even with the most reliable suppliers, yet I was overruled. Aldrich allowed Alfa to sell organometallics, defining metals as "all elements to the left in the periodic table of the boron, silicon and arsenic diagonal." Alfa could also sell all boron and arsenic organics, but phosphorous organics only with Aldrich's specific permission. We kept arguing about silicon organics and particularly about whether borane.THF was organic.

These arguments made me receptive to Milt's proposal, in the spring of 1967, that Ventron acquire Aldrich's half of Alfa. We exchanged Aldrich's interest for 14,200 shares of Ventron, then worth $700,000, and agreed not to compete with each other for a period of ten years beginning in January 1968. During those ten years I was to be a consultant to Alfa and remain on its board, and Aldrich was to receive $50,000 per year.

Whether or not this was a good deal for Aldrich depended on the value of Ventron stock, which fluctuated widely, and on Alfa's growth compared to Ventron's, but at least we were no longer so involved in bickering, and as of 1978 Aldrich was free to go into inorganics and Alfa into organics.

I remained good friends with Milt, and invited him to join the Aldrich board. To my regret, he resigned in the summer of 1970, partly because Aldrich did not compensate its outside directors handsomely. As Milt wrote in his letter of resignation, "Your compensation of your directors carries with it your implicit appraisal of their value to Aldrich." This was not really true, because I had appreciated Milt's advice, although with the grains of salt used by scientists for MBAs. But I was frugal, often too frugal.

While Milt was a director of Aldrich, he again suggested a merger with Ventron, proposing a complex deal worked out by Andrew Kahr. It involved a tax-free exchange of a Ventron convertible preferred stock for 80% of Aldrich's stock, leaving the other 20% in the hands of the public. I declined, largely because I thought Aldrich's future brighter than Ventron's.

Working with MHI-Ventron-Alfa had at least three great pluses. Aldrich learned a good deal about inorganics. We also learned about the important applications of sodium borohydride so that we were later receptive to Herbert Brown's suggestion for collaboration leading to the foundation of Aldrich-Boranes. And I got to know Dr Michael Strem.

Long before I met Herbert, I was familiar with some of his papers on the use of boron hydrides for the reduction of organic functional groups. By 1958 MHI had produced the first million lbs of sodium borohydride

133

at its Danvers, Massachusetts plant, followed by millions more from the Danvers and a new Elma, Washington plant. Of course I was interested in Ventron's most important product, and in Herbert C Brown, the man who had developed its many applications.

It was from Milton that I received my first impressions of Herbert, the man. Chemists already knew of his fight with Saul Winstein and Jack Roberts in the non-classical carbonium ion controversy. Today, most have forgotten the details of that argument, but remember the heat generated. Derek Davenport has described some details of their fight in the *Aldrichimica Acta*[1] dedicated to H C Brown on the occasion of his seventy-fifth birthday. Milton often commented on how demanding Herbert was in his patent negotiations, but there was no question about the enormous importance and potential of sodium borohydride and hydroboration, recognized most clearly when Herbert received the Nobel Prize for Chemistry in 1979.

I did not meet him until 1972 when he called to ask whether he might visit Aldrich. He wanted our help. He had developed his hydroboration, a technique for the easy preparation of compounds otherwise difficult to make. He had suggested to several large companies—du Pont, Exxon, Searle, Kodak—that they start a company to use this technology. Each had shown initial interest, but lost it when they found that there was as yet no million-dollar demand for any hydroboration product. "Hundreds of compounds that cannot be made easily otherwise?" I inquired. "Yes, indeed," said Herbert. So Marvin Klitsner and I arranged to visit Purdue to spend a day with him. By the end of that day we had a handshake agreement that Aldrich would start a wholly owned subsidiary, Aldrich-Boranes, with an initial capital of $250,000, to make hydroboration reagents and products, and we would pay Herbert a 10% royalty on sales of the first $2,500,000, 7-1/2% for the next $2,500,000 and 5% thereafter.

In 1972 we still had a good relationship with Ventron, the sole US manufacturer of sodium borohydride, the key starting material, so I showed the details of this proposed contract to Milt and asked whether Ventron would like to join Aldrich as an equal partner. His reply was brief, "No, you are paying Herb too much."

We all make mistakes. Milt's decision was one, but few are as serious (and with hindsight, as hilarious) as the *JACS* referee's report in 1956 on Herbert's seminal paper with B C Subba Rao on hydroboration:[2] ". . . there is nothing new about the reaction. The fact that the addition of diborane to alkenes takes place in ether solution in a few seconds at zero degrees is a mere convenience. Moreover the reactions produce organoboranes for which there are no known applications. Consequently rejection is recommended."

We foresaw a great future for hydroboration. Following Herbert's suggestion, we hired Clinton Lane, one of his PhD students, experienced in hydroboration. Clint joined us in September 1972 and soon he and his assistants were making hundreds of products and reagents. In 1977 Aldrich purchased a chemical plant built by the Schlitz Brewing Company in rural Sheboygan County, some fifty miles north of Milwaukee, with 140 acres of land, subsequently expanded to 550 acres. ". . . the true significance of my own situation has finally hit me," Clint wrote at the time of Herb's seventy-fifth birthday celebration. "Here I am in a chemical plant which will eventually be devoted exclusively to the operations of Aldrich-Boranes, and Aldrich-Boranes is a company organized exclusively to develop the technology discovered by HCB and his research group."

Of course sales of Aldrich-Boranes products have continued to increase, and so have Herb's royalties, although now only at 5%. In the early years, we sometimes had minor disagreements with him. These were seldom about details of the contract, more often about our efforts in developments, but the differences were never serious—nothing like the disagreements Milt had described.

We greatly expanded the Sheboygan plant, no longer devoted exclusively to Aldrich-Boranes products. Once we learned how to handle one highly air-sensitive material like diborane safely, we could handle other air-sensitive materials like the metal alkyls safely. Clint has become the executive vice president of Aldrich.

After we bought the Schlitz plant near Sheboygan, we moved Aldrich-Boranes there. Schlitz had built it to make a beer additive, diethyl carbonate, which decomposes slowly to form alcohol and carbon dioxide. What a wonderful additive for beer! Alcohol and foam. But then a scientific paper appeared in Rumania, I believe, claiming that diethyl carbonate might form minute quantities of possibly carcinogenic heterocyclics. That was the end of diethyl carbonate in beer, and Schlitz sold this specially designed plant. It was an over-reaction, because there may be a thousand identifiable chemicals in beer, and the chances are that some of them may be carcinogenic if taken in large enough quantities. We all know that peanuts contain aflatoxins, some of the most carcinogenic compounds known, yet how many love peanuts and peanut butter!

We wanted to drain the water from lagoons at the new site into Lake Michigan, but it took a year to get permission because it was discovered that the water contained four parts per billion of cadmium; 2 ppb was the limit. Schlitz had never used cadmium, nor did we. The Wisconsin Department of Natural Resources found that the wells in the area that fed the lagoons contained 4 ppb, but at first regulators did not know this. Sometimes I did not know whether to laugh or cry until I remembered Marvin's maxim: "When in doubt, laugh."

Of course we asked Herbert Brown to join the Aldrich board of directors in 1972 and then the Sigma-Aldrich board in 1975. However, in 1979, the year Herb received the Nobel Prize, Aaron Fischer and Tom Cori suggested very strongly that he should retire from the board; the good reason given was his age. Little did we know that for many years afterwards, he and his associates would turn out great research work with many new, practical applications. The Nobel Prize presentation read:

"Herbert C. Brown has systematically studied various boron compounds and their chemical reactions. He has shown how various specific reductions can be carried out using borohydrides. One of the simplest of these, sodium borohydride, has become one of the most used chemical reagents. The organoboranes, which he discovered, have become the most versatile reagents in organic synthesis. The exploitation of their chemistry has led to new methods for rearrangements, for addition to double bonds and for joining carbon atoms to one another."

In April of 1979, in his last letter to the Sigma-Aldrich board, Herb wrote:

"Over many years my students and I had been exploring a new area of chemistry, that of organoboranes, with major promise in synthesis and chemical manufacture. I tried repeatedly to interest one of the major chemical companies in exploring the possibilities of this area of chemistry, but without success. Company after company expressed interest. They would authorize and pay for a market survey. This would establish that the compounds had not been manufactured or marketed in the past year and they would lose interest.

"Only Alfred Bader showed imagination and courage. After he heard my story, he decided to go ahead to test the market for borane chemistry. As you know, Aldrich-Boranes is doing very well. Sales are far from being market-limiting and are growing as fast as the space, equipment, and personnel permit.

"There are still numerous new developments in chemistry and biochemistry coming out of our research laboratories. Regrettably, our large chemical companies have apparently lost the ability to take such new developments out of the research laboratory into the market place. All too often, developments that had their origin in the research laboratories of the U.S. are today being introduced to the market by industrial organizations in Japan and West Germany, not in the U.S.

"Sigma-Aldrich still has this ability. I believe that organizations which take advantage of these new developments will be far more profitable than those that stay with old, well developed areas. Apart from the greater opportunities for financial return, I believe that the bringing of these new research developments to the market place represents a major contribution to the research workers of the U.S. and a major contribution to the well-being of this country.

"When we were discussing taking over the Israel development, there were some questions raised as to whether we might not be spreading our executive talent out too thinly. It may be that we are. If so, I hope that you will make a major effort to add to our executive capabilities and will continue to expand Sigma-Aldrich's capacity to bring new research developments to the market place and to emphasize that function.

"This is an area where we can be idealistic while greatly improving the financial prospects for Sigma-Aldrich."

Purdue honored HCB on his seventieth, seventy-fifth and eightieth birthdays, and we were happy to be able to help with exhibits of old master paintings there. His great work continues, and we look forward to celebrating his next milestone.

The third advantage of our collaboration with Ventron was getting to know Dr Michael Strem. Mike and I have a good deal in common. He majored in history and chemistry, received his PhD in chemistry from the University of Pittsburgh, loved soccer as a boy and wanted his own company. He started Strem Chemicals in 1964 and Ventron offered to become his equal partner in 1965 in exchange for laboratory space in the Danvers plant and help with sales through Alfa. For a time I served on Strem's board and enjoyed that more than serving on Alfa's—there was no bickering. Mike specialized in the manufacture of metal carbonyls, small-volume ligands, particularly phosphines, and in platinum group organometallics used as homogeneous catalysts. Sales grew nicely, reaching the first $100,000 in 1968, the first $1,000,000 in 1981 and $5,000,000 in 1993. Strem and Aldrich became each other's satisfied customers, and I was often told by academics around the world that the only supplier who treated them as personally as I did was Michael Strem. In 1977 Mike was able to acquire the other half of his company and has been growing independently ever since. I encouraged him to stay independent but suggested that, if he ever did want to merge, he should think of Aldrich.

My friendship with Mike led to my being invited to Boston for his wedding to Ann, a charming young lady, and that morning I bought a

137

beautiful sketch on paper in Marika's, an antique store on Charles Street. Marika, a colorful Hungarian who specialized in antique jewelry, thought the sketch to be 19th century French and priced it accordingly. Cleaning revealed it to be an early work, of about 1580, by Annibale Carracci, the great Bolognese artist, and I can admire it now at the home of Ralph Emanuel, also a good friend of Mike's.

Alfa's sales of inorganics continued to grow. I tried to help, but we could not agree whether borane.THF was organic according to our original definition of 1963. With the formation of Aldrich-Boranes, this was of particular interest because Herb owned a patent on this reagent and had turned the rights over to the company.

I was so certain it was organic that I suggested to Milt that we ask Professor Eugene Rochow to arbitrate. Gene was a famous inorganic chemist who had come from General Electric to Harvard where I listened to his lectures in organometallic chemistry in 1949. He became a director of Alfa and a consultant to Ventron. I knew he had told Milt that he thought that borane.THF was inorganic, but I felt confident that a simple presentation would persuade him. Gene had suggested two lower figures as his fee, but Milt felt that whoever lost the case should pay $500 assuming it took no more than one day of Gene's time, but more if it took longer. It seemed such a relatively simple question that I did not believe it could possibly take a day—until I saw Ventron's position papers, one of them forty-three (!) pages. Gene asked Ventron for a copy of Aldrich's agreement with Herbert Brown. This struck me as totally irrelevant, until I saw Gene's nine-page opinion. This ruled borane.THF to be inorganic *and* wrote that the agreement forming Aldrich-Boranes violated article 5 of our original Alfa agreement of 1963, which stated that Aldrich would not engage in the principal business of Alfa and MHI. Herbert Brown had tried hard to interest Ventron before he came to Aldrich; I had offered Milt a half interest, which he declined (because "we were paying Herb too much"); and Milt had never suggested that Aldrich-Boranes violated the 1963 agreement. When I protested to Gene that his comments about Aldrich-Boranes were irrelevant to whether or not borane.THF was organic, he sent me one of the strongest letters I have ever received. ". . . I spent a month on this case, to the exclusion of all else; it occupied all my thoughts, day and night. On March 19 I sent in my considered judgment, for which you have paid me only $1.20 per hour . . . Hence your charges are false and unwarranted, and have reduced my respect for Aldrich to the vanishing point." I must truly have hurt Gene's feelings, and I apologized in a long letter that ended, "From a commercial point of view the matter is quite unimportant, but from an emotional point of view this was important both to Mr Lauenstein and me because each of us was convinced of the rightness of his position. I am just sorry and now I have the added chagrin of having hurt your feelings so deeply."

Where did we go wrong? I fear that choosing Gene as arbitrator was a form of arrogance: I was so certain I was right that I believed even a director of Alfa and consultant to Ventron could be convinced. Of course I know that it is possible to be convinced and mistaken, but I still believe that we were right. We should have chosen an outside arbitrator.

More important—we should not have gone into the joint venture with MHI in the first place. Such joint ventures seldom work. Each party expects more from the other, and there is such a waste of emotion. Had we hired a really good inorganic chemist in 1963, we could have done it alone. A survey of chemists conducted by the Harvard Business School in 1968 showed that Aldrich was the preferred source for organic and Alfa for inorganic research chemicals. In 1978 Aldrich did hire an excellent inorganic chemist, Dr John Long, to compete with Alfa, and before long Aldrich's sales of inorganics overtook Alfa's.

My fears about Milt's ability to control Ventron's conglomerate materialized in 1975. He had done very well with sodium borohydride. In 1955, about 80% of sales had been to one customer, the Navy. By 1975 most of its customers were commercial, particularly in the pharmaceutical, textile and pulp and paper industries. The Danvers plant was operating around the clock and an almost identical plant was built in the State of Washington to be close to customers. Most of the acquisitions however were faltering or had been sold, and in 1975 sales and earnings were flat. Ventron's stock had peaked at close to 100 in 1968, but by 1975 was down to about 25. Milt owned only about 2% of Ventron's 540,000 shares; the other directors a total of only 2300 shares. Clearly Ventron was ripe for a takeover by a company that could see the great potential of sodium borohydride.

The first offer of $36 per share in cash came from the French oil and chemical company, Elf-Aquitaine, in May 1976. Milt resisted it strongly; Jacob Kaplan, the largest individual stockholder, owning 11%, was for it. Milt found a white knight in the Thiokol Corporation, which offered $44 per share in August 1976 provided that Thiokol gained control. Ventron's board unanimously recommended acceptance and Thiokol acquired over 96% of the stock.

Aldrich declined Thiokol's offer, feeling that Ventron would grow so well that the value of its stock would rise substantially.

In 1978 Thiokol merged Ventron into Thiokol and offered $45 per share for the outstanding stock. Aldrich took Thiokol to the Superior Court of Massachusetts, where the valuation case was heard before Judge J J O'Leary in 1982. We thought that we had a very good case: Ventron had grown since 1976, had a bright future, and we believed the stock was worth much more. We were disappointed when the judge found against us; disappointed and even more eager to compete with

Alfa, now owned by Thiokol.

Again a large company did not know what to do with a small, entrepreneurially driven company. Alfa tried and failed to compete with Aldrich in organics, whereas Aldrich did very well with inorganics. Eventually Thiokol decided to sell Alfa, touting it as the world's premier supplier of inorganic research chemicals. It found a buyer, in Johnson Matthey, the British supplier of platinum group metals. I remember visiting Johnson Matthey in Royston, near Cambridge in 1984, before their purchase of Alfa, when they told me, with great assurance, that they were entering the organic research chemicals field and building a versatile pilot plant. Aldrich placed some trial orders, which were never filled. Inorganic research chemicals were closer to Johnson Matthey's expertise than organics, yet I venture the guess that they erred in their acquisition of Alfa.

Alfa/Ventron and Steward Stafford, Alfa's president since 1963, decided to part company in 1971 and Stafford became a vice president and director of PCR in Gainesville, Florida. PCR, Peninsular ChemResearch, had an interesting history. Founded in 1953 by Professors George Butler and Paul Tarrant of the chemistry department at the University of Florida, it had grown nicely, selling mainly fluorine-containing monomers and polymers, some of its own manufacture and some purchased. In 1962 a business investment company, J H Whitney and Co, purchased a 28% interest in PCR and in 1966 the Calgon Corporation bought the company for about $1,600,000 in Calgon capital stock. I could not help but reflect that Aldrich might have had a similar history. In 1968 Calgon became a subsidiary of Merck and Co, and Merck, like other highly profitable giants such as J & J and Eastman, had little interest in a small fine chemicals business. So the seven managers of PCR were able to buy it back from Merck, using a loan and guarantee from the New Venture Capital Fund of Dow. By agreement, Stafford became the eighth stockholder, the vice president of the research chemical division and a director of the company. How much stock he would be allowed to buy would depend on the sales increase generated by him. The ambitious goal was to quadruple the sales of the research chemical division by 1976, from an estimated $500,000 without Stafford, to $2,000,000 with him.

Stafford joined PCR in May 1971. Early in September, he wrote to many of our suppliers, requesting quotations on products supplied to Aldrich, including a few made exclusively for Aldrich. Some of our suppliers wondered what our relationship was to PCR. As president of Alfa, Stafford had learned a great deal about Aldrich, but not about our suppliers. Only an insider could have supplied that information. The insider was Richard Vitek, who had been our sales manager from 1964 to 1967 and had become Stafford's friend. Vitek was really not effective in sales, and in 1967 we had given him six months' notice to find another position, which he did with Camag, the Swiss supplier of chromatographic equipment in which Aldrich owned a 40% interest. We thought that we had parted amicably until we learned that Vitek had given Stafford lists of our bestselling products and their suppliers. Stafford had paid Vitek all of $1000 for "consulting".

In September 1971 Aldrich made claims against PCR, Stafford and Vitek, within days of receiving details from our suppliers. PCR's management reacted speedily and honorably, returned our confidential material and Stafford's worksheets that same month, and then agreed not to sell any of the products involved for a period of years.

I do not know why PCR waited until January 1974 to dismiss Stafford, who then left the fine chemicals business and joined Dixie Lime Rock of Ocala, Florida, a company mining lime rock and phosphate.

Our second joint venture was the formation of Aldrich-Europe with Janssen Pharmaceutica, wholly owned by Johnson & Johnson. The experience was very different, at times enjoyable and challenging, yet essentially disappointing.

Janssen Pharmaceutica is located in the small Flemish town of Beerse, near the Dutch border town of Breda. I first visited them in September 1959 when the business was still independent, and met Bert van Deun, at that time in purchasing, but also involved in selling intermediates made by the company. The company was then owned by Dr Paul Janssen and his family, who three years later sold it to J & J for $7,000,000.

Paul Janssen is one of the world's finest medicinal chemists, whose work has led to more pharmaceutical products on the market than those of any other scientist. I understand that he has been nominated for the Nobel Prize in Medicine, but that prize is rarely given to industrialists.

Although I chatted with Paul on every visit to Beerse, my dealings were almost exclusively with Bert, who soon became my close friend. Aldrich purchased more and more compounds from Janssen, and in 1962 became Janssen's US sales agent, distributing their attractive 114-page catalog of many research intermediates. By the late 1960s, when we were working well together, Bert suggested that Janssen and Aldrich should cooperate to market research chemicals on the Continent. I felt we were not entirely satisfied with the performance of our own company, EGA, which we used for this purpose, and we inquired whether Janssen would be interested in purchasing EGA and thus having exclusive distribution on the Continent. J & J would not however allow Janssen to purchase a chemical operation outside Belgium. Later, Bert told me that he also had misgivings because he felt that if Janssen were to buy EGA, it would soon be making research intermediates required by Janssen, and no longer the many compounds required by Aldrich.

141

Still, we were so interested in working together that we set up a distributorship agreement in which Janssen organized a division, Aldrich-Europe, wholly owned by Janssen. The agreement was to be binding for twenty years from May 1970, subject to Janssen having the right to terminate after ten and fifteen years, in which case they would undertake not to sell the same chemicals for the remainder of the original period.

Aldrich was to share with Janssen its knowledge about purchased chemicals, its analytical data and all the information needed for the compilation of an Aldrich-Europe catalog paralleling the Aldrich catalog. Janssen was to pay Aldrich a 10% commission on Aldrich-Europe net sales, except for smaller commissions on Janssen-originated items and on bulk sales. Aldrich was to give Aldrich-Europe a 40% discount and to sell in Europe only through Janssen and EGA. For the first five years this joint venture worked quite well, ruffled only by occasional and understandable complaints from EGA and Aldrich-Europe about each other's activities.

Just as years earlier I had thought and hoped that Upjohn might want to purchase Aldrich, I thought and wondered whether J & J might be interested. However, they were doing so well with pharmaceutical acquisitions, particularly with that of Janssen, that they had little interest in buying a chemical operation. Janssen must have been J & J's most brilliant acquisition—at a cost of $7,000,000 it now produces some 25% of J & J's total profits!

During Aldrich's merger negotiations with Sigma in 1975, it became very clear that the Sigma executives did not like the Aldrich-Europe agreement, and some time later I was told that it was really the major stumbling block to our merger. Shortly after the merger, Tom Cori and David Harvey visited Paul Janssen, whom they thoroughly disliked. Since Paul also disliked Tom, the collaboration went downhill. David decided that the paragraph in the 1970 contract calling for Aldrich and Janssen to provide each other with purchase price information could well be against EEC law, and so that exchange was discontinued.

About 1980, J & J became very concerned about Janssen's many contracts around the world. I believe that the reason was that some European companies had been found guilty of pharmaceutical price-fixing, and Janssen and J & J were very concerned about EEC law.

Their attorneys questioned the validity of our 1970 agreement and asked the professional advice of Professor Walter van Gerven, an eminent Belgian lawyer. In a highly technical six-page opinion of February 1982, he concluded, ". . . it will appear from the foregoing that the validity of the agreement and of each of the specific clauses dealt with above is, to say the least very doubtful." This led to a serious and really quite friendly discussion about how the joint venture could be terminated. I was sorry for personal reasons, as I so enjoyed working with Bert.

Tom and David however were delighted because they had been against the agreement from the very beginning and it was clear that Paul Geuens, the manager of Aldrich-Europe, was also satisfied because he felt that he could do a better job alone.

In an agreement of June 1982, we spelled out the details for termination of the 1970 contract. Aldrich-Europe's name would be changed to Janssen Chimica, which would continue to pay a 10% royalty on its sales until the end of 1984. This would be scaled down to 7.5%, 5% and 2.5% in the years between 1985 and 1990. Janssen Chimica could sell all over continental Europe, but not in Britain until the end of 1986 or in the United States until the end of 1989.

Years later Bert told me that the carefully considered opinion written by Professor van Gerven had been written sincerely. Had Janssen Pharmaceutica been really happy about its collaboration with Sigma-Aldrich, surely a way could have been found to continue the collaboration within EEC law; but there was such personal dislike between some of the principals that van Gerven's advice was readily accepted.

Janssen Chimica subsequently made substantial efforts to market fine chemicals around the world, but I do not think that they succeeded particularly well. The key factor to success in any fine chemical company is the availability of good chemists, and although Janssen Pharmaceutica of course has superb chemists, they have been interested almost exclusively in medicinal research.

When Janssen Chimica began selling in the US in 1990, they decided to appoint Spectrum, a small chemical distributor, as agent. Spectrum advertised very aggressively, but advertising alone is not enough.

To me, it was clear that in time J & J would insist that Janssen Chimica be sold. But who would buy it or—a more relevant question—what was there to buy? Since the split with Aldrich, Janssen Chimica had built its reputation on being a low-cost supplier of common solvents used by Janssen Pharma in large quantities, and a supplier of important pharmaceutical intermediates. Would a buyer of the chemical company have access to these? Riedel de Haen, the German fine chemical supplier owned by Hoechst, was one of the first to consider the purchase, but eventually decided against it. There usually is a buyer however for every company, and Fisher Scientific bought it early in 1994. Fisher has been a respected name in the fine chemical business for many years, with a roller-coaster corporate life. It was purchased by Allied Chemical in 1981, then, via Allied Signal, became part of Henley and finally in 1991 again became an independent, publicly-owned company. Fisher paid a little over $30,000,000 for the company with sales of $30,000,000, guaranteeing the jobs of the seventy-five Belgian employees and, I am sure, hoping that they would be comfortable with the new owners.

At the same time, Fisher purchased the research chemical business of

Eastman Kodak, the oldest in the United States. It goes back to the First World War when the US government asked Eastman to fill the void due to the unavailability of German chemicals, and during all this time Fisher had been Eastman's most important distributor. Until about 1950, Eastman had a virtual monopoly in research chemicals—"no one can compete with Eastman," my boss at PPG had told me in 1951—but since Eastman paid little attention to this, its market share and thus Fisher's also declined. Finally Eastman told Fisher that it would either close the fine chemicals division or sell it to Fisher for very little. Fisher's purchase of the Eastman division made much better sense than that of Janssen Chimica, and not just because the Eastman division cost so much less. Some years ago Fisher commissioned a very interesting and thought-provoking study on how to compete with Sigma-Aldrich. I could have given them the key to success at no cost and in one sentence: All will depend on people, on really good and imaginative chemists who can think internationally. There were none such at Janssen Chimica.

Bert van Deun is one of the brightest chemical entrepreneurs I know. J & J must have recognized his ability because in 1985 they moved him to the US, in charge of Cilag Chemie, which J & J had acquired in 1959. Cilag had long been a rather sleepy division, always chafing under comparison with Janssen Pharmaceutica, but under Bert's tutelage, they have done very well. Bert and Mia van Deun have remained our good friends. They have become serious collectors of Dutch and Flemish 17th century paintings and visit us regularly to view our most recent acquisitions. We have a ball talking about art and chemistry around the world.

After the dissolution of Aldrich-Europe, we started companies in various countries, and I was particularly concerned about how well Aldrich Benelux would perform, competing geographically so closely with Janssen Chimica. Luckily we found an enthusiastic chemist, Max van Laere, to head that company. Despite having to beard the lion in his den, Max has pushed our sales up year by year.

Surprisingly, Tom Cori put Peter Gleich, an accountant who had been the company's treasurer, in charge of the European operations. Peter is neither a chemist nor does he speak foreign languages well, which was perhaps one of the reasons we encountered such rapid turnover in our management of Aldrich Chemie in Germany. Some three years ago, Peter became head of SAF, the bulk chemicals division handling all the bulk sales of Sigma, Aldrich and Fluka. Again, his lack of chemistry and languages must have been a disadvantage. Peter has always been most loyal to Tom Cori and Aaron Fischer, but I do not think that is qualification enough to head our important European and bulk sales efforts.

People are the key to success in every venture—joint or otherwise. Alfa never had what I regarded as really good people, and Aldrich did better alone. Aldrich-Europe had Bert van Deun until J & J moved him to Cilag, which they considered more important. I think that in time Sigma-Aldrich management may realize the importance of our European business and put a multilingual chemist entrepreneur in charge.

REFERENCES:
1. *Aldrichimica Acta*, 20, 1 (1987)
2. *JACS*, 78, 5694 (1956)

12

Sigma-Aldrich

At the time of the merger of Sigma and Aldrich, I knew relatively little about the history of Sigma or about its chief officers. The main attraction of the company was its leading position as a supplier of biochemicals.

Sigma's entry into biochemistry was almost accidental. Two brothers, Aaron Fischer and Bernard Fishlowitz, Washington University graduates in engineering, had started a firm, Sigma's parent company, Midwest Consultants, but both having other jobs, they needed someone to manage it. Fresh with his BSc in chemical engineering in 1936, Dan Broida applied and the brothers had the wisdom to hire him. The company's first products were diverse—shoe polish, dyes and cosmetics, followed by the production of saccharin after Dan returned from military service. One day Louis Berger, a biochemist at the VA hospital who had received his MSc from the Nobel Laureates Carl and Gerty Cori, asked Dan whether he could use the Sigma laboratory to extract adenosine triphosphate (ATP) from rabbit muscle. Louis had learned the technique while working for the Coris, and he taught Dan the process, which Sigma still uses, although rabbits proved too small and today they use horses. ATP is a major source of energy in living beings and so of great interest in research. Soon Sigma had the purest product and was the first to offer stable, crystalline ATP, as well as many of its derivatives. Researchers could concentrate on their research instead of spending many hours preparing the starting materials.

Shortly thereafter, Professor Oliver Lowry, of the Washington University School of Medicine, asked Dan to produce a phosphatase substitute to measure acid and alkaline phosphatase in the blood; and Sigma-Diagnostics was born. Louis Berger joined Sigma in 1953, became its vice president in 1963 and retired to San Diego in 1974.

Dan, handsome and abrasive, was immensely hard-working and needed little sleep. He announced in the Sigma catalog that any scientist needing help could call him person-to-person collect any time of the day or night at 314 993 6418. Dan meant it, and learned a great deal talking to his customers.

Dan, who was Sigma's only salesman, insisted that every order for products in stock—and over 95% were in stock—must be shipped the day it was received. Sigma prices had to be the lowest and included postage. Advertisements were infrequent and simple, and visits to conventions and exhibitions were shunned. Despite learning so much from academics, Dan regarded many of them as idiots. PhD stood for "Piled higher and Deeper." Academics however were a class higher than bureaucrats, SOB became "Son of a Bureaucrat," and he revelled in twisting their tails. When the federal government decreed that all reagent catalogs had to be 11 x 8 1/2 ins in order to fit neatly onto bookshelves, Dan said that he would comply if the government paid for the catalogs, but as long as Sigma supplied catalogs free, they would stay 9 x 6! Sigma, like Aldrich, refused to give government agencies (and large customers) any discounts. Dan commented, "Sigma's prices are the lowest and we pay the postage. When that bureaucrat told me that we would get a contract at once if we raised prices and gave the government a 1% discount, I told him where to go."

When a researcher at a university objected to what he considered Dan's reactionary attacks on government bureaucracy and threatened never to buy another Sigma product, Dan replied that Sigma would gladly cooperate, but would he please clarify whether Sigma's computer should reject only his orders, all orders from his department or orders from the entire university? There was no reply. You could not help but admire Dan, even when you disagreed with him.

Dan disliked and was unwilling to help his competitors. He refused to sell anything to any of them. Naturally, that feeling was mutual, yet only Sigma's biggest competitor at the time of the merger, Calbio in San Diego, protested to the government that the merger of Sigma and Aldrich might produce a monopoly.

One of the first discussions of the merged board highlighted one of Dan's idiosyncrasies. At his insistence, Sigma had long refused to sell any products to Merck because they had refused to sell Sigma actinomycin for resale, explaining that they could not keep up with the demand of their medical customers. "If Merck will not sell us actinomycin," Dan declared, "we will not sell them any biochemicals." Merck had to get around this by buying through a small New Jersey college. In contrast, Merck was one of Aldrich's best customers. I had long admired their respected president, Max Tishler, also a Fieser student, and I numbered many Merck chemists among my friends. The new Sigma-Aldrich board voted to sell Sigma products to Merck, with only Dan dissenting. Some years later we acquired Makor in Jerusalem, a manufacturer of fermentation products, including actinomycin, and offered Makor's product to Merck, who has been our good customer for this ever since. Dan also refused to sell to Parke-Davis because he felt their major product, chloromycetin, was dangerous. That matter was settled quietly somewhat later.

I had known Dan for many years and always found him difficult, and so had feared before the merger that I would find working with him very

147

awkward and working with Aaron Fischer straightforward, if not easy. Surprisingly, I was mistaken on both counts.

Dan and I respected each other, and while we agreed to disagree on matters like the sales to Merck, disagreement never degenerated to a personal level. In fact, the longer I worked with him the better I liked and respected him. He was tough, and you could never win an argument with him, but that did not matter when the argument was important. Dan's refusal to sell to Merck, for instance, was irrational, and the board voted against him 8:1. Yet Dan's hard work, imagination and intelligence had propelled Sigma to become the world's premier supplier of biochemicals, and with a more balanced management, his idiosyncrasies could do little harm, but his hard work could do much good.

I had known Aaron only since 1974 as chairman of Sigma. He was always suave, well spoken and intelligent, and he would ask more searching questions than anyone else I knew. I was staggered when one of his nephews came up to me before the merger, after a talk I gave at the Minneapolis Art Institute, and asked me whether I realized "what I was getting into" working with Aaron. I first realized Aaron's lack of compassion when he urged us to fire Bernie Edelstein, secretary and director of Aldrich. Since joining us in 1962, Bernie had become my friend but did not hesitate to disagree with me on company policy when he thought I was wrong. I tend to be pragmatic, goal-oriented, and too short with people. He would always take time to talk to employees, encourage them and look at all sides of human problems. Sadly, he was a severe diabetic. Before the merger, Aaron asked me whether we should not retire him, and I said, "Certainly not. He has been a most loyal employee, and I don't know how long he has to live." He recovered briefly when his sister donated a kidney, and a year later Aaron said to me, "You promised me that Bernie would be dead. He is not. Now fire him!" Of course I did no such thing, and sadly Bernie died in 1983. As Aaron tried to treat Bernie, so he treated Dan.

At the time of the merger it was clear that the ablest younger men in the company, Tom Cori and David Harvey, were the most likely successors to Dan, Aaron and me.

Tom was the only child of Carl and Gerty Cori, brilliant biochemists of Czech origin. Both had received the Nobel Prize in medicine in 1947 for their work in biochemistry at Washington University in St Louis. Tom was just 10 when his parents became Nobel Laureates; he decided on biochemistry also and received his BSc from the University of Wisconsin in 1959 and his PhD from Washington University in St Louis in 1969. His parents knew Sigma well, and Tom joined the company as a production chemist in 1970. He became a vice president of Sigma in 1975, its president in 1976 and a director of Sigma-Aldrich in 1977. Dan often referred to Tom as "our president in spe", and that and the many references to his parents, the Nobel Laureates, may well have irked Tom.

David Harvey came from a working-class family in Birmingham, England and won a scholarship to Oxford, where he graduated with a PhD in organic chemistry. He then spent several years with Shell, travelling all over Europe, before joining our English operation in 1974. David is immensely hard-working, very analytical and speaks German well. He was soon put in charge of our German operation.

David succeeded me as president of Aldrich, and was elected a director of Sigma-Aldrich in 1981. Ralph Emanuel had worked closely with him and had assured Marvin and me that we could depend on him for independent thinking and that he would not be swayed by pressure or emotion. In that Ralph was sadly mistaken.

The first months of 1980 proved to be critical for the future of Sigma-Aldrich. Marvin and I had a lengthy and heated discussion with Aaron Fischer in St Louis in January when Aaron told us that he had finally been able to persuade Dan to retire as chairman of the board at the annual meeting in May, although he would remain a director. Aaron went on to say that he had discussed the succession with several directors, and the decision was that Tom Cori should become chairman of the board and CEO, the most important position, since I was not willing to be "kicked upstairs" to the position of chairman. I objected, saying bluntly that I was not willing to continue serving as president under such circumstances. I cited as my reasons Tom's abrasiveness and his treatment of people. Aaron asked me for a specific example, and I gave him the first that came to mind, a recent occurrence. A chemist at Roche had suggested that we make a compound by a fermentation process patented by Kodak. I wrote to the inventor who replied very graciously that Kodak would license us under its patent, and he would send us the fermentation strain so that we could do the microbiology at Sigma. Tom saw no reason to bother with a patent license. Aaron told me: "That attitude of Tom's is my doing." If only Tom could have had Marvin instead of Aaron as his mentor!

On February 3, Dan flew to Milwaukee, where Marvin and I talked to him all that Sunday afternoon. It became clear that he did not really want to retire, and had agreed only because Aaron had threatened to walk away from the company if he did not agree. Dan, who really respected Aaron, did not want that to happen. Roma, Dan's charming wife, who accompanied him on many of his travels, later told me how deeply hurt Dan had been by this episode.

Dan was very ill at the time with cancer, but none of us knew how close he was to death. Perhaps if Aaron had known, he would not have pushed him quite so hard. After all, he had made Aaron a very rich man. After Dan's death on October 12, 1981, Aaron and Tom recommended that the company set up a Dan Broida scholarship memorial for children of Sigma-Aldrich employees.

The February 1980 board meeting in St Louis was hectic. Ralph Emanuel did not attend every meeting, but had flown over for this one partly because his vote with respect to Dan could make the difference in deciding the succession. Ralph still remembers the look Aaron gave him when he made his unexpected entrance.

Dan reluctantly agreed to retire as of October 1, 1980 and after much acid discussion it was agreed that I would relinquish the presidency of Sigma-Aldrich, becoming chairman of the board and chief executive officer. Tom would become president and chief operating officer. It was ironic that Dan, who had so resisted the merger of Sigma and Aldrich, was supported by three directors from Aldrich—Marvin, Ralph and me.

Aaron later managed to persuade a majority of the directors, all but Marvin Klitsner and myself to force Ralph from the Sigma-Aldrich board of directors. My discussion about this, alone with Aaron the evening before the crucial directors' meeting, was most heated and distasteful. Ralph had built our English operation, knew British business practices and had been a most helpful and constructive director, who had done far more to advance the interests of the company than any of the outside directors. But Aaron insisted he had to go.

The disappointing aspect of this fight was that David Harvey, my successor as president at Aldrich, and the man we thought would eventually head Sigma-Aldrich, sided with Aaron against Ralph. David's vote for Ralph could have made a difference. Ralph had hired him in 1974 and had constantly pushed him ahead and urged his promotion.

Why did David, who best knew how valuable a contribution Ralph was making, join Aaron and Tom in their vote against Ralph? I believe there were two reasons for his votes with respect to Dan and Ralph. Perhaps he simply believed that Aaron had the upper hand and could call the shots. A more complex reason may have been that David seemed to be mesmerized by Tom, clearly the ablest younger man at Sigma. He has often said to me, "Tom is by far the most intelligent man I have ever known." Tom is indeed very intelligent, hard-working and ambitious, and on any matter of importance to him, David seemed to support him.

The differences over Dan and Ralph were an utter waste of emotion, utilizing great effort that could have been spent much more effectively building Sigma-Aldrich. Tom and David were the obvious successors to Dan, Aaron and me, and had we been able to work together harmoniously, they would be in exactly the same positions as they are now, but heading an even better company.

Early in 1980 I got a clear indication of what Tom is really like. "Alfred," he said, "the problem with you is that you want to be liked, even loved. I don't have a single friend in the world, not one." He also described the founders of Sigma, "Dan Broida is hard outside, soft inside. Aaron Fischer is hard outside and inside." I do not know who is harder, Tom or Aaron. Probably Tom.

Our relationship with Aaron took an odd and unexpected turn in the summer of 1985 when he announced that he wanted to diversify his holdings and sell much of his interest in Sigma-Aldrich. Had he lost faith in the company's ability to continue its growth once his own guidance would no longer be available? Aaron persuaded his sister-in-law and the Broida family to join him, and he asked me whether I would also join in trying to find a buyer for the company. I declined. Together, the Sigma families owned about 40% of the stock, and Aaron asked Goldman Sachs to find a buyer. That was easier said than done: only a very large company could have bought us, and we were selling at a high multiple. Also, the management was strongly opposed to a sale. Tom and David were particularly upset, understandably so. For years they had done everything Aaron wanted and backed him in his effort to get Dan to retire and to remove Ralph from the board. Luckily, Goldman Sachs could not find a buyer, and the three Sigma families agreed with Aaron to offer 1,500,000 shares in a secondary underwriting by Goldman Sachs, with Sigma-Aldrich buying an additional 500,000 shares at the net sales price. I was happy with the secondary offering which disposed of two-thirds of the Sigma families' holdings and broadened the outside shareholdings, but I opposed the company's purchase of 500,000 shares. At that time there seemed to me much better ways to spend $30,000,000, but the board of directors overruled me.

During the pendency of the secondary offering, the price of Sigma-Aldrich stock approached $70, and it is not unlikely that Aaron and the other Sigma families hoped to get that kind of price for the 2,000,000 shares. I learned later that a large stockholder, perhaps disturbed by the prospect of the company borrowing money to buy back 500,000 shares at close to $70 per share, offered a large block to Goldman Sachs via another broker, and the price of the stock moved down rapidly from the upper to the lower $60s. Aaron, Goldman Sachs, and perhaps others, made the erroneous assumption that I was behind that offer. I did not and would not have had anything to do with it, yet Aaron has scarcely spoken to me since and at board meetings just glared at me.

The underwriting was a success, and the stock then moved steadily higher. Within a year and a half it was selling at over twice the price of the secondary offering.

While the merger of Sigma and Aldrich has been exceedingly good for stockholders and has brought some advantages for customers, it brought many problems for some of its employees, particularly at Aldrich and later at Fluka.

The management styles at Sigma and Aldrich were very different. At Sigma, and eventually at Sigma-Aldrich, decisions were made at the top

151

of the pyramid, with little or no discussion with the managers who had to carry out the policies. At Aldrich, there had been a great deal of discussion—perhaps at times too much—but every manager knew why decisions had been made. There was much more profit-sharing, and Aldrich benefits were better. Dan, like me, had limited his salary to $40,000 a year at the time of the merger, but when Tom became CEO, the salaries of the very top people, and their bonuses, moved up markedly—but only those of the very top people.

Dan mistrusted suppliers. If a compound became a good seller, he wanted it made at Sigma, and some 60% of Sigma's sales were Sigma-produced. Dan was totally forthright, and Sigma's catalog is the only one in the world that specifies whether the product is purchased: pfs, indicating "prepared for Sigma". Aldrich made only 40% and Fluka 20% of the compounds they offered, and the chemicals made at Aldrich and Fluka were still listed as pfs in the Sigma catalog.

Many of Aldrich's suppliers had become my good personal friends—contradicting two of Tom's three frequent sayings. One is, "There are no friends in business." Second is, "I don't trust anyone—why should I trust you?" I have trusted many of our suppliers and have seldom been disappointed. At the time of the merger, Aldrich's relationship with its suppliers was an eye-opener to the purchasing people at Sigma, who had not known how to speak so openly and so constructively to suppliers. At Aldrich, I tried to insure that every letter was answered. Of course, one cannot say yes to every request, but each letter merits an answer. At Sigma, the policy was to write very little—telephone if important; if not, do nothing.

Tom's third saying, "Our goal must be 2000 in 2000"—sales of $2 billion in the year 2000—struck me as erroneous as the first two. To Dan and me, growth was important but our goal had not been to reach so many millions in sales, but to become the best suppliers of fine chemicals. Best does not mean the largest—though we became that—nor the fanciest, just the most reliable in quality and service. I admired Tom for his striving for excellence in service, but not for his goal of $2 billion in sales.

It is in service and quality that Aldrich learned most from Sigma. At Sigma, employees did not leave for the day until all products that could be shipped were shipped. If a compound is white when pure, it had to be white to be offered. If Aldrich had the choice between offering a building block 98% and yellow at $6 per 100 grams, or 99% and white at $18, we would probably pick the former. To biochemists, high purity is essential; to synthetic chemists, price is sometimes more important than high purity.

The greatest difficulties with my successors at Sigma-Aldrich were not about how to improve a product line or service, but almost entirely about how to treat people.

Shortly after the merger, for instance, I was told by Professor Nelson Leonard at the University of Illinois in Urbana, an old friend and one of Aldrich's first stockholders, that the university had patented several purines, which Sigma had added to its catalog without permission. If the patents were valid, Sigma could not offer these compounds legally without a license from the university. Nelson had written to Sigma many times, twice by registered mail, without receiving a reply. When I inquired, Aaron told me to let the university sue; if the patents were found valid in court, Sigma would pay. When I checked the sales of the patented compounds at Sigma, I found them to be very small; at most, a few hundred dollars per compound. I was really embarrassed and suggested that I settle the matter personally by giving the university 100 shares of Sigma-Aldrich, then worth about $4000. I was glad the university accepted. Aldrich paid many chemists a 5% royalty on sales for teaching us how to make interesting compounds, and did so even without patents being involved. I do not think for a moment that was giving the store away. It cost us several thousand dollars to develop a new procedure, and to pay 5% for five or ten years seemed eminently fair. But to refuse even to answer a patent owner!

Chemists often asked me how Aldrich was able to advertise the availability of new products that had only just been published. The answer was simple: many of our friends sent us their manuscripts before publication.

Another patent argument concerned me even more. A competitor of Sigma, Research Organics in Cleveland, headed by Dr Marvin Sternfeld, received two US patents on a series of six biological buffers with the catchy names AMPSCO, CAPSO, DIPSO, MOPSO, POPSO and TAPSO. Sigma was selling them without a license. Research Organics filed suit, and in 1982 Sigma had to agree to pay a 7.5% royalty and to cite the two patents in the Sigma catalog. In 1989 I discovered that the compounds were selling quite well but that Sigma was paying a royalty on only one—an oversight, I was told. I suggested that we calculate what should have been paid and pay the difference plus interest. We did so. I also recommended that we tell Sternfeld of our mistake, but was overruled. He must have been surprised when the royalty for 1989 jumped to $6828 from $1672 in 1988.

At the annual meeting in May 1983, Tom assumed my duties as chief executive officer; I continued as chairman and David became chief operating officer. Year after year our annual reports had told our stockholders that the previous year had been the most successful in the history of our company, and I had every reason to hope that our team of intelligent, hard-working executives would continue that steady growth. In fact, the next eight years were, to me, among the happiest and most productive of my life. No longer burdened by the responsibility of being CEO, I could concentrate on doing what I did best: being an ambassador for the company, finding many new products, making real friends in academia and industry, negotiating large purchase contracts, and improving our catalog and the *Aldrichimica Acta*.

I probably became unpopular among our directors by being an internal whistle-blower, but the manner in which serious mistakes throughout the company were brushed off really bothered me, so much so that I brought some to the attention of the audit committee. Thus, for instance, Sigma had mistakenly billed a Swiss company for $2553 instead of $12,765 and when our honest customer pointed this out, he was told that the original invoice was correct. Similarly, our old friends at Loba in Vienna were paid twice for an invoice of AS120,700, about $10,000, but it took two years and finally a letter from Loba to me before Aldrich acknowledged that we really had made a mistake. Less serious—except that US Customs might think we were trying to reduce customs duties—were the many errors in Aldrich Chemie's invoices to Aldrich Milwaukee. I always tried to alert our internal auditors first, but often nothing happened. Eventually, in frustration, I wrote to Jim Weinberg, the chairman of the audit committee:

"It is, of course, a testimony to the loyalty of our customers and suppliers that they complained so loudly, but how many others are there out there who just pocketed our money, laughing all the way to the bank when we underbill or overpay. Errors in our favor, all will bring to our attention."

I worried much more about the thinness of top management, about Tom's reluctance to put really able scientists onto our board, about less and less information being shared with the board, about our compensation policy and the rapid turnover of management in Europe. However, I made many new friends among customers and suppliers and clearly earned my salary, which had not changed for years.

In time—once Tom had found a successor as president—I looked forward to his becoming chairman, and I chairman emeritus, continuing with my work, perhaps working only eight hours a day five days a week. If perhaps at one time David had been seen as Tom's successor, Tom now stated openly to the other directors that he did not see David in that capacity, telling David that their age difference was too small. I personally think that David is more responsible for the company's profitability and growth than Tom, but he is under Tom's thumb.

At the board meeting in November 1990, Don Brandin, the chairman of the company's compensation committee, told me that we should avoid the kind of fight the company had had with Dan, and that I should resign as chairman at the next annual meeting, allowing Tom to become chairman and president.

After considering this point carefully, I wrote to Don on February 6, 1991:

"... the cases of Dan and me are as different as chalk and cheese. You know what Dan was like, immensely able and hard-working, but also autocratic and had problems in sharing authority with anyone. Since Tom became president and CEO and I chairman, Tom has made all the important decisions and I have tried hard to do that which I think I do best—as I will outline.

"Unfortunately there is only one director, David Harvey, who knows in some detail what I do, and how consistently hard I work. Certainly none of the members of the compensation committee know, and so I would like to outline this to you."

That outline, with many examples detailed the ten areas of my work, and I continued:

"Naturally the time will come when I should cease being chairman, and perhaps continue as honorary chairman, and do whatever I can to help the company. That should be when Tom has a really competent successor in place as president, and one or perhaps two younger executives have learned carefully what I do. Right now, Don, our management is terribly thin and that scares me no end.

"Tom is very much a loner—you know his favorite statements—'I don't trust anyone, why should I trust you?' and 'There are no friends in business,'—and yet, through his ability and hard work he has done wonderfully well guiding Sigma-Aldrich. Yet what if ... he is in his fifties, without clear succession. His life and the company's future would be much more secure if he found a really able successor he can trust and if he would work also with me sincerely. He knows that I have not challenged his authority, nor do I present any threat."

On February 14 Marvin and I had a very long phone conversation with Don Brandin, during which Don kept reiterating that the compensation committee was unanimous that I should retire in May because Tom would find it easier to find a president if he were both chairman and president. It was a matter of "simple equity"; he had been CEO for eight years, had done an excellent job and was now perceived "as an inside guy" while I was on the outside! Don assured us, "We are leaning on Tom very hard to bring in a president." Marvin told Don that he could understand the committee's decision "if Tom weren't the CEO ... but as CEO, he is in complete charge and has complete responsibility." I assured Don that I would welcome becoming chairman emeritus when we named a new president. This suggestion fell on deaf ears.

Tom called me on Monday, February 18, just before the next board meeting in St Louis, and told me to take an earlier flight than I had planned so that I could meet Don Brandin to discuss my proposed retirement in May. When we met, Don explained that he was a very sick man, although he sounded very vigorous to me. He repeated what he had told Marvin on the phone, that Tom deserved the chairmanship, that as chairman he would find it easier to locate a president and that my remaining as chairman gave the wrong signals to the investment community, who probably thought that I was the man who wielded the power. He and the entire compensation committee were absolutely determined that I must tender my resignation "gracefully" or I would simply be forced out. He also explained that in his personal opinion David was not the right man to succeed Tom but that he would make certain that we had a successor to Tom as president within a year.

David had already explained to me that he accepted that he and Tom were too close in age and that we needed a man some ten years younger.

During the directors dinner that evening, I gave the compensation committee my written proposal that I remain as chairman until the appointment of a president or until the annual meeting of 1992, whichever was the earlier.

In the morning I presented my case calmly, to Tom and the members of the compensation committee, and then left while they made their deliberations.

The board of directors meeting started at about 9.30. Don reported that his committee was unanimous that I should resign at the annual meeting in May, but since they had been unable to obtain my agreement, no action was to be taken until the nomination committee meeting after the annual meeting, at which time I would be forced to resign. They had given me the option of either promising to resign now and receiving the title of chairman emeritus or being forced out completely in May.

The annual meetings had always alternated between St Louis and Milwaukee, and it was Milwaukee's turn in May. Tom had agreed and, in fact, my secretary, Marilyn Hassmann, had already made all the necessary reservations in Milwaukee. Yet Don now proposed and clearly had the majority to move the meeting to St Louis. When I remonstrated and reminded Tom that he had promised to have the meeting in Milwaukee, he just waived that aside and said, "So what?"

At that point I asked for a short recess to take counsel with Marvin, the only director on whom I could rely. Marvin felt that the vote would go against me and so I agreed to tender my resignation. Don then reconvened the compensation committee meeting, which he asked me to attend. As chairman emeritus I was to continue my work and my compensation would remain at the existing level. Details were to be worked out with Tom who suggested that I continue at $180,000 for one year. I pointed out that I would also be receiving director's fees and pension benefits of over $20,000 a year, and left him to work out the details. The following year's compensation would then depend on how well I did.

Tom also asked me to make lists of the work I was doing; for instance, lists of bulk purchases in which I was involved, lists of academics who had been really helpful, lists of people who might supply us with library compound collections, lists of suppliers I knew well. I was also to pick five old master paintings for catalog covers and twenty for *Acta* covers, and write essays to be used with each. All of this I agreed to, and carried out in the next few months.

When we reconvened, David made an impassioned speech about how much he had learned from me and what a great deal-maker I had been in building the company. I thought to myself that with such a speech and 80¢ I could get a cup of coffee.

It was all such a waste of emotion. I should not really have been surprised. It was a repeat of the Dan and Ralph shows.

Almost ironically, on my return home I was faced with all sorts of really challenging problems: should we consider buying a company in England, what could I do to assure the continuing supply of a raw material vital to Sigma, could I find sources for an acid important in getting a $2,000,000 contract from Roche? I believe I responded positively and effectively to these and many other important requests.

The 1990 annual report, which came out in April, announced that Tom would be elected to the additional position of chairman at the annual meeting, and I would become chairman emeritus.

During the next few months of 1991 work proceeded smoothly; I found lots of new products and made many productive visits to customers and suppliers. In October, Tom told me that my compensation would be stopped. I demurred, explaining the obvious: I did not need the money, but termination of compensation would demean the value of my work. Tom was adamant, and I had the choice of either continuing my work without compensation or retiring completely. Of course the answer was simple: I so enjoyed my work that I wanted to continue. As subsequent events developed, I wonder whether Tom really expected and hoped that I would refuse.

After the November board meeting I reminded Tom of Don's assurance that a potential successor as president would have been found within a year of my giving up the chairmanship. Tom just waved this aside, saying that in time they would need several men, not one. To my knowledge, none has been found so far.

13

My Expulsion

November 15 is a special day in my life. On Thursday, November 15, 1941, I had arrived at Queen's University, scared and wondering whether I could succeed, starting so late in the academic year.

Fifty years later, on Friday, November 15, 1991, Queen's had planned some special festivities to mark the anniversary of my arrival. In the morning I gave two lectures; one on challenges at Sigma-Aldrich, in the chemistry department; the second, "Adventures of a Chemist Collector," in the department of art history. In the evening there was a fine dinner, hosted by Principal Smith, followed by a third lecture, on Jan Lievens, in the Art Centre. I had already given a lecture on Josef Loschmidt the day before, and was to give another, "The Bible through Dutch Eyes," at the Art Centre on Saturday afternoon. All in all, it would have been a wonderful weekend, had it not been for a most threatening phone call from Tom Cori, after the first lecture on that Friday morning. He said he had to see me and refused categorically to discuss the matter over the phone. I asked whether we could meet in Canada on Saturday or Sunday, but he said that was impossible for him because he had discussions with people from Warburg and Goldman Sachs, and was receiving certain honors at Washington University. I could not go to St Louis since I was flying to England later on the Sunday, and so Tom ordered me to meet him at the Russell Square Hotel in London at 1 pm the following Wednesday, November 20. He said he would fly over specially, and I was to give him several hours.

At the Sigma-Aldrich board meeting the previous August, Tom had told the board that management were planning to sell about 10% of their stock. Subsequently, the papers reported that Tom, David and Peter Gleich, company secretary, had sold 10,000, 7500 and 5000 shares respectively. I was sorry to see this because it might indicate that they had doubts about the company's future. Just a few days earlier, my son Daniel had told me that his trust was selling covered options as a way of maximizing proceeds from the sale of stock. I was considering making a substantial gift to Queen's University, so as Marvin and I flew back to Milwaukee after the board meeting, I asked him what he knew about covered options. He said he thought they provided a good way for me to achieve what I had in mind. For example, Sigma-Aldrich stock was selling for $43 that day. If I sold an option for January at $45, I would receive $2 for the option. If the stock rose above $45 and the option was taken up, I would get $47, but if the price dropped, I would still have the $2 and could re-offer the stock later. It sounded good to me. On August 15 I sold an option for 10,000 shares. Tom, David and Peter had sold for about $42 per share; $47 seemed preferable, especially as Queen's was to benefit.

I had no intention of selling stock for myself. I had never sold any since the first offerings of Aldrich in the sixties. I did not join the Fischers and the Broidas, who have sold substantial blocks in the last ten years, although I have given stock to many universities, and early in 1991 I committed a substantial gift to Queen's. On the day before that threatening call from Tom, I had given Principal Smith a check for $1,000,000 and told him of my gift of optioned shares.

On Wednesday, November 20, I was confronted by both Tom and David in a meeting which lasted exactly seventeen minutes. They demanded that I sign a letter of resignation which they produced and told me that the contract for my work the following year without compensation, which Tom had drawn up and which we had agreed verbally on November 12 in St Louis, would not be renewed. Tom said he had discussed the option sale with all the directors (except Marvin, who had just undergone a heart by-pass operation), and all had agreed that a director who was "betting against the company" by selling options should not remain on the board. But of course I was not betting against the company; I just wanted to maximize the gift to my *alma mater*. I was the only major stockholder who had never sold any Sigma-Aldrich stock—and I had wondered whether their outright sale might not more realistically have been described as betting against the company.

The meeting had its comical aspects. Just a few weeks earlier Tom had chided me about sending him Xerox copies of my correspondence. He complained, "It is a waste of money, and you know how careful I am with the company's money." Yet now both he *and* David had flown to London to spend just seventeen minutes to get rid of me. Needless to say I refused to sign the letter of resignation, but have kept it, although I hardly need any reminder of that meeting. In the end, I suggested to Tom that he allow me to record the gist of what they had told me, and he replied sharply, "We don't have time for that, get out of here." At least I had been saved the several hours I had been instructed to reserve for him.

In the weeks following the November 20 meeting in London, I continued my work at English universities, interrupted only by visits to a Belgian and a Dutch chemical conference and three days holiday in Leiden, to let paintings take my mind off my worries. Many lectures and visits with some of England's finest chemists and their many suggestions reinforced my certainty that I was a useful link between academics and our company. But how many of our directors knew this?

Sigma-Aldrich stock rose in November and December, the option was exercised and Queen's University received about $60,000 more than Tom had received for the same number of shares.

Isabel and I returned home just before Christmas, and I tried to speak to each of the directors personally, by telephone, to explain that Marvin and I had not been betting against the company. The longest discussion was with Jim Weinberg, the most financially experienced of them all. He kept reiterating that directors of public companies "just know" and had been told by their managements, that they should not trade in options. The Sigma-Aldrich management had certainly not told me, and a long letter to Jim Weinberg (Appendix 1) went unanswered. In any case, there is a clear distinction between trading in options and the sale of shares by selling a covered option. The most equivocal responses came from directors Tom Urban, the president of Pioneer Seed, and Don Brandin, the retired chairman of Boatmen's Bank. "I clearly understand Tom Cori's position and yours," Urban told me. "But we can't both be right," I replied. Urban then responded, "That is right, too." You cannot argue with that! Don, Cori's close ally for years, told me that he was happy that he would miss the next board meeting; he had long ago made plans to go to Africa. When I reminded him that I had resigned as chairman the previous year on the basis of his assurance as chairman of the nominating committee that they would find a potential successor to Cori within twelve months, he claimed not to remember that promise! The strongest response came from Andy Newman, CEO of Edison Brothers Stores in St Louis. "Don't give me all this crap, all your *ex post facto* explanations. You bet against the company, you should be out, and what you do is your call."

For many years I had really paid attention to our customers, suppliers and employees, and little to our board of directors. That was a serious mistake. Our outside directors did not fully understand what went on in the day-to-day operations of the company, and none replied to the letter (Appendix 2) that I sent to each of them just before the annual meeting.

At the last full board meeting Marvin and I attended in St Louis on February 18, 1992, everything was cut and dried. At the nominating committee meeting preceding the meeting of the full board, Marvin and I pointed out the differences between selling covered options and speculating with options, and made a clear case that we had not bet against the company. When you sell a covered option, as I did, you must continue to hold the shares even if the price declines. That is not the case when you sell the shares outright. No one on the committee commented or asked a single question. Minutes later they presented to the board a previously prepared resolution, nominating all the directors except

Alfred Bader

Dr. Alfred Bader has had a long and very distinguished career.

Since founding Aldrich Chemical Company 41 years ago, Dr. Bader has been instrumental in building Aldrich into one of the world's foremost suppliers of high quality, fine organic and inorganic chemicals.

A native of Austria, Dr. Bader went to England and eventually to Canada, where he received several degrees from Queen's University in Ontario. Later he also earned a PhD. degree from Harvard University in Cambridge, Massachusetts.

While working in Milwaukee, he received permission from his employer to start a small business on his own, which he did in 1951 in a rented garage. When, in 1954, his employer decided to move its Milwaukee operations to Pennsylvania, Dr. Bader opted to remain in the city he had grown to love and formed Aldrich Chemical Company. It grew and prospered under his able leadership and guidance.

The early success and growth of Aldrich was due to his enthusiasm and creativity which attracted other able chemists and to his stamina and drive which were widely admired by his co-workers.

In 1975, he and Dan Broida, then the President of Sigma Chemical Company in St. Louis, led the effort which resulted in a merger of Sigma and Aldrich that year to become today's Sigma-Aldrich Corporation. Dr. Bader served as President of the new Sigma-Aldrich Corporation, with Dan Broida as Chairman. In 1980, Broida stepped aside and Dr. Bader became Chairman, a position in which he served with honor and distinction until his recent retirement.

Throughout his career, Dr. Bader has traveled extensively meeting customers and suppliers, giving lectures and becoming well known among leading chemists throughout the world. He has been the driving force in accumulating a collection of 39,000 rare chemicals which Aldrich makes available to the research community. Over the years, he has also personally helped many deserving chemists at universities with grants to underwrite their research.

Dr. Bader also has won renown as an art historian and a student of the Bible. His collection of the works of seventeenth century Dutch Masters is considered one of the finest private art collections in the world. He was named a fellow of the Royal Society of Arts in London for his achievements as an art collector and historian and for his research in art restoration.

Sigma-Aldrich has benefited significantly through the years from the influence and guidance provided by Dr. Bader. The entire Sigma-Aldrich organization is deeply grateful for his valuable contributions.

Please Bother Us.

Tom Cori's appreciation, prepared early in 1992 and withdrawn from the 1991 annual report.

A Letter To Chemists

Alfred Bader

Many of my chemist friends around the world have contacted me to inquire why I am no longer with Sigma-Aldrich. It is difficult to respond to each of you individually and so I have chosen this means of replying.

Some of you know me as the man who founded Aldrich over 40 years ago and built it into your favorite supplier of research chemicals. Many of you know me as the chemist collector who finds paintings for Aldrich's catalog and Aldrichimica Acta covers. Some of you know of the ABC's of my life—art, Bible and chemistry and the Alfred Bader Chemical Collection of research samples from some of the world's greatest chemists. Many of you know me as the chemist who has visited your laboratory with Isabel, his wife, and asked: "What can we do better?"—and surely you know that we meant it. For years we have been an important link between research and Sigma-Aldrich, and many of your suggestions have led to new products for Aldrich and Sigma.

On November 20 of last year, my successor at Sigma-Aldrich as CEO, Dr. Tom Cori, and Dr. David Harvey, the Chief Operating Officer, flew to London specially, to demand that I resign as a director of the Company because, in their words, I had 'bet against the Company.' That 'bet' consisted of a sale of an option on 10,000 shares of Sigma-Aldrich stock. Dr. Cori said that all the directors, except myself and Marvin Klitsner, who was undergoing heart bypass surgery at the time, had held a long telephone discussion about that sale, and had decided that I was no longer fit to work for the Company. I was flabbergasted, refused to resign and attempted to point out how erroneous that interpretation was.

The events leading to this November 20th meeting are simple. In the summer of 1991, I heard about option sales as a conservative way of marketing a limited number of shares at a price somewhat above the current market. I have never personally sold any stock in Sigma-Aldrich but have given a great deal of it away to universities around the world, to the ACS, and to many other institutions.

For some months I had intended to make a gift to my alma mater, Queen's University. With the intention of maximizing the gift, I sold a call option covered by 10,000 shares of my Sigma-Aldrich stock. This option, which sold on August 15 for $2⅝ per share, gave the buyer the right until mid-January to purchase these shares for $45 per share. The University's practice—like almost every institution's—was to sell stock immediately on receipt, and the market was then about $41 per share. So instead, I turned over to Queen's the optioned shares and the option proceeds.

Interestingly, Dr. Cori sold 10,000 shares in August, Dr. Harvey, 7000, and Mr. Gleich, the Company's secretary and treasurer, 5000 shares, all at $41⅜. The option which I sold was taken up in January at $45, making the total proceeds $47⅝ per share, so that Queen's University received some $60,000 more than Dr. Cori for the same number of shares. My *gift* represented less than one third of 1% of my 3,600,000 shares. Dr. Cori's *sale* of about 10% of his stock was a personal sale. As the only major individual stockholder who has *never* sold any of his stock, I have been 'betting *with* the Company'

with the biggest part of my assets. To accuse me of 'betting against the Company' is rubbish.

After the November board meeting in St. Louis just eight days before Dr. Cori's meeting with me in London, Dr. Cori and I had agreed that I should continue to work as chairman emeritus, without compensation, doing what I love doing—helping chemists and helping Sigma-Aldrich grow as a world leader in providing research chemicals. At that time, Dr. Cori said forcefully, "Keep working, Alfred; I have known many people who have retired and were dead six months later." Then in the November 20th meeting in London, he said that a man who had 'bet against the Company' could not continue in any capacity.

Between then and the next board meeting in St. Louis in February, when the new slate of directors was approved for the annual meeting of stockholders in May, I tried to explain to Dr. Cori and the directors that I had not 'bet against the Company.' I gave a short presentation to the nominating committee stating that I would love nothing more than to continue working for the Company, not primarily for my own sake but in the best interests of chemists and Sigma-Aldrich. Minutes later, the committee presented to the board a previously prepared resolution in which Marvin Klitsner and I were excluded from the slate of directors. Marvin and I cast the only dissenting votes.

Ever since November 20th, I have wondered why Dr. Cori decided that I must stop working for the Company, even though I had agreed to work without compensation. This is at his discretion. Many of you have heard my lecture "The Challenges at Sigma-Aldrich," which outlines the history and aims of the Company, and know how supportive I have been of our management; so Dr. Cori's decision seems absurd, and I believe we will all be the losers. For many decisions there are *stated* reasons and *real* reasons. The stated reason is that I had 'bet against the Company.' Did he have other reasons? Only he knows and he has not told me.

I will miss my visits with many of you and the excitement in your work which you have shared with me. I would be happy to continue to respond on a personal basis to any calls for help and advice you may care to make; my fax number at home is 414 962 8322.

Above all, Isabel and I want to thank you for the many wonderful experiences we have had with so many of you. Our lives have been so much richer because of you, and we hope that chemistry world wide has been better because of our work.

Sincerely yours,

Alfred Bader

Alfred Bader
P.O. Box 93225
Milwaukee, Wisconsin USA 53203

Distributed in April 1992

A letter to chemists, distributed in April 1992.

Marvin and me. We cast the only dissenting votes.

Tom tried to ease me out gracefully by preparing a fulsome, obituary-like appreciation to be included in the company's 1991 annual report, and said in his proposed letter to shareholders:

"A review of Alfred Bader's many achievements during his 41 years with Aldrich Chemical and Sigma-Aldrich follows this letter. Dr. Bader, named Chairman Emeritus in 1991, and Marvin Klitsner will not stand for reelection to the Board of Directors in 1992. We have gained from their many years of dedicated service and are grateful for the important contributions they have made."

At the next Aldrich board meeting in March, Tom watched me carefully when I was handed the draft of this testimonial, yet may not have observed that I was having a hard time not to laugh out loud.

I prepared an open letter to chemists which I submitted as an advertisement to *Chemical & Engineering News*, the magazine going to all members of the American Chemical Society. Professor Ernest Eliel, the President of the ACS, and Michael Heylin, the Editor, called me to explain that they could not accept such a letter as an advertisement, but I was told that a detailed article would appear in the April 6 issue. As a result, Tom removed his praise of me from the annual report.

Many articles followed, in the *St Louis Post Dispatch* (April 16), the *Milwaukee Sentinel* (May 2 and 6), the *Canadian Chemical News* (June), *Chemistry in Britain* (June), and even a brief piece in *Forbes* (June 11), all quite accurately giving the story in varying detail.

I gave my open letter to chemist friends at three symposia Isabel and I attended in April, one honoring Gilbert Stork on his seventieth birthday, one for Herbert Brown's eightieth, and the third for that greatest of organic chemists, R B Woodward, on the seventy-fifth anniversary of his birth. Thereafter, I received many letters from friends all over the world. I never realized how many friends I had. The simplest and pithiest letter came from the able Danish chemist, Niels Clauson-Kaas, who wrote, "... I can, about the new leadership, only cite, what my father often said (mostly to me): *wie kann man nur so dumm sein.*" The most poetic came from Carlos Seoane in Madrid, and I framed it for my office.

When successful men retire and are feted, they may wonder how much of the praise is sincere. Often, much of it is for show, as was Tom's prepared testimonial. But when a man is thrown out, he learns who his real friends are.

Some did more than just write letters. They telephoned Tom, who was forced to spend many hours reiterating that they were not in a position to judge the issue, and that he could not tell them what I had done! Two of Britain's greatest chemists, Professor Ralph Raphael from Cambridge

Carlos Seoane Prado

DOCTOR EN CIENCIAS QUIMICAS
CATEDRATICO DE UNIVERSIDAD
Fax: 34-1-5433879

Avda. de El Ferrol. 2 - 9.° 1
Teléfono
28029 Madrid

Dr. Alfred Bader
2961 N Shepard Avenue
Milwaukee
53211-Wisconsin
U.S.A.
FAX: 07-1-414-962-8322

8.4.92

Dear Alfred:

Not very often in a lifetime does one receive such a deeply engaging letter. A *Letter to Chemists* that a chemist, husband and father feels compelled to read, disturbed, to his family at the dinner table as a teaching of life.
A sad event, very true. But not a sad life.

Not many people can show such a full, fruitful and rich life.
Not many people can start with nothing, less than nothing, at fourteen and build Aldrich.
Not many people can have and deserve thousands of friends around the world, a whole profession indebted to him for his help of decades, to whom send a letter knowing it will be understood.
Not many people has created a new concept in his field and is unique in his approach to something.

Not many people can show excellence in chemistry, business, art and life.
Not many people, deprived from C, can still have A and B as a happy and essential part of an exemplary life. (And let's wait until September to see whether C is there).
Not many people has the privilege of pursuing and enjoying a passion no one on earth can spoil. Not many people can loose so much and keep still more.
Not many people has helped two generations in a family and made such a lasting impression in both of them.
And, certainly, not many people has a gift named Isabel.

A man like that does not have the right to complain. He must be grateful for a life very few people can have. He has the duty to be happy, the duty to Chemistry, to Bible, to Art, to his friends, to his family, and to himself.

For us, chemists of the world, as always and forever, a bit of Alfred's soul will pop out every time we open an Aldrich bottle.

From now on, it is your turn: *Please, bother us.*

Un abrazo muy fuerte.

Carlos

Letter from Professor Carlos Seoane, one of hundreds of letters received from around the world.

University and Professor Steven Ley from Imperial College, met him in London in May and reported on that two-hour meeting in the September issue of *Chemistry in Britain*.

At the annual meeting in May 1992, everything was again cut and

Letters to the editor of Chemistry in Britain.

dried, but although the annual report omitted all mention of Marvin and me, both the St Louis and Milwaukee newspapers reported at length the story of my dismissal.

Why did Tom want me out? Of course there were many differences between us, but when he became CEO I never challenged his authority. At the time of the merger in 1975 Sigma was twice as big as Aldrich and even more profitable; and I tried to persuade rather than dictate policy to both companies. In some areas I succeeded, in others I did not.

Among the objectives not achieved to my satisfaction were the improvement of the Sigma catalog, our policies on pricing, and our method of recruiting top people.

The Sigma and Aldrich catalogs are as different as two chemical catalogs can be. At Aldrich we tried to make the catalog as much a handbook as possible. We have an excellent man, David Griffiths, checking the consistency of nomenclature, so important to customers looking for specific compounds. In 1975 the Sigma catalog had a cluttered cover, and the chemical nomenclature was inconsistent and often wrong. It is better now, but many scientists still ask why the Sigma catalog does not at least give the structures and information that could so easily be transferred from the Aldrich catalog. I have never known a company as imbued by the NIH ("not invented here") syndrome as Sigma.

Our experience in Spain will document my frustration with some of the pricing policies. I had not visited Spain while Hitler's friend, Franco, was in power, but our first visit in 1986 was an eye-opener. Spain is a beautiful, fast-growing country, its chemistry is improving, and we made good friends quickly. During that visit we realized what a handicap it was for Spanish chemists not to have a Sigma-Aldrich España. Air shipments from St Louis came quickly, but truck shipments from Aldrich Germany and seafreight from Milwaukee often took months. Spanish dealers enjoyed large mark-ups, but they saved customers the bother of customs clearance and having to buy checks in marks or dollars. Naturally we urged the establishment of a Sigma-Aldrich España, and the company found a capable, hard-working manager, Carlos Calpe, for an office in Madrid. I believed Spanish chemists would be able to order directly from our new office, save the dealer's mark-up, pay in pesetas and save time and money.

Isabel and I really looked forward to our second visit in November 1990, thinking that Spanish chemists would thank us for making their lives so much easier. We were in for a rude shock. After my first lecture at the Universidad Complutense in Madrid, the first question had nothing to do with the subject of my talk on Josef Loschmidt, but was, "How dare you come to Spain after what you have done to us?" The questioner, Vice Dean Roberto Arche, obviously had the sympathy of the entire audience, and I just hope that he and the hundreds of other Spanish chemists who asked the same question, more or less politely, realized how flabbergasted and chagrined we were.

What had happened was clear. For years Spanish chemists had used the Aldrich Chemie catalog to order products from Germany. Now they had the Spanish catalogs, and could compare the two. The prices in pesetas were over twice those in the German catalog!

On our return home, I was told that someone—I was never able to find out who—had erred by a factor of two when converting German mark prices into pesetas. The mark then stood at about 60 pesetas, but the conversion used was 125! Naturally I urged that we just own up to this mistake and slash Spanish prices across the board. I was told that this was not immediately practical, but that all expensive items, particularly our own books, would be reduced sharply. That was in fact done, but I was also told that in the next catalog, for 1992-93, all other Spanish prices would be brought close to our German ones.

In the autumn of 1991, before the pricing of our European catalogs was completed, I reminded management of this, and I was assured that the price disparity would be corrected. Sadly, it was not. The rate of exchange was then 65 pesetas per mark, but the rate used was 109, a discrepancy of 68%—better than the previous 108%, but still very unsatisfactory. What a way to treat chemists in an entire country. And no wonder the vice dean in Madrid had been so angry. I fear that our slo-gan, *Por favor, moléstenos,* had a very hollow ring to it, and I have been ashamed on this account ever since.

In August 1992 our best Spanish friend, Professor Carlos Seoane of the Universidad Complutense, the secretary general of the Spanish Royal Society of Chemistry, visited Milwaukee and discussed this serious prob-lem with Dr Jai Nagarkatti, who had succeeded David Harvey as presi-dent of Aldrich. Sadly, Carlos came to the conclusion that the original "mistake" of doubling prices may in fact have been deliberate.

My third major disappointment has been the manner of recruiting of people. At Aldrich, I had always tried to promote from within, but when excellent people became available locally I tried to hire them. John Biel, for example, was a world-class medicinal chemist who came to us from the Lakeside Laboratories in Milwaukee in 1962 when we were still a relatively small company. I was really sad when he left to become vice president of Abbott Laboratories in 1968 and happy when he offered to return to Aldrich in 1975. Alas, he died suddenly and unexpectedly of a heart attack, just at the time of the merger; had he lived, his strength would have made a great difference.

I first met Bill Buth at the Kolmar Laboratories in Milwaukee in the fifties. He joined Aldrich in 1960 and for some twelve years installed many of the systems that allowed us to grow. Like myself, he was really interested in art and science, and he was a fine sculptor. He left Aldrich in 1971 to start his own art gallery.

I was so proud of the excellent research chemists we attracted although I was too penny-pinching and lost some of them. Among the very best were Ed Warawa, who left for ICI for personal reasons, and John Campbell who came with a PhD from Queen's. I hoped that in time he would become my successor at Aldrich. At the time of the merger, we decided to promote him to vice president, but his face fell when I told him, and he indicated that he had heard some horror stories about the treatment of chemists at Sigma, and decided to accept an offer from General Electric. He too could have made a great difference.

Almost all the other vice presidents in Milwaukee were chemists who joined us on graduation or shortly thereafter. Bob Gorzek, in charge of operations, came from St Norbert College and the Navy; competent and caring, he must have found the pressure difficult and took early retire-ment in 1994. Chuck Pouchert, who built our analytical department and is the father of our spectral libraries, studied at Carroll College; Hank Koppel, who built our first production department, was at the University of New Mexico and the Midwest Research Institute; Dr Ike Klundt was hired as a research chemist by John Biel, from Wayne State University. We soon realized that Ike's forte was as a link with our cus-tomers. This devoted and loyal man became progressively more discouraged by the way Tom and David treated him, and he left us after almost thirty years, for semi-retirement in Colorado. We never used an executive search firm to hire our executives. Ours is a complicated business, and it seemed to me wiser to let our people grow with us.

Tom has paid many thousands of dollars to headhunters, hiring senior executives from other companies, giving them contracts and then firing them. The worst situation was at Aldrich Chemie in Germany. One man after another was hired as joint managing director, at a salary much higher than that of Dr Alfred Griesinger, who has remained there for thirty years, most of that time as a managing director, while the new and better paid men fell by the wayside.

For some years, Sigma had an excellent president, Dan Fagan, a good peptide chemist, very people-oriented. He had been promoted to this position by Tom, who had ample opportunity to observe him as an executive. In November 1991 he was asked to resign because, I was told, he was not decisive enough. Ron Wolfe, Dan Fagan's successor, asked Tom why he thought that he, Ron, could succeed where Dan had failed. Tom's reply was clear, "If you fail, you will be fired also!" When I called Ron to confirm that this conversation had really taken place, he hesitated for a moment before saying, "Yes, but if you publish this, I will have to deny it." On August 31, 1994, Tom and David announced that "Ron Wolfe, as of today, is no longer employed by Sigma-Aldrich as President of the Research Business Unit."

After the merger, Sigma-Aldrich set up a very generous stock bonus scheme for our executives, paying both in stock and cash. I always supported the plan but urged that a larger share of the bonus should accrue to the presidents and vice presidents of Sigma and Aldrich. In the years after Tom took over, about half of it went to him. Indeed, four Sigma-Aldrich executives received most of it—Tom, David, Peter Gleich and Kirk Richter.

I suggested larger stock bonuses for the officers of the subsidiaries, and in November 1992, after my dismissal, I submitted a motion to be voted on by stockholders at the annual meeting, recommending that at least 30% of the bonuses be given to executives other than the top Sigma-Aldrich officers. The company's St Louis law firm, Bryan, Cave, reacted as if the company's future depended on this vote, and the SEC ruled that Sigma-Aldrich did not have to submit my motion to a vote of stockholders. I hope that my raising the issue nevertheless resulted in greater consideration being given to executives other than the very top management.

My disappointments might suggest that I have regretted the merger. This is not really so, for three reasons. First, there have been many successes. Sigma, Aldrich and Fluka are much better companies now than they were in 1975. Second, my family and I are very much wealthier than we were then, and can give more away. Buying Herstmonceux Castle for Queen's, for instance, would have been unthinkable before the merger. Third, I was able to enjoy some of the best years of my life after I ceased having the responsibility of being the company's CEO.

Isabel and I really enjoyed our many visits to chemists around the world. We got to know them well, and I took pleasure in trying to teach our people everything we had learned during those trips. The first and second visits to a chemistry department were often slightly awkward, but by the third, the academics knew that we wanted, and were able to help, and they reciprocated by offering us many ideas for new products, which we promptly passed on to Milwaukee and St Louis. We spent about six months a year travelling, both in North America and Europe. I still have copies of several of my letters, each containing many pages with individual comments, marked to the attention of the person responsible. There were always new product suggestions for Steve Branca, our new products manager, often accompanied by literature references and sometimes even experimental details. Lists of new products offered by chemical companies went to the purchasing department and the occasional complaint was passed to our analytical department. Marilyn Hassmann, my secretary, promptly sent copies to each employee involved, and on my return and three months later, I went through the letters again. Details of commercial intelligence, about major bulk products, our competitors and our operations abroad, went to Tom and David. Copies of all my letters went to Jai and David, just as copies of all my letters sent from Milwaukee went to David. No one could complain that I did not want to share all I learned. Unfortunately the directors, other than Tom and David, knew little or nothing about my work.

I regard it as a pity that an intelligent, able CEO should have been willing to deprive himself, his team and the company of several more years of effective, valuable help with new products, customer relations, purchasing and other profit and growth producing activities, and that the board supported him.

After my expulsion, my name had to disappear from articles submitted to the *Acta* and from the thousands of labels with the words: "Alfred Bader Chemicals." These were first replaced with ABC labels, but even that was too close for comfort, and the new wording became: "The Sigma-Aldrich Library of Rare Chemicals." It hardly matters that the cover of the new rare chemicals catalog is no longer the familiar man with the open mouth, but a good alchemical painting by David Teniers. It does matter that the catalog is priced at $79! To charge for a sales catalog elicits surprise best expressed by our former cover. Must the "bottom line" govern everything? I had been so proud of the Library's service, the thousands of free computer printouts guiding chemists to the 50,000 products we offered, and the possibilities of good for mankind that came from the Library—from a drug for Alzheimer's disease to a fungicide that doubles rice production. Fortunately what really counts is that the Library carries on and thousands of research samples still come to it every year and will continue to help many scientists.

Since my dismissal, the company's performance has been mixed. In 1992 sales increased by 11%, less than our goal of 15%, with earnings increasing by an impressive 20%. In the light of subsequent events, it might be asked whether Tom tried too hard to prove that he could do better without my help than with it; did he squeeze expenses so hard that while the bottom line was helped in 1992, subsequent earnings suffered from poorer service? In the meantime, the stock price reached a high of 59, then slid back into the 40s, and in July 1994 dropped down to a low of 30 following an unprecedented announcement of flat quarterly earnings. The company had always reported earnings on the morning of a regular board meeting. This particular announcement came late one afternoon, well ahead of the scheduled meeting, and was followed by a teleconference the next morning. Until then, analysts had predicted the customary increases, without contradiction by the company, and were shocked by the turn of events.

Reasons given in the teleconference for the disappointing quarter, and a prediction of flat earnings for the balance of the year, included a discussion of the well-known difficulties in the pharmaceutical industry and the fact that profit margins were lower in the newly acquired businesses and in the company's steel business. Analysts may well have wondered whether these were the real and the only reasons. There was no discussion about whether the flow of good new products had been hurt by the absence of close contact with the academic community, whether the earlier squeeze on expenses had adversely affected service and the back order situation, or whether bulk sales had hurt the bottom line. Analysts and shareholders responded by selling three million shares in a single day at sharply lower prices. Some of them, no doubt, wondered whether the management had not recognized earlier what was happening, or whether it had, but failed to say so—in either case, a circumstance that would not do much for confidence. For whatever reasons, the company's unblemished record of growth had been broken, the confidence of the investment community damaged and possibly the morale of employees lowered. The stock, which had been trading at a price/earnings ratio of about 25, had dropped to a multiple of about 14—at least temporarily. Perhaps the market overreacted initially.

I certainly do not mean to imply that anyone—least of all, myself—is irreplaceable. However, I cannot help but wonder whether any of the directors have asked themselves if it might have been better to have heeded my urging to assign an understudy to me rather than dispense with my services with no replacement prepared.

I am confident however that Sigma-Aldrich has so many good things going for it, including many very able people, that with some needed reinforcement of top management, it will continue to be a leader in its industry.

From a personal point of view, it is gratifying to know that even if my work as a "chemist helping chemists" was not fully appreciated by the directors and CEO of the company that I helped to found and build, it was more fully appreciated by the chemical community as a whole. Among the manifestations of this recognition were honorary doctorates conferred upon me by the Universities of Wisconsin in Milwaukee and Madison, Purdue, Queen's, Sussex and Northwestern. The capstone came from the American Chemical Society, which announced that I would receive the 1995 Charles Lathrop Parsons award, the society's highest honor bestowed for outstanding public service. I had never dreamed that I might one day deserve this award and be in the company of some of the outstanding figures of our times—my academic grandfather, James Conant; Roger Adams, the greatest organic teacher of his day; Glen Seaborg, the Nobel Laureate; Arnold Beckman, the father of Beckman instruments and the Beckman Center; and so many others. Nor had I dreamed that *C & E News* would describe me as a "fascinating mixture of ego, modesty, and almost boundless energy". Me, modest? What next? I was proposed by my friends Leo Ochrymowycz, E J Corey, Gilbert Stork and Leon Mandell. My cup runneth over. But the award is really largely for Aldrich and what it has done to revolutionize chemical research.

APPENDIX 1

January 28, 1991
Via Fax 212-357-9888

Mr. Jim Weinberg
Goldman, Sachs & Co.

Dear Jim:
I really appreciated your call on January 11 and your taking so much time to discuss my dismissal.

What has astounded me since November 20 is how all nine directors could feel that Marvin and I have been betting against the Company by selling options for stock we own. I now understand, of course, the strong views that all the Board members have against option transactions. I hope you took away from our conversation a firm conviction that had I known of these views in advance, I would never have written a call option on 10,000 of the 3.6 million-plus shares I own.

The Board seems to believe I must have known transactions in options were beyond the pale because all public companies disapprove of them. Jim, of the things that matter to me, Sigma-Aldrich has been the most important. Because this has been my focus, I have not, unlike a number of the outside directors, served on the board of any other public company. You told me other public companies counselled their directors to avoid option transactions. Sigma-Aldrich did not. Surely the Board is not saying a director is required to have inborn knowledge that option transactions are akin to insider trading and must be shunned.

And while perhaps I can be criticized for not checking with Tom Cori in advance (even though the Company has not articulated any policy that would even suggest I do so), if I had sought information about options from the publications available in any good library, I would have found that covered call writing is a conservative strategy, and one that has been used on a wide basis for many years by money managers and fiduciaries. A 1979 article in the *American Banker* (the leading journal for that industry) says

> "there is a consensus among conservative investors
> and regulators that covered call option writing *per se*
> is a prudent strategy. The Comptroller of the Currency
> and numerous state insurance commissioners have
> authorized covered call writing as appropriate for
> institutions under their jurisdiction."

The Board can reply that conservative strategy and prudence notwithstanding, an option transaction by a director in the stock of his company is a horse of another color—a "bet against" the horse the director is riding. The financial literature on options does not, however, view writing a covered call as a "bet against the company." Rather, the covered call writer "should be *mildly bullish*, or at least neutral, toward the underlying stock." (My underlining; the quote is from *Options as a Strategic Investment*, published by the New York Institute of Finance.)

I know you have read my December 9, 1991 memo to the Board and I will not take up your time with repetition. But I still do not understand how the Board can say that writing a covered call (which, if the price of the stock declines or does not rise enough so that the buyer of the option can exercise it profitably, leaves the writer with the *same* investment in the underlying stock) is a "bet against the company" while refusing to condemn an outright sale of shares (which divests the seller of all future economic risk for those shares) as a far stronger "bet against the company."

My comparison is not hypothetical. Really, I am not faulting Tom Cori's sale of 10% of his Sigma-Aldrich shares nor am I faulting the contemporaneous sale of equivalent percentages of their stock by other senior executives. I am still "betting with the company" to the extent of 99.7% of my pre-call holdings. These sellers "cashed out" to an extent that after their sales they owned only 90% of their pre-sale positions. Isn't the Board using a double standard in concluding I transgressed by writing an option carrying with it only the possibility of selling a miniscule percentage of my stock when it does not also censure those who engaged in outright sales of far greater percentages of theirs? In fact, I believe that none of us should be censored.

Of course, I don't question the sincerity of the directors, just their understanding of what happened. I talked to each individually, and was shaken most by Andy Newman's reply. You know what a thoughtful person he is— and how much the Edison family has done for St. Louis. And so when Andy told me curtly, "Don't give me all this—all your ex post facto explanations. You bet against the Company, you should be out, and what you do is your call.", I realized the depth of the misunderstanding. The record is clear: I have never sold a single share of Sigma-Aldrich stock, and I promised the gift to Queen's University in April and— most importantly, selling covered options is not a bet against a company— it is an attempt to maximize proceeds of a sale, and Queen's has always sold the stock I gave them.

So Andy is mistaken to talk about ex post facto reasoning, though right about my next call. And unless I am satisfied with the directors' decision on February 18, I will fight as hard as I can to make certain that chemists and others know exactly what happened. They will then be able to decide who is right.

Unfortunately, none of the outside directors really knows what I have done for the Company these last years. Last year I sent you a resume about my work, but did so uneasily because it sounds too much like blowing my own horn. Yet the fact is that many of the suggestions for our best selling new products came in through me and our future growth depends on developing new products. Our Aldrichimica Acta, nurtured by me has become the best chemical house organ in the world; the authors of our best papers in the Acta are the winners of the Bader awards in the U.S., Canada and Britain. I have been involved in many bulk purchases and sales— just last month we finalized on the sale of several tons of a product for which I had encouraged the use and for which I found just the right manufacturer in Czechoslovakia—a supplier unknown to us until my last visit there. That product will earn several hundred thousand dollars for us this year. Nor is this an isolated instance. Luck? Of course, but the harder I work, the luckier I get, and I have been working very hard being the link between our Company and chemists around the world.

Since my forced retirement I have been swamped by phone calls and letters from around the world, even though there has been no official announcement yet. The enclosed sample, from one of Britain's most distinguished professors, says it more clearly than I can.

Resumes often sound like this, but this resume is different, as I have agreed to work without salary. All I want is to continue doing what is best for the Company. You, the outside director with the most experience in our Company will, I hope, take a leadership role in helping the other directors to understand that.

What surprised me was Tom Cori's uncertainty about all this. He called me on Friday morning, December 27, to ask how I felt about the matter, and I explained that I thought the directors had made a bizarre mistake. He, Tom, knows how much I do for the Company. Tom replied thoughtfully that he would mull over all this, and let me know. On Sunday he called me to say that he could not change the decision. It may be that Tom believed that in fact some of the directors felt so strongly that he could not change the decision.

I appreciated talking to you, and if you would like any more information, please call me at my home anytime today or tomorrow or after February 11. On Thursday morning, January 30, we are going on a trip to California universities— supposedly the last for the Company— and we'll return on February 11.

Best personal regards,
Alfred

APPENDIX 2

Letter sent by certified mail to the following directors on April 22, 1992. None replied.

Donald N Brandin	Retired Chairman of the Board and Chief Executive Officer, Boatman's Bancshares, Inc, St Louis, MO
Dr C Tom Cori	
Dr David R Harvey	
Dr David M Kipnis	Chairman and Professor, Department of Medicine, Washington University School of Medicine, St Louis, MO
Andrew E Newman	Chairman of the Board, Edison Brothers Stores, Inc, St Louis, MO
William C O'Neil, Jr	Chairman of the Board, President and Chief Executive Officer, Clin Trials, Inc, Nashville, TN
Jerome W Sandweiss,	Attorney at Law, St Louis, MO
Thomas N Urban, Jr	Chairman of the Board and President, Pioneer Hi-Bred International, Inc, Des Moines, IA
Sidney J Weinberg	Limited Partner, The Goldman Sachs Group, New York, NY

Mr Andrew Newman
St. Louis, Mo.

Dear Andy

Having been excluded from your nomination for director, I will take this method of transmitting to you some of my concerns.

First, I must reiterate my strong conviction that it was contrary to the best interests of the corporation to have eliminated the opportunities for evaluations which, as a director, I would be in a position to provide the Board with respect to acquisition possibilities and other opportunities in the chemical industry, and many other aspects of the business which should relate to policy decisions.

Also, at the risk of appearing to be immodest, utilizing my years of involvement in chemical business, my close relationship with world leaders in chemical research, and my knowledge of the industry which would continue to lead to many profitable bulk transactions, sources of new products and continued contribution to profits through the ABC rare chemical collection, I think that termination of my services to the corporation was contrary to the best interests of the company. Accordingly, Tom Cori's reversal of our prior agreement to continue my services without compensation, and the Board's failure to urge him to continue those services, was short-sighted and detrimental to the bottom line and continued growth of the company. I will not repeat here what I have attempted to point out to all of you over the past months—that my single transaction of selling calls covered by 10,000 of my 3,600,000 shares in an effort to maximize my gift to Queen's University was not a justifiable basis for those decisions—especially absent any stated company policy or prior warning.

From my perspective, those decisions could even now be reversed if, in the best interests of the company, you and Tom were to reconsider at this time. If you do not do so, I do urge that at the very least some senior person or persons be given the specific responsibilities of undertaking the tasks I was performing. One of those is to serve actively as a positive link between Sigma-Aldrich and the scientific community and other sources of new products. I am aware that one of the difficulties in the corporation's doing so—so much the greater is the error in dispensing

174

with my services at this time—is the absence of sufficient depth in the top management. All of you have recognized this situation, but have failed to recognize some of the underlying causes and failed to see to it that something is done about it.

The principal reason given me by Don Brandin last spring, on behalf of the Nominating Committee and the Board, for requesting that I relinquish my position as chairman, was to provide Tom with a better opportunity to put in place within the year a potential successor. Not only has that not occurred, but to my knowledge no report was made to or requested by the Board with respect to what steps, if any, were taken to accomplish this goal. All of you know that Tom has said to you and to David Harvey that he does not regard David as his potential successor as C.E.O. Whether or not he is correct in this, so long as that is his view, it is his clear obligation to locate someone promptly whom he and you find qualified to be a suitable successor.

Aside from the above, I am deeply concerned that a significant factor contributing to the difficulty in strengthening the ranks of management is the style of "management by fear" which is perceived by some of our own personnel, in part, at least, from the peremptory manner in which senior executives, such as the immediate past President of Sigma, are promoted or recruited and then dismissed. Dan Fagan's abilities and characteristics were well known, or should have been, when he was selected for the position of President of Sigma. It is not difficult to appreciate how this can dampen the desire of other Sigma and Aldrich executives (some of whom could be the best source of candidates for higher management positions) to advance too close to the top. Likewise, such actions create anxiety among those already in high management positions; this is not conducive to their best performance. The handling of my own case accentuates this situation. If this can happen to a founder, others might conclude that noone can count on consistency in decisions relating to retention and/or promotion in the management team. I am convinced that more should be done on the positive side to improve that spirit. One such step, to which I have referred in the past, is the recognition of at least some executives of the subsidiaries through more generous participation in the Executive Stock Bonus Plan. In the past, even the presidents of the major operating entities have at times been completely excluded from participation and at times included in relatively nominal amounts. The continued success of the company overall depends to a large extent upon how these executives carry out their responsibilities.

The company has enormous momentum which will carry it forward for some period of time. However, unless you recognize and act constructively on the foregoing matters, continued growth may not occur. I do not know how or whether the Board will attempt to inform itself of, and take corrective measures with respect to these and other important matters to continue the growth and prosperity of the company. However, in my judgment it is the obligation of the Board as well as the management to find appropriate ways of doing so.

Sincerely,
Alfred Bader

14

David and Daniel

Some dates in life are more important than others. August 17 is one
that keeps recurring in my life story. On August 17, 1873 my grandfather, Moritz Bader, married my grandmother, Hermine Freund, in
Prague. On August 17, 1951 the Aldrich Chemical Company was incorporated, and at 10 am on Sunday morning, August 17, 1958, David
Martin Bader was born at Columbia Hospital in Milwaukee. It was a
difficult birth. Danny started in labor after a spaghetti dinner late on
Saturday, but the baby was healthy, and that was what mattered. We had
hoped for him for years, and named him David after David Mayer in
Vienna, and Martin after Martin Wolff in Canada.

David grew into a fair-haired, rather bashful boy with a beautiful
singing voice and good hearing—so unlike his father who cannot carry
a tune. For many years I have derived great pleasure listening to David
sing, a reminder of the Biblical David who soothed away the troubles of
King Saul. I would so love to be able to join in myself, and it fills me
with happiness when he sings beside me in synagogue.

Daniel Joseph Bader was born on January 24, 1961, a snowy Tuesday
afternoon, at Mount Sinai Hospital in Milwaukee, after just a few minutes' labor. Danny chose his names, Daniel after her family name, and
Joseph because she admired the Biblical Joseph's organizing ability in
Egypt. People who know what I think of Joseph as a son and brother in
the Bible have asked me how I could give my own son that name. I tell
them that there are also traits in King David's character which I do not
admire; if you read his last speech you will see what I mean. Yet there
was much good in both David and Joseph.

Daniel was a chubby, noisy baby with a mass of dark hair, and it soon
became clear that the two boys were quite different temperamentally,
although they almost always got along well. Daniel, although younger,
was more venturesome. Many a time when something unusual was
served at table, David would turn to him and ask, "Is it good, Daniel?"
and when Daniel had made up his mind about it, David would follow
his lead. We loved our sons and hoped for a third whom we would have
called Benjamin, the youngest, and of course we would have loved a
daughter. Yet I cannot possibly have been as good a father as I should,
and probably could, have been. I spent a lot of time travelling on business, and when at home, I was so busy at Aldrich that I usually came
home dead tired. Happily, I could always console myself that Danny was

succeeding wonderfully in being a good parent.

The years when the boys were small were also the years of greatest challenge and danger to Aldrich—one false step and the company might have gone under. Danny and I worked very hard for the company, but she managed also to be a caring, loving mother and to look after the house we bought in 1957 for $27,500—a major expense, but preferable to continuing to live in the flat we had rented since our marriage. It was the only house we ever inspected. We were delighted by the wooden panelling in the living and dining room which provided such a great backdrop for paintings, and we loved the neighborhood, within walking distance of Temple Emanuel, where I taught, and the University of Wisconsin and Lake Michigan. We never regretted the purchase, and I hope to die there.

Fortunately by the time the boys were born we were able to afford household help. First came Odessa, a lovable roly-poly black woman, who came mainly as a babysitter. When she left us, we found Abby, an American Indian, who stayed with the family for years, retiring only recently. Odessa saw the boys through their early chicken-pox and measles, bumps and tumbles, and Daniel's strep throats. Abby cleaned and brought order and tidiness to a very busy household, while Danny continued to work half days at Aldrich. We entertained many guests, who often stayed overnight, because I always tried to get to know customers and suppliers personally, and the best way to do that seemed to be to invite them to stay with us. As Daniel quipped in a recent interview, "We were all on the hotel staff."

Finding good schooling for the boys proved a serious problem. I was very conscious of my deficiencies in Jewish education. I had learned little Hebrew until I went to England at 14, and little about the substance of Judaism until I was interned. David Mayer had given me the taste, but Friday evening and Seder discussions are not enough. Teaching at Emanuel had shown me how little the kids there knew. Although there had been a Jewish day school in Milwaukee when I arrived in 1950, it had failed. I worked with Rabbi David Shapiro, Marvin Klitsner and others to start a viable day school, the Hillel Academy, which has managed to survive and still flourishes today. The beginnings were difficult. Funds were short, good teachers hard to find, and financial support from the Jewish community did not come until we proved successful. I was one of the first presidents, and David became one of the first students, Daniel following. Both attended for eight years, learning less than I had hoped, but more than I had done as a boy.

Some of the teachers were inadequate, one was actually physically abusive, and non-orthodox children—including our boys—felt discriminated against. Daniel seemed to feel this more than David, and perhaps that is one reason he now works so hard to improve Jewish education of all kinds in Milwaukee. Adverse experiences do not necessarily have adverse results in later life; they can sometimes have very positive results.

A special problem for David was the discovery that he was dyslexic, which caused him to read painfully slowly. He was eager to do well and, by concentrating on every word in any reading assignment, he forgot the general theme. Reading for enjoyment was slow, but he managed to skim and remember the theme. I cannot have been an easy parent. I was too demanding, perhaps even inviting competition and an inferiority complex, but the boys also learned from me. I remember driving home from synagogue one Saturday morning and seeing two policemen handle a black drunk very roughly, too roughly. I was so proud that David and Daniel, and of course Danny also, were really upset and joined in my protest. "You shall not stand idly by the blood of your neighbor," is the Bible's most important commandment for human relations. It is easy to become a life member of the NAACP, but more difficult to risk being hit by an irate policeman.

We had a rough basement where the boys played in poor weather. They were particularly fond of a train set and a racecar set, which they tinkered with for hours, joined by half a dozen neighborhood boys who met in their "club house". In the winter they could go sliding or tobogganing and ice skating in the ravines and rink in Lake Park, a few minutes from the house. David loved building things, a sturdy tree house in our small garden, for instance, and many go-carts that he ran up and down the street. Both boys belonged to the bowling league at the Hillel Academy and as Daniel says, "every boy won a trophy." David became particularly interested in judo at the Jewish Community Center and the YMCA.

Danny hoped that the boys would develop her love of music. She had a collection of classical records which she played in the evenings, and both boys took private music lessons. David tried his hand at the violin, but found the trumpet more exciting, and played it in the school band throughout his years at Riverside High. Daniel took flute lessons for five years, but was definitely more interested in stage lighting and electronics. A love of music and theater has however remained an important part of both the boys' lives, although now they form part of the audience.

The choice of high school was a difficult decision. There was no Jewish high school in Milwaukee, so we had three options: to send them to the nearest Milwaukee high school, Riverside, almost an inner city school; or to a suburban high school where Milwaukee residents had to pay tuition; or to a private, elitist school. I considered myself a liberal democrat, and looked down on private schools, and even on sending kids to the public schools in the fancy suburbs. I myself had gone to very ordinary schools in Vienna and Hove; should not our children also learn about life in a public high school? I equated Riverside with the

Sperlgymnasium and sent the boys there. What I did not realize was how very rough Riverside was and how very poor its educational standards. In Vienna one could learn a great deal at the gymnasium, and in neither Vienna nor Hove had I been in the slightest danger of being attacked by my fellow students. Within his first few days at Riverside however David was beaten up by some toughs because he was a Jew. The education was not good, and since neither boy did particularly well, they found college difficult; but it was only there that they realized some of their potential. If only they could have gone to the camp school on the Ile aux Noix!

In the summers of 1968 and 1969 we sent the boys to Rehovoth in Israel to spend a few weeks with the cousins of David Mayer, to improve their Hebrew and give them a feel for what Israel was really like. I am sure the Mayers made them very welcome, but their children were older, and perhaps David and particularly Daniel were too young and felt alone. Their love for Israel has continued however and both have been back many times.

Some years they spent a few weeks at a Jewish summer holiday camp nearby, and they made many visits to Danny's parents in Aberdeen, South Dakota. I found that town very dull—there were no academic chemists and no art, and I was always concerned about how things were going at Aldrich and eager to get back to work. But the boys were happy there, particularly David, because Lloyd Daniels loved woodwork and was delighted to have two grandsons he could help with their building projects. There was also a small cottage near a lake where Lloyd's father had built a number of canoes, a new one each year—what a model for David!

Twice we all went to Europe in the summer. I wanted the boys to spend part of their vacation in Neuberg an der Mürz—the fourth generation of Baders to do so—and to meet our best friends, Franz Sobek in Vienna and Ralph Emanuel in London. Of course I combined the family's holiday with visits to suppliers and our European affiliates.

David and Daniel developed very different interests. David liked motors. He spent months taking car motors apart and reassembling them. In a short essay about the boys, written in 1976, Danny wrote of David, "My older son is a car nut. I was rather shaken up one day after returning home from work to find two huge wheels sitting in my living room, looking as if they owned the place. My son's car, a 1968 Ford Torino which he almost never drives for fear of rust, is a black, shiny, rustless automobile with inside carpeting, an 8-track player and bucket seats. All his necessary errands are done with his mother's beat-up station wagon." That same summer, Lieve van Deun, the elder daughter of our good Belgian friends, stayed with us. Lieve was a pretty and intelligent girl. When she left, her last words, looking at David, were, "If only I was a motor."

Describing Daniel, Danny wrote, "My younger son is a very likeable, outgoing young man. He has a great interest in people, working with them, talking with them or just being with them. He is a very enterprising young fellow, what my husband calls a wheeler-dealer. In his first week of high school, he got a job in the school office and became friendly with all the school administrators and teachers. He loves work. Since he was fifteen, he has been working with the audio-visual department of the Milwaukee Board of Jewish Education and is now an apprentice with the stage crew of the Milwaukee Repertory Theater."

From ages 15 to 18, the boys spent part of their school holidays working at Aldrich—David in prepack and Daniel in shipping. Eventually I wanted David to have a chance of working in Europe, so I sent him to spend the summers of 1974 and 1978 with our German company. During the second summer he worked quite closely with David Harvey, who was to succeed me at Aldrich and who was then in charge of our German company. Both Davids have told me that they enjoyed working together. David Bader thought he had learned to speak German, and so he had, but with a strong Swabian accent. Daniel began working in Aldrich's computer department when he finished high school. He really enjoyed it and did so well that Dick Koehler, his supervisor, wanted to give him a raise, which I quashed because I was afraid he might be getting special treatment. When I went to Europe on my next trip, Dick put through for the raise and Bernie Edelstein approved it. I was surprised when I learned about it, but Daniel kept the raise. After two years, he left to go to college, and I was somewhat relieved because I knew that Tom Cori, Sigma's successor to Dan Broida, did not want Dan's children at Sigma and would not want mine at Aldrich.

After high school in 1976, David went to Queen's University, but became terribly discouraged when he realized how much better prepared the Canadian youngsters were, and he left after one term. Life was easier at the University of Wisconsin in Madison where he graduated with a degree in structural engineering in 1981. He then worked for six months with a dyestuff manufacturer in Philadelphia. He liked the city but not the work, so he returned to Milwaukee, bought a house near us which he and a good friend refurbished, and studied architecture, receiving his MSc in 1986. Structural engineering and architecture were clearly the right combination for David. Daniel also had problems of a different nature, rough friends, but he stuck with his studies and got a degree in business and computer technology from the Rochester Institute of Technology in 1987. When I opened my art gallery in 1992, Daniel installed all the equipment and left a note: "This office is now electronically equipped! The fax machine faxes, the copier copies and the computer computes. Now all we need are a few people to operate the technology. The techno-whiz-kid." What a blessing for a computer-illiterate father, who knows nothing about motors either, to have two such sons!

David and Daniel were truly shaken by our divorce and at first were quite unbelieving. They had always been close to Danny, had no inkling of what was happening between 1975 and 1980, and even thought we were joking. Many young men would simply have turned away from Isabel; not David and Daniel. Today there is a great rapport between them. Isabel and her mother flew from London to Chicago early in 1982, on one of the coldest January days ever, and I remember how happy I was when Daniel offered to drive to O'Hare with me to pick them up. We packed blankets and liquor in the car, just in case we were stranded in -26°F weather. Although the flight was many hours late we got home safely. Since then, David and Daniel have come to know Isabel better and better, and we are one family.

The divorce was hardest on Danny, emotionally, although not financially. When we married in 1952, I wanted to share everything with Danny and made certain that she owned half the shares in Aldrich. After the boys were born we gave stock in Aldrich to trusts set up for them by Marvin. We sold Aldrich stock only twice, a few thousand shares through the Marshall Company in 1966 and 100,000 shares through R W Baird in 1967. That left us with over 460,000 shares between the trusts, Danny and me—72% of Aldrich. Danny and I had no financial arguments whatever during our divorce; I was just happy that she and the trusts had so much.

David and Daniel dated some non-Jewish girls. David was quite serious about an intelligent, attractive French Canadian architect. Naturally we discussed the matter, and what could I say? Certainly not, "You must not marry a non-Jewess." All I could do was to explain my conviction. As Martin Buber wrote so eloquently in that little book *Drei Reden über das Judentum,* which I have read on many Days of Atonement, what sets Jews apart is not that we are better or more clever, but that many of us— sadly not all—are more angered when we see evil. As I used to tell my students at Sunday School, "Most of the time when you think something is none of your business, you are mistaken." "Justice you shall seek" is the corollary of "You shall not stand idly by the blood of your neighbor." This is why so many of the world's great teachers of morality and social reformers have been Jews. But this is certainly not a black and white matter. There are of course a great many non-Jews who are appalled by evil. They may be sincere and idealistic Christians who, when they learn about Judaism, are attracted to it. Isabel and Danny became totally convinced, sincere Jewesses.

When Danny returned from a vacation in Mexico in 1988, she discovered why she had been feeling so unwell for months. She had ovarian cancer. Neither an operation nor chemotherapy really helped, and the months before her death in November 1989 were sheer agony. The last time I saw her out of the hospital, she was listening to David singing the Book of Jonah on the afternoon of Yom Kippur, and on flying back from England I was shaken to see her often just semi-conscious during her last days.

Danny's will, drawn up by Marvin as were Isabel's and mine, left almost everything to the Helen Bader Foundation, largely to help causes of special interest to her. In the years after our divorce, Danny worked at the Milwaukee Jewish Home, mainly to help Alzheimer's patients, and this is one major area supported by the foundation. Danny had always given generously to help the disadvantaged, the homeless and the abused. She supported the Legal Aid Society, which provides free legal counsel to the poor, and she was deeply interested in education, particularly Jewish education in Milwaukee and Israel.

The five directors of the foundation are David and Daniel, Marvin, Richard de Vey, the husband of Danny's only sister Marjorie, and Jere McGaffey, who became the attorney for all of us when Marvin moved to Israel. At first, like me, the foundation owned a large block of Sigma-Aldrich stock, but of course it sold part in a rising market in order to diversify. Daniel then had a brilliant idea: why not become the director of the Helen Bader Foundation full time, of course without pay? He had not enjoyed his first job after graduation with a small radio station in upstate New York which he may have taken mainly to be close to friends in Rochester, but when he moved to Madison in 1988 to be close to Danny, he was well appreciated by a local computer software company. It cannot have been an easy decision for him, but it was a great one for us all. As director of the foundation, Daniel assembled an excellent staff of specialists in each of the four areas of concentration, and the foundation has given over $7,000,000 a year to help people, just as Danny wanted. In 1994 it placed one of its staff members in Jerusalem and completed its staff diversification by adding the former president of the Milwaukee Public School Board, a woman intimately familiar with inner-city problems.

David's professional progress has been very different from Daniel's. After graduating, he joined a large firm of architects in Philadelphia in 1986, where he stayed for three years.

The eighteen months of Danny's illness were very hard on both David and Daniel. David made frequent visits to Milwaukee to see his mother, and the constant travelling and long hours of work affected him seriously. After her death, he decided he needed time away from work and enrolled in courses at the Pennsylvania Academy of Art. He had often said how much he would like to study drawing, and he enjoyed and benefitted greatly from the months he spent there. He also had the great good fortune to meet a lovely girl, Michelle Henkin, an artist who has captivated us all. Michelle is the daughter of a very interesting man, an engineer, MD and inventor of medical devices. When Isabel and I walked away from Faith and Mel Henkin's home in California after our first meeting with them, we said, "They seem too good to be true," but their intelligence and goodness are real.

In 1992 Michelle and David were married in Pennsylvania by Rabbi Peter Mehler who had helped Danny so greatly during her last illness in Milwaukee. David now has his own architectural office in a small town, Washington Crossing, providing computer-imaging services and animation for architects and their customers. He is working immensely hard to make his business grow, but he also loves dealing in old master paintings—I wonder where he learned that?—and Michelle is no less keen. Time and again we have compared notes about upcoming auctions and discovered that we were interested in just one painting—the same painting. "David, you wouldn't bid against your father, would you?" I was so proud when I heard that they had sold their first three old master paintings, working with Otto Naumann. One of these, sold to the Metropolitan Museum, was by a Rembrandt student. But we were even prouder when their daughter Helena was born in October 1994—our first grandchild.

Daniel met a delightful, caring girl, Linda Callif. The announcement of their engagement was delayed because Linda wanted to find a position as a social worker in Milwaukee without being known as Daniel Bader's fiancée. For the last nine years she has worked at a Madison shelter for the homeless, a demanding job if there ever was one. Her parents used to come to Rabbi Shapiro's synagogue, and we have really enjoyed getting to know many of their family. Linda and Daniel arranged their wedding date for the end of October so that Michelle, David and the new baby would be able to join them. Isabel and I have already been asked in Milwaukee, "Are you perchance related to Linda and Daniel Bader?" and near Philadelphia, "Are you related to Michelle and David Bader?"

15

A Tribute to Universities

At Aldrich, as I have explained, our main interest was in organic chemistry. Because 90% of the world's best organic chemical research is done in 10% of the universities, we tried to visit those universities that were known for their research. We got to know hundreds of academics all over North America, as well as in Europe from Edinburgh and Glasgow in the north to Florence in the south. An autobiography cannot become a Baedeker to the chemistry departments of the Western world, but I feel impelled to mention a few of the friends we made.

Until fairly recently, the best organic work in the US came from Columbia University, despite its outmoded laboratories and poor location in New York City. This was largely due to the genius and warmth of one man, Gilbert Stork, who built up a team of great chemists. He was on the junior faculty at Harvard while I was a student there and helped me far more than my professor. At Columbia, as in every chemistry department, we were allowed to visit the students in their laboratories, and Isabel and I remember meeting many of Gilbert's students on the sixth floor of Chandler, then two or three years later as postdocs in Cambridge or at the ETH, and perhaps a year or two after that in their first academic positions. These chemists did not need convincing that we really wanted to help.

Gilbert guided me in a very special way. For many years he gave us a list of excellent chemists who had just started their academic careers, to whom we personally offered a few thousand dollars to enable them to help their students. Our funds could not compare with the many thousands granted by the NIH and the NSF, but they were totally unrestricted, and required no accounting. It was just our simple way of thanking chemists in general, so many of whom had helped us.

I believe that Harvard is again one of the best schools in the country. It has always had some of the ablest chemists, but they often had their own fiefdoms and did not work together. Fieser was very jealous of Woodward; Paul Bartlett, though always friendly, held his own group almost isolated on the third floor of Converse; and it would have been unthinkable for a Woodward student to discuss his problem with Fieser or Bartlett.

I have long thought it was a mistake that after the appointment of R B Woodward, no member of Harvard's junior faculty was given tenure.

Gilbert was passed over, and Harvard's loss was Columbia's gain. Surely some excellent young chemists must have refused positions at Harvard because there was no hope of tenure. On one of my visits I bet George Whitesides that they would still not have given tenure to a junior faculty member by the end of 1994. Now I sense a spirit of real collaboration between the senior faculty—E J Corey, David Evans, Yoshito Kishi, Stuart Schreiber and George Whitesides—and I was really happy to lose my bet when Gregory Verdine was given tenure.

My family and I were surprised and delighted when the Harvard Chemistry Department invited all of us to an "Alfred Bader Day" and symposium in May 1992. Professor Hisashi Yamamoto of Nagoya University and Dr Chi-Huey Wong of the Scripps Research Institute spoke about their work; and I had an opportunity to talk about Josef Loschmidt's chemistry. The lectures were held in the old Mallinckrodt basement lecture hall where I had learned so much from Paul Bartlett's lectures in Organic Chemistry 5. What an experience to spend such a day with the Harvard faculty! Gilbert Stork came to Cambridge specially, and I had the opportunity to hug Warren Stockwood, who had planted the idea of Aldrich in my mind in 1949. I often look at the photograph taken that day with E J Corey and Dudley Herschbach and I feel happy all over.

Yale had a rather sleepy chemistry department until Harry Wasserman went there from Harvard around 1950, and it improved steadily by choosing great teachers—Sam Danishefsky and Stuart Schreiber among them. Stuart has now gone to Harvard and Sam to a joint appointment at the Sloane Kettering Institute and Columbia, and Yale's future depends, as always, on people.

We always enjoyed our visits to Cal Tech and Stanford, for very different reasons. Jack Roberts was a father figure to chemists of my generation. To me, physical organic chemistry seemed the source of all wisdom and Paul Bartlett, Saul Winstein and Jack Roberts its great teachers. Federal funding for chemical research now concentrates mainly on medicinal applications, but this has not changed my admiration for Jack, and he and Peter Dervan always welcomed us enthusiastically.

We know many of the chemists at Stanford, where, unlike Berkeley, parking was so easy! Stanford was a collection of fiefdoms—very different from Harvard, but fiefdoms nonetheless. Carl Djerassi and Gene van Tamelen taught there. I have known Carl longer than any other chemist. He lived just a few blocks from my home in Vienna, and we went to the same two schools, Carl a year ahead of me, until July 1938. He was the only boy I knew who had a table tennis table, and all of us looked up to him as the ringleader of much mischief in the Sperlgymnasium. "*Karli: Du wirst an einem Galgen enden*" ("You'll end up on the gallows"), I once heard a teacher exclaim—how wrong he was! Years later, Carl invited me to his home, and I was surprised to meet his well-behaved children—could these really be Karli's offspring? Carl and I have much in common, our Viennese Jewish background, our involvement in companies, and our serious interest in art, and yet we do not know each other really well. It is a pity: friendship cannot be turned on like tap water, and we have never had an opportunity to spend much time together. We have been too busy.

Gene van Tamelen was a Stork student when I was at Harvard, and he and Leon Mandell were my two best friends. Gene invited me to spend Christmas 1948 with him and his fiancée, Mary Houtman, in their hometown, Holland, Michigan. That was a great experience. Mary came from a large family, and I had never seen people live and work together so lovingly and well. Gene accepted a position at the University of Wisconsin in Madison on graduation, and I am sorry to say I was too busy at PPG and Aldrich to visit them there very often. Like other brilliant chemists in Madison, Gene was offered a professorship at Stanford, and at first did truly excellent work, until he realized what financial potential there was in Californian real estate, after which his work in chemistry declined.

The man I came to know and appreciate most at Stanford was the self-effacing Harry Mosher, a great chemist, loved by his students. I once asked his permission to call a reagent he had developed Mosher's Reagent. This has become very important for the determination of optical purity of alcohols and amines. Most chemists would love to have such a reagent named after them, but Harry demurred, saying, "This was developed with several of my students and to name all of us would result in too clumsy a name." We listened, but luckily others did not, and despite his reluctance, the reagent is now universally called after him.

As a student at Harvard, I never went to the chemistry department at the neighboring MIT, although I knew of the good work being done there. Once I started travelling for Aldrich, I visited both universities on each trip to Boston, and Barry Sharpless soon became a good friend. Barry moved briefly to Stanford, and while there continued his work on one of the great discoveries of the century—metal-catalyzed asymmetric epoxidation. In 1979 Aldrich was very pleased to publish his first review paper on this work in the *Aldrichimica Acta*; and I was delighted when Barry told me later that this paper had over 1000 citations, more than he had received for any other paper.

I have sometimes thought that Barry and his wife, Jan, wondered whether they might be happier running their own chemical company. Barry's grandfather had started the Sharpless Chemical Company, so the attraction would be understandable, but I do not think they would have welcomed the business details. Barry's boyish enthusiasm for research is truly infectious, and he seems really happy now at the Scripps Clinic in

HETEROCYCLICS

The Aldrich Chemical Company announces that it has been appointed U.S. salesagent by the Fluka Chemical Company of St. Gallen, Switzerland, for the following heterocyclics:

(handwritten) 1,2-(2-pyridyl)-1,2-ethanediol

	10 g.	100 g.	1 kg.
Bis-(2-pyridyl)-glycol	$ 5.00	$ 45.00	$
Bis-(4-pyridyl)-glycol	6.00		
2-Cyano-6-methylpyridine	5.00	35.00	
2-Cyanopyridine	5.00	30.00	
3-Cyanopyridine	7.00	60.00	
4-Cyanopyridine	5.00	35.00	
2,6-Dicyanopyridine	5.00	35.00	
6,6'-Dimethyl-alpha-pyridil	4.00	22.00	
4,6-Dimethylpyridine-2-aldehyde	5.00		
6,6'-Dimethyl-2-pyridoin	3.00	20.00	
6,6'-Dimethyl-alpha-pyridyl glycol	6.00	50.00	
2,6-Dipicolinic acid			
2,6-Dipicolinic acid dithioamide	5.00	35.00	
Isonicotinic acid thioamide	5.00	35.00	
6-Methyl-2-picolinic acid	3.00	20.00	
6-Methyl-2-picolinic acid thioamide	5.00	35.00	
6-Methylpyridine-2-aldehyde	5.00	17.00	150.00
4-Methylpyridine-2,6-dialdehyde	6.00		
Picolinic acid		13.00	120.00
Picolinic acid-N-oxide	5.00	40.00	
Picolinic acid thioamide	4.00	25.00	
alpha-Pyridil		11.00	90.00
Pyridine-2-aldehyde		11.00	100.00
Pyridine-3-aldehyde	4.00	30.00	
Pyridine-4-aldehyde	5.00	17.00	150.00
Pyridine-4-aldehyde hydrate	3.50	12.50	110.00
Pyridine-2-carbinol-6-carboxylic acid	6.00	50.00	
Pyridine-2,6-dialdehyde	4.00	25.00	200 00
Pyridine-2,6-dicarbinol	6.00	50.00	
2-Pyridoin		10.00	85.00
Pyridyl-2-carbinol	3.00	20.00	
Pyridyl-3-carbinol	6.00	50.00	
Pyridyl-4-carbinol	4.00	25.00	
2-Pyridylhydroxymethylsulfonic acid		7.00	65.00
3-Pyridylhydroxymethylsulfonic acid	3.00	20.00	
4-Pyridylhydroxymethylsulfonic acid		6.50	
Quinoline-2-aldehyde	5.50		
Quinoline-4-aldehyde hydrate	5.00		

All prices are net, f.o.b. Milwaukee, three to six week delivery.

Aldrich CHEMICAL COMPANY, INC.
161 W. WISCONSIN AVENUE
MILWAUKEE 3, WISCONSIN

(handwritten) 6-Hydroxymethyl-2-pyridinecarboxylic acid.

PLEASE TURN OVER

Charles Hurd's first corrections, 1953.

San Diego. He assigned some of his patents to Stanford, others to MIT. In the past, neither the professors nor the universities benefitted financially from great inventions, but gradually this is changing.

One of the first academics ever to help Aldrich was Charles Hurd at Northwestern. He is a stickler for correct chemical nomenclature and he went through the first Aldrich catalogs, carefully noting our mistakes. That was truly a great help. As our catalog became a handbook, the correct nomenclature became a model for many chemists. Charles' help, together with the hard work of our specialist, David Griffiths, had a great impact. I still read all issues of *C & E News*, the weekly publication of the ACS, and cringe when I see mistakes in advertisements by chemical companies for new products. If only Charles could help them also! I was very pleased when I learned that he had purchased 400 shares of Aldrich stock in our first public offering in 1965, stock which he has kept. Charles is well over 90, but still draws attention to any glaring mistakes he spots in our advertisements.

Not every chemistry department we visited was chosen because of its excellence. The University of South Florida in Tampa has a good department, but it is not one of the greatest in the country. At first we went there for the sheer joy of seeing my old friend, Leon Mandell, with whom I could reminisce about our late evening hours at Albiani's on Harvard Square in the late forties, when we discussed chemistry with Gene van Tamelen. During one of our visits to Tampa, we met George Newkome and heard about his exciting chemistry with directed polymers, which Aldrich advertised widely.

The chemistry departments closest to Aldrich in Wisconsin, at UW Milwaukee and Madison, have always helped us, and we have many good friends at both. UW Eau Claire is a special case because of one man, Leo Ochrymowycz. There is no graduate school at Eau Claire, but Leo is an outstanding teacher, and many of his good students went on to Aldrich.

We got to know the chemists at the University of Pennsylvania well, particularly after my son David moved to Philadelphia, and we have to thank Amos Smith for sending Aldrich Stephen Branca, one of its ablest chemists.

Our relationship with Purdue has been very special. Many chemists there have helped us, including Ei-ichi Negishi, Nathan Kornblum, Phil Fuchs, John Frost, Derek Davenport, Jim Brewster, Robert Benkeser, but the overpowering figure there is Herbert C Brown, the father of hydroboration and Aldrich-Boranes.

I first met Bob Benkeser in the early sixties when he was quite depressed because one of his students had fraudulently reported a great discovery, the first aromatic silicon compound. The paper had to be withdrawn, and the student's PhD rescinded. Benkeser, a most outgoing man and a Gilman graduate, withdrew into his shell. Gradually he recovered and was his old self when he told me in the eighties about the fate of a paper he had submitted for publication. It concerned his facile reduction of aromatics with calcium at room temperature, which the referee had indicated should not be published because the results simply

paralleled those of the Birch reduction. In fact the Birch reduction is satisfactory for gram quantities, or quantities so large as to justify building
a safe plant to handle sodium and liquid ammonia. For medium-scale
reductions in the kilo range, Birch reductions are difficult, whereas the
Benkeser reduction is much easier. It would be amusing to compile a collection of the astounding reasons given for the rejection of papers. We
made many of the Benkeser reduction products at Aldrich and advertised them widely.

When it came time to dedicate an *Acta* to Herbert Brown, we thought
we would invite contributions from Jim Brewster and Derek Davenport.
Derek's interest in the history of chemistry led him to chronicle the hilarious rejection of Herb's seminal paper on hydroboration and some of his
arguments with his peers. Jim, shy and modest but a brilliant chemist,
had a wonderful idea for his essay. I never imagined that one could use
such esoteric quotations from the apocryphal book Ecclesiasticus to
highlight the story of Herb's accomplishments. These two articles combined with a paper on the utility of chiral organoboranes, Brown's chemistry, made for a truly memorable issue for Herb's seventy-fifth birthday,
and we chose an *Alchemist* by Thomas Wyck for the cover which was
printed in shades of brown.

Of course, Canadian universities have long been close to our hearts,
and not just Queen's and the University of Toronto, which is Isabel's
alma mater. Almost every year we spend at least a week travelling from
Montreal to Ottawa, Kingston and Toronto, visiting dozens of good
chemists in the universities and at the National Research Council in
Ottawa. From time to time, we have also visited the Western universities, and once had a delightful speaking tour to all the universities in the
Maritimes.

On our summer trips to Europe, we travelled with chemists from our
subsidiaries to visit some of our most important suppliers and also many
of the universities. Of the European universities, the ETH in Zurich, the
University of Basel, and the Technical University in Vienna stand out in
our minds. The chemistry department of the ETH is one of the very best
in the world, and over the years we developed a delightful schedule for
our day there. The cheerful welcome we invariably received from Silvia
Sigrist, Professor Dieter Seebach's secretary, always set the tone for our
entire day there. We could depend on Albert Beck, Seebach's right-hand
man, to give us a true appraisal of our service and to discuss problems
he had with shipments from Aldrich Chemie in Germany. I was delighted to see Professor Seebach's brilliant paper on peptide chemistry in a
recent *Acta*. I had long hoped we could present one of his papers there.
Professor Vladimir Prelog, the Nobel Laureate, usually invited us to
lunch and was never without some memorable, and usually humorous,
stories about chemists. When I first met Professor Albert Eschenmoser,

one of the ETH's outstanding researchers, he was on the board of directors of Fluka, and so considered us competitors. At one time, he complained strongly about our acquiring Bob Woodward's collection of research samples, but as he got to know more about what Aldrich was trying to do, and also about how helpful the Library can be to research chemists around the world, his attitude softened.

In Basel, I used to visit Professor Kuno Meyer, also known as Krötenmeyer because his work in the School of Pharmacy involved the isolation of steroids from Chinese toads. We always discussed the chemistry of these interesting lactones, and I ordered them for Sigma and Aldrich. He passed away shortly after his retirement, but our visits to the city continued because we had met the most distinguished organic chemist in Basel. Professor Tadeus Reichstein, born in 1897, is one of the oldest chemists in the world. He arrived in Zurich from Poland as a youngster of 9, studied chemistry at the ETH, where he began his academic career, and then settled at the University of Basel. His first well-known work was his synthesis of Vitamin C in 1933, a synthesis still used today. This was followed by his best known work, on corticosteroids, where he systematically isolated and determined the constitution of the constituents of the adrenal cortex. As Professor Eschenmoser detailed in the issue of the *Helvetica Chimica Acta* in 1987, dedicated on the occasion of Reichstein's ninetieth birthday, he has mastered three fields of natural product chemistry—isolation, structure determination and synthesis—as hardly any other chemist has done. Until very recently, he continued with his work on the isolation and structure determination of compounds from ferns.

In recent years we have enjoyed spending an evening with him at his home, surrounded by a garden full of ferns. He allowed us to acquire his magnificent collection of research samples, including many steroids and many plant extracts for our Library of Rare Chemicals. We had an interesting discussion at the time. As was our custom, I offered to pay for the collection, but he told me that in his eighties he had absolutely no need for money, and his children were also well off. We settled the matter happily when I suggested that Aldrich send a substantial check to each of two charitable organizations. One was Mazon, a Jewish organization that feeds the hungry; the other was Amnesty International.

I enjoyed going through Reichstein's collection of research samples which spanned some sixty years of work. It was like having chemical history unfold in my hands. During our next visit I asked him whether there was not some further way that we could thank him, and he told us about his inaugural lecture at the ETH in February 1931, which had never been published. It was a most interesting lecture, in German, on the true meaning of alchemy. Marisa Fulton Hart, a good friend in Bexhill who is multilingual, helped us with the translation, which Aldrich then offered in both English and German versions to anyone interested.

There is a convenient night train from Basel to Vienna which I took every year, but I was not a regular visitor to the universities there until the 1980s when my good friend, Paul Löw-Beer, introduced me to a remarkable young chemist, Dr Christian R Noe. Christian was then Privatdozent, or assistant professor, at the Technical University, the school from which both Josef Loschmidt and my grandfather had graduated. Christian is one of the most enthusiastic, able and hard-working chemists I have ever met. If he has one flaw, it is that he scatters his great energies in too many directions. Besides doing exciting research at the university, he has been a consultant to industry and also helped start a chemical company in Hungary. Over the years we have spent a great many hours together, discussing everything from chemistry to paintings and postage stamps

When Bill Wiswesser brought his work on Loschmidt to my attention, I shared it with Christian. After Bill's death, Christian and I worked together diligently to document Loschmidt's major contributions in chemistry. Recently, we have been joined in our efforts by my old friend, Dr Robert Rosner, who for many years was sales manager of Loba and who on retirement went back to university to study the history of Austrian chemistry of the 19th century.

When I first met Christian, he was working in a large laboratory where, despite sharing one desk with some of his assistants, he managed to turn out great research. I was really disappointed that he was not offered a professorship in Vienna, but he accepted the professorship and directorship of the Pharmaceutical Institute of the University of Frankfurt.

Alfred Griesinger and Gerd Backes, our ablest chemists at Aldrich Chemie, had such a good rapport with German universities that it was less important for me to visit Germany. Nevertheless, our visits to most of the major universities in both parts of Germany were really fruitful, and two of the best collections of research samples in our Library of Rare Chemicals came from Professors Dimroth, father and son, in Marburg and Professor Siegfried Hünig in Würzburg, whom we have come to know and appreciate. In Würzburg, two of my major interests, chemistry and the Bible, converged. I love talking to fellow travellers, and on one trip from Vienna to Würzburg got to know Professor Klaus Wittstadt, who teaches church history there. We have spent many happy hours with him and his family both at their home and in ours.

Because of the smaller size of the country, it is so much easier to visit the best universities in Britain than in the US. Cambridge and Oxford are just an hour by train from London, the great universities in the Midlands are easily visited by car, and the Scottish universities are also close to each other.

Cambridge, Oxford and Imperial College probably have the best chemistry departments in England, and we were always welcomed there. Ralph Raphael is such a father figure and has such wonderful stories to tell, that he is great fun to be with. Our friendship with him and Prudence has made Cambridge special for us. Our two-day visits always include a pub lunch with Roger Sansom, the chemistry departments's stockroom manager, invariably glad to see us and brimming with suggestions, and Chris Sporikou who runs a small production laboratory to scale up preps for academics from the gram to the 100 g scale. Talks with the academics always produced many fine ideas. Dudley Williams wrote a splendid article about Ralph for the *Acta* which we dedicated to him on his sixty-fifth birthday. Andy Holmes, the exuberant Australian, helped us greatly with acetylenes. Most exhilarating however was the chance to spend hours talking to students, among the best in the world, and to round off the day with a fine Chinese dinner with Ralph and Prudence.

Although Professor Alan Battersby was always happy to tell us about his work with alkaloids and porphyrins, we did not get to know him at all well until we travelled with him and his wife from Urbana to Ames for his Gilman lecture. After an eight-hour drive, the four of us were ready for a good meal, but unfortunately the Chinese restaurant we found could not compare with the one we go to in Cambridge. Just recently Aldrich was able to acquire Alan's exciting collection of alkaloids for our Library.

Down in a small, cluttered basement laboratory, Chris Sporikou and two assistants, make all sorts of interesting new products. We arranged with Ralph for Chris to give us the details of his preparations; in return we would pay Chris for the write-ups and pay the chemistry department a royalty based on our sales of the products. Imagine my delight when I learned that in one year we sold over $100,000 worth of just one substituted nitropyridine for which Chris had given us the procedure!

Personal relationships are very important. Unfortunately, we never really got to know Jack Baldwin, the professor at Oxford, but other academics there, Stephen Davies and George Fleet, for instance, always made us welcome. We were happy that Stephen Davies was the first chemist to win the Bader award that we had recently established through the Royal Society of Chemistry.

The next award winners, Dudley Williams at Cambridge, Willie Motherwell at Imperial College, Roger Alder at Bristol and Andy Holmes also at Cambridge, were among the very best chemists we knew in Britain. I remember asking Ralph Raphael many years ago what he could tell me about Willie, and his reply said it all, "Willie is wonderful. He has only one fault, he doesn't know how good he is." He shared the large laboratories on the top floor of the old chemistry building of

SIGMA-ALDRICH EXECUTIVES

With Dan Broida, Milwaukee, 1976.

With Tom Cori, David Harvey, Peter Gleich and Kirk Richter, St Louis, 1984.

With Tom Cori, St Louis, 1985.

DAVID AND DANIEL

At an art exhibition in Kalamazoo, 1968.

David.

Daniel.

R B Woodward and Albert Eschenmoser.

Vladimir Prelog.

Tadeus Reichstein.

Albert Eschenmoser and Ernst Vogel.

FRIENDS IN VIENNA

Franz Sobek, Vienna, 1970.

Ala and Paul Löw-Beer, Vienna, 1988.

With Robert Rosner at our annual dinner.

Auf Wiedersehen. The Löw-Beers, Noes and Dr Peter Schuster, 1991.

Bert van Deun.

McGill, 1993. Jack Edward, Alan Shaver and Masad Damha.

Cambridge University, 1985. Chris Sporikou, Roger Sansom and Ralph Raphael.

Imperial College, 1991. Robyn Motherwell, Steven Ley, Willie Motherwell and John Emsley.

Winnipeg, May 1994. Edward Piers.

Spain, August 1994. With Carlos and Margarita Seoane.

AMERICAN CHEMIST FRIENDS

Collecting chemicals with Gilbert Stork.

With Tom Wickersham, Gilbert Stork and Ike Klundt in the Aldrich pilot plant.

Robert B Woodward, 1977.

Leo, Judy Kay and Tara Ochrymowycz.

Barry Sharpless.

With Lloyd Fletcher.

HERB BROWN'S EIGHTIETH
BIRTHDAY
Purdue exhibition, 1992: 'From
Private Collection to Corporate
Identity.'

Below With Sarah and Herb
Brown.

A happy day, October 1990. E J
wins Nobel Prize.

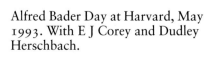

Alfred Bader Day at Harvard, May
1993. With E J Corey and Dudley
Herschbach.

Archibald S. Couper.

Josef Loschmidt.

William J Wiswesser.

Christian R Noe.

Imperial College with Steven Ley and his students—as crowded and unsafe a workplace as I have seen in any university—and yet there was such enthusiasm among the students and such great chemistry! I would make myself at home in the tearoom adjoining the laboratories and discuss chemistry for hours. Steven, then the chairman of the department, is one of the most helpful, enthusiastic and down-to-earth chemists I know, and one of the best. Now that he has accepted the chair at Cambridge and Willie is at University College, Imperial College will not be the same to me, although I will be assured of a great welcome by John Emsley, who excels in writing about chemistry and edits the college's chemical monthly.

The other London colleges also have good chemistry departments. University College has a great tradition, and I think that Willie's acceptance of the chair will rejuvenate the department. It will not be easy to follow in the footsteps of Sir Christopher Ingold, but I know that Willie will try.

One of the English universities I know best is the University of Sussex in Falmer, which can be reached easily by train from Bexhill. The department is distinguished by the friendliness of the academics and the impossibility of finding your way around the building. The architect who designed it must have been challenged to plan a building with the most difficult geography. Despite many visits and their bestowing on me an honorary Doctorate, I still despair of making my own way from one office to the next. Dr David Walton is usually the first academic I visit. He wrote to me many years ago about his silylation reagents, but unfortunately I did not realize how really important they were, and we were late in offering them through Aldrich. In the last few years, he has worked with Professor Harry Kroto, doing pivotal work on Buckminsterfullerenes, a form of carbon perhaps present in outer space. The discovery has really shaken up scientists, who wonder how many others there are to be made. David truly cares for people. He has been deeply involved in trying to upgrade the teaching of chemistry in Sri Lanka, where he spends considerable time trying to help their universities. Two other Sussex friends are Jim Hanson, a bio-organic chemist who has suggested many interesting compounds to Aldrich, and Professor Michael Lappert, a metal organicker who has sent some of his best graduates to Aldrich in Gillingham and to Sigma in Poole.

I really used to enjoy visiting Sheffield University largely because of the enormous enthusiasm of Dr Fraser Stoddart and his students and associates. Fraser was doing truly exciting work on large ring compounds, and I really think that if that work had been done just a few years earlier, he would have joined the other chemists who won the Nobel Prize for related work. The person I have known longest, although not best, at Sheffield is David Ollis, the professor of organic

193

chemistry whom I met when he was with Bob Woodward at Harvard. He once lit into us for providing funds to help Fraser Stoddart's students, by saying, "We don't need you. Anyone who really needs funding for research in Britain can get it easily", to which Isabel replied in astonishment, "I just don't believe you." I am sure all chemists would agree that funding is particularly tight in Britain. Clearly David had strong feelings about Fraser at the time, and I was amused later to see a glowing note about Fraser's achievements when he was leaving to take up the chair in Birmingham. The note was written by David in language usually reserved for eulogies for recently departed friends. In 1991 Fraser invited me to give three lectures in Birmingham, and we were amazed and happy to see that now, away from the battleground of Sheffield, he and David, who also moved to Birmingham, were on excellent terms.

All three universities in the Manchester area, UMIST, Manchester and Salford, as well as many other universities such as Liverpool and Birmingham, welcomed us sincerely, and we really enjoyed visiting them because close contact with academics became increasingly important to Aldrich. In the beginning, our priority was to find good suppliers. In the 1950s practically everything was purchased, and even now about 60% of Aldrich compounds come from suppliers around the world. As our capability increased to produce new compounds ourselves, we relied more and more on teachers and students to report their new discoveries and to help us with their expertise. Many a professor has given us his method and Aldrich has often been ready to advertise the key compound suggested when the manuscript appeared in print. Although all our visits to universities began in the hope of getting to know our customers better, and perhaps of finding exciting new compounds, they often became pure personal pleasure for Isabel and me.

For several months after my dismissal, I could not sleep. We still travel a good deal and I am invited to speak at many universities, so we see many of our old friends, but it is not quite the same. I sleep well now, but once or twice a week I dream that Isabel and I are visiting an old academic friend who is suggesting a new reagent.

16

Joseph Loschmidt—The Father
of Molecular Modelling

The greatest chemical breakthrough of the 19th century was a basic understanding of the carbon atom, the foundation of all organic chemistry. In March 1858 the German chemist August von Kekulé published a paper showing that carbon is quadrivalent and that one carbon atom can be linked to another carbon atom. This was quite revolutionary at the time, and Kekulé's fame rests on this paper and his publication in 1865 of the structure of benzene as a ring of six carbon atoms, an idea which, he claimed twenty-five years later, had come to him in a dream. Perhaps as much as a half of organic chemistry is aromatic, namely based on benzene as its simplest unit. The dyestuff industry is based on naphthalene and anthracene, of two and three fused benzene rings; most medicinal products are aromatic. The simplest, aspirin, is a simple benzene derivative. Until the structure of benzene was understood, aromatic chemistry was at an impasse.

Early this century Richard Anschütz, a German organic chemist, student of August von Kekulé, later his secretary and then successor in the chair of organic chemistry at Bonn University, began working on a two-volume biography of Kekulé, published in 1929, years after Kekulé's death in 1896. During his investigations, Anschütz made two discoveries, both calling into question Kekulé's great discoveries. The first concerned Archibald Scott Couper, a young Scottish chemist whose work on the reaction of phosphorus pentachloride with salicylic acid Anschütz was studying. Kekulé had tried to repeat Couper's work which, when he failed, he had dismissed as probably fraudulent. Yet by following Couper's method exactly, Anschütz had succeeded. Eager to learn more about Couper, Anschütz wrote many letters to chemists who might have known the man, and was finally able to piece together the life and work of this brilliant chemist who had studied in Glasgow, Berlin and Paris, and had had a meteoric rise and fall. Albert Ladenburg and Adolf Lieben mentioned that, while they and Couper were studying in Paris under Professor Wurtz, Couper independently hit on the idea of the quadrivalence of carbon and presented a paper to Wurtz, for submission to the French Academy. Submission was delayed, and Kekulé's paper was published first. Blaming Wurtz for the delay, Couper became very angry and abusive, and Wurtz expelled him. Returning to Scotland late in 1858, Couper became a laboratory assistant at Edinburgh University, but suffered a mental breakdown followed by sunstroke from which he never recovered fully. All the important details of his life were uncovered through the voluminous correspondence with Couper's friends and with a well-known chemist in Edinburgh, Alexander Crum Brown, who in turn located Couper's relatives. I was recently fortunate enough to acquire much of this correspondence and have been able to study Anschütz's investigations first-hand. It makes fascinating reading. Eventually, in 1909, Anschütz published his findings, both in German and English, undermining one of Kekulé's claims to fame.

Anschütz's second great discovery came a year or two later when he read a footnote in Kekulé's famous paper of 1865 in which he states that his structure seems preferable to the modifications proposed by Loschmidt and Crum Brown. Of course Anschütz knew Crum Brown well, but what was Loschmidt's chemical work, he wondered? Once again he set to work. He found an abstract of a book by Loschmidt in Liebig's *Jahresberichte* of 1861, but this 38-word summary really gave no inkling what the chemistry was all about, and at first, Anschütz could not find Loschmidt's book. It was not in Kekulé's library or in any of the university libraries he checked. Eventually Franz Deuticke, an antiquarian bookseller in Vienna, supplied a copy, and Anschütz was staggered when he read it.

Loschmidt's circular structure of benzene and many other aromatic compounds, some of them unthought of before 1861, seemed very clear to Anschütz who then undertook a very arduous task. Loschmidt's *Chemische Studien*, an octavo booklet, published in 1861, is not only very rare but is exceedingly difficult to read. The language is highly technical, often including words which Loschmidt coined. The type is small and the seven foldout plates, illustrating the 368 structures to which the reader has to refer, fall apart easily. Anschütz re-formatted the book so that the structures accompany the text, and the re-publication of 1913 is very much easier to read. He posed the obvious question: had Kekulé actually seen Loschmidt's book or had he been told about his structures by a third party? In a curt ten-word sentence he stated categorically that Kekulé had not seen it, but later, following his discovery of a letter dated January 4, 1862 to Professor Erlenmeyer in which Kekulé ridiculed Loschmidt's structures as *Confusions formeln* (sic), he published his belief in his 1929 biography that Kekulé must indeed have seen Loschmidt's book.

The re-publication seems like an act of atonement by a student for the omissions of his teacher, quite unknown in the annals of science. Indeed, were it not for Anschütz we would know hardly anything about the chemical work of either Couper or Loschmidt, and Kekulé's claim to fame would be unchallenged. In 1906 Anschütz wrote to Crum Brown referring to Kekulé as "My chief and venerable friend of many years", yet I wonder whether there was not a serious generation conflict between Anschütz and Kekulé.

It is an interesting coincidence that Ladenburg and Lieben, who became well-known chemists, also had indirect connections with Loschmidt. Ladenburg had worked with Kekulé in Ghent in 1865, before joining Wurtz in Paris. While Kekulé was the first to postulate a cyclohexatriene concept for benzene, Ladenburg was the first to propose a hexagon, with *carbon* atoms in the corners. Lieben was one of Austria's ablest organic chemists who must have known Loschmidt personally, yet never referred to Loschmidt's *Chemische Studien*.

Loschmidt's small 54-page book contained 121 structures with benzene rings, many of them correct. This was a private publication which Loschmidt paid for himself, although at the time he was a poor and scientifically unknown teacher in a Realschule in the Praterstrasse in Vienna. In the same year, Kekulé published a textbook that was to become universally well known. There he stated that one cannot depict formulae of constitution, that is formulae showing the position of atoms in molecules. Yet that is exactly what Loschmidt's work did, and there is no record of anyone paying the slightest attention to Loschmidt's book, except Kekulé and that brief abstract which appeared in Liebig's *Jahresberichte*.

Loschmidt titled his book *Constitutions-Formeln der organischen Chemie*—Formulae of Constitution in Organic Chemistry. The book in the British Library and the copy owned by Anschütz were entitled *Constitutions-Formeln der organischen Chemie in graphischer Darstellung*. However, the copy in the National Library in Vienna is entitled . . . *in geographischer Darstellung*. It probably is a galley proof, yet geographic is so apt: Loschmidt did try to depict molecules in space. *Constitutions-Formeln* led to Kekulé's ironic play on words in the letter he wrote early in 1862 to his friend, Professor Erlenmeyer, in which he referred to Loschmidt's *Confusions formeln* (sic)—formulae of confusion. Kekulé's only other mention of Loschmidt is the footnote in his paper of 1865, but he does not give a reference to Loschmidt's book. Nothing more was published about these *Constitutions-Formeln* in the 19th century despite the fact that Loschmidt had presented formulae not just for benzene and related compounds but also for many other organics. For instance, he was the first to show double and triple bonds as we show them today, and the first to show heterocyclic rings and sugar molecules correctly. His work was, however, ignored.

Until the mid 1980s I knew nothing about Josef Loschmidt except that he was connected with the Avogadro-Loschmidt number, the number of molecules in a liter of gas. I have found the investigation into his life and work exciting not only because of what I have learned about Loschmidt and the famous Kekulé, but also about other less well-known but remarkable chemists of the 19th century.

197

It was Dr William Wiswesser who brought Loschmidt to my attention when he submitted a paper on his work to the *Aldrichimica Acta*. Bill's great contribution to chemistry was the Wiswesser Line Notation, the WLN, which made possible the single line depiction of every molecule, no matter how complicated. At a time when computers were in their infancy, this was so useful that Aldrich offered its catalog in WLN. Unfortunately Bill's paper dealt mainly with Loschmidt's structures as forerunners to the WLN, and I found it too narrowly focused, so put it aside.

A quiet, self-effacing man who worked for the US Army, Bill channelled his energy, of which he had a great deal, into the WLN, and in Loschmidt he had made a great historical discovery. He believed that this almost unknown chemist was the forerunner of the WLN, and he wanted the world to know. By the 1980s the *Aldrichimica Acta* went to over 200,000 scientists worldwide. It had featured brilliant papers by some of the world's ablest chemists, and was cited widely. Bill hoped we would publish his paper in the *Acta* and kept saying, "Please read Loschmidt's book of 1861." Finally I did read the Xerox copies he sent me, and I was truly astounded. My involvement with Loschmidt had begun.

When I first saw Bill Wiswesser's copies of Loschmidt's book, I wondered whether we might be dealing with a very elaborate hoax. Had the original version been written by Anschütz and not Loschmidt? I enlisted the ablest Viennese chemist I know, Christian R Noe, to dig for information in Austria. From the National Library in Vienna he obtained a microfilm of Loschmidt's book, which I persuaded Aldrich to reprint despite concerns that no one would want to pay for a chemistry book of 1861. This was no hoax, and I believed the work was of such interest that it should be available. Since the Anschütz version of 1913 was much easier to use, that too was reprinted, and we helped Bill to broaden his paper which was then published in 1989. Knowing that Bill was very ill after his second heart attack, I sent him the first copy by special delivery and shared his happiness, promising that I would carry on his endeavors to publicize the work of this most innovative chemist of the 19th century.

Bill had been invited to present a paper on Loschmidt at a meeting of the Division of the History of Chemistry of the American Chemical Society in Boston, to be held in April 1990. This had been planned as a 100-year anniversary of the *Benzolfest* in Berlin on March 11, 1890, a tremendous party held in the Berlin City Hall sponsored by the German Chemical Society to honor Kekulé for his publication of the cyclic structure of benzene twenty-five years earlier. Sadly, Bill died in December just a few days after he had received a copy of his article, and with the continued support of Christian Noe, I undertook to present the paper at the meeting which was chaired by John Wotiz in Boston. In preparation,

Christian and I studied Loschmidt's work much more thoroughly, and the result of my talk, before an overflow audience, has been an even more intense involvement with chemists and chemistry in 19th century Europe. A number of papers were given at the meeting on various aspects of Kekulé and the *Benzolfest*. Some discussed other chemists of note in the 19th century, others dealt with Kekulé's dream, real or imagined. Certainly the audience was really excited and asked many questions, some of them very critical. John Wotiz later published *The Kekulé Riddle* which includes most of the papers presented at the meeting. A number of chemists from different countries have taken strong views on the whole subject. I have received over eighty invitations to present talks on Loschmidt and with Christian Noe have written several review papers.

Anschütz had lamented the fact that the book was privately printed and said, "If only Loschmidt had published his views in a widely read chemical journal . . ." Anschütz did not ask himself which journal would have accepted a theoretical paper from an unknown high school teacher. In an attempt to find out how widely the book had been circulated, I contacted the Harvard Library and the Library of Congress. Neither had Loschmidt's book. When next in England, I visited the British Library and was able to see their copy of the 1861 edition, as well as the invoice of 1863 from a bookseller on the Strand, the price—20 Neugroschen. The book was indeed published in 1861 and some people did buy it! When I next visited Vienna, I called on Franz Deuticke, the bookseller who had supplied Anschütz with his copy, but they had no other copies and did not know how many had been printed. However, I was given a catalog of 1863, showing the works offered for sale by the printer, Carl Gerold's Sohn, and there, on page 55, was Loschmidt's *Chemische Studien* offered for 20 Neugroschen. Since then an old friend, Robert Rosner, who is working for his second PhD, this time in the history of Austrian chemistry in the 19th century, has brought to my attention a paper by a friend of Loschmidt. Alexander Bauer, the grandfather of the Nobel Laureate, Erwin Schrödinger, wrote in 1913 that Loschmidt had given him copies of his book to distribute during a trip to France and Britain in 1862 to scientists who might be interested. Only one of them, the French mathematician Liouville, showed any real interest.

There has been strong criticism from some historians of chemistry of what Wiswesser, Noe, Rosner and I have been writing. The first argument is that Loschmidt did not really think of benzene as six carbons in a circle; he just used the circle as a symbol, a lucky break for him. While it is true that he did not know the exact structure of benzene in 1861, neither did Kekulé in 1865. Loschmidt did think of six carbons in a circle and his many aromatic structures are based on that. Time and again Loschmidt postulated the various possible structures of a molecule under consideration and then pointed to the one he preferred. In discussing benzene he showed a diallene structure and wrote, "... *könnte man fast versucht sein* ..."—one might be tempted to consider this—but then he clearly preferred the circular structure. Some historians have misunderstood the phrase to mean that Loschmidt in fact preferred the diallene structure, yet he did not use it in any of his 121 aromatic formulae.

Another criticism has been that Loschmidt did no experimental work to substantiate his proposed structures. Probably this is true, but it is an argument that can be made against all purely theoretical work. It has also been argued that in 1890, at the very time of the *Benzolfest*, Loschmidt published a short paper about the structure of benzene, referring to Kekulé's formula, but not mentioning his own earlier work of 1861. Is this not proof that he considered Kekulé as the discoverer of the circular structure of benzene? Yet many of Loschmidt's contemporaries and friends have written about this unmaterialistic, self-effacing man who wanted to avoid controversy at all costs. He wanted his work to be used, not praised, but is modesty a good reason to deny credit?

An ingenious argument was put forward by Professor A J Rocke in *Chemistry in Britain*: "Kekulé himself did not recognize Loschmidt as a predecessor for the benzene structure because he *cited* Loschmidt's *benzene proposal* in his first paper on the subject. If he had consciously taken the idea for benzene from this obscure source, or regarded the Loschmidt structure as similar to his own, the last thing he would have wanted to do was to draw attention to it." (My emphasis.) It is useful to read the original literature: Kekulé did not "cite" Loschmidt's benzene proposal. Rather, he wrote in passing, "*Elle me parait préférable aux modifications proposées par M M Loschmidt et Crum Brown.*"

Beginning with Anschütz, there have been chemists who pointed out that Kekulé's formula was superior to Loschmidt's because one can predict ortho, meta and para isomers with the former. I am not certain this is correct. About p-phenylenediamine, Loschmidt wrote that "just looking at that structure shows the possibilities of isomers"; I presume he meant ortho and meta.

Kekulé may have been the first to think of benzene as a cyclohexatriene, an improvement over Loschmidt's six carbons in a circle, but with bonding indeterminate. Yet it is most likely that his dream was based on the Loschmidt circle he had seen four years earlier. To paraphrase John Wotiz: When you cite a dream, you don't have to give footnotes.

We have been faulted many times for stressing the importance of Loschmidt's work because it was already well known. "Noe and Bader are wrong in believing that Loschmidt's work is not appreciated; in the *Dictionary of Scientific Biography*, more space is devoted to Loschmidt than to Kekulé," Alan Rocke wrote in *Chemistry in Britain*. Of course Loschmidt's work is appreciated, but as that of a physicist, not as the father of molecular modelling or as the chemist who first depicted benzene as a circle with six carbons. I have yet to hear even one of the thousands of chemists who have heard my Loschmidt lecture say, "I knew all this before." In a short essay on gas laws which accompanies the *Chemische Studien* of 1861, Loschmidt states that the overall aim of his work is *"einen tieferen Einblick in die Constitution der Materie zu gewähren"*. Loschmidt must have been deeply hurt by the almost total neglect of his work by chemists, and from then on concentrated on physics. His most important paper was published in 1865, the calculation of the Loschmidt number. That number gave the size of the molecules; the *Chemische Studien* gave their shapes. Both were part of his aim "to provide a deeper understanding of the constitution of matter".

I was rather staggered by the sharpness of the attack on our work. Professor G P Schiemenz of Kiel University ridiculed Wiswesser's paper and, in a slide talk where he showed a tombstone above an open grave, suggested that Wiswesser was dead and should be allowed to rest in peace. Schiemenz wrote: "to date molecular modeling back to 1861 is just anachronistic." In Darmstadt, Professor Klaus Hafner, director of the Kekulé Museum began discussion after my talk by saying, "The most dangerous lies in the world are half-truths, and you have just heard half-truths." In response to an article that Christian Noe and I wrote for *Chemistry in Britain*, Professor W B Jensen, the editor of the *Bulletin for the History of Chemistry* accused the British publication of "tepid academic yellow journalism". We were just presenting "historical hobby horses" like many "who have been knocking on our door for years with an entire herd of equally dubious hobby horses, ranging from the supposed charlatanism of Lavoisier and Linus Pauling, to the homosexuality of Justus Liebig and the duplicity of Charles Darwin.". When does someone really interested in history become an historian? Unfortunately the editor of *Chemistry in Britain* did not publish Dr Jensen's letter. I invited Professor Jensen to come to my talk on Loschmidt at an ACS meeting in Chicago, but he did not have time. Yet some very able chemists have listened and approved. The three times that I was most concerned about the reaction that would follow a talk were at the ETH, the Bader Symposium at Harvard and in the chemistry department of the University of Marburg, where I first talked about Loschmidt to German students. Would they jeer, I wondered, and chase me out? They did not. They laughed where I hoped they would, and understood, and some of the world's ablest chemists, Albert Eschenmoser and Vlado Prelog at the ETH, E J Corey and Gilbert Stork at the Harvard Symposium, understood and approved.

The heat engendered by my championship of Loschmidt may be because Kekulé has become such a status symbol for the superiority of German chemistry in the 19th century. Indeed he was a great experimentalist and can be considered the father of the German chemical industry. He was also a consummate politician, quite a different man from Loschmidt.

Josef Loschmidt was born in a village in Bohemia in 1821, the eldest son of a poor farmer. He had the good fortune to be recognized by the village priest as having exceptional abilities. His parents were persuaded to send him to high school, and he went on to the University in Prague and then to the Technische Hochschule in Vienna. On graduation with the equivalent of a BS in chemistry and physics, he and a friend with whom he had developed the production of potassium nitrate founded a company which unfortunately failed in 1849. He then accepted various jobs in Styria, Bohemia and Moravia before returning to Vienna in the early 1850s, where he worked first as a private tutor and then in 1856 qualified as a high school teacher in chemistry and physics. He became friends with two of Austria's ablest physicists, Josef Stefan and Ludwig Boltzmann, younger men who realized that this high school teacher was studying some of the most important scientific problems, and Stefan helped him obtain a position as Privatdozent, assistant professor, at the university in 1866. Within four years he was given an honorary doctorate, having become an associate professor in 1868. His advance continued to full professor in 1872 and in 1875 to chairman of the physical chemistry laboratory and professor of physics to include physical chemistry. Two years later he became dean and in 1885 was elected to the senate of the faculty of philosophy. He died on 8 July 1895.

Some years ago I was able to acquire many of Loschmidt's manuscripts, left by his widow to a niece who sold them to a chemist in Vienna who had received his PhD for a thesis on Loschmidt. What strikes one most forcefully when reading these papers is the enormous diversity of Loschmidt's interests. There are works on chemistry and physics, mineralogy, crystallography, economics, customs duties, even anti-semitism.

Friends have asked me why I have worked so hard on Loschmidt. Is it because he taught just a few houses away from where I lived as a boy? Certainly not. Why have my friends, Professor Noe and Robert Rosner, spent so many hours delving into his life and work? All of us feel that the *Chemische Studien* of 1861 was one of the great works of organic chemistry. In the early 1900s there were still some eminent scientists who believed that we would never be able to depict molecules. Thanks mainly to X-rays and NMR, we now know that they were wrong, and this depiction is one of the greatest achievements of this century. The father of this molecular modelling—not just of benzene but of many other molecules and, most importantly, the father of the concept that this was possible—was Josef Loschmidt and we hope that chemists around the world will honor his memory at the 100th anniversary of his death in July

1995. We hope, too, that there will be another *Benzolfest* in 2061, honoring the right man in the right year.

The more I think about Loschmidt, the more I think about Anschütz. Ninety-nine out of a hundred chemists would have read a reference to Couper or to Loschmidt, and let it go. Not Anschütz. The many letters to Crum Brown and the painstaking re-publication of Loschmidt's *Chemische Studien* prove his persistence and his dedication to the truth.

FURTHER READING:

Josef Loschmidt *Chemische Studien*, Vienna 1861, reprinted by the Aldrich Chemical Co., Inc., catalog No. Z18576-0

Josef Loschmidt *Konstitutionsformeln der Organischen Chemie in Graphischer Darstellung* reformatted by Richard Anschütz *Ostwalds Klassiker der exakten Wissenschaften No. 190*, Leipzig 1913, reprinted by Aldrich Chemical Co., Inc., catalog No. Z18577-9

Leonard Dobbin "The Couper Quest", *J.Chem. Educ.*, *11*, 331 (1934)

William J. Wiswesser "Johann Josef Loschmidt (1821-1895): a forgotten genius", *Aldrichimica Acta*, 22, 17 (1989)

Christian R. Noe and Alfred Bader Chapter 16 in *The Kekulé Riddle* edited by John H. Wotiz, Cache River Press, Vienna, IL 1993

Christian R. Noe and Alfred Bader "Facts are Better than Dreams" *Chemistry in Britain*, p. 126, February 1993

Alan J. Rocke "Waking up to the facts?" *Chemistry in Britain*, p. 401, May 1993

Günter P. Schiemenz "Goodbye, Kekulé? Joseph Loschmidt und die monocyclische Struktur des Benzols" *Naturwissenschaftliche Rundschau*, 46, 85 (1993)

Günter P. Schiemenz "Joseph Loschmidt und die Benzol-Formel. Über die Entstehung einer Legende" *Sudhoffs Archiv 78*, 41 (1994)

17

Paintings

I have been buying, selling, trading and giving away paintings for many years, as many as 200 a year during the last decade. It was a natural extension of my dealing in stamps and much more interesting. Once Aldrich was in a firm position and I could give a little more time to this "dabbling" in art, I decided to start a company, Alfred Bader Fine Arts, to keep track of my enjoyable pastime.

With my dismissal from Sigma-Aldrich finalized in May 1992, it became clear that I had to move into a gallery—where else could I hang the dozens of paintings that were in the Aldrich offices? I had the good fortune to find a fine apartment in the Astor, a friendly old-fashioned hotel, near downtown Milwaukee and the lake, and less than ten minutes' drive from home. Even better fortune was heralded by a phone call from Marilyn Hassmann, my long-time secretary at Aldrich. She needed a change and wanted to take early retirement from the company—did I have a job for her? My "yes" was immediate, with one proviso: that she would not insist on leaving me at 65.

Marilyn is competent, hard-working, loyal and—best of all—straightforward and outspoken. She has no hidden agenda—if she does not like something, she tells me right away, clearly and distinctly. When I call the office, it always gives me great pleasure to hear her greeting, "Alfred Bader Fine Arts."

I spend about a third of my time dealing in paintings, a third writing and lecturing and a third trying to help chemists, particularly in small companies. Marilyn is experienced in all these areas. There was no need to teach her anything, and I can leave her safely in charge while I travel. I really enjoy working with her.

My mode of buying and selling changed in 1992. I had never bought very expensive art, paintings that cost millions. We were well off, but since I had never sold a single share of Sigma-Aldrich stock before my dismissal, we did not have millions in ready cash. I have in any case always considered it much more fun to pay a few thousand dollars for a work that might prove great and valuable after cleaning.

Selling old master paintings from a gallery in Milwaukee is pretty hopeless. What few old paintings Milwaukeeans—including the Milwaukee Art Museum—buy, usually come from prestigious and very expensive New York galleries. Even Chicago does not have a single old master gallery! So I teamed up with two excellent old master dealers, Dr

Otto Naumann, an art historian who specializes in Dutch paintings in New York, and Clovis Whitfield, an Italian art specialist in London. Generally, I buy works that strongly appeal to me, and Otto and Clovis offer them for sale.

Our first major purchase gave Alfred Bader Fine Arts a lot of publicity, but also subjected Otto and me to some quite unjust criticism. The painting was a major Rembrandt portrait of the famous Remonstrant minister, Johannes Uyttenbogaert (plate 2). The Rembrandt Research Project had accepted this work as genuine, pointing however to its flattened condition. Many experts had questioned how much of the original paint surface remained, which is why Sotheby's had estimated the value of the painting at only £3,000,000. I was enchanted by the sitter's face, and Otto argued that this might well be the last great Rembrandt to come to market in my lifetime. The condition was a problem however and we asked our restorer, Charles Munch, to fly to London to examine the painting. Charles assured us that careful relining and cleaning would greatly improve the appearance. It is one of the master's best documented works, because the sitter noted in his diary on April 13, 1633, "Today I was painted by Rembrandt." The face was magnificent, but whether the hands were by Rembrandt or by an assistant, only cleaning could tell. Otto and I decided to bid to a hammer price of £6,000,000, plus one bid, if we were on the wrong side of the bid. Luckily, this great work was knocked down to us for just £3,800,000—to our great relief and to Sotheby's, who feared it might not sell. The pound was then worth almost two dollars, so that we had been prepared to pay over $12,000,000.

Just days after the sale, Otto learned that the Rijksmuseum in Amsterdam was seriously interested in purchasing this work, particularly as the Remonstrant community there was willing to make a sizable contribution. We were in a quandary. Selling it quickly at a relatively modest profit to the Rijksmuseum would be a real feather in our cap; having it cleaned and being patient would net a far greater profit. After long discussions, we decided to offer the portrait to the Rijksmuseum for $10,000,000, loan it to the museum for its consideration until the beginning of December and give them three years to pay, should they require time.

When Isabel and I visited the Rijksmuseum at the end of November, on our way to an exhibition in Dordrecht, they were not yet sure whether they could raise the money, and we really did not know whether to hope for a negative or positive decision. On December 1, we learned that the Rijksmuseum would indeed purchase the portrait and pay for it promptly. The director gave us the news and announced the purchase in the Dutch press. Then all hell broke loose: how could the Rijksmuseum pay so much, why had it not bid for itself, why give an American dealer so large a profit? One Dutch dealer, Hans Cramer, wrote an essay in which he chided the museum for paying too much! I did not know whether to laugh or cry. I certainly do not know of any Dutch dealer who would sell me, at a comparably modest profit, a great painting that he had just bought. More pertinent: if the Rijksmuseum had bid at auction, determined to buy the portrait, it would have had to pay much more than $10,000,000.

Cramer's essay, published in the *NRC Handelsblad*, a respected Dutch paper, accused the Rijksmuseum of conspiring with us *before* the auction—a conspiracy which Cramer pointed out was a criminal offense in England. The director of the museum, H W van Os, published a clear account of the true facts in the *Bulletin of the Rijksmuseum*.

This brouhaha even spilled over into the American press. *Art & Auction* published a piece alleging that Otto and I had misled the museum by claiming that we were making a profit of only 10%. What nonsense: when we agreed in July on the price to the Rijksmuseum, we had no way of knowing what our profit would be, because we did not know what the dollar cost would be, having not yet purchased the pounds sterling to pay for the painting. In any case the museum could easily have decided against the purchase on December 1. When I faxed the editors of *Art & Auction* that their article was so close to libelous that I could not tell the difference, their attorney replied promptly that the magazine would publish my letter, explaining the reality of the situation.

Many great purchases followed. A wonderful *Entombment* by Rubens, from Christie's in London in December 1992, went to the J Paul Getty Museum. Another surprising find was a large *Crucifixion* (plate 3) by Amsterdam's first really good painter, Jacob Cornelisz van Oostsaanen, dated 1507, which appeared at Sotheby's in New York in January 1993. I had looked at paintings by Oostsaanen before—none that I remember of this high quality—and thought that all such works were in museums. Yet here was a really well-preserved panel, of quite beautiful color, without provenance or documentation and hence given a modest estimate.

In some ways the most exciting painting I bought as a dealer was neither the Rembrandt nor the Rubens, but a German altarpiece *circa* 1510 which came up at Sotheby's in London in December 1993. George Gordon, one of the old master experts there, allowed me to look at several pictures in his office a few days before the sale. Four of the paintings were German, 16th century, consigned for sale by a small church in Shropshire to which they had been given a century ago. I understand that the church insured them for a mere £250 and worried about the condition of the panels as icicles sometimes formed on them in the winter. Sotheby's put the highest value on the earliest of the four, a *Crucifixion*, probably from Alsace, but I found it rather wooden and in fact it did not sell. To me, the center of a large altarpiece, a *Lamentation* (plate 4), with a later Albrecht Dürer monogram, was stunning, among the best German works of that period I have ever seen. The wings were offered as a separate lot and depicted the same donor as the center panel, but I suspected that they were painted slightly later and by a different hand, and I did not bid on them. Otto and I decided that I should bid to £1,000,000, plus one bid. The next day a friend at Christie's told me that they had expected the altarpiece to fetch several millions, and we were delighted that the hammer price was £210,000, more than Sotheby's estimate, but much lower than we expected. The wings, which were cut down, went to a dealer for a mere £35,000. I silently thanked George Gordon for having left me alone to study the altarpiece so closely, just as he had left Charles Munch and me alone with Johannes Uyttenbogaert.

Sotheby's had assured me that the export permit would be granted quickly, so I was surprised when informed that the National Gallery in London objected to the export and that the Reviewing Committee would meet soon to discuss whether export should be approved or denied. The committee reasoned that the altarpiece was of such importance that it fell under one or more of three criteria, called the Waverly criteria: (i) closely connected with British history, (ii) of outstanding aesthetic importance, or (iii) of great significance for study. George Gordon urged me to attend the meeting of the committee in the National Gallery, and Isabel and I flew over specially.

Earlier Otto had told me that he believed he knew the artist of the altarpiece, a Thuringian painter known as the Master of the Crispin Legend, about whose work a lengthy article had just appeared in the *Record* of the Art Museum of Princeton University. If Otto's theory were correct, we had bought the work of a minor German artist, although perhaps his best picture; but the more I studied the illustrations in the Princeton article, the less convinced I was. Certainly they were similar, with shades of Dürer, Altdorfer and Cranach, but there was a difference in quality.

As I waited for the meeting to be convened by the committee's chairman, Jonathan Scott, I watched my painting being carried into the room where we were to sit in a semi-circle; I recognized two of the committee members, Jack Baer, a respected dealer I have known for many years, and David Scrase, a most helpful art historian at the Fitzwilliam Museum in Cambridge. I was to sit beside Neil MacGregor, the Director of the National Gallery, and Dr Susan Foister, the gallery's expert on northern Renaissance paintings, neither of whom I had met before. I then did something that made me realize, on reflection, that indeed I was still, even at close to 70, a *Spitzbub*. I got up and sat on the floor next to the painting, wetted my finger and put some saliva over the monogram in the lower lefthand corner. "I do this only with my own paintings," I said, "but look: at least the D of the monogram is floating, in case any of you think this might actually be a work of Albrecht Dürer. It is not."

I had feared that I would be surrounded by a group of stuffed shirts, but I was wrong. The meeting was relaxed and informal, and within minutes I began to enjoy it. Neil MacGregor presented the gallery's case: there are few such early German works in British public collections, almost none is a *Lamentation* or even the central panel of an altarpiece; the convincing identification of the donor as that of a member of the Brandenburg-Ansbach family greatly increases the interest in the fine example; and the artist must have worked with Dürer whose work is not well represented in British collections. Mr MacGregor ended by saying that he hoped that the wings might yet be reunited with the central panel.

I had brought my tape recorder and was told by the chairman that I could tape only my own words. I began by saying that I felt badly about the way the matter had been handled. The church wanted to use about half the money to build affordable housing but had not yet been paid. If the wings were so important, why had the gallery not bid? It could have been certain of its ability to stop the export of the centerpiece the moment the bidding went over £100,000, the threshold for export denial. Beyond that I could do nothing but agree with the director about the beauty and great importance of the painting and that it should indeed be in the National Gallery. I said that I had already discussed this with Dr Naumann and we were willing to sell to the gallery for much less than the limit we had set for ourselves, just as we had agreed to sell the Rembrandt portrait to the Rijksmuseum for well under our limit. "I have no argument with you," I stated. "I think the painting should stay at the National Gallery at a reasonable price, but do decide quickly, so that the church gets paid."

I was asked whether I would be willing to sell the painting to another British museum, and I said yes. I would sell it to a private British collector, but not at so low a price. After a few questions, Neil MacGregor, Dr Foister and I were asked to leave the room. Dr Foister assured me that she did not believe the altarpiece was by the Master of the Crispin Legend; we all wanted it to be acquired by the National Gallery but, alas, there was no money. Within ten minutes we were called back into the room and told by the chairman that some members of the committee had thought points (ii) and (iii) of the Waverly criteria to be applicable, yet the majority had voted for granting the export license. Just minutes after 3 pm I rushed from the gallery to Charing Cross station to catch the 3.15 train for Hastings, in ample time to view the paintings in a small auction house in Battle, where an auction was to begin at 6.30

that evening.

Ever since leaving the National Gallery that day, I had been elated about the fair treatment I had received and almost looked forward to purchasing another great painting with export denied at some time in the future. Yet before the day ended, I came close to making a purchase I would have regretted. In the Abbey Auction House in Battle, I spied a delightful little panel of a Dutch couple making pancakes, close to Adriaen van Ostade. When I asked Mr Ellin, the auctioneer, what he thought it would bring, he said that such a good copy might fetch £200—£300. How did he know it was not stolen, I asked. He knew the owner, a young man who had inherited it, who had at first brought in the fine carved frame for sale, and later had been encouraged to bring the painting also. During the auction, only a dealer from Kent and I bid beyond a few hundred pounds, and I sensed Isabel's worry as the bidding went into the thousands. She knows that my expertise is in Rembrandt students, not in genre paintings, and she was relieved when I stopped bidding at £4000. The successful buyer was upset: if I had not come, he would have bought this blue gem for a few hundred pounds. If he was upset then, he had more bad news to come.

As *Art & Auction* wrote in its May issue, "It's so hard to find good help: a former Buckingham Palace footman has been charged with pilfering a 17th century painting by Adriaen van Ostade . . ." The painting had not yet been missed, but Sarah Lidsey at Phillips recognized it when the buyer brought it to the London salesroom for an evaluation. That would have been all I needed to mar such a great day—to buy a painting stolen from the Queen!

Otto Naumann, most knowledgeable about Dutch 17th century works, is a man justifiably respected for his integrity. In the art trade, so much is done on a handshake, but some handshakes are better than others, and it is good to know that your partner is reliable. He has helped enormously with recent major acquisitions. Not that we were able to purchase all the great paintings on which we had set our sights. In that Sotheby's New York sale where we bought the Oostsaanen, we failed to buy an enchanting portrait of a well-known 15th century composer, Jacob Obrecht, in its realism very close to Hans Memling. The frame was dated 1496, two years after Memling's death, and posthumous works are hard to sell unless one can prove that the frame was completed later. We need not have worried: both the Getty and the Kimbell museums bid for this painting even though the authorship might never be universally accepted—and the Kimbell won out at a hammer price of $2,200,000.

Bidding on such major works is a long way from my first efforts. When I was a child in Vienna, my mother's apartment was filled with paintings, mostly 19th and 20th century Viennese works, and even then

I knew that I did not like them. But I became very interested in paintings and at some point—I do not remember where or when—I realized that my preference was for Dutch and Flemish 17th century works: not the innumerable tavern interiors or even the landscapes and still lifes that are most desirable commercially, but historical paintings, particularly Biblical ones, and portraits—works that displayed invention and originality.

My first old master painting came from Paul Drey, a distinguished New York dealer, whose death in the 1950s precluded his selling me more than just two pictures. During our first meeting, we discovered that his family's gallery in Munich had sold paintings to my father and perhaps also to my grandfather. Dr Drey invited me to look around his gallery, and the painting I liked best was a study of a man with an open mouth (plate 5). Would I be willing to pay $50 per month, for sixteen months? It was the first and only painting I bought in installments, and what pleased me most was that Dr Drey trusted me and allowed me to take the painting with me. Later it was used as the cover of Aldrich's catalog of the Alfred Bader Library of Rare Chemicals, and reproductions of the painting hang in many laboratories, often with hilarious captions!

Buying from Dr Drey's gallery was very much the exception. Generally, I preferred to acquire dirty old paintings in antique stores and at auctions, hoping that cleaning would reveal great works. I considered the large commercial galleries in New York, London and Amsterdam just too expensive, although with hindsight, and compared with today's prices, I am sure they were not. My greatest Dutch successes are still in my collection, but I gave my best Italian, French and German works to the Queen's University Art Centre and to other museums.

The Noordeinde in the center of The Hague is a street lined with antique stores, and I still marvel at the good fortune that led me, in the late 1950s, into just one of them, owned by Han and Saskia Jüngeling. Han had been a dealer for many years and, like me, liked to buy unknown works, judged on their quality only. He would go to the small auctions, particularly in Amsterdam and London, to buy unillustrated works with low estimates. Over the years, I have bought well over a hundred works from Han, and since his death, from his widow Saskia, who was trained by her father, a restorer of paintings.

The two most memorable works I bought from Han are illustrated here. Han thought that the *Mary Weeping* (plate 6) might be one of Jan Vermeer's earliest works. I was certain that it was earlier, and Benedict Nicolson, the expert on Terbrugghen, identified it as one of that artist's late works, confirming my initial feeling. The portrait of a dour old man, Jacob Junius (plate 7), was identified by Wolfgang Stechow as a late work by Jan Lievens, the artist who greatly influenced Rembrandt in Leiden in the 1620s, and was in turn influenced by him. There is a myth that Lievens was really competent only while he was an artist in "Rembrandt's Shadow", as he was called in an exhibition in Braunschweig in 1979. The *Jacob Junius*, painted in the 1660s, certainly shows that late in life Lievens was a great portraitist.

One other dealer from whom I have purchased many fine paintings, always priced reasonably, in London, is different from any dealer I have ever met. His main effort has been to find fine works at minor auctions, often outside London. He has an excellent eye and is very much a loner, operating from a small office near Christie's. He is totally honest, but rather pessimistic, and I think it is his pessimism that has kept him from becoming as commercially successful as many other London dealers.

I like to think that my enthusiasm for some of the paintings he has sold me has brought him as much pleasure as the paintings have given me. At first horrified by the price he mentioned for a Gerbrand van den Eeckhout, who is one of my favorite Rembrandt students, I was thrilled when I actually saw *The Rest on the Flight to Egypt* (plate 8), signed and dated 1653. Of the many Dutch paintings I have bought from him, this is my favorite.

Over the years, I have spent much time with dealers and art historians, but relatively little with collectors. Among the exceptions was Franz Sobek, a distant relative in Vienna whose parents had been friends of my mother. Oddly, we were related through both my parents' families, so Franz had some Jewish ancestors. However, he was a religious Catholic, a Christian Socialist who had served in the police administration under Kurt Schuschnigg, and had been sent to Dachau in 1938 where he was kept for five and a half years. I remember his sister Mitzi coming into our Jewish neighborhood on Friday afternoons after the Anschluss, carrying a large basket of food, gifts for her Jewish friends. There were some decent Austrians. Mitzi died of a heart attack nine days after Vienna was liberated. In April 1945 Franz became vice president of the first free Austrian government, and later managing director of the state printing works. The counts von Sobek had large properties in Bohemia which were confiscated by the Communists, and he told me once that some of the new Austrian government's first expenditures were paid for with gold that he had buried in his garden before the war

He had been an ardent collector of Viennese clocks since boyhood, but he also knew a great deal about paintings. He really understood my passion for collecting and knew all the major antique dealers in Vienna as well as many collectors who were willing sometimes to sell their treasures. He was happy to help me and always took a day or two off to accompany me when I visited Vienna. I stayed with him whenever I returned and felt a little uncomfortable only on my very first night in his guestroom, surrounded by a dozen crucifixes and statues of Jesus and Mary.

Some time in the 1950s, Franz became the head of the Austrian government's attempt at restitution to Jews. He found the work very difficult. The Austrians were much less sincere than the Germans. They talked about compensation but were unwilling to spend money for the purpose. In appreciation of his efforts, the Austrian Jewish community presented Franz with a large gold medal, which he gave to my son David, who cherishes it. Late in his life Franz told me he wanted to leave me one painting that would give me real pleasure for the rest of my life—*St Vitus's Cathedral in Prague* (plate 9) by Rudolf von Alt, 1850. Von Alt is best known for his watercolors; his oils are very rare and Prague has long been my favorite city. What a gift!

Franz died in 1975 after a long illness, leaving his fine collection of clocks and a rococo castle, the Geymüller Schlössl, to the city of Vienna. It is now the Sobek clock museum.

With one exception, there has never been anyone really knowledgeable about old master paintings in Milwaukee, although several art historians have worked in the city for short periods of time, and I have always been delighted to have someone close to home with whom I could share my interest and discuss puzzle paintings. In the early 1960s I met Ann and Harry Moore from Chicago, both lovers of old masters, and Harry, like myself, is a dealer. We have spent many hours together over the years, combining business with pleasure. The great experts in old masters, however, are all over the world, mainly on the East Coast and in Europe, and I have tried very hard to learn from them and visit them as often as possible.

I have never known anyone quite like Wolfgang Stechow at Oberlin, in knowledge and human kindness. I look at his photograph in my office every day, saddened by the inscription, *"gut, dass wir uns später doch noch kennengelernt haben!"* (Better late than never.) We knew each other for only a few years before his death in 1974, but I learned so much from him. He had a wonderful eye for quality, was careful and almost always correct in his attributions, and had a great knowledge not just of Dutch 17th century art, but also of Renaissance and even modern works. And what a giving man, truly a human masterpiece. I have kept the many letters he sent me and it still gives me great pleasure to re-read them.

Why did such a great scholar remain at a small Ohio college that does not even offer a PhD in art history? However, Oberlin does have a fine art museum with a collection of old masters, largely amassed with the help of Wolfgang's knowledge, and it also has a great school of music. We visit his widow Ursula from time to time, and clearly she is still active and happy at Oberlin, within walking distance of great art and music, her husband's second love.

The first art historian I got to know well was Ulrich Middeldorf, whom I met when he was chairman of art history at the University of Chicago. I vividly remember the advice he gave me on my very first visit in 1951: "When you consider buying a painting, look first at the drawing; don't buy it if it's badly drawn. Buy on quality, not name. Pay little attention to expertises written by art historians; a really good work doesn't need an expertise and a bad one is not improved by one." Over forty years later, I still remember his advice whenever I am offered a painting. Yet despite his advice, I still love the works of Aert de Gelder, Rembrandt's last student, who was a poor draftsman and yet so painterly, so close in spirit to Rembrandt.

Ulrich and his family moved to Florence in 1954, where he became director of the German Kunsthistorisches Institut. For years I paid him an annual visit in June, catching the night train in Lucerne on a Friday evening and arriving in Florence around 5.30 in the morning. I would leave my luggage at the station, walk slowly to the Middeldorf home just the other side of the Arno, and drink four or five capuccinos at a little cafe before Ulrich came out at 7 am to pick up a newspaper. We would then spend the day discussing the forty or fifty photographs I had brought along, of paintings I had just bought or was considering. He was less interested in attributions than in quality and condition, and he knew so much about many related fields—medals, textiles, literature of all ages. He had a wonderful library that was eventually acquired by the Getty Trust. We have often visited his widow, Gloria, since Ulrich's death in 1983, but just as Vienna is not the same without Franz Sobek, so Florence is not the same without Ulrich Middeldorf.

In the same way that I associate Florence with the Middeldorfs, so Munich is synonymous with Walther and Ellen Bernt. I first visited their home in the Mottlstrasse in 1954, and usually spent two hours every year discussing past and prospective acquisitions. Walther had compiled the best illustrated reference work on the lesser known Dutch and Flemish 17th century artists—three volumes on paintings and two on drawings, and had amassed a wonderful archive of thousands of photographs of paintings. He knew far more about Netherlandish paintings than most academics, and wrote expertises only for works of quality, and always for the same fee regardless of the value of the painting. His opinion was so well respected that few collectors in central Europe would buy Dutch paintings without a Bernt expertise. Mindful of Ulrich Middeldorf's advice, I did not ask for expertises, just advice, which was always given most generously.

Of course, anyone writing thousands of expertises must make some mistakes, and Walther might occasionally have attributed a painting by one Rembrandt student to another, but never a work of a student to the master himself.

During my visits, there were usually paintings leaning against the bookcases in the Bernt living room, awaiting expertises. These paintings were often owned by dealers or parties willing to sell, and Walther sometimes introduced me to the owners. Some of my best paintings entered my collection that way.

Walther was totally honest, as straightforward as a man could be, and yet his very success generated a lot of jealousy and criticism from dealers who wanted "upgraded" expertises and from academics who were doing less well financially. Ellen Bernt, who also has an excellent eye and great knowledge, has continued Walther's work with expertises and still receives us with tea and cakes and most helpful criticism of our recent and prospective acquisitions.

I have heard that students, and even some mature adults, are afraid of Werner Sumowski, professor of art history in Stuttgart; they would not be if they knew him well. He looks so impressive, with his shock of white hair, and he speaks and writes very incisively. He has written two encyclopedic works on Rembrandt students, one on their drawings—ten volumes so far—and the other on their paintings, in six volumes. His work on the paintings alone, a Herculean undertaking, illustrates over 2000 examples and contains an enormous amount of information. I have spent many an evening studying these volumes.

Werner does not travel much, preferring to work almost entirely from photographs, and of course, as with almost every art historian who makes attributions, some of them have been questioned. Job's saying is applicable here: "Shall we take the good from God and not the bad?" Werner has helped thousands like myself to understand Rembrandt students better, and if I find it hard to believe that his attributions of two of my favorite paintings (plates 10 & 11) to Johann Ulrich Mayr and Heerschop are correct, it does not really worry me.

For years now we have visited Werner and his adoptive mother annually, in the company of Alfred and Erika Griesinger and Helge and Doris Herd. We usually spend a couple of hours in Werner's home, discussing Rembrandt school paintings, and then go out to dinner together. Helge used to work at Aldrich, and now has his own consulting firm. The Griesingers and the Herds both have fine collections of art, albeit largely more modern, and we have all benefitted from Werner's knowledge.

Since 1968 a group of eminent Dutch scholars known as the Rembrandt Research Project (RRP) team, have been studying paintings attributed to Rembrandt, separating what in their opinion are works by the master from those by his students and followers. With three volumes published to date, they have covered about half Rembrandt's works, through 1642, the year in which the artist painted *The Nightwatch*. The RRP has been most careful to assemble all the details of provenance, copies, condition, X-rays and iconography of every painting discussed. No artist's work has ever been examined so carefully and yet, while the physical facts presented are correct, a few of the conclusions are unconvincing. Nonetheless, of major importance are the discoveries by the RRP that some paintings may be partly by Rembrandt and partly by his students, and that Rembrandt signed and sold some workshop paintings as his own work.

The team's decisions have caused considerable controversy, but from their studies and Sumowski's works on Rembrandt students, one fact has become crystal clear: some of the students were great painters. In the 1950s I began collecting the students' works at very low prices. Most major auctions at the time included some, but today very few come on the market, and when they do, they are much more expensive.

For many years, works like *The Man with the Golden Helmet* in Berlin, *The Polish Rider* in the Frick Museum, and *David Parting from Jonathan* (RRP C84) in the Hermitage, have been considered among Rembrandt's finest paintings. If indeed Drost and Bol, respectively, painted the last two, as the RRP panel believes, then they were painters of ability comparable to that of Rembrandt. My own belief is that Rembrandt did not paint *The Man with the Golden Helmet,* but did paint the other two. However, if one studies the greatest works of Rembrandt's best students, Carel Fabritius, Eeckhout, Drost and de Gelder, one realizes what great art they produced. No wonder that many of their works were long attributed to Rembrandt.

The panel has effectively dispelled the idea that all Rembrandt's paintings were great works of art. Some of the accepted portraits of the 1630s are plain boring: just look at his self-portrait with a poodle in Paris (RRP A40). Because it is so clumsy, its authenticity has long been doubted, but the panel has now shown convincingly that it really is by the master. He was human after all, and had his "blue Mondays".

Some of today's greatest art historians have sought to distance Rembrandt from his students. Consider the latest great Rembrandt exhibition in Berlin, Amsterdam and London in 1991-2, entitled "Rembrandt: The Master and His Workshop." It cost several million dollars to assemble 83 paintings, 51 "authentic" Rembrandts, three or four works by Jan Lievens, and the rest by Rembrandt pupils. It would be hard to fault the choice of the Rembrandts, except that almost all were works from accessible museums, well known to most serious students of Dutch art. Some of the students' works however were mediocre and some were misattributed. Since the exhibitors' stated intention was partly to show good pictures that had once been attributed to Rembrandt, why did they include second-rate paintings in such a major exhibition? Perhaps they wanted to demonstrate what a great gulf exists between Rembrandt and his students. But does such a gulf exist? If only they had chosen the best works of the finest students, it might have been clear that there is no gulf.

The organizers missed a golden opportunity. If they had shown *The Flight to Egypt* (RRP C5) from Tours and *The Scholar by Candlelight* (RRP C18, p.84), paintings the RRP attributes tentatively to Dou, together with authentic works by Dou, it would have been clear that Dou never had it in him to paint the former works; and that might have caused them to wait before attributing the beautiful *Tobias and His Wife* (RRP C3, number 55 in the exhibition) to Dou. Similarly, exhibiting the Hermitage's *David and Jonathan* next to authentic Bols would have been very instructive. Or they could have shown RRP C69, the Beresteyn portrait of 1632 from the Metropolitan Museum, now attributed to a student whom Professor Bruyn has identified as Isaac Jouderville. If that portrait had been hung next to the insipid concoctions really by Jouderville, even Professor Bruyn might have changed his mind. Perhaps some day I will be able to help with an exhibition of works of Rembrandt students, showing how great they really were.

It is a self-centered way to look at paintings, but whenever I see such an exhibition, I ask, "Would I buy this or that painting for my collection if it came up at auction?" With at least nine works in that Rembrandt exhibition, the answer was no. Of course, I now wear two hats, that of dealer and that of collector. As a dealer I would purchase any of those nine, if the price were right, but they would not enter my personal collection.

The work of the RRP has had some beneficial side effects. One is the help that a C rating (namely, a work not considered to be by Rembrandt) gives to buyers of fine paintings. In 1979 Christie's in London offered a study of Rembrandt's father (RRP C22, plate 13), pointing out that the RRP did not accept it as a work by the master. I was able to purchase it most reasonably, at a fraction of the price an A number would have commanded, although many competent art historians share my view that this work is an authentic Rembrandt. Horst Gerson has even reproduced it in color in his catalog of authentic Rembrandts, and Julius Held has published his belief that the father's blindness, depicted here, led to Rembrandt's great interest in the story of Tobias. When I thanked Professor Joshua Bruyn, the senior scholar at the RRP, for his help in enabling me to acquire *Rembrandt's Father*, he gave me a very strange look, and I really felt like giving him a great big hug. But what of the poor seller?

Another benefit is the light that Rembrandt studies have thrown on Jan Lievens. Until recently, the accepted wisdom has been that Lievens was almost a Rembrandt student, a painter *"im Schatten Rembrandts"*. All one has to do is to stand in one spot in the National Gallery in Ottawa and look at two works, a large Lievens of *Job* and a large Rembrandt of *Esther* (RRP A64), painted at about the same time, and ask which is the better work. There is no doubt it is the one by Lievens, a great artist. Of course, Rembrandt influenced Lievens, but the influence applied the other way also. Grudgingly, the RRP panel has come to the same conclusion, and in Volume II they re-examine RRP A32, the portrait of *Rembrandt's Mother* at Windsor Castle, at first attributed to Rembrandt, and now rightly acknowledge it as a work by Lievens.

Another portrait of *Rembrandt's Mother* (plate 14) by Jan Lievens, in my own collection, shows what a great colorist Lievens was; someone, long ago, added Rembrandt's monogram, but I certainly do not need that to enhance the painting's value in my eyes. So far, I have purchased seven paintings by Lievens and sent three of them to Queen's University. Depending on my mood, I am fondest of my *Rembrandt's Mother*, or that dour old man *Jacob Junius* (plate 7) painted some thirty years later. Lievens "in the shadow of Rembrandt", the shadow was only in our minds!

My two favorite kinds of acquisition have been Biblical subjects by Rembrandt students, and truly great works by as yet unidentified artists. As Isabel and I wrote in the introduction to a catalog of paintings given to Queen's University:

"In the field of art so many collectors and particularly museums are often influenced in their purchases by the name of the artist rather than the beauty of the work involved. An ugly Renoir is worth many thousands of dollars; a beautiful unsigned and unattributed painting of the same period may be impossible to sell, at least to a museum. The signature of Renoir, one hopes, guarantees authenticity, and that may be more important to an acquisition committee and to many a collector than beauty, which is so difficult to measure. That is where collectors like us have a chance. We have always tried to buy on quality only, preferring unattributed paintings in the hope that in time art historians will discover the artist. We will die with many such puzzles in our estate—things of beauty that challenge and tantalize, and with many more paintings to which the right names have come during our ownership."

Among the most beautiful puzzles in our collection are two Biblical works and one portrait of a young girl (plate 15). I first saw *Joseph and the Baker* (plate 10), attributed by Professor Sumowski to Johann Ulrich Mayr, when it was in the collection of Morris Kaplan, a Chicago attorney. I fell in love with it on first sight, and on successive visits to Mr Kaplan, made higher and higher offers. Mr Kaplan always declined, saying it was his favorite painting and not for sale. After his death, most of his collection was sent to Sotheby's in London, and in the 1968 sale catalog this wonderful painting was not even illustrated. No one was much interested in unattributed

Rembrandt school paintings in those days, and I was able to buy it for £2600, a small fraction of the price I had offered Mr Kaplan. Rembrandt taught his students how to depict communication between people. "Three days from now you will be dead!" Joseph's words to the baker (Genesis 40, 19) could not have been described more intensely. The subject was painted often by Rembrandt students, but as far as I know, this artist, I believe from Delft around 1650, was the only one to represent just the baker. The butler would distract from the intensity of the scene.

The second Biblical painting (plate 12) is as great a puzzle. In the collection of the Earls Spencer at Althorp, this *Angel Appearing to Hagar* (Genesis 16, 8) was attributed to Domenico Fetti. I rather think it is Dutch, *circa* 1620, and when I again see such beautifully painted shot silk, I may have found the artist. It is indicative of the spirit of the Bible that the first time an angel appeared to man after the expulsion from Eden, it was to a fugitive Egyptian slave. When I showed a transparency to our friend Christopher Brown, the curator of the National Gallery in London, he told me that he had very bad news for me. "This has been a Spencer painting since the 17th century, and you will not get an export license." To which I could reply that I did not need one; Lady Spencer, the Princess of Wales' stepmother, had sold this painting so cheaply that no export license was needed.

At first, I bought only Dutch and Flemish 17th century paintings, but gradually art historian friends caused me to reconsider this policy. One was Ulrich Middeldorf, another was Anthony Clark, whom I met by chance. When an elderly Viennese collector in Washington wanted to sell his paintings, I bought the Dutch old masters, but wondered who might be interested in buying the large Batoni of a pope receiving the French ambassador. I took counsel with Wolfgang Stechow, who suggested Tony Clark, long the director of the Minneapolis Institute of Art, who was delighted to purchase it directly from the owner for $12,000, which he suggested was a great deal fairer than the $4000 the owner was asking. Tony's specialty was 18th century Roman art, but his knowledge and background as a painter made him enthusiastic about art of all periods. I have also kept his many letters, which I still enjoy reading. People like Stechow and Clark bring so much to their institutions, and there must be thousands of great works in museums because art historians like them have been so helpful to collectors.

Late one December I visited Tony in Minneapolis and told him that, because it was he who had kindled my interest in Italian paintings, I wanted to give Minneapolis a large Dosso Dossi (plate 16), the Italian work in my collection which he liked best. Tony's face fell and he said, "Don't do that. I have just been fired by the museum and am going to the Metropolitan. The Dosso will look equally good there." I soon realized that he was not well treated in New York either, and he took time off to study in Rome, where he died of a heart attack.

When I first saw the Dosso, it was one of a pair with a very curious dealer in Tel Aviv. Mr Rosner had no gallery but sold paintings from his one-room apartment, where perhaps fifty paintings were stacked under and beside the bed. I wanted to buy the pair, but he said "No, you'll pay me so much ($3,000) for one that I will not need to sell both." So I picked one of the Dossos and also a much less expensive 18th century landscape, and asked Mr Rosner to ship both seafreight from Haifa and to insure the landscape for $1000 and the Dosso for $10,000. I was worried when I received the shipping papers, showing the landscape insured for $10,000 and the Dosso for $1000. But Mr Rosner soon reassured me, "Both are in one box, and if the ship sinks, you'll get $11,000. I had to get export licenses, and when those bureaucrats in Jerusalem thought that an American had paid $10,000 for that landscape, I got the license right away. Renaissance paintings they don't understand and valued at only $1000, why worry?" The Dosso is now much admired at Queen's University.

The other art historian who sparked my interest in Italian art was Benedict Nicolson, the editor of *The Burlington Magazine*. We spent only one or two evenings a year together, meeting at his home, and then having supper at a simple Italian restaurant nearby and talking about my recent acquisitions. He was interested in art in all its forms, and had written the definitive books on Terbrugghen, Georges de La Tour, the followers of Caravaggio and Wright of Derby. He was a great wordsmith, and many of his editorials in *The Burlington* still echo in my mind. I always looked forward to his help, which was given with such enthusiasm and bolstered by his encyclopedic knowledge. I well remember one evening in 1974. I had just come to London from Holland, where Han Jüngeling had sold me a *St Jerome Working by Candlelight* (plate 17), perhaps by Abraham Bloemaert. I had no photograph, and so had to describe the painting to Benedict, verbally. As he listened, his eyes lit up and he said, "There is a print of just that subject by Cornelis Bloemaert after a long lost work of his father, Abraham." Within minutes, he showed me a photograph of the print, and the puzzle was solved. I still own that long lost work. He and Efim Schapiro lived only a few blocks apart. They were as different as chalk and cheese, yet both loved paintings, and I miss them.

Astrid and Christian Tümpel are art historians with interests parallel to mine, especially the subjects of Rembrandt and the Bible. I first heard of their work from Egbert Haverkamp-Begemann, who spoke of the interesting insights Christian had into the iconography of Biblical paintings, many of which were clearly wrongly described in auction catalogs and even in museums. I met them first in 1975 when they were returning from Sacramento to Hamburg, where Christian was a Lutheran pastor. He and Astrid had written the catalog for an exhibition of pre-Rembrandtist paintings being held in the E B Crocker Art Gallery. It was the first pre-Rembrandtist exhibition ever, and although I was unable to see it myself, I was very impressed by the catalog and was delighted when the Tümpels accepted my invitation to visit us in Milwaukee.

Christian was writing a book on Rembrandt, which was published in 1977 by Rowohlt in Germany, and Astrid soon wrote the authoritative work on Pieter Lastman, Rembrandt's teacher in Amsterdam. Since that visit, we have spent many happy hours with them, discussing paintings and puzzling iconographies. We felt it was a pity that Christian's book was not available in English, for he had some new and insightful thoughts on the master's works, so Isabel and I spent many hundreds of hours translating it into English. Sadly for us, Christian was later persuaded by Mercatorfonds, his new publisher in Antwerp, to expand the book greatly, adding several chapters and giving his opinion about the authenticity of paintings then attributed to Rembrandt. We did not have the time to translate these additional chapters, and the publisher engaged a professional to finish the work, which took several years to complete. Mercatorfonds delayed publication of the English version and then unfortunately mixed up Christian's scheme for indicating which of the paintings he considered autograph and which were workshop. By the time it finally did appear, the first of the volumes on the works of Rembrandt by the Rembrandt Research Project had already been printed, and a whole new and comprehensive presentation of the master's works was being prepared for English-speaking art historians. Perhaps it would have been better if Christian had left decisions of authenticity to the committee and had offered his little book in English in the early eighties when there was a real scarcity of new works on Rembrandt.

It may be that Christian had difficulties similar to mine in deciding between professions, except that I never had any doubt that my life's work was to be a chemist helping chemists. Even now that I have become an art dealer, I still try to help chemists, whereas Christian left the ministry, and he and Astrid moved to Nijmegen where he accepted a professorship in art history at the university. While her health permitted it, Astrid worked as curator of a museum nearby, and while continuing to write, the Tümpels have mounted some fine exhibitions of Biblical paintings of Rembrandt and his school.

Of course, we have come to know many younger art historians as well. Some seem more interested in the sociology and the hidden meanings of art than in connoisseurship, but I am confident that some will develop into historians of the stature of Wolfgang Stechow.

My close connection with the Queen's Art Centre began in 1967 when

Frances Smith asked whether I would consider donating a painting to the Agnes Etherington Art Centre. I was pleased to be asked and felt that Queen's would be a good home for the *Salvator Mundi* that had belonged to my grandfather. An early 16th century Italian painting, it did not really fit into my own collection, and from then on Queen's became the "home" of choice for beautiful paintings which I could not pass up, but knew were not really for me. When David McTavish began teaching art history there in 1973, I realized his competence and real love of old masters, and my ties with art and art history at Queen's strengthened.

David's specialty is 16th century Italian drawings, but his interests are wide-ranging and his enthusiasm infectious to students and friends alike. In 1986 the Art Gallery of Ontario lured him away to become its curator of European art, and Queen's was lucky to be able to persuade him to return and to become head of the Department of Art in 1989.

David eventually had the unenviable job of being both chairman of Art and director of the Art Centre at Queen's. He has worked hard to establish a PhD program in art history and if he succeeds in his second goal, building a larger art museum, his great efforts will have been particularly worthwhile. To me, the PhD program was the more important goal, because together with the good department of conservation, a strong Canadian collection and the old masters we have already given to the university, it would establish Queen's as the best art history department in Canada. We have come a long way from my student days when there was neither an art history program nor an art gallery at Queen's. The present Agnes Etherington Art Centre is so small that it could not possibly house our entire collection. Of course, some people must have asked the question we have asked ourselves: if we can give Queen's £6,000,000 to buy a castle—the story of which I shall tell later in this book—why not a similar sum for an art museum? The castle seemed like a unique opportunity, whereas there are museums that could house our entire collection without additional building, and it is not our style to spend many millions building a museum. We have nevertheless given Queen's the funds for a chair in Northern art history and US$2,000,000 as seed money for the museum; and, if that cannot proceed, I am sure that they will find another good use for our donation.

Two other younger friends are Bill Robinson and Volker Manuth. I first met Bill when he was working towards a PhD at Harvard University under Seymour Slive, one of America's great teachers. I have always been fond of Harvard's Fogg museum because I had my first lessons in art history there under Jakob Rosenberg, and I have tried to keep in contact with the Dutch specialists there. In 1977 Bill started working on Nicolaes Maes, a Rembrandt student in the 1640s. That was a really difficult task, because Maes started as a really good history and genre painter but eventually developed into a rather repetitive painter of seemingly innumerable fashionable stilted portraits. The difficulty never seemed to faze Bill, but I think he has given up the idea of writing a *catalogue raisonné* of Maes' works. He is one of the most gentle and helpful people I know. How many other art historians ever pick up the phone to recommend a collector to consider a particular painting coming up at auction? I was saddened when the Morgan Library took him to New York and happy when he returned to Harvard as the Fogg's curator of drawings.

I can only imagine what Wolfgang Stechow was like in his thirties, but in my mind's eye I see him as very much like Volker Manuth. Volker's first interest was in Dutch Biblical paintings, which were my first love as well. He started with the works of Jan Victors and then concentrated on Gerbrand van den Eeckhout, one of Rembrandt's best students, who became his master's good friend. Volker got his PhD at the Free University of Berlin, where he then became a lecturer. We first met when he offered to come to Stuttgart to spend an afternoon and evening with us and Werner Sumowski. I did not know what to expect when I met this somewhat intense bearded man in the Stuttgart museum, but by the evening I hoped that we would become close friends—which indeed we have.

Volker has a very good eye for quality, makes attributions cautiously and sensibly and takes a great deal of time to help others. The Rembrandt Research Project has asked him to work with them on a part-time basis—a great honor for any non-Dutch art historian, particularly a German, especially since he was the first non-Dutch person to be asked. We were happy when he accepted Queen's offer of the Bader Chair in Art History, to begin in 1995.

Egbert Haverkamp-Begemann, originally Dutch, one of America's best teachers of art history, invited Volker to spend a few months at the Institute of Fine Arts in New York in 1991, and I would venture to say that students at the Institute learned as much from Volker as he learned there. Egbert is one of the world's most widely travelled scholars and hates to miss any important exhibition. He comes to the Midwest occasionally and we love showing him our new acquisitions. It was really in his honor that we established the fellowships for students at the Institute. Egbert tried to bring a Czech art historian out of Czechoslovakia to study in New York during the Communist régime. Although she was denied permission, it gave us the idea of establishing travelling fellowships in the Czech Republic, now that it is free. Recently Egbert became a member of the Rembrandt Research Project, surely the apex of a distinguished career, and is happy to be back in Holland at least part-time.

My relationship with the Milwaukee Art Museum has been up and down and essentially disappointing. Edward Dwight became the director of the Art Center, as it was then called, in 1955 and was the first director I got to know well. I liked him immensely. He was a sensitive, kind, soft-spoken man, and knowledgeable, particularly about American 18th century paintings. He organized some great exhibitions, one of the Peale family for instance, of great American still life painters. Unfortunately, he made one public and one private "mistake" which so embittered his life here that he left, or perhaps was asked to leave, in 1962. The public "mistake" was to purchase a large and beautiful *St Francis* by Zurbaran in Mexico for $60,000. He was repeatedly and sharply attacked by the Milwaukee daily papers for spending so much money for such a painting. In fact, it was a fine purchase, but Ed was too sensitive to shrug off the criticism.

The private "mistake" was a clash with Eliot Fitch, a Milwaukee banker, member of the Art Center's board of trustees and chairman of its acquisition committee. I remember attending an auction at Parke Bernet in New York where a 16th or 17th century depiction of a man counting money was sold for $600. It was in poor condition with a great deal of later overpaint and so $600 struck me as a high price; I speculated, somewhat prophetically, that a banker must have bought it. A few weeks later, Ed Dwight asked me to visit his office to give my opinion of a proposed donation to the Art Center. And there was that painting! Mr Fitch had bought it, obtained a local appraisal for $15,000 and wanted to give it to the Art Center. Of course I told Ed what I knew, and Ed objected to the gift, but Mr Fitch as chairman of the acquisition committee forced its acceptance and Ed left to become director of the museum in Utica. His departure was a real loss to the Art Center. I do not think the painting was ever exhibited there, but it was given on loan to the Milwaukee Public Museum, where it probably is still in storage. A couple of years later an IRS agent asked me about several donations, this among them; I again related the facts, and the value of the donation was reduced from $15,000 to $5000.

Ed's successor was Tracy Atkinson, a pleasant, straightforward man who knew his limitations as an art historian. I felt very comfortable with him, and since by then I had a little more free time, I became even more involved with the Art Center, donating some thirty paintings, mostly old masters, and I undertook to curate an exhibition "The Bible through Dutch Eyes" in the spring of 1976. Tracy thought I might have great difficulty borrowing old masters from museums, yet every one of the sixteen museums I approached was helpful. The National Gallery of Canada loaned their *Job*, probably Jan Lievens' greatest work, and the exhibition was particularly strong in the works of Rembrandt's students. The purpose was not to emphasize the works of individual artists, but to illustrate how well the Dutch in the 17th century studied and understood the Bible. Rabbi David Shapiro and many art historians helped in the preparation of the catalog, which was dedicated to the memory of Wolfgang Stechow. Unfortunately the Art Center ordered only 2000 catalogs, which sold quickly. When we wanted more, the printer told us that the plates had been thrown out; the Art Center had never before reordered any catalog.

Tracy Atkinson left Milwaukee that summer to become the director of the Wadsworth Atheneum in Hartford, a move that surprised me because the museum has one of America's great old master collections, and Tracy knew relatively little about old masters.

I hoped that our growing collection would end up in the Milwaukee Art Center, recently renamed Milwaukee Art Museum. While I had not been asked to join the board of trustees—surely because I was too critical—my rapport with the directors and the staff was good, and it seemed to me to be the logical destination: I had built Aldrich and become wealthy in Milwaukee, and had formed my collection there. The director from 1977 to 1984, Gerald Nordland, changed my thinking.

Often when I found a painting that I thought would fit into the museum's collection, I bargained with the seller as hard as I could and then gave the museum a check for the purchase, avoiding hassles with the IRS. There was then no need for an appraisal. Shortly after Dr Nordland became director, I found a beautiful early work on slate by Leonard Bramer, in fine condition, for only $7000. Leonard Bramer was a Delft artist; I already owned three of his works and the fourth, a *Denial of St Peter*, would be a great addition to our museum. Dr Nordland disagreed however: "$7000 for a small, dark painting?" he questioned. Why, for that we could buy a good modern work!" I am really sorry that his total lack of interest in old masters on this very first encounter precluded my involvement with the museum for the next seven years, and changed my mind about the destination of our collection.

In 1985 Dr Nordland was succeeded by Russell Bowman, who was also more knowledgeable about modern works, but without Nordland's disdain for old masters. Our Art Museum recently spent over $1,000,000 for a work by Jasper John—money given specifically for a modern painting. I do wish it had the funds to hire a curator of the many fine old master paintings it possesses. A good curator could make such a difference and help the growth of that section of its collection.

Milwaukee has three other public collections of paintings. The most ambitious is that of the Haggerty Museum at Marquette University, with many paintings housed in a fine building. Two of its curators, Barry Hannegan and Jane Goldsmith, for whom we had a high regard, were asked to leave after only a year. The Milwaukee Public Museum is excellent in many areas, but so many of its paintings just gather dust in storage, as do many of those among the fewer paintings at the museum of

ART HISTORIANS

Ulrich Middeldorf.

Walther Bernt.

Wolfgang Stechow.

Egbert Haverkamp-Begemann.

ART HISTORIANS

Anthony Clark.

David McTavish.

William Robinson.

Werner Sumowski.

Otto Naumann.

Volker Manuth.

PLATE 1: Paulus de Lesire, *The Quillcutter*. Our first painting on a catalog cover, 1967.

Right PLATE 2: Rembrandt van Rijn, *Portrait of Johannes Uyttenbogaert*, 1633.

PLATE 3: Jacob Cornelisz van Oostsaanen, *Crucifixion*, 1507.

PLATE 4: *Lamentation*, German, *c.*1510.

PLATE 5: *Man Surprised*, believed to be a portrait of Adriaen Brouwer.

PLATE 6: Hendrick Terbrugghen, *Mary Weeping*, *c.*1625.

PLATE 7: Jan Lievens, *Jacob Junius*, *c.*1660.

PLATE 8: Gerbrandt van den Eeckhout, *Rest on the Flight to Egypt*, 1653.

PLATE 9: Rudolf von Alt, *St Vitus's Cathedral in Prague*, 1850.

PLATE 10: Rembrandt student, *Joseph and the Baker*, c.1650.

PLATE 11: Attributed to Jan de Bray, *Portrait of a Girl*.

PLATE 12: *Angel Appearing to Hagar*, Dutch, c.1620.

PLATE 13: Rembrandt van Rijn, *Portrait of his Father*, *c*.1629.

PLATE 14: Jan Lievens, *Rembrandt's Mother*, *c*.1629.

PLATE 15: *Portrait of a Girl*, Dutch, *c*.1640.

PLATE 16: Dosso Dossi, *A Learned Man of Antiquity*, *c*.1535.

PLATE 17: Abraham Bloemaert, *St Jerome Working by Candlelight*.

PLATE 18: Jan van Noordt, *Joseph Selling Grain in Egypt*.

PLATE 20: Jan de Corduba, *Still Life*.

PLATE 19: Michael Sweerts, *Self-portrait*.

PLATE 21: Pieter Claesz, *Still Life*, 1646.

PLATE 22: Cornelis van Poelenburgh, *St Christopher.*

PLATE 23: Jacob van Ruisdael, *Coup de Soleil*, c.1670.

PLATE 24: Jacob van Ruisdael, *Winter Landscape*, c.1660.

PLATE 25: Rembrandt student, *St Jerome*, *c*.1630.

PLATE 26: Artist unknown, *Head of a Young Man*.

PLATE 28: Abraham van Dyck, *The Widow of Zarephath and Her Son*.

PLATE 27: Domenico Fetti, *Jacob's Dream*. *Right* Collector's seal.

PLATE 29: Rembrandt student, *Hendrickje Stoffels as Venus with Cupid*, c.1650.

PLATE 30: Constantijn Verhout, *Portrait of a Brewer*, c.1660.

The Laboratory, a publication of the Fisher Scientific Company.

PLATE 31: Cornelis Bega, *The Alchemist*, c.1660.

Dedicated to Professor Robert Burns Woodward on his sixtieth birthday.

PLATE 32: *Aldrichimica Acta* dedicated to R B Woodward, 1977.

Above right PLATE 33: Rembrandt School, *Head of an Old Man, c.*1660.

Right Dr Efim Schapiro, *c.*1970.

PLATE 34: *The Good Samaritan*, believed to be Dutch, *c.*1640.

JOHN WHALLEY

PLATE 36: *Linda with Matthew* (pencil).

PLATE 35: *Farm Scale* (tempera).

PLATE 37: *Still Life with Jug* (oil).

Barry Young, Isabel, Linda and John.

Isabel in Bexhill. The freckles are still there.

With Isabel's mother, Stella Overton.

Isabel with my sister Marion.

Surface-cleaning an old painting with
Carlos Seoane, Jr.

An Aldrich party with Marilyn
Hassmann, to my right, and Delores
Menehan, to Isabel's left.

In our new gallery.

Michael Hatcher.

With Vladimir Matous at Milotice Castle.

With Vera Bader Weber, her son and
grandson at Milotice.

AT MY SEVENTIETH BIRTHDAY PARTY

Above With Bill Schield and Marvin Klitsner.

Above right With Jane Furchgott and Charles Munch, standing, Marvin and Jane Klitsner, and Gloria and Leonard Parker.

Below Helena with her two proud grandfathers, 1994.

Below At Daniel and Linda's wedding, 1994.

Below right At David and Michelle's wedding, 1992.

AT HERSTMONCEUX CASTLE

With knights.

With Isabel, Agnes Benidickson, and David and Mary Smith, leaving in a landau.

Left Under the Queen's flag (photo. Eleanor Bantell).

Below David Smith.

the University of Wisconsin, Milwaukee. We really like Milwaukee, but not its art scene.

I have tried to share my love of paintings with others, and there are several serious collectors of old master paintings in Milwaukee whose collections I have helped to build. Many chemists have listened to my talks on art restoration and one, at Eli Lilly, became an impassioned collector and art historian as a result. Lee Howard started as a physical chemist at Lilly in Indianapolis and was then promoted to be a manager at Lilly's plant in Clinton, Indiana. Lee's first love was American and English portraits of the 19th and early 20th century, and he now has a distinguished collection. He also became very interested in Indiana artists. I have never understood why the artists of some American states—Indiana and California, for instance—are so much more appreciated than those of other states.

In 1969 the Milwaukee Auction Galleries sold many paintings from the estate of John L Lewis, the head of the United Mine Workers of America Union, among which was a beautiful water color by an Indiana artist, Otto Stark. I knew next to nothing about Stark, but Lee Howard bought the watercolor from me and began to study the artist's work. This culminated in Lee acting as guest curator of a scholarly Stark exhibition at the Indianapolis Museum of Art in 1977. That exhibition showed the artist's skill so clearly that today his works bring many thousands of dollars.

Pat and Lee Howard also appreciate John Whalley's work and helped the Sheldon Swope Art Museum in Terre Haute mount a Whalley exhibition in 1988. Many collectors are mesmerized by artists' names and fame. The Howards really look for quality. They loved a group of works by Richard Andriessen (1865-1910), an American who studied in Munich but was totally unknown. I bought my first fine *Torso of a Male* by the artist in an antique store in Cincinnati. The dealer's assurance that it was Spanish 17th century was laughable, and I was delighted to find a large group of Andriessens, including many strong portrait drawings in a Cincinnati flea-market.

Lee's decision to concentrate on studying and dealing in art when he retired from Lilly really pleased me. He is such fun to work with that I was happy to trade my Andriessens with him for two old master paintings. He recently mounted a travelling exhibition of over thirty Andriessens and prepared a catalog for the Indiana University Art Museum in 1991. Seldom has an exhibition of non-Dutch 17th century paintings given me such pleasure, and this fine artist's works are at last becoming better known.

Isabel has pointed out that my first purchase and sale of a Rembrandt was important to me after my dismissal from Sigma-Aldrich, to prove my ability in the art field also; but I have always enjoyed finding really good works of art, often by quite unknown artists, buying them for very little and selling them inexpensively to friends like the Howards.

I am addicted to antique stores and auctions. When I came to Milwaukee in 1950, I was delighted to find Al Schrager, an enthusiastic and totally honest auctioneer, running the Milwaukee Auction Galleries. Al was a small, slight young man who had begun his career in the auction business in the 1930s as an employee of a local house, the Wall Auction Gallery. He had come up through all the collecting, carting, sorting of everything from junk to beautiful furniture, paintings and objects d'art, and was fascinated by the business. He had seen all sorts of shady dealings, and determined that if he ever owned his own galleries, he would run a strictly honest shop. I have spent some wonderful hours in his gallery in search of good paintings that I could buy for a song in the early days, if I was lucky.

Al always disliked reserves and gave no price estimates in his catalogs. That certainly made for more exciting auctions. The great burden of modern auction houses is the high reserves demanded by sellers. Consequently thousands of pieces are bought back, cluttering and depressing the market. Al avoided all that, but he was lured to California in 1973 and the MAG changed hands, location and commercial practices.

One of these changed practices led to an interesting hassle. It happens fairly often, sometimes several times in one auction, that after the hammer falls, a bidder who has been overlooked speaks up and the auctioneer reopens the bidding. Under the new management, bidding was sometimes reopened on a lot that had been sold an hour or two earlier. This caused great consternation and anger to the first buyer. In fact, the conditions of sale in the auction catalog included the clause, ". . . the auctioneer, in his discretion, may re-offer and resell the article in dispute at any time prior to the conclusion of the session," but the logical conclusion to this illogical condition was that every buyer had better stay to the very end of the auction lest his purchase be re-offered.

Early one evening in 1980, I bid on a fine collection of art books, and the auctioneer recognized me as the buyer, for $700. I left the gallery to get a soft drink when someone hurried out to tell me that my lot was being re-auctioned. A bidder claimed to have been overlooked and bidding had been reopened. I rushed back and joined in. I had to bid, no matter how high, for if someone else bought the lot, I would have two parties to fight. So long as I bought it myself, my argument would only be with the auction house. The difference was $1100 and Mrs Janice Kuhn, the president of the MAG, unswayed by the unfairness of this practice, insisted that those were her conditions. The case came before the Circuit Court of Milwaukee County. Unfortunately Marvin Klitsner could not plead for me, as his law firm had done some work for the

MAG, but Craig Zirbel, a young attorney just out of law school, agreed to take my case on a contingency basis and did an excellent job. The auction gallery was represented by Quarles & Brady, one of Milwaukee's prestigious law firms, which pointed to the gallery's clearly stated conditions. Craig Zirbel pointed to the illogic of these conditions and, in a beautifully brief decision, Judge Patrick Sheedy agreed with us. After the verdict, Mrs Kuhn made two surprising statements. "You wouldn't have sued me," she said, "if I were a man." Little did she know me. The second was: "I will pay if you will agree not to have the decision recorded. Otherwise I will appeal." I had of course sued in order to get the decision recorded so that there would be a clear precedent for the future. The decision was recorded, the gallery paid and there was no appeal. Mrs Kuhn considered briefly not allowing me to bid in her auctions, but her attorneys wisely counselled against this. The business developed other problems, such as not being able to pay consignors, and the MAG had to close.

The fun goes out of an auction when you are not happy with the way it is run, and I was not alone in remembering wistfully the days when Al Schrager had been in charge. What pleasure we had when Al and his charming wife and partner, Bonnie, returned to Milwaukee in 1985 to open a new auction house, the Schrager Auction Galleries. Quiet and unassuming, now white haired, but still wearing his jaunty bow tie and his impish smile, Al is again providing a wonderful service to people in and outside the state, both to those who have goods to sell and to those who are addicted to the hunt for hidden treasures.

My enjoyment of paintings has taken me searching in beautiful estates and tiny garrets, into great auction houses and flea-markets. I love discoveries, not only of material value, but of great beauty. And getting to know the people involved in art has enriched my life.

18

Trophies of the Hunt

Walther Rathenau, the statesman of the German Weimar Republic, is reported to have said that any Jew who claims to enjoy hunting is a liar. Well, I could not bring myself to hunt animals, yet I have been a hunter all my life, in my ABCs—in Art, Bible and Chemistry.

I have scoured the world for chemicals to add to the Aldrich catalog, and for collections of research samples for my other ABC, the Alfred Bader Chemical Library.

I have searched for Biblical commentaries for pure enjoyment, for use in teaching and for help in understanding the iconography of many Dutch 17th century paintings.

I am never happier than when hunting for dirty old paintings that might be hidden treasures. The following brief descriptions are of eighteen trophies of my hunt in the world of art.

1. *The "Foggy Girl"*[1,2] *attributed to Jan de Bray* (plate 11)
In November 1967, I flew from Chicago to London on my way to Brussels for a meeting with our friends at Janssen, but that Thursday morning we were fogged-in at Heathrow and told that there would be no flights leaving for Brussels that day. Naturally, I took the tube into central London to see what the next day's sale of old master paintings at Christie's had to offer. There I saw this beautifully sensitive *Portrait of a Girl*, marred only by a foggy varnish, and I have thought of her as my "foggy girl" ever since.

The next year the Paine Art Center in Oshkosh asked me to act as curator of an exhibition of Dutch 17th century paintings, and I put her onto the cover of the catalog with this description:

"The portrait of the girl depicted on the cover of this catalog is a thing of great beauty, exceptionally broadly painted, lit from the right (which is uncommon in Dutch paintings), a girl obviously plain and yet charming. Valentiner thought her to be Hendrickje Stoffels, Rembrandt's mistress, by Barent Fabritius. At the Netherlands Institute for Art History (the RKD) in The Hague it is given to Jan de Bray; other art historians have suggested Willem Drost. It matters a great deal to the commercial value of this painting, were it to be sold, but not one iota to its intrinsic beauty."

The attribution to Jan de Bray was first made by Dr S J Gudlaugsson, the Director of the RKD, and was confirmed by Wolfgang Stechow. Recently, Professor Sumowski has published it as a work by Hendrick Heerschop, which I find difficult to understand.

2. *Joseph Selling Grain in Egypt*[2] *by Jan van Noordt* (plate 18)

The Galerie Fischer in Lucerne holds two major auctions of old master paintings annually, in June and November, and my trips to European chemists were often planned around these Friday afternoon auctions.

In June 1964 I purchased what seemed to me a very strange and exciting painting that Fischer had called *The Counting of the Children in Bethlehem*, attributed to Rembrandt's last student, Aert de Gelder. I could not recall any such counting, and I was certain that the painting was not by de Gelder. Although quite large, it was frameless and easily carried on the night train to Florence. I was anxious to show it to Professor Middeldorf the next morning. Ulrich agreed that I had certainly bought a fine and exciting work, but he thought it might be later than 17th century, closer to Venetian artists like the Tiepolos, or perhaps even early 19th century. Like me, he was sure it had nothing to do with the counting of children in Bethlehem. The subject of the painting remained a fascinating puzzle for a couple of years. At first I wondered if it might depict King Solomon and the two babies, one dead and the other alive, in his famous judgment, but the rest of the figures did not quite fit: what were those almost Daumier-like people on the left doing in the scene? The answer came in an unexpected way. We very much enjoy going to synagogue on Saturdays, particularly to listen to the reading of the Torah. I had not thought of listening for art historical reasons, but one Sabbath when I heard the description of Joseph in Egypt (Genesis 42) with a white cloak and a gold chain, trading the Egyptians' children for the grain hoarded during the seven good years, the penny dropped. That was the scene depicted in my painting.

When I checked at the RKD in The Hague, I found that an eminent art historian, Dr Hans Schneider, had attributed this painting to Jan van Noordt, an Amsterdam artist in the middle of the 17th century, who was greatly influenced both by Rembrandt and his Flemish contemporaries. That attribution has been generally accepted. Dr Efim Schapiro owned a similarly exciting painting by van Noordt, *The Massacre of the Innocents*, which I bought and have since donated to Queen's University. I now have several other works by this amazingly versatile but little-known artist who foreshadowed the style of the 18th century. He certainly deserves a monograph.

3. *Self-portrait*[2,3] *by Michael Sweerts* (plate 19)

This is one of my most exciting acquisitions, one of the many fine paintings I first saw in the home of Dr Walther Bernt. He told me that he considered it a very fine portrait, and although he thought he knew who had painted it, he was not certain and would not tell me.

The owner was a dealer in Munich, Dr H Fetscherin, who had a gallery specializing mainly in those sweet story-telling, 19th century Munich school paintings. Fetscherin knew it was a fine work and thought it was by the Flemish portraitist, Pieter Franchoys.

I liked it very much and was happy to buy it because it reminded me of the famous self-portrait of the Flemish artist, Michael Sweerts, which I had seen at Oberlin College. The skull had been overpainted, probably by a Victorian who objected more to the finger poking into the skull's nasal cavity than to the skull itself. In the 17th century, skulls were used very often as symbols of the transitoriness of life.

The first thing I did on returning home with the painting cleaned was to send a photograph to Wolfgang Stechow, hoping he would confirm my suspicion that it was by Sweerts. After two weeks without a reply, I finally phoned him. "It is a fine portrait," he said. "Who painted it?" I replied that I had hoped he would confirm the attribution to Sweerts. A long silence followed until he said kindly, "Alfred, I can see what you mean. It is Flemish with Dutch overtones. It was painted about 1660. It is very intense. But you can't go around the world calling every intense Northern portrait Sweerts. That is not good art history." I asked his permission to send the portrait to Oberlin for direct comparison. Seldom has any communication given me more pleasure than an airmail, special delivery letter from Wolfgang, telling me that with the two portraits side by side, there was no doubt that the painting was indeed a self-portrait by Sweerts, and in some ways more characteristic than the one at Oberlin.

When I contacted Walther Bernt, he congratulated me, telling me that he had indeed believed that Sweerts was the artist, but that he had been reluctant to make so important an attribution lightly, and he was delighted that Professor Stechow had confirmed his belief.

I then wrote a brief article about the matter, which I sent to Benedict Nicolson for publication in *The Burlington Magazine*. He thought it a fine article, but could not accept it because he did not believe the attribution. I had planned to attend a conference on Caravaggio in Cleveland, and knew that he would be there also, so I took my painting with me. When Benedict saw it in his hotel room, he had only to look at it very briefly before assuring me that he would after all happily accept my article, which appeared in *The Burlington Magazine* in 1972.

Michael Sweerts was a very strange artist. Born in Flanders in 1624, he studied in Rome, returned north in the 1650s and worked for a time in Amsterdam. In 1662 he stopped painting and joined a Catholic mission to the Middle East. We know of a number of letters from the head of the mission to their bishop in Marseilles, complaining about the artist's deep depressions. He veered from a happy, outgoing man to a man deeply depressed. Of course, someone as confident as the painter portrayed in Oberlin and as concerned about the vanity of life as he appears in my portrait might not have been the easiest man to live with. The mission expelled him, and he travelled to Goa in India, where he died in 1664.

4. *Still Life by Jan de Corduba* (plate 20)

Generally, I prefer Biblical and historical paintings and portraits to landscapes and still lifes, but occasionally a still life really excites me. I have often urged Isabel to help me find a really good Willem Kalf, to me the "Rembrandt" among still life painters. His works are rare and often not in good condition. As I have explained, reputation is not all-important to me, however, and some years ago Han Jüngeling in The Hague offered me a still life by Jan de Corduba, which I really could not reject. I had never heard of Jan de Corduba and was surprised to learn that he was a Flemish artist who worked mainly in Vienna, for I had never seen any of his works as a boy; but then I had been looking for postage stamps.

The painting is an almost mystical vanitas with many of the common paraphernalia: a violin, playing cards, a calendar, music, a globe and of course a skull. What enchanted me was the composition. All the paraphernalia are crowded into the lower half in a triangle. The upper half is illuminated by a simple glittering oil lamp.

Time and again I have found that my son David shares my taste in paintings, and I was delighted when he told me proudly that he had recently discovered and purchased another still life by Jan de Corduba at an auction in New York.

5. *Still Life by Pieter Claesz* (plate 21)

My sister Marion, who has lived in England since 1949, in Burton-on-Trent, has sometimes wondered during my visits whether I had come to see her or the local antique dealers. I can hardly blame her for asking.

In 1954 I visited Mr Richards near the railway station, who told me that his house, just three blocks away, was full of paintings. Of course I invited myself to his home and saw many Victorian canvases in large crumbling frames. Most of them struck me as mere daubs, the sort of things that could be bought cheaply all over England. Above the couch in the living room, however, hung a beautiful, albeit dirty, Dutch still life. I asked about its value, and Mr Richards told me that several dealers had offered him £30 to 40 for it. I said that I would be happy to pay £100, but his face fell as he explained: "I recently married my second wife, and she's much younger than I am and so I have to be careful and, darn it, I gave her the painting as a wedding gift. But did you say £100?"

He called Nora, his wife, and reminded her that he had paid only £12 to the previous owner. She insisted that it was a wedding gift and not for sale. Then Mr Richards had a brilliant idea: "Nora, ever since we got married you have been bugging me to buy you a washup. Why don't you take the £100 and buy your blooming washup?" So I traded this beautiful still life by Pieter Claesz, monogrammed and dated 1646, for a kitchen sink.

6. *St Christopher by Cornelis van Poelenburgh* (plate 22)
Professor Middeldorf suggested during one of my visits to Florence that I consider buying the little moonlight scene with St Christopher from the widow of a well-known art historian, G J Hoogewerff, who had attributed it to Adam Elsheimer. Indeed, Elsheimer did paint such a composition, probably on copper, but it has long been lost, although it was recorded in an etching by Wallerant Vaillant. Like many artists, Poelenburgh must have been fascinated by Elsheimer's little gems, and painted this scene at least twice. The Amsterdam dealer, Pieter de Boer, owned one version.

When I returned from Florence, I showed my panel to Professor Horst Gerson, then at the RKD in The Hague. He looked at it most carefully and said that he would like to compare it with de Boer's version and arranged for us to meet at the Singer Museum in Laren, for direct comparison. I liked both versions, so different in tonality. Mr de Boer thought his version better, pointing to a monogram on his which was absent from mine. Gerson's comment reassured me: "Some paintings need monograms." Horst Gerson liked his witticisms. I remember a dealer once asking his opinion of a mediocre painting. When Gerson turned up his nose, the dealer apologized, "I can't bring you only first-class works; sometimes I am curious even about second- or third-rate ones." To which Gerson replied, "I wouldn't mind if you brought me third-rate works, but when they are tenth-rate, I get discouraged."

In fact, I really liked both de Boer's silvery and my own golden version which I was able to compare again in a more leisurely fashion in the great Elsheimer exhibition in Frankfurt in 1966. Monet was not the first artist to depict similar scenes in different lights.

7 & 8. *Landscapes*[2,3] *by Jacob van Ruisdael* (plates 23 & 24)
The Dutch in the 17th century really excelled in landscapes but, strangely, I have never been particularly attracted by the works of the most popular landscape artists, van Goyen and Salomon van Ruysdael. They look so much alike to me. The greatest landscape painters were Jacob van Ruisdael, Philips Koninck and Hercules Seghers, and I am happy to have three totally different Ruisdaels and two Konincks in my collection. Only great good luck could add one of Seghers' magical masterpieces;

but then I had thought the same about Philips Koninck's long views until I bought my first at Christie's in London. So hope springs eternal.

I saw my first Jacob Ruisdael in 1960 in Dr Bernt's home in Munich where it had been sent by an Augsburg industrialist, W Grovermann. He had recently married, and his wife insisted that his many fine old masters be traded for impressionists. I felt sorry for him, but I was only too pleased to buy this romantic wooded landscape, which I so admired, for DM60,000. When I showed photographs to several art historians however I began to worry. They all said much the same, that it was a fine landscape but it was 18th century, and the signature must be a fake. I was really torn. I loved the work, and how could I hurt Dr Bernt who had written the expertise? What relief I felt when Professor Seymour Slive, the world expert on Ruisdael, called it a *"coup de soleil"* and assured me that it was a fine late work by the master.

My next van Ruisdael was one of his rare winter landscapes. When I saw it at Christie's in London, I thought of Wolfgang Stechow's words, written about another, very similar painting:

"There is nothing comparable with this in Dutch seventeenth-century landscapes; and outside of landscapes, only the deep gloom that spreads over a religious tragedy through the technical and colouristic discrepancies, Rembrandt's 'synthesis of the visible and the invisible' here inspired Ruisdael: the very fact that all outward, imitative features of such an 'influence' are missing, is eloquent, for this can be expected of the fruitful relationship between two very great artists.

"It is as though greatness in the interpretation of winter as a drama had been preserved for one single artist: Jacob van Ruisdael." *(Dutch Landscape Painting of the Seventeenth Century*, p. 97, Phaidon, London, 1966)

I find it hard to decide which of my Ruisdaels I like best. It really depends on my mood.

9. *St Jerome, Rembrandt Circle, c. 1630* (plate 25)

Shortly after Professor Sumowski's Volume V on Rembrandt students appeared, we spent a happy afternoon and evening looking through it with him. One of the very first paintings illustrated was a real surprise: a *St Jerome* described as "of exquisite quality" in the collection of Lewis G Nierman in Plantation, Florida. Naturally one of my first phone calls after returning to Milwaukee was to Lewis Nierman. I had no idea where Plantation was but the telephone operator knew. I told Mr Nierman that I liked the painting, and asked him to think of me if he ever wanted to sell it. He laughed and explained that he would be happy

233

to sell it; he was a retired paintings dealer from New York. "Make me an offer I can't refuse," he said. I replied that if he wanted $1,000,000, that it would be too much, but if he wanted $10,000, I would send him my check immediately. He laughed once again, "You are right. The price is in between." I urged him to think about it and promised to call him again in two weeks. We arrived at a satisfactory price, but when I offered to send my check, he suggested that I first see the painting because it looked very different from the illustration. Two days later it came by Federal Express and I liked it even better than the illustration.

But who had painted it? The relationship to Rembrandt is clear because in 1631 van Vliet did an etching after a lost Rembrandt closely related to this painting. There is also a much weaker copy in Aachen. The first artist who came to mind was Gerard Dou, but I had never seen a Dou quite so good; I do not really like his early works and was relieved when Ronni Baer, the Dou expert, reassured me that this was not by him. In any case, the painter's identity is a delightful puzzle.

So often in life, one good thing leads to another. Since that first purchase, we have visited Lewis Nierman whenever we are in Florida, and have bought a number of fine paintings from this sensitive and caring dealer.

10. *Portrait of a Girl,*[1] *Dutch, c.1640* (plate 15)
One painting that caused me a sleepless night was this portrait of a modest young girl by an unknown artist. We viewed the auction the day before the sale at Christie's in London, and both Isabel and I fell in love with her. We have many portraits of old men in our collection, and although many Dutch artists of the Golden Age painted children, this was the first time we had seen one so enchanting. Would other collectors be as affected as we were by her simple beauty? Would we be successful in securing her?

The sleepless night was forgotten in the thrill of being able to take her home. We cannot be sure where this portrait was painted. Certainly it was done in Holland about 1640, but by whom?

She is such a serious young girl, with her direct gaze and trusting eyes. What hours of pleasure we have spent with her, and we are delighted that all who see her are as captivated as we are. She graced the cover of the Aldrich catalog in 1990-1 and thousands of chemists shared our joy.

11. *Head of a Young Man,*[2,3] *artist unknown* (plate 26)
It is often easier to tell what a painting is not, than to decide what it is. When I bought this portrait of a boy from a Milwaukee dealer, I thought at first that it might be a Bolognese portrait, perhaps by Carracci, because it looked similar to one I had bought in Boston.

The previous owner, who had purchased it in an antique store in

Vienna in 1926, had obtained an expertise from a "pseudo expert" in New York, who had attributed it to the famous Dutch artist, Frans Hals. The painting was in fact exhibited as a Hals in the Milwaukee Art Center. When the owner died, the attorney for his estate wisely sent a photo to Seymour Slive, the world's real expert, who replied that it was not by Hals.

The portrait is in excellent condition and so intriguing, but who painted it, and where and when? Many of the world's ablest art historians have tried to answer this particular question and have come up with many different solutions, none of which is generally accepted. Some have suggested that it is indeed Bolognese, perhaps by Annibale Carracci or one of his brothers, about 1580 or 1590. Another eminent art historian was convinced that it was painted a little later by the Bolognese artist, Guercino, while still another scholar suggested that it is Roman, between Vouet and Bernini. There is a group of art historians who think that it is not Italian at all, but perhaps by a Dutch artist working in Italy about the middle of the 17th century. One suggestion has been the elusive Willem Drost when he was painting in Italy.

Will this wonderful puzzle ever be solved? I am sure it will, though perhaps not in our lifetime. Some day an art historian will look at it and point to another, signed work by the same artist, painted in exactly the same manner. Attribution will greatly enchance its commercial value but not its beauty. Even now it is clear that we each got a great bargain, the previous owner when he bought it in Vienna, and I about fifty years later in Milwaukee.

12. *Jacob's Dream*[2] by Domenico Fetti (plate 27)

Ever since the *Aldrichimica Acta* began, a painting—usually an old master—has been on the cover. This *Jacob's Dream* appeared on the 1982 *Acta* dedicated to Gilbert Stork.

When the painting came up for sale in April 1980, it was so covered by layers of dirty varnish that Christie's in London, who operate two auction galleries—one on King Street for better works and the other in Kensington for minor works—put it into the Kensington sale. It was attributed to one of the Carraccis. Cleaning revealed not only that the painting was in excellent condition, but that it was by Domenico Fetti, an artist who also worked early in the 17th century in Rome, Mantua and Venice. Fetti often produced several versions of a composition, and the best known one of this subject is in Vienna.

The painting had been sent to Christie's by its owner in Dorset, who had inherited it but knew nothing of its previous history, although it must have belonged to a collector whose seal is burnt three times into the back of the panel. I have not yet determined the identity of the seal, although I have tried.

The Bible is the book of dreams *par excellence*: dreams of individuals, dreams of a people, dreams of all mankind. It is surely no accident that the very first well-known dream in the Bible is not that of a king or of a general but of a man at the lowest point in his life, when he is homeless and hunted, yearning for God's promise that He would return him to his homeland.

The vision of a ladder with angels going up and down is unique in Biblical imagery, and *Jacob's Dream* has inspired many artists over the centuries. The Fetti is my favorite Italian painting in our collection.

13. *The Widow of Zarephath and Her Son*[2] *by Abraham van Dyck* (plate 28)

When I first saw this painting in Walther Bernt's living room, he told me that it had been attributed to Nicolaes Maes, but said he was certain that it was really by another, rarer Rembrandt student, Abraham van Dyck. After I purchased it, Jane Furchgott and Charles Munch cleaned it and Jane discovered Abraham van Dyck's signature. I used the painting on the cover of the catalog for the exhibition "The Bible through Dutch Eyes".

For a long time the painting had been called *Grace before a Meal*, but Christian Tümpel pointed out that it was really a *Herauslösung*, an isolation of one or two figures from a larger composition. Rembrandt and his students loved to paint such isolations. Indeed, in the museum in Copenhagen, there is another painting by the same artist which shows the third figure, Elijah, who has come to save the widow and her son from starvation. Van Dyck painted yet another version of the same scene, now in the Sarah Campbell Blaffer Foundation in Houston. The Copenhagen and the Houston paintings, certainly by the same hand, were attributed to other Rembrandt students, but the signature on mine assures that all three are by Abraham van Dyck. Surprisingly, he was also an excellent portraitist, and recently I acquired a fine signed and dated portrait of a woman. I know of several very similar portraits that have long been attributed to Rembrandt, and in time, Abraham van Dyck's work will be described in a monograph, illustrating his versatility.

14. *Hendrickje Stoffels as Venus with Cupid*[2,3] *by a Rembrandt student c.1650* (plate 29)

Should one ever buy a painting described by an experienced auction house as a copy after a well-known painting? The answer is, generally, no. Auction houses employ very competent professionals who want to describe their works as optimistically as possible to encourage bidding. However, they look at thousands of works each year, and occasionally miss real gems.

This painting was sold at Sotheby's in New York in 1988, described as a "copy of a work in the Louvre, formerly attributed to Rembrandt (see A Bredius, rev by H Gerson, *Rembrandt*, 1969, p 177)". The entry was illustrated by a mediocre black-and-white photograph, one of the few black-and-white illustrations in the lavishly produced catalog. Serious collectors were unlikely to give such an entry a second thought, I hoped.

My purchase of the work illustrates two interesting points of great potential value to connoisseurs. If the photograph of a painting looks better than the original, beware. If, on the other hand, the original looks much better than the photograph, as was the case here, then it may be a good painting. The second point concerns first impressions. To the real connoisseur, these are most important. Potential buyers are offered all sorts of paintings, often accompanied by glowing descriptions. If your first impression is bad, you are probably making a mistake if you try to convince yourself that the painting must be good because of its provenance or because it has been illustrated in many books.

In this case, I was surprised when I saw the painting; my first impression was excellent. Although it was covered by a thick, discolored varnish, enough of the fine, even craquelure was visible to assure me that it was a 17th century work. I knew the Louvre version well, and I looked carefully at this picture before the sale. A copy of an old auction catalog entry affixed to the back stated that the painting was signed but that the signature was hard to read and that the painting measured 122 x 100 cm. The painting offered at Sotheby's was 98.5 x 83 cm, and had clearly been cut down on all sides. I was the only bidder.

As I discuss this painting with many experts, the jigsaw puzzle is gradually taking form. Volker Manuth told me that the picture was sold twice in Berlin auctions in 1933, as by Ferdinand Bol. The information on the back came from the second of those auctions, so the painting must have been cut down after that, perhaps to facilitate getting it out of Germany.

We know that one of Rembrandt's creditors was Harmen Becker, a serious collector in Amsterdam. The inventory of his estate in 1678 lists one *Venus and Cupid* by Rembrandt hanging in the living room, and another, after Rembrandt, in the back hallway. How many other copies existed?

The attribution of the Louvre painting to Rembrandt has been questioned for some years, and Ferdinand Bol has been suggested as its author. The quality of my painting is high, but it looks closer to Willem Drost than Ferdinand Bol. Rembrandt scholars believe that several paintings long attributed to Rembrandt, for instance the *Polish Rider,* are really by Drost. His works will surely be studied in great detail and in time these mysteries will be solved. Jacques Foucart, curator of Dutch

237

paintings in the Louvre, has agreed that the two pictures should be shown side by side, but only after the Louvre version has been cleaned. We may have to wait some time for that to be done, and for a solution to our mystery.

15. *Portrait of a Brewer by Constantijn Verhout,*[1,2] *c.1660* (plate 30)
The only painting in our collection that I ever purchased in Canada is also one of the most satisfying. It is a small portrait by Constantijn Verhout of the Delft brewer, Cornelis Abrahamsz Graswinckel. Although he was the Kerkmeester of both the Nieuwe Kerk in Delft where Vermeer was baptised and the Oude Kerk where Vermeer was buried, Graswinckel was known as *Het Delfter Israelit* because of his Jewish appearance. In a home for old people long supported by his family, there is a much more formal portrait of Graswinckel wearing a skull cap, rather than a fur-trimmed *Streimel*. Indeed, if we did not know for certain that this is Graswinckel, he might well be taken for a Jew.

He lived in a marvellous age and is likely to have known Carel Fabritius and Vermeer personally. One wonders why Verhout, an artist from Gouda, was chosen to portray a brewer from Delft. If only paintings could talk, and we could know why they were painted, probably right in Graswinckel's brewery, De Drie Ackeren in the Voorstraat.

Constantijn Verhout is a very rare artist: only three signed works are known. A second depicts this same brewer and includes the Graswinckel coat-of-arms, and a third, in the museum in Stockholm, is a beautiful study of a student asleep beside a pile of books. Verhout must have painted other works, probably now attributed to more famous artists. Because his signatures were overpainted or removed, Vermeer's name too was almost forgotten for 200 years!

In gratitude to our many friends and customers at Upjohn, I agreed to send many of our paintings to the Kalamazoo Institute of Arts in the autumn of 1967. Tony Clark, the Director of the Minneapolis Institute of Arts, was invited to speak for the opening of the exhibition, and he described this little painting wonderfully well:

"The Verhout portrait of an unpretentious brewer is as beautiful a piece of still life painting, and as original, daring, and elegant a work of art as anything I know. It is also, for all its intense simplicity and tiny format, as classical and potent as the finest Greek statues of the late archaic and early classical period. It is utterly clean and fresh, and as moving and great a piece of human creation, technique and insight as possible to make."

Tony captured my feelings so accurately. If only I could write like that! My reaction to paintings is immediate and it usually takes me only a minute or two to decide whether something will fit into our collection, but I shall never be able to describe any painting as well as Tony.

16. The Alchemist[1,2,3] by Cornelis Bega (plate 31)

I first saw this composition in 1952 on the cover of *The Laboratory*, a publication of Fisher Scientific Company, and I just could not help laughing. It showed Bob Feller, one of the country's ablest experts on restoration, working as no expert would, with the painting in the frame, on an easel, next to a 12-liter flask! When I asked Bob about the photograph he explained that he had not worked on the painting at all. Fisher wanted to publish the article "A Scientist Looks at an Old Master", and their photographer asked Bob to pose in a particular way and took the picture as he imagined Bob would work.

So when Christie's in London offered *The Alchemist* in 1969, from the collection of one of England's greatest collectors, John Sheepshanks, I was familiar with the composition, and was happy to buy it. When I sent a photo to Fisher, however, their director of public relations called me in some agitation to tell me that Fisher had sold over 9000 reproductions. They had the original and mine must be a copy. That was not nearly as clear to me as to him, and on my next trip to Pittsburgh, I took my painting along, first to show Bob Feller and then to compare it with the version in the Fisher Museum.

Bob assured me that he thought both versions were period and the signatures on both were genuine. Direct comparison convinced me that both were beautiful and quite different. The Fisher painting was on panel, small and pinkish in tone. Mine was on canvas, and somewhat darker. Many details were different. Thus the logical conclusion was that both versions were by Bega. Perhaps a customer admired the first version and commissioned a second. The only question—a purely academic one—was which version came first.

In 1971 I published a paper in the *Aldrichimica Acta*, suggesting that mine was the first and Fisher's was an improved second version. In 1983 Mary Ann Scott, the expert on Bega, compared both pictures while they were on loan to the Fogg Museum, and wrote, "I agree with your conclusions on the precedence of your picture, which may have been painted about 1660."

The story has a rather sad ending. The Fisher family may have concluded that a second version was not as valuable as a first—I did not think that at all—and sold theirs to Herman Shickman, a New York dealer, for $27,000. This was much more than I had paid for mine, but Shickman later sold the Fisher panel to the Getty for $100,000. Still, Bega might have been pleased to know that his two versions adorned the publications of two chemical companies in America.

17. *Curtain*,[2,3] *Bolognese, c.1700*

Just hours after I bought this curious *trompe l'oeil* from a gallery in Vienna, I became scared. Tearing the paper off the back of the picture I saw a large seal inscribed "KÖNIGL. SÄCHS. GEMÄLDE-SAMMLUNG"—"Royal Saxonian Art Collection". Had I bought one of the many paintings stolen from the museum in Dresden during the last war? Dr Mayer Meintschel, the director in Dresden, reassured me. The painting had not been stolen, but had been sold in the 19th century because they could not identify the artist! This seemed to me a curious reason to sell a painting.

It is a picture of a picture, for the drapery casts its shadow on a flat surface. Perhaps a version exists without the drapery, and an art historian may some day identify the painting, which is said to be of the meeting of King Alexander with Roxana, the Persian princess.

Most experts believe it to be Bolognese, *circa* 1700, although the artist is still unknown. Professor Middeldorf told me that he had filed a photograph of it under T for Textiles.

As I was buying the painting, a man came into the gallery and, noticing it, exclaimed, "Remove that curtain so that I can see the picture!" That request has been repeated many times. It was a natural for the cover of the *Acta* (plate 32) dedicated to R B Woodward, who had made many discoveries in chemistry. It was a good cover, too, for the collected *Acta* articles: open the cover and see what is inside.

18. *Head of an Old Man, Rembrandt School c.1660* (plate 33)

One of the great auction sales of old masters in my lifetime was that of the Erickson collection at Parke Bernet in New York in November 1961. It included three works believed to be by Rembrandt. The most important, *Aristotle with a Bust of Homer,* was bought by the Metropolitan Museum for $2,200,000, then a record price for an old master.

But the painting that moved me most was one which Jakob Rosenberg of the Fogg Museum had used as an example of the artist's sympathy with Jews. I still remember the day Rosenberg discussed this painting. As I was leaving the Converse Laboratories, Fieser met me on the stairs and asked where I was going. When I replied that I was off to the Fogg to listen to Rosenberg, he said in mock disgust, "Alfred, you haven't made up your mind yet whether you want to be a chemist or an art historian." Forty-six years later I am still not sure, but I do believe that the love of both has kept me sane. Accepted by Rembrandt experts at the time, this study of an old man was expected to bring $60,000, and in 1961 I felt I could afford that for such a superb portrait. I was staggered to see how much others were willing to pay. A London dealer acting for a collector in Birmingham bought it for $180,000!

Since then, members of the Rembrandt Research Project must have told the owner that they do not consider this a work by Rembrandt but by one of his students. So it was valued at only £60-80,000 when it was offered at Christie's in London in April 1993. I was in a quandary. Should I bid and if so, how high should I go? If another collector loved it as much as I did, it would sell for a very high price, but most works at auction are bought by dealers, who are unlikely to pay the reserve for an unattributed painting. So I gambled, did not bid and was elated when I learned that the painting was unsold and that my offer after the auction was accepted. It was less than I had been prepared to pay in 1961, but I had missed the joy of looking at the painting for thirty-two years. Since then I have spent hundreds of hours studying it in our living room and have often carried it into our bedroom for a last look before putting my arms around Isabel and falling asleep. What serenity, what knowledge of the world is mirrored in this old man's face! It is the same great painting whether or not it was painted by Rembrandt. What great opportunities for collectors have been unwittingly created by the RRP!

REFERENCES:
1. Used on an Aldrich catalog cover
2. Used on an *Aldrichimica Acta* cover
3. Illustrated in *The Detective's Eye*, a Milwaukee Art Museum 1989 exhibition catalog

19

Efim Schapiro

O ne of the most interesting collectors I ever knew was Dr Efim
   Schapiro, who lived at 37 Arundel Gardens, near Notting Hill
   Gate in London. I met him in the early 1960s and saw him
almost every time I visited London until his death from a brain tumor on
August 8, 1977. Efim Schapiro, the son of Israel Schapiro, an MD and
businessman in Vilna, was born there on November 27, 1899. When he
was still a child, his uncle took him to St Petersburg where he attended
the gymnasium and passed the matriculation examination, winning the
gold medal in 1918. It must have been an exciting time for a boy from
a provincial town—he told later that he even witnessed the storming of
the Winter Palace. He studied for three years at St Petersburg University,
reading classical philology, history of the Middle Ages, art history and
oriental languages. Even as a boy he often visited the Hermitage, saying
later that it was his spiritual home. The best teacher in art history there
was Count Valentin Zubof, who became Schapiro's first mentor.
Schapiro also worked towards a medical degree, studying under Pavlov
who was the father of modern physiology and a legendary figure to
thousands of medical students. Pavlov's work on conditioned reflexes
with his famous dogs has entered common usage. Schapiro never finished his medical studies. In 1923 he went to Germany and continued
his art history studies at the University of Würzburg in 1925, receiving
his PhD two years later. His dissertation dealt with the *Mir Iskusstva*
(World of Art), a group of 18th and 19th century Russian painters, and
their place in the history of Russian painting. He later joked about how
easy he had found it to write his sixty-page thesis in this field, almost
unknown in the West.

Mir Iskusstva was also the name of a periodical, founded in 1898 by
Sergei Diaghelev and his friends, which reflected their interest in French
culture, the architectural splendors of St Petersburg and nostalgia for the
18th century. One of the most important artists in this group was
Alexandre Benois, whose paintings Schapiro collected. They became
friends when both were exiles from Russia. Benois was one of the few
people Schapiro loved as well as admired.

In 1926 Schapiro made his first journey to Paris to study Russian art,
but most of his time between 1923 and 1938 was spent in Berlin, working partly as a music critic for Russian newspapers and also as a private
tutor in art history.

Even as a young man Schapiro was an imposing figure—self-confident, knowledgeable, fluent in several languages, with a total recall of what he read. He was a great raconteur, particularly in Yiddish, and he had the ability to excite his listeners, especially about paintings. One day in 1927, for instance, the 27-year old Schapiro found himself seated beside Jacques Fryszman, a 17-year old student, on a train from Berlin to Würzburg, where Jacques planned to study chemistry. They started talking and discovered that both were Jews with roots in Eastern Europe. Schapiro invited the young man to attend his lectures in art history, and within weeks Jacques became convinced that he preferred art history to chemistry. Jacques Fryszman received his PhD with a thesis on Dutch landscape drawings around 1600, moved to Paris in 1933 and remained a good friend of Efim Schapiro throughout his life.

Schapiro married before he left Russia, but lived with his wife only a short time. She died during the siege of Leningrad by the Nazis, but their daughter survived, as did Efim's sister, Maria Amnuel, now still living in Moscow. Apparently he had little feeling for his daughter and did not mention her in his will.

To escape the threat of the Nazis, Schapiro moved from Berlin to Paris in 1938. His good friend, Dr Fryszman, helped him find a pleasant flat overlooking the Musée Légion d'Honneur, and he continued to give lessons in art history and write about music. Susini, the well-known Corsican-born Germanist and radio executive, also employed him to work for French radio. When the Germans overran Paris in May 1940, Schapiro escaped with many government officials and executives of Radio France to Bordeaux, and from there in a small boat to England. The British suspected him at first and interned him on the Isle of Man where he joined many thousands of German Jews. However, he was released quickly after A E Popham, the well-known British art historian, vouched for him. Soon the BBC employed him in its Russian section, where he worked until the end of his life.

He had great difficulty sleeping at night and so volunteered as a night-time fire-watcher throughout the war, and then frequently spent the mornings inspecting the paintings that were coming up for auction in London, buying those he thought the best and most reasonably priced. During and just after the war, many great paintings could be acquired for less than £100, and there were few experts like Dr Schapiro interested in buying them. In this way, he built up a large collection of old masters, seldom paying more than a few pounds or at the most a few hundred pounds for any of them. He chose paintings purely for their quality and because they appealed to him, not because of attributions. He never had any restored or framed, and they were either hung or just stacked all over the place in Arundel Gardens, where he lived with Mrs Trude Mugdan, and in the house of another friend, Susanne Lepsius.

Richard Kingzett, in his book *Agnew's 1892-1992,* writes about eleven collectors whom he remembers. The first is John Paul Getty and the fourth is Dr Efim Schapiro, who was as different from Getty as any collector could be. Schapiro cannot possibly have been a good customer of Agnew's, but then Richard Kingzett writes about collectors because of their interest to him, not because of their pocketbooks. "Struwwelpeter hair streaming behind him, he took exhibitions at the run, a manic smile of glee overtaking his features when he spotted a wrong attribution." This surely accurately describes Schapiro visiting exhibitions, but Kingzett is just too kind a man to mention how he pushed people aside to get a really good look.

Dr Schapiro had a reputation for being stubborn, opinionated and very difficult to deal with. He also had the reputation of walking into museums, shoving visitors aside, demanding briskly, "Let me through. I want to look at these paintings." Being with him however was great fun as he was so knowledgeable about all sorts of paintings and could tell the most hilarious stories in German, Yiddish and English. It was wonderful for me to spend time with a collector who was as excited about paintings as I was and with whom I had so much else to share.

Early in 1971 however I had one very unhappy experience with him. He told me of a wonderful large *Tobias and the Angel* by Abraham Bloemaert, from the collection of the Earl of Burlington. It was being offered by Paul Wengraf, a seasoned and well-known dealer originally Viennese, who owned the Arcade Gallery in Old Bond Street in London. Wengraf handled many hundreds of fine paintings and had a great reputation. When Schapiro told me about this painting, I rushed to the Arcade Gallery. The story of Tobias has long been one of my favorite Biblical stories, and here was what seemed to be a masterpiece, 86 x 66 inches, i.e. museum size. I was delighted when Wengraf sold me the painting for £6500.

A day or two later I had my annual dinner with Benedict Nicolson, who always asked me what I had purchased recently in London. Proudly I showed him the photograph of the *Tobias,* and he looked at it carefully, shook his head and said, "Alfred, you have bought a pastiche. This is not by Bloemaert." I did not want to rely on just one opinion, so I rushed a photograph to Professor Wolfgang Stechow at Oberlin, who replied identically: "this is not an original." I returned the painting to Wengraf, who was very understanding but explained that he might find it difficult to refund £6500. I agreed to leave the funds with him in an arrangement whereby he would buy paintings chosen by both of us and sell them, keeping half the profit and turning half over to me. Within a relatively short time the £6500 was repaid, and I learned that working with Wengraf was a pleasure. Schapiro however was exceedingly angry when he learned that I had returned the painting on the advice of

Benedict Nicolson and Wolfgang Stechow. He wrote me a scathing letter, ending by saying that I should never ask his opinion about any painting again. I replied, explaining all the circumstances, but it was two years before he talked to me again.

The story has a curious ending. Wengraf sold the painting to a Swiss dealer, who in turn sold it to Richard Feigen, a dealer in New York, whose belief that the painting was a genuine Bloemaert was strengthened by Professor Marcel Roethlisberger, the world expert on Bloemaert, who wrote that it was a fine, original work by the artist. This helped Feigen to sell the painting at a good profit to the New Orleans Museum of Fine Arts in 1979. Since then however Professor Roethlisberger has changed his mind and in his recent book on Bloemaert writes, "Had the original vanished, the question of authenticity would be difficult to decide." At some time in the past the original was cut in two; the right part with Tobias and the angel has long been in the Hermitage; the left, entitled *Herdsmen under a Tree,* was offered at Sotheby's, London in December 1993. They pointed out that it was the missing left portion, and I was tempted to buy this original, partly for nostalgic reasons, but a hammer price of £26,000 seemed a lot for a fragment. The New Orleans Museum has exchanged the studio copy with Richard Feigen for an undoubtedly authentic Bloemaert of *John the Baptist Preaching.*

Fortunately by 1974 Schapiro was allowing me to visit him again, and I was careful never to ask his advice about any other purchases. When the Milwaukee Art Center asked me to be the curator for an exhibition in 1976, "The Bible through Dutch Eyes", I asked Schapiro for his help and was delighted that he loaned us eleven of the seventy paintings in that exhibition.

Some time during the sixties, Schapiro told me that he was leaving his paintings to the Hermitage. When I asked him why he, a Jew, would leave his paintings to a museum in a communist country that had treated Jews so badly, he replied, "I learned most of the art history I know at the Hermitage. There were great paintings there long before communism and there will be great paintings there long after communism. But right now, they cannot purchase any paintings, and I would like to have my collection there."

In his will, written on August 16, 1971, Schapiro named Mrs Susanne Lepsius and Mrs Stefanie Maison as executrices. The relationship between him and Susanne Lepsius was a very close one. She was the great-granddaughter of the famous Egyptologist, Professor Richard Lepsius, and was attractive both physically and intellectually, as well as being a competent translator of English books into German. Schapiro chose Mrs Maison, a great expert in French art and a well-known art dealer, at Mrs Lepsius's suggestion. The widow of K E Maison, the famous expert on Daumier, she combines great charm with real knowledge in art. Each of the executrices was left one painting of her choice. Mrs Lepsius chose an octagonal *Ceres* attributed to Frans Floris, and Mrs Maison, a sketch by Cornelis van Haarlem.

Schapiro's was a most curious will, just two pages, and it was to cause enormous difficulties for Mrs Lepsius and Mrs Maison. Clause 4 of his will states:

"I GIVE AND BEQUEATH to my Trustees for their own use and benefit absolutely all my pictures prints manuscripts works of art and scientific collections. Without impose (sic) any enforcable obligation on my Trustees I declare that it is my wish that the objects referred to in this Clause shall be given to the Museum known as The Hermitage situated in Leningrad USSR and I request but do not require my Trustees to give effect to my wishes as to the disposal of such objects during the lifetime of my Trustees and after their respective deaths which I shall express in any written document signed by me subsequently to this Will."

After Schapiro's death in 1977, Christie's was asked to prepare a list and appraisal of 280 paintings and two pieces of sculpture. That, of course, caused difficulties for the trustees because the British government wanted a large sum in estate duties on the appraised value of £633,450 before the paintings could be turned over to the Hermitage. Since the museum was unwilling or unable to pay the tax, the trustees had to sell many of the paintings to pay the estate tax.

Some 130 of the lesser works were sent to Christie's to be stored in a cavernous warehouse near Victoria Station, where I was given the opportunity to look at them. It was a hot July afternoon, and I was told that I could pick any that appealed to me for negotiation with Mrs Maison, but that Mr Reid of Christie's had only two hours to give me. I do not recall ever working as hard as during those two hours when David Reid showed me the paintings. Luckily, it does not take me long to decide whether I like a painting, and yet after looking at 130 at the rate of about one a minute and selecting four that I liked, I was completely drenched with sweat when I left the warehouse.

Mrs Lepsius and Mrs Maison worked immensely hard to dispose of much of the collection through auction at Christie's. As many of the paintings had not been cleaned for years, many were unframed and a few had been damaged by rain water, a number had to be offered time and again before finally finding buyers, often at really bargain prices. At the end of the day, the Hermitage was given one painting as a token, a *Crucifixion* by Marco Palmezzano, signed and dated 1531, which Schapiro had purchased at Christie's in July 1946 for 32 guineas and which Christie's now valued at £15,000. There was no binding obligation that the collection go to the Hermitage, and when the estate duties were finally paid, the trustees sent the fine collection of old master drawings to an old friend of Dr Schapiro's, and also gave some remaining paintings to friends.

When considering Christie's valuation of these 280 paintings, one must remember that the period during which they had to be sold, from 1978 through the early 1980s, was a time of flux when most fine old master paintings were appreciating considerably in value. Still, studied with the aid of hindsight, it is clear how little meaning can be attached to such a valuation. Eeckhout's beautiful *Jacob's Dream*, Sumowski No 481, signed and dated 1672, was valued at £3000. It was unsold in Christie's auction in 1979, and I was able to purchase it after the sale for £1300. One of the most important paintings in the collection was Mattia Preti's *Jesus and the Woman Taken in Adultery*, which Schapiro had bought at Christie's in 1946 for 10 guineas and was valued by Christie's in 1978 at £25,000. It was sold in December 1980 at Christie's for £90,000. One of my favorite paintings, Jacob Pynas's *Stoning of St Stephen*, monogrammed and dated 1617, was valued by Christie's at £8000; I bought it in November 1979 for £7000, and have given it to Queen's University. Another of my favorites is the painting of *Jesus with the Samaritan Woman at the Well*, which was attributed by Christie's to Eeckhout and valued at £3000 and sold to me in 1979 for £2200. I have since had the painting cleaned. The date of 1634 has appeared, although the signature had been removed. The painting is certainly not by Eeckhout, but is, I believe, a fine early work by Govaert Flinck. Yet another intriguing painting is the beautiful interior with two Eastern Europeans, monogrammed and dated 1649 by the Master IS, a very gifted artist as yet unidentified. Christie's valued this work at only £600 and offered it in 1982, but in the catalog the illustration was cropped. I purchased it for £1800, and after the sale was approached by a dealer who explained that he had been asked by a Dutch museum to bid very much higher, but had missed the bidding. Naturally I declined to offer the painting. In all, I have been able to purchase over 10% of the collection, and some of them have become among the most treasured in our own collection.

There were a few horror stories. Christie's lost a surprising number of paintings, nine in all. Then there was a painting by Frans Floris of a Roman emperor, estimated at £500. It was offered in November 1978, and remained unsold at £240. It was offered again in May 1979, but did not reach the reserve. Then, finally, it was sold after the sale for £10! This is a painting offered by Christie's with the full name Frans Floris—for £10! Jacob Pynas' beautiful mountainous landscape, signed and dated 1628, valued at £8000, was bought in 1979 for £8500 by Sam Nystad, the well-known dealer in The Hague, who sold it to the

National Gallery in London. Schapiro's favorite painting was Giulio Romano's *The Weaning of Hercules*, which had belonged to King Charles I and to the Duc d'Orleans. Purchased by Schapiro at Christie's sale of paintings belonging to the Earl of Ellesmere, in October 1946, for 80 guineas, it was valued in 1978 at £22,000 and sold for that sum in 1979. I wonder what such a mannerist masterpiece would bring today.

Schapiro particularly liked two Dutch artists, Cornelis van Haarlem and Leonard Bramer. He owned eleven paintings by van Haarlem or attributed to him at the time, and eight by Bramer. In 1992 the Haggerty Museum of Marquette University in Milwaukee had a Bramer exhibition. On the catalog cover was a Schapiro painting valued by Christie's at £4500 and sold to Richard Feigen in 1979 for £2800. Feigen sold it to Jack Kilgore, a young New York dealer, who valued it at $95,000 and sold it to the Detroit Museum of Fine Arts. A second Bramer, *Circumcision*, which sold at Christie's in 1949 for 50 guineas, was valued in 1978 at £1750 and sold to Feigen in 1979 for £2200. He now values it at $125,000. I think that Schapiro would have been particularly delighted at the growing interest in Bramer, which will increase still further after a scholarly exhibition planned in Delft.

Schapiro had purchased a beautiful pair of allegories of summer and autumn by Nicolaes Berchem at Christie's in 1945 for 32 guineas. Christie's valuation was £25,000 for the pair, and they were sold in 1979 for £35,000 and £32,000. The allegories of all four seasons are known, and Schapiro's two were sold recently by the Noortman Galleries to a private collector.

Two of the most romantic works, Boucher's *Toilet of Venus* and *Story of Psyche,* enchanting grisailles, sold by Christie's in 1941 for 42 guineas and valued in 1978 at £15,000, were claimed by the daughter of his friend, Mrs Mugdan.

One of the finest works of Jean François de Troy entitled *Time Unveiling Truth*, 80 x 82 inches, signed and dated 1733, was valued at £20,000. I remember seeing it hanging over the mantelpiece in the largest room of Mrs Mugdan's house. It was unsold at £13,000 in 1979 and purchased by the National Gallery after the sale for £10,250.

Clearly Schapiro would have liked his collection to go to the Hermitage, if possible. What—if anything—went wrong? The answer to that depends on what his real intention was. He was an astute collector, and he must have known that the meager cash in his estate could not possibly pay the British inheritance tax. He must also have known that it was unlikely that the Hermitage would pay.

Both Schapiro's executrices were mature women, knowledgeable in the art trade. Mrs Lepsius had been employed by Christie's for some years. Both women worked very hard to bring order to the estate. About 80% of the paintings were interesting but relatively minor works, and many were unframed and in need of restoration. Both may have thought of selling the entire lot to one dealer, but in that case they would certainly have been criticized for selling too cheaply, no matter what the price. So they did what seemed most sensible, they sold at auction. Today, the major works are in great art galleries and with collectors who really appreciate them. Maybe that is what Efim Schapiro really wanted; in any case, I think he would be pleased with the outcome.

I would like to thank the late Mrs Susanne Lepsius, Mrs Stefanie Maison, Dr Jacques Fryszman and Dr and Mrs Max Rendall for their help in writing this chapter.

20

John Whalley

I have my good friend Barry Young to thank for meeting John Whalley. For many years I enjoyed travelling with Barry, Aldrich's eastern sales manager, visiting customers all the way from Boston to Philadelphia. He is such a happy person, also interested in antiques, and our customers loved him. I was saddened when he left Aldrich and joined Fluka, but then came back into the fold when Sigma-Aldrich purchased Fluka, only to leave again shortly after I was dismissed.

Late one evening in March 1981, Barry took me to visit his brother William, who lives in Lima, New York, where I saw a stunning tempera painting of an old woman. It was a masterpiece, and Bill told me that it was the work of his neighbor, John Whalley. Although it was then about 10 pm, we could see through the window that Whalley's lights were still on, so we called on him.

John was born in Brooklyn in 1954, and from an early age his parents encouraged him to paint and draw. He studied at the Rhode Island School of Design where he received his Bachelor of Fine Arts degree in 1976, the year he married Linda, a delightful fellow graduate. Both John and Linda were interested in religion and in helping disadvantaged people. At one time John had planned to enter the ministry, and to this day has still not decided whether he would prefer to be a painter or a social worker.

That Monday evening in 1981, John seemed quite depressed and it quickly became clear why: he had recently exhibited twenty-eight of his paintings at the Gallery Zena in Boston, and every one had been returned unsold. What could be more discouraging to a young artist? I was unfamiliar with John's technique, painting in tempera, but I loved some of the works and immediately purchased two of them. John explained that working in tempera is a slow process and that he also did water colors and drawings in pencil. I liked his temperas by far the best, and during the years that followed, purchased a good many of them. Finally in 1986, John listened to my oft repeated advice that he should also paint oils on canvas, a less time-consuming process, and he has in fact turned out some beautiful oils. Plate 35 shows the *Farm Scale,* one of his finest temperas; plate 36, a beautiful, pensive sketch of Linda and their son Matthew; and plate 37, a lovely still life in oils done in 1986.

What John wrote in one of the catalogs exhibiting his works is so very apt, "I much more enjoy taking everyday unbeautiful things in the prop-

250

er setting and painting them beautifully if I can, rather than taking a beautiful thing and painting it all right. I like to take something unbeautiful and bring out the beauty in it." He has certainly done that in many of his still lifes.

In the winter of 1981, Linda and John moved to a school for abused children in Harrison Valley, Pennsylvania, way off the beaten track and not very far from the New York border. There they worked closely with the children, and I am sure no one could have done a more thoughtful job. John spent some of his spare time painting, but free time in such a residential home is very limited, particularly as their first son, Matthew, was born in 1982.

During the next few years, Isabel and I visited the Whalleys several times, buying many beautiful pieces. In August 1984, I arranged an exhibition at the art gallery of Purdue University, showing the works of two of my artist friends, John Whalley and Charles Munch. During our visits to the Whalleys in Harrison Valley, it became clear that John had very little time for painting, and it seemed that he would be happier if he were able to paint full time. I suggested that I become his limited agent, buy a number of his paintings fairly regularly on a first-choice basis, and pay him a guaranteed salary that would increase annually. The idea appealed to him, and I asked Marvin Klitsner to draw up a contract. John discussed it in detail with his father and his attorney, and during our next visit to Harrison Valley, signed it in April 1986.

John and Linda left Harrison Valley in the summer of 1986 and moved to Standish, a small town near Portland, Maine. He then began his life as a full-time painter. He and Linda now had two healthy boys, Matthew and Benjamin, and some of John's happiest drawings and paintings have been of these youngsters. I kept urging him to paint more studies while the children were young, but alas he spent most of his time on still lifes, beautiful but not as moving as the studies of the children.

During the summer of 1986, John sent me a number of slides of his new work, and I picked several items for purchase, under the terms of our contract. All was well, I thought.

In order to promote his work, I arranged with the art department of the University of Wisconsin in Eau Claire to have an exhibition in April 1987. There were seven of John's works from our collection, and several of his paintings that were offered for sale. The university invited John to come to Eau Claire to lecture and to talk to students in the fine art department about his work and technique. We looked forward to what we believed would be a particularly interesting and enjoyable event that would please him.

We met John in our motel room on April 8, and within minutes it was clear that he was very unhappy. In a discussion lasting until midnight, he explained that he found it difficult to live on $24,000 a year and had

251

taken a loan from his father. I pointed out to him that he was free to sell his paintings to others and that in fact I knew that two of the paintings which he had sent to Eau Claire had already been sold, which alone would give him an additional $3000. He said that other dealers were reluctant to buy from him because they felt that with my having first refusal, I would take the best paintings. That, of course, is a matter of opinion and taste, and I was certain that John had many paintings that both dealers and individual collectors would purchase.

John's second worry was that, while I had paid the $2000 per month promptly, I had not taken $2000's worth of paintings every month. He calculated that by the end of the first year of the contract, I would have paid him $24,000 but would have taken only about $15,000's worth of paintings, leaving a $9000 carry-forward for the year following. He told me that he found it very difficult to live with such a burden, although I pointed out that he would never have to repay the money other than in works of art.

His third problem was my five-year option beyond the first three years of the contract. He said he had not initially realized the implications of this option and that, while I was happy for him to teach or attend courses to further his work in art, he did not want to be obliged to dedicate all his working time to art.

What was clear in this rather heated discussion was that John was not only unhappy, but believed that his output had suffered because of what he saw as a burden. Of course, I explained more than once the reason for the option. It takes time for an artist to become well known. I had arranged for exhibitions and had printed 20,000 beautiful reproductions of his *Farm Scale*, but John Whalley had certainly not yet become a household name. I had already worked hard and might well represent him for three years without any of his paintings selling for substantial money. This explanation did little to satisfy him, and at one point he referred to himself as "being indentured" to me.

The effect of his feeling "indentured" was very clear. Until he signed the contract, he had painted little, but had been a versatile artist, painting still lifes, portraits, and also animal pictures. I had found the portraits of his children by far the easiest to sell, but since the signing of the contract, he had painted only still lifes and seemed to resent my suggesting portraits. Time and again, he referred to the fact that other well-known artists received many thousands of dollars for their works, while even his most expensive paintings fetched only a few thousand dollars.

Clearly the only thing to do was to tear up the contract and to let John go his own way, so we assured him in May that we would release him from the contract and hoped that from then on he would again be able to paint some wonderful works.

There had been no question in my own mind that the contract was fair. I had shown it to several artists and dealers. The former thought that most young artists would be happy to have the security, effort in promotion and freedom to sell to others. Dealers pointed out that they wanted exclusivity and generally took paintings only on consignment, to be paid for after sale. But all that was immaterial. John felt "indentured" and we certainly did not want him to live like that.

Under the contract, he still owed us works to the value of about $8000, and we visited him later that year and picked some of his paintings, mainly older works, to balance the books. Most of these paintings were works that had not been my first choices, but by then I was as anxious as John to settle the matter.

I have been deeply disappointed by how little John has been painting since. At first he took a job in Maine, renovating houses, and then in the summer of 1990 he moved to Fort Lauderdale and accepted a position with Daybreak, a religious organization attempting to help youngsters who were into drugs and prostitution. The organization actually sent John to Colombia for study and to Brazil, with his family, to set up an orphanage.

We have visited John and his family several times in Florida, and he has shown us some of his works, mainly very large drawings that I would find very difficult to sell. He is working with two galleries, one in Maryland and the other in Florida, but I understand that they have not been very successful in selling his works.

Isabel and I hoped that his experiences in South America might prove an inspiration to him. I believe that John has both the talent and the genius to be a very great artist and to bring a great deal of pleasure to many people. His work reminds me of that of Andrew Wyeth, and yet it has a character all its own. I think that in time John will be considered one of the very good American artists of the late 20th century, but, alas, he has still not decided whether he wants to be a painter or a social worker. Of course I understand his desire to help people, but in the long run the beauty of his works will bring such pleasure. Just recently, he has again begun working on beautiful small still lifes in oil, and I certainly hope he will continue.

21

The Getty: A Cautionary Tale

There must be thousands of people around the world who would like to sell something of value—a work of art, a whole collection, or a library—to the Getty, for no other organization has as much money that must be spent on art, and it is common knowledge how voraciously the Getty has been buying. To many of the sellers, often the widows or estates of art historians and collectors, the Getty is *the* great hope. This account is written to urge such sellers to deal with the Getty cautiously and with the advice of counsel, and not to assume that the Getty Trust will always deal fairly—for as this shows, that is not always the case.

Professor Ulrich Middeldorf was one of the great art historians of our time. He left the chairmanship of the University of Chicago in the early fifties to become director of the Kunsthistorisches Institut in Florence where he helped thousands of young art historians and collectors. His great connoisseurship was in Italian Renaissance art, but his knowledge was not limited to his specialty, and he was always willing to help everyone interested in art. Over the years he accumulated a wonderful art historical library. In July 1980 Professor Middeldorf sold his library to the Getty Museum for $220,000 with the proviso that he would be paid $1000 per month while keeping his library and that, upon his death, the Getty Museum would have the library shipped to California, and the unpaid balance of the purchase price would be paid to Professor Middeldorf's widow. So far, so good—a willing buyer, a willing seller, a fair agreement.

Professor Middeldorf died in Florence in February 1983. His American widow, Gloria, then in her seventies and in poor health, was quite unfamiliar with business matters and had no counsel whatever about tax laws. Professor Middeldorf had repeatedly asked the people at the Getty for tax counsel, which had been denied, and neither he nor his wife had known where to turn for help. The Getty had the library picked up after Professor Middeldorf's death and Mrs Middeldorf asked that the payment of $1000 per month be continued. Now, however, the situation had changed. The library was at the Getty and surely Mrs Middeldorf should have been offered interest on the considerable balance due. Instead, in May 1983, she received a contract from Barbara J Capodieci, the Getty's trust counsel, saying, in paragraph 1, "The Getty agrees to pay the $193,000 which it owes to Mrs Middeldorf in monthly $1000 installments. *The unpaid balance of the total purchase price of $1000 shall not bear interest.*" [My italics] Since this makes no sense, I presume that a line was omitted in typing. Luckily, Mrs Middeldorf also had the right at any time to demand payment of the balance due. Without counsel and without any financial experience whatever, she just signed this agreement in May 1983.

When Isabel and I visited her in June 1984, Mrs Middeldorf showed us the contract and asked for our advice. Of course we pointed out that at $1000 a month without interest, the principal would be gone within sixteen years, whereas the interest that could then be earned on US bonds paying 12-14% was about twice the $1000 per month, with principal intact. We urged her to ask the Getty for principal and accrued interest, and to invest this in US government bonds. The Getty paid the principal, but we were astounded to learn that it refused to pay interest. So I wrote to Harold Williams, the president of the Getty Trust, pointing out the absurdity of the contract, ending my letter with a personal appeal: "Keep in mind that the agreement was drafted by your attorney, that Mrs Middeldorf, a woman in her seventies, was without benefit of counsel, and that less than three months had passed since her husband had died. As an attorney and former head of the SEC, you will understand the implications of all this, and so I feel certain that you must have been unaware of the details of the contract, and will now be anxious to see this matter put right."

Unfortunately, I was mistaken. Mr Williams replied promptly, alleging that the Getty had the impression—erroneous in fact—that Mrs Middeldorf was advised by tax professionals and that she was very knowledgeable about her financial matters. He added that no interest was due for the period of over a year during which the Getty held the principal because, "Funds being used to pay Mrs Middeldorf are not in an interest-bearing account."

This reminded me of a statement attributed to him [*Industry Week*, Sept 3, 1984, p.37] about the treatment of boards: "The way to handle boards is to treat them like a mushroom. Keep them in the dark, water them well, and cover them with horse manure." At least the latter applied to Mr Williams' treatment of Mrs Middeldorf. His arrogance is not limited to boards of directors.

In reply, I confirmed that Mrs Middeldorf had taken no legal advice at the time she signed the Getty agreement and was certainly not knowledgeable about taxes or business matters. I wrote that "there is no just basis for depriving her of interest on the deferred payment while at the same time deducting $1000 payments from principal." Mr Williams had studiously refrained from commenting on the gibberish about interest in the Getty contract, and I find it difficult to believe that the Getty board is so financially incompetent that it would leave almost $200,000 lying

255

for over a year without interest.

Mr Williams quoted the letter that Mrs Middeldorf had written in April 1983 in which she had asked that the $1000 per month payments be continued. There had been no reference to interest in her letter. "We honored the transaction as she requested it," he wrote. "For you to be going around the art history community indicating that we have, in some way, taken advantage of a poor widow is totally inappropriate."

I discussed the matter with two art historians whom I respect immensely. One was Professor Seymour Slive at Harvard University who had received his PhD from Professor Middeldorf at the University of Chicago; the other was Professor Egbert Haverkamp-Begemann at the Institute of Fine Arts of New York University. Both tried to help, but to no avail. Professor Slive talked to Mr Williams personally, while Professor Haverkamp-Begemann wrote to Dr John Walsh, Director of the Getty Museum, stressing that my action was a plea for justice. Dr Walsh then wrote kindly to me that he "felt the greatest regret that the Getty's behavior should be seen as callous" and he turned the matter over to Dr Kurt Forster, Director of the Getty Center. One of Dr Forster's associates, Dr Herbert H Hymans, wrote to me that "since Mrs Middeldorf has always had the option to receive the entire amount due her at any time, payment of interest would be inappropriate." The Getty staff and bureaucrats worldwide love the word "inappropriate," but logic is not improved by buck-passing. If you have $200,000 in a bank, you can withdraw funds at any time, but you do not lose interest on the balance. The Getty is not a bank, of course, but surely Mrs Middeldorf should have received the interest earned by the Getty on her principal.

Professor Haverkamp-Begemann put it most clearly when he wrote to Dr Hymans: "It isn't what the Getty did, but what it didn't do." They didn't set out to deprive Mrs Middeldorf, but they didn't ask the obvious questions, they wrote a nonsensical contract and, when challenged, put up a stonewalling defense. I wrote to Mr Williams in January 1985, suggesting that "we settle this unpleasant matter by submitting all the facts for arbitration."

I ended that letter to Mr Williams, "I am truly sorry that you are in such an unhappy corner—surely unhappy for Mrs Middeldorf, for you, for me and for all who know about it. You must be a very able man to be in your position, and also very proud, and that makes it difficult for you to say, 'Perhaps there is more to this than met my eye at first.' Only a great man could now say, 'Yes, we could have done more to help Mrs Middeldorf.' *I hope that you have that greatness.*"

In May, Dr Myron Laskin, curator of the Getty Museum, a Milwaukeean whom I have known for many years, telephoned me. When I sought his help, he asked, "Why do you get involved, what business is it of yours?" I have also asked myself that question, and I think the answer is twofold. I could not ignore the commandment in Leviticus XIX, which I have quoted before, "You shall not stand idly by the blood of your neighbor." I was convinced that a defenseless widow had been mistreated. Secondly, I felt guilty. For many years I had visited Professor Middeldorf once every summer, arriving in Florence on the 5 am train, and from 7 am until late in the afternoon we had discussed all sorts of matters concerned with his expertise. Never once did I have the wit to ask him whether I could help him with business matters.

He was such a great person, who helped so many people. As Dean Avraham Ronen of Tel Aviv University put it so clearly, "His heart knew no limits. He was always ready to listen to a young beginner, no less than to the greatest celebrity. You can hardly find an article or a book on Italian art that does not acknowledge Middeldorf's generous help in solving some of its problems, and only he could offer his advice and help to so many, because he knew so much." Scores of art lovers relied on him, from the great historians to the novice collector, such as I was in the 1950s. As Sir John Pope-Hennessy wrote [in *Apollo*, May 1983], "Ulrich Middeldorf was that rare thing, a scholar who realized himself most fully through the self-effacing encouragement and disinterested help he gave to other scholars." Such was the man, yet the Getty had the gall to stonewall his widow, and to refuse her interest.

The representations of art historians having produced no results, and hoping that Mr Williams might listen more carefully to a fellow financier, I asked Jim Weinberg, a partner in Goldman Sachs and a director of the company of which I was chairman, to speak to him. He did so in April. Finally on June 4, Mr Williams wrote to Mrs Middeldorf that he regretted the misunderstanding and sympathized with her difficulties. He enclosed a check for $26,800 for the interest on the unpaid balance. Isabel and I learned of this one Sunday evening in June while at a chemical convention in Frankfurt. It was one of the happiest evenings of our lives.

I do not believe for a minute that Mr Williams or anyone else at the Getty set out to short-change Mrs Middeldorf deliberately. Why should they? They have to spend millions annually to remain a tax-exempt foundation, and the amount involved was so small.

Mr Williams' first reaction to Mrs Middeldorf's and my letters was that of many a proud bureaucrat who has to face serious criticism: stonewall the critic. He never commented on the unintelligible wording of the contract sent to Mrs Middeldorf. When stonewalling proved ineffective, he tried passing the buck—to Dr Forster and to Mr Hymans who wrote that Mrs Middeldorf was not entitled to interest because she could have withdrawn the principal at any time.

For many months the thoughts of some of the country's ablest art historians—Egbert Haverkamp-Begemann, Seymour Slive, John Walsh—

made no impact on Mr Williams whatever. Only when an eminent financier, Jim Weinberg, a partner in Goldman Sachs, interceded did Mr Willliams listen.

All's well that ends well. But the lesson is that even when dealing with one of the wealthiest trusts in the world, it is advisable to have competent legal advice.

22

Caveat Donor

I have derived real pleasure in my life from being able to establish prizes, scholarships and awards for students in Canada, the United States, Britain and the Czech Republic. This is surely rooted in the enormous benefit such awards provided me when I was a student at Queen's University and later at Harvard. Without them, I could not have continued my studies.

My first opportunity to repay came in 1948, while I was still a graduate student at Harvard. The circumstances were very sad. Martin Wolff, who had just begun signing his letters "Daddy Wolff", died suddenly of a heart attack. He was a man of modest means, with five daughters, four of them unmarried, and I was staggered to learn that he had left me $1000 in his will—a princely sum at a time when my income as a teaching fellow at Harvard was $100 a month. With the memory of this truly good man clear in my mind, I asked Queen's University to use the money to establish the Martin Wolff prize in civil engineering. I was recently reminded of the passing of time when a student at Queen's wrote to tell me that he was particularly happy to have won that prize as his father had won it some thirty years earlier!

Different institutions treat scholarship funds very differently. When I wanted to start a travelling fellowship for students in art history at Harvard, I learned to my dismay that to establish an award of $10,000 a year would require capital of $200,000. Harvard pays only 5% on capital; this may be in the long-term interest of future generations, but students need help now. In contrast, the Institute of Fine Arts in New York, another important institution that teaches art history, pays 10%, and I established three such fellowships there, but I have been disappointed that in some years awards were not made because there were no suitable students. The American Chemical Society required over $100,000 to set up the $3000 Bader award in bioorganic/inorganic chemistry; the Canadian Institute of Chemistry and the Royal Society of Chemistry wanted less than half that. Best of all has been Queen's University, which has consistently returned over 10% on capital—praise the Lord for its Scottish tradition of frugality!

Sometimes I just walked away, as I did at first at Harvard. Later I reconsidered. On other occasions a little discussion was needed. The directors of the Royal Society of Chemistry, for example, were at first taken aback at the suggestion that awards should not be open to professors. In Britain there is generally just one professor of organic chemistry at each university, and many academics of great competence, who would be called professors in North American universities, do not hold professorships. Funding is much easier for professors, and so I wanted awards to go to really good organic chemists who had not yet become professors. Fortunately the directors of the RSC eventually understood my point of view.

An unforeseen problem arose. After the first award was given to Dr Stephen Davies at Oxford and the second to Dr Dudley Williams at Cambridge, we were told that in all likelihood all the Bader awards would be given to Oxbridge chemists; and it was suggested that we establish another award specifically for the other universities. Isabel and I met Professor Charles Stirling, now at Sheffield University, and chairman of the awards committee, to discuss this matter, and I have seldom heard Isabel quite so outspoken. We did not want to duplicate the award, because we knew dozens of brilliant chemists who are neither professors, nor academics at Oxbridge, and who were eminently eligible for an award. Of course we understood the problem: life at Cambridge and Oxford is so comfortable and fulfilling that many brilliant academics there ask themselves why they should leave and accept the hurly-burly of a university chair elsewhere.

Sometimes the discussion to establish a prize has been distinguished by the beauty of its brevity. Such was the case with all the awards at Queen's and recently with a £1000 annual award in the chemistry department of Imperial College. The latter took just a few minutes' discussion with Dr B P Levitt who then graciously permitted me to use the scheme as a model at many other British universities.

Only once have I been really flabbergasted by the way an institution treated an award. The one singular case was at Sheffield University. Dr William J P Neish, a chemist, had worked there for many years, mainly on purines, pyrimidines and xanthines. His book *Xanthines and Cancer*, was published recently by the Aberdeen University Press. Willy is a delightful person, an impish, straightforward Scot with a wonderful sense of humor. He helped us greatly with his chemistry, would not accept payment for his research samples, which came to our Library, and when he retired I suggested that the Aldrich Chemical Company show its appreciation by establishing a prize in organic chemistry in his honor. This is, I believe, the only award for students ever established by the company; the others were our personal gifts.

Unfortunately, the professor at Sheffield whom I knew best, David Ollis, a brilliant organic chemist whom I had first met at Harvard when he was working with Professor R B Woodward, was away when Isabel and I next visited Sheffield, and so we discussed this matter with Peter Maitlis, the professor of inorganic chemistry. It was clear that Professor

Maitlis was not enthusiastic about a prize in organic chemistry. He wrote in July 1987:

". . . it would be much more appropriate (and useful) to establish an 'Aldrich Lecture' or a 'William Neish Lecture, sponsored by the Aldrich Chemical Company', than to have a student prize."

to which I replied immediately:

". . . a lectureship would help academics, while a scholarship or student prize would help students. While we do try to help a good many academics around the world, I feel that in this specific case helping students is more appropriate."

After some correspondence with Professor E Haslam, the professor of organic chemistry, about how the students should be picked, I wrote to him:

"Of course we are totally in accord with your suggestion that the award be given to a student in any course of organic chemistry as recommended by all the academic staff and the teaching review committee. What is important to us is that it be awarded to a student in a course of organic chemistry."

Professor Haslam, then head of the department, advised me that the prize of £200 awarded annually and in perpetuity in the name of Dr William Neish would require £3000, and on December 12, 1987, I sent Professor Haslam by registered mail the Aldrich check "to endow in perpetuity the Dr William Neish prize in a course of organic chemistry. The course will be selected by your department before the end of June 1988, and the prize of £200 will be awarded for the first time in 1989 . . . Please send me a copy of the 1989 university handbook describing this when it appears."

I never received the handbook, which announced that there would be three awards annually "one each in Inorganic, Organic and Physical with Theoretical Chemistry." In July 1989 Dr Neish sent me details of the first prizes; there were three awards of £80.

The small prize had been split into three still smaller prizes, and two of them had been given to physical and inorganic graduates who were going into industry! I assumed that the change had come about at the suggestion—or at least with the approval—of Dr Neish, so I wrote to him, "If you approved, we approve. If not, I'll try to get the terms changed." Dr Neish's response was as clear as could be: he had neither been consulted, nor even told!

261

"Had I been consulted I would have recommended that a single prize be given in organic chemistry as I am sure you intended and which I believed would be done."

No one in Sheffield had ever asked me whether I objected to the prize being split.

There followed some increasingly acrimonious correspondence between Professor Haslam, Dr R Brettle, the new head of chemistry, Dr Neish and me. Finally, Dr Brettle wrote:

"The Department is not prepared to offer a prize in Organic Chemistry, associated with Dr. Neish, on the terms you proposed. I have therefore instructed the University to refund the full value of your gift and the cheque should reach you at Bexhill shortly. All references to the William J. P. Neish Prize will be deleted from University publications."

Clearly donors do not have the right—at least not at Sheffield University—to specify that a prize should be given to a student in organic chemistry.

Why did this happen? As I wrote to Dr Brettle:

"I don't believe for a moment that the decision to split the prize came from Prof. Haslam. Rather, it is likely to have come from non-organic professors, and Prof. Haslam, out of a mistaken sense of loyalty, may be trying to cover some internal argument."

I have kept the voluminous correspondence. However, this story has a happy ending. The Department of Chemistry at Aberdeen University, Dr Neish's *alma mater,* has accepted the funds with the assurance that the William J P Neish Prize will go to one student in organic chemistry. We have come to know Willy Neish better. He is a fighter for what is right, as I try to be. When Queen's University gave me an honorary LLD in 1985, I said in my acceptance, "I am especially happy to be awarded the degree of Doctor of Laws because I have sometimes secretly wished that I were a lawyer, and my good friends know how I have always enjoyed a fight when I knew—or thought I knew—that I was right."

Also we discovered another facet of Dr Neish—aka Gullielmus the Poet, who sent us ten stanzas which began:

Who is this fellow, Neish by name?
From the ranks of lowly prats,
Some say he is a chemist
But we hear he worked with rats.

He may well be a chemist
And perhaps not bad, you say!
But to link him with Organic
Would dishonour Kekulé.

We were just sorry that the students at Sheffield were the real losers in this affair.

Our experience in Sheffield was the low point of our attempts to help students. Perhaps the most satisfying was our involvement with Project SEED, an effort by the American Chemical Society to assist disadvantaged students. While president of the ACS, the late Professor Paul Gassman, an old friend at the University of Minnesota, suggested that we get involved, and the Helen Bader Foundation, Isabel and I pledged $100,000 a year for three years. I was asked to speak in 1993 at the twenty-fifth anniversary of Project SEED, and tried to explain our involvement.

"Paul was a very old friend, and I listened when he urged me to become involved in Project SEED. But what did SEED mean? Summer—Educational—Experience—for the Disadvantaged. I knew what summer and education and experience meant, but who was really disadvantaged, or how can it be defined? I have just been studying the works of Michael Faraday and Josef Loschmidt, two of the world's greatest chemists. And one can probably say fairly that each as boys could have been defined as disadvantaged. In my own mind, the most disadvantaged kids might really be the children of very able and rich people who are so busy that they don't hug them enough. But that is another matter.

"I like to think of Project SEED more in terms of what the word SEED really means—the SEED, the beginning of a really good life.

"Allow me to share with you a little bit of my own personal philosophy.

"*The New Yorker* recently told the story about Sir Bertrand Russell, the late, great philosopher, who, when lunching with an acquaintance late in his life was asked: "Sir Bertrand, you are today not only one of the greatest philosophers and best known atheists, but also the oldest great atheist. What would you say if at the end of your day you find that you are standing before the pearly gates and realize that you have been mistaken? Sir Bertrand replied without hesitation, 'I would say, "God, You did not give us enough evidence."'" —You did not give us enough evidence. You and I know that there are millions of good, intelligent atheists, just as there are millions of good and intelligent people who believe in God. But, my friends, please don't worry, I am not going to give you a talk on theology. Let me just say that I do believe, and that to me one of the most important sentences in the Bible is the sentence at the very beginning of Genesis, where the Bible tells us that God said, 'Let Us make man in Our image.' Please note that He did not say, 'Let Us make a white man or a black man or a yellow man, a Christian, a Jew, a Muslim, in Our image' but that all of us are made in God's image. Clearly, some people are much smarter than others. Many of you could easily beat me up, some are very much stronger than others, yet there is some of God in each and every one of us and to me it seems that this is the only rational basis for democracy. And that, of course, gives everyone, disadvantaged or not, the right to a good education. The right to equal opportunity.

"But back to Project SEED—when I listened to Paul Gassman he explained that Project SEED gave opportunities to high school students for one summer. But then I thought back to my own days as a student, and I remembered how happy I was when a paint company in Montreal offered me a summer job. I really enjoyed it, and of course the fabulous salary of $130 a month. And, I was so happy when the Murphy Paint Company asked me to return to them during the next summer at no less than $160 a month. And during that second summer I learned so very much more and I could do so very much more than I had done in the first summer. In any first summer job, you spend a lot of time finding out where the beakers are and where the toilets are, and you can surely be far more productive in a second summer. And so my family and I offered to help Project SEED II on a three-year trial basis, and I very much hope that all of you who have taken part in Project SEED II will agree that a second summer is more productive than a first."

One of the most amusing incidents after my dismissal from Sigma-Aldrich in 1992 involved Aldrich's chemical library and Project SEED. During the war and for some years thereafter, *Beilstein*, the extensive encyclopedia of compounds, had been offered by the Alien Property Custodian in reprint at the unbelievably low price of $45 per set of 49 volumes. Each new volume of *Beilstein* now sells for several thousand marks! I personally bought ten sets, and in the fifties and sixties traded nine of them for chemical journals, such as the first 100 years of the German *Berichte*, a long run of *Chemical Abstracts*, and others. I placed them in the Aldrich library for use by its chemists, who understood that they belonged to me personally, as indeed did about half the books in the library, which was undoubtedly the best chemical library in Milwaukee.

In September 1992 I gave a list to Jai Nagarkatti, the president of Aldrich, and to Steve Branca, a very able chemist in charge of new products. Both knew that I owned the books. I proposed several alternatives to Jai, stating that in exchange for relinquishing my rights, my preference was that Aldrich should give $25,000 to Project SEED. There would be no need to refer to me, and this way the library at Aldrich would remain intact, and good use would be made of it by the chemists, for whom I continue to have the highest regard. An alternative suggestion was that my books be divided between two Wisconsin schools, Carroll College and the University of Wisconsin in Eau Claire from which several of Aldrich's good chemists have come.

Jai promised to provide help with packing and shipping if we were not able to reach an agreement whereby Aldrich kept the books and made some reimbursement for them. Finally, in March 1993, David Harvey told Jai that he could make the decision himself. Jai thought that $25,000 for Project SEED was a large expense for one year, so I suggested $5000 a year for five years. Surprisingly, Jai then said that Aldrich could purchase microfilms of the books less expensively, and told me to ship the books to Carroll and Eau Claire. I thought this was a mistake because microfilms are much harder to use. I wrote to the schools offering them a choice of books, and sent a copy of my letter by certified mail to Jai.

Then on April 28, I received a certified letter from Kirk Richter, the controller of Sigma-Aldrich in St Louis, stating that I could not remove the books without first proving my ownership. I faxed Marvin a copy of Kirk's letter, adding that I did not know whether to be happy or unhappy. I have always enjoyed a good fight, and I was being given the opportunity. Marvin's reply was a classic: "If you don't know whether to be happy or unhappy about this, be happy."

I sent Kirk copies of my letters to Jai and a copy of a draft letter from Jai to the ACS concerning Project SEED, then considered which attorney might best represent me in a lawsuit, and awaited developments.

Despite the agreement made at the time of the merger that annual meetings would alternate between St Louis and Milwaukee, the 1993 annual meeting was held in St Louis. I had thought of going to ask all sorts of embarrassing questions, but Marvin counselled against it: "I never think it pays to try to make your points in the other fellow's court, especially when the other fellow has full control of the proceedings and a packed court."

David Harvey called me from the meeting in St Louis to ask whether he could meet me the next morning to discuss two matters, the library and some papers that required my signature. German commercial law requires that a *person* own 5% of Aldrich's German company, and when

I stepped down as chairman in 1991, I had turned over my ownership of those shares to Peter Gleich, the treasurer of Sigma-Aldrich. However, because of an oversight by the company, the transaction was not carried out before a notary public, which made it invalid in German law, and David and the company's German attorney had subsequently urged me to sign a power of attorney. Reminding them of Tom Cori's statement during those horrid seventeen minutes in London that "a man who bet against the company couldn't do anything for the company," I contended that "anything" meant everything, including signing papers, and declined to sign.

I had not thought that I would ever see David in my gallery, but there he was, sweet as could be, the following day as arranged. He had looked at the books I claimed as mine, and said he would now agree to pay $25,000 to the ACS, at once, not over five years, provided that I also signed the power of attorney. Furthermore, he would help Carroll and Eau Claire by sending both of them the Aldrich libraries of spectra, with a retail value of over $3000. This struck me as a good deal—after all, I had refused to sign the German papers just to be awkward—but I worried that if Tom heard about this amicable settlement, he might countermand it. So I agreed, provided I could go to Aldrich in an hour and make sure that the check was mailed to the ACS then and there. This we did. *Ende gut, alles gut.*

Of course, as so often, this fight was an ego trip on my part, but my satisfaction largely arose from the help it gave project SEED. I was reminded of what the late Don Haselhorst, a director, said to me after a particularily difficult argument with Tom and Aaron, "Nice guys don't always finish last."

David was probably not as amused as I was when he received a letter from Professor Ochrymowycz of Eau Claire thanking him for the libraries of spectra and saying that "The volumes will be placed in our library with a dedication to Dr Alfred Bader and Aldrich Chemical Company in recognition of the donors' generosity."

When I told Marvin about all this, he replied, "The solution to the matter of your books was, indeed, most satisfactory. Although neither of us could think of it at the time, there was a very good reason for your holding off on signing the German share transfer document."

There is no Project SEED in Britain, so Isabel and I tried to start one on a small scale. For years many of our academic friends in London have been at University College, and at the end of 1993 Willie Motherwell became professor of organic chemistry there, moving from Imperial College where he was one of the best and most caring teachers. We agreed to fund four bursaries for three years at University College for students from areas with predominately poor traditions of higher education. The college planned to invite about fifty students to a two-day summer school in order to get to know them before awarding the bursaries. Unfortunately plans for 1993 were changed, the "summer school for sixth formers" was reduced to one day—which was filled up almost completely with chemical demonstrations, lunch, tea and biscuits—and there was hardly time to get to know the students, only forty of whom turned out. Five applied for bursaries and three were awarded. In 1994 fifty-two students attended the two-day summer school, which we hope will result in more applications. If this project proves successful by 1995, we plan to fund it fully and encourage other urban universities in Britain to join the scheme.

In 1966 Marvin and I had set up the Bader Klitsner Fund of the Milwaukee Jewish Community Foundation with gifts of Aldrich (and later Sigma-Aldrich) stock. Along with the Helen Bader Foundation, this fund has financed many educational projects in Israel. We also supported a co-educational Jewish high school in Milwaukee, wondering how such a school would have helped David and Daniel if only it had been in existence at the time, but money alone could not assure success. Some right-wing orthodox rabbis in Milwaukee strenuously objected to a co-ed school, and it failed after struggling for eight years.

My roots are in the Czech Republic, a victim of geography if there ever was one. The Czechs are a down-to-earth, hard-working people. Under Thomas Masaryk, Czechoslovakia was one of Europe's most democratic countries with a high standard of living. We have tried to help Czech students in chemistry and art history, but surprisingly it has not been easy.

In art history, we suggested a travelling fellowship of $15,000 for a student to study any baroque artist anywhere for six months. We did not know how to fund such a fellowship in perpetuity nor whether it would really work, so we pledged $15,000 a year for three years. In the first year, 1993, only two art historians applied. The younger was chosen, a man of 41 with an established position at the Institute of History of Art in the Czech Academy of Sciences, who used the funds to look at paintings in museums in western Europe. We met him and found him to be a caring, thoughtful man who appreciated the travel grant, but of course the purpose of the fellowship was to help students. Our communication had been through Dr Milena Bartlova, a young and very able art historian who had been offered a Bader Fellowship from the Institute of Fine Arts in New York, but had not been allowed by the Communists to leave because she was not a member of the party. We had met Milena and her mother, the late Rita Klimova, years before, and knew what thoughtful people they were. After the velvet revolution, Rita had been the country's first ambassador to the United States. Clearly the fellowship for 1993 had been inadequately advertised. Milena then recommended that the $15,000 fellowship might best be changed into three $5,000 awards, so in 1994 seven students applied and three were selected. If that success rate continues in 1995, the only problem remaining will be the funding in perpetuity. Western institutions know how to do this; Czechs do not—yet. Luckily we met the staff of the Charter 77 Foundation, now called the Foundation for a Civil Society, who are dedicated to helping Czechs and have shown us the way.

To help Czech chemists, we adopted a two-pronged approach. One was to set up four fellowships in perpetuity, at Columbia University, Imperial College, the University of Pennsylvania and Harvard University, to enable graduate students to get their PhDs in organic chemistry.

The first of these was at Columbia, which received eight applications. The chosen student is doing so well that Professor Turro told me with a smile that if the department could get many such Czech students, it might forgo Americans! There is no fear of that, because, sad to say, there are not enough Czech students! Imperial College only had four applications and Pennsylvania had only one applicant, who accepted another fellowship before hearing from them. This is not a problem we foresaw, and it may resolve itself once the first graduates return and talk to other students about their experiences abroad. The fourth fellowship, at Harvard, was only set up in 1994, and the first student has accepted. The success of the fellowships depends on publicity and the return of the students to the Czech Republic. We certainly do not want to encourage a brain-drain.

Our second approach was to encourage chemists within the Czech Republic by establishing an annual award for the best young organic chemist, such as we have set up elsewhere, where chemists are nominated by their peers, and a committee makes the choice. At first, the Czech Chemical Society suggested an elaborate foundation, complete with president, administrator and seven board members—I presume all paid—to hand out the prize of a few thousand dollars! Communist bureaucracy still lingers. Establishing the award in perpetuity presented another problem. Under existing Czech tax law, interest on capital, even for such a foundation, might be taxable, and the Czech Republic has as yet no long-term bonds. Again, we shelved the problem for three years by giving the funds for three one-year awards to the Foundation for a Civil Society, which will give 110,000 Czech crowns to the Czech Chemical Society annually. In three years we hope to figure out a way to set this up permanently.

To follow up all these details is quite a chore, and I understand why the Helen Bader Foundation has a professional staff. Giving intelligently is difficult. I do not mean writing checks to the Salvation Army or Amnesty International, but to new causes.

However, raising funds for established causes can be even more frustrating. Some time in the sixties, the Milwaukee Jewish Welfare Fund, which helps here and in Israel in a sensible and well-organized manner, asked me to become a volunteer fund-raiser. I attended one meeting, which I so disliked that I begged off. Competent men whom I liked and respected sat around a big table and discussed the prospective contributions of others, most of whom I also knew. "So and so gave only $5000 last year, just look at his new home, he can do much better," or "This poor fellow is just going through a divorce and she is taking him to the cleaners, $3000 is out." Such intrusive behaviour, although perhaps necessary for success, was not for me. Asking for donations was even more frustrating. I was asked to approach a friend, a well-to-do pediatrician, yet hard as I tried, I could not raise his contribution beyond $150.

There have been hilarious moments: in 1993 I received an eloquent letter signed by the wife of one of Milwaukee's best known company presidents, asking for a large contribution to Milwaukee's United Performing Arts Fund. With it came a note, enclosed in error, "Dr. Bader is a founder of Aldrich Chemical now Sigma-Aldrich . . . He has significant means! Alfred is an art collector and is not known for his generosity . . . with Isabelle . . . we might get at least Golden Circle." What an unfortunate enclosure; we can live without belonging to the Golden Circle of donors.

Only once did I put considerable effort into raising funds for a cause which I knew was worthwhile and where I could make a difference. Robert Burns Woodward (1917-1979), as I have said earlier, was one of the greatest organic chemists ever, perhaps the greatest. He helped me a good deal during my two years at Harvard, made many suggestions to Aldrich and inspired thousands of chemists. I proposed to the Beckman Center for the History of Chemistry that it mount a Woodward Exhibition while many of his friends, co-workers and students were still alive. You know what happens when you make such a suggestion: the answer is "A great idea, provided that you go out and raise the funds." The minimum was $50,000; double would be preferable. With the help of my good secretary, surely that would be easy. I thought that by writing a few letters, or perhaps even just one, the money would be assured. After all, Bob Woodward had helped many companies and for years headed Ciba-Geigy's Woodward Research Institute in Basel; maybe that great Swiss company would fund the exhibition entirely. I was staggered by Ciba-Geigy's reply, signed by two of their executives, Dr F L'Eplattenier and Dr G Haas:

"We think that Ciba-Geigy from all chemical companies has most contributed to the fact that R. B. Woodward could actually become a 'living monument' by his scientific work and publications during his lifetime. In our opinion it will not further increase his reputation to organize a special exhibition years after his death."

When I shared this astounding nonsense with some of Switzerland's well-known chemists who had also been Bob's good friends, they were as flabbergasted as I was. Professor Prelog made the pithiest comment: "To think that the writer was my PhD student!"

I responded strongly in a letter to Ciba-Geigy:

"Please do not misunderstand: the exhibit will take place whether Ciba-Geigy supports it or not, but for the firm with which Professor Woodward worked so closely to refuse support in this way seems astonishing. This is an exhibition which will be made while many of Professor Woodward's colleagues and students are still alive and can contribute vivid recollections and documents of this remarkable scientist.

"He became a legend in his own day before working with Ciba-Geigy, although it is certainly true that your company supported his research most generously and hoped to accomplish great things with his help. Those who were challenged and inspired by Professor Woodward, the greatest chemist of our time, would consider it not only hurtful, but untrue, that without Ciba-Geigy Woodward would not have become a 'living monument.'

"I am constantly amazed how much in life has its precedent in our greatest book, the Bible. 'And there came a pharaoh who did not know Joseph' (Exodus I, 8)—who did not want to know Joseph, who had saved Egypt from starvation. And there came a management to Ciba-Geigy that did not want to know Woodward."

There was no reply. Stonewalling is practised in Switzerland also. What was even worse, Ciba-Geigy may have influenced the other pharmaceutical companies in Basel against helping. The four major Basel companies, Ciba-Geigy, Roche,

The first response to our "Please bother us" ad.

Sandoz and Lonza, meet in a group called *Kontaktgruppe Forschung* to consider requests for help. For many years I had bought most of Lonza's new products for Aldrich through Dr Peter Pollak, a thoughtful and accomplished chemist, and was confident of his help. Yet he had to write that the group had turned down the request and, "as its weakest partner", he could do nothing. Still, where there is a will there is a way. When we asked Sandoz, its Basel office turned us down, but Sandoz US sent us a handsome contribution.

Thus it was not all frustration, just an eye-opener to corporate giving, and there were some happy surprises. The largest contributions came from the Dreyfus Foundation, American pharmaceutical companies and du Pont, but donations were international, as might be expected, given Woodward's influence worldwide. Four German and two Japanese companies contributed, as well as Ontario Hydro. Some companies, like Polaroid, turned us down, but with good reason: Polaroid had recently made a major gift to Harvard to establish a Woodward Chair. Edwin Land, however, the founder of Polaroid, asked what sum I expected. When I replied that I had written to him personally as Woodward's friend and that $1000 would be great, he sent a check for $2000 by return mail. Among others, the Woodward family and Sarah and Herbert Brown helped personally. The happiest surprises came from individuals.

Finally we raised well over $80,000 and the financial viability of the exhibit "Robert Burns Woodward and the Art of Organic Synthesis" was assured. Arnold Thackray, director of the Beckman Center, assembled an excellent advisory committee that worked hard to assure not just the correctness, but the beauty of the exhibition and of the brochure written by painstaking historians, Mary Ellen Bowden and Theodor Benfey. Some on the committee, Roald Hoffmann, of the Woodward-Hoffmann Rule, Albert Eschenmoser who had succeeded with RBW in the mind-boggling total synthesis of vitamin B_{12}, and Jacques Gosteli, the manager of the Woodward Research Institute, had been among Woodward's closest collaborators. Others had been his students; some, like Gilbert Stork, his contemporaries and close friends; and his daughter, Crystal, added many personal touches. The opening of the exhibition in Philadelphia in April 1992 left nothing to be desired.

Within three weeks in 1992 we attended three wonderful festivals, a celebration for Gilbert Stork on a boat circling Manhattan, another for Herbert Brown's eightieth birthday with a loan exhibition of our paintings at Purdue, and now this gala event for the world's greatest chemist. I realized that, although Sigma-Aldrich wanted to expel me, my friendships with chemists and my work would continue.

23

Dance with the IRS

"The purpose of the IRS is to collect the proper amount of tax revenues at the least cost to the public, and in a manner that warrants the highest degree of public confidence in our integrity, efficiency and fairness," or so an Internal Revenue Service poster states.

One reason for the growth of museums all over America in the last century is that until quite recently donors could deduct the appraised value of their donated art from their taxable income. As a result of the substantial increase in the value of art, many donors have preferred to make gifts to museums rather than incur the income tax payable on sales of their property. While these donations of collectors and estates have made a tremendous difference to the scope and quality of the art in American museums, the practice has undoubtedly led to many abuses, which the IRS has investigated and in recent years has tried to stop.

As an art appraiser I have been involved in local cases. Some years ago, for instance, a Milwaukee industrialist gave a small museum a work valued by an Italian "expert" at $120,000, which the donor deducted from his income. The IRS asked Victor Spark, a well-known New York dealer, and me to appear as the government's witnesses in the tax court trial in Chicago, and we testified that the work had a value less than a tenth of that claimed. When the judge decided on a value of $12,000, I thought he was being rather generous. I have no idea how many over-valuations have escaped the vigilance of the IRS, but certainly museums have benefitted in the long run.

I myself donated many paintings to many museums, and have tried to obtain fair appraisals. My tax returns have been audited regularly, and on one occasion in the sixties, the examiner commented that I was the only donor he had ever encountered whose valuations were lower than those obtained by the government. Silly? Perhaps, but the last thing I needed was trouble with the IRS.

In order to set a more even standard of appraisal of valuable works as well as to avoid costly litigation, the IRS set up an Art Advisory Panel which it describes as "made up of some of the most experienced and widely acknowledged art experts in the United States. Some are major art dealers who have many years of experience in their respective fields . . . Panelists are from the foremost auction houses . . . The others are widely respected scholars and art historians with extensive museum experience." Fairness was assured by this assembly of scholarship and experience. Or so you would think.

My first contact with this panel came as a result of my gift of three old master paintings to Queen's University and one to the Milwaukee Art Museum in 1988. Dr Otto Naumann provided appraisals totalling $113,000.

To me, the most moving of the four is a Dutch *Good Samaritan* (plate 34) painted in the first half of the 17th century. The painting was included in an exhibition of the thirty-six most important pictures I had given to Queen's, which was shown in seven art galleries across Canada during 1989 and 1990. In the introduction to the catalog, I wrote: "And who painted that invitation to kindness, *The Good Samaritan* (cat. 12), a marvel in color, surely Dutch, done early in the Golden Age? A firm attribution would greatly enhance its commercial value, but as it is not for sale, this does not matter. Some day an art historian will have a wonderful time recognizing the artist and publishing the discovery."

Various attributions have been made. Shortly after I bought the painting in the 1970s, Dr Walther Bernt suggested Lambert Jacobsz., a pre-Rembrandtist. Professor Linda Stone, an art historian at the University of Kansas, thought it might be by Jan Lievens. If by Jacobsz., it is one of the best of his works I have ever seen. A French gallery recently had a work by him of similar quality, also a large New Testament subject, but my offer of $60,000 was refused. If *The Good Samaritan* is by Lievens, it must date from his middle period, of which we know little. I loved the painting when it hung in my office and was proud to have it grace the cover of an *Aldrichimica Acta,* and now I am happy to have it among the best at Queen's. When Dr Naumann valued it at $30,000, I told him I just wished I could find a dozen works of that quality at auction; I would be delighted to buy all I could find if I could get them that cheaply. Otto is one of the most honest dealers I know, and mindful of our friendship, he was careful to value it conservatively.

My 1988 tax return was audited in 1991, and the Art Advisory Panel, meeting in October, valued our four paintings at a *total* of $40,000! Of the fifteen members, the two most knowledgeable about old masters, Dr William Jordan, formerly of the Kimbell Art Museum, and Adam Williams, of the Newhouse Galleries, did not attend that meeting. The report, which was signed by Wiley C Grant, the staff appraiser, and Karen E Carolan, the chairwoman of the Commissioner's Art Advisory Panel, contains some of the most preposterous statements about art I have ever seen. *The Good Samaritan* attributed to Lambert Jacobsz. and a comparably beautiful *Jacob's Dream* by Paolo de Matteis were dismissed with the comment: "No public sales of other works by these artists could be located, however, the panelists considered the public and private sales of other large 17th and 18th century paintings of religious subjects by relatively minor artists. The panelists recommend a value of

$10,000 each." It seems to n.e that these two sentences must be a "boilerplate" attached to large works that are considered mediocre by experts who are unfamiliar with old masters. The two old master experts on the panel, Dr Jordan and Mr Williams, must have spent many thousands of dollars on large paintings of religious subjects, buying purely on quality, and must know that some works by Jacobsz. and many by de Matteis appear at auction every year. Auction records on artists are provided on request by the Centrox Corporation whose records show that no less than twenty-seven works by or attributed to de Matteis were sold through large auction houses in 1991-2.

The IRS advised us in July 1992 that we owed $17,522 in additional tax and that we must inform the Regional Director of Appeals promptly if we disagreed. We did indeed disagree, and were visited at home by Gary Haley, a very friendly IRS agent who recommended that we obtain another independent appraisal. George Wachter, the director of Sotheby's Old Master Paintings Department in New York, has had many years' experience of auction sales, and I asked him for an evaluation of the four paintings; his total was higher than Dr Naumann's. Of *The Good Samaritan* he wrote: "The painting . . . is an extremely beautiful picture by a Rembrandt follower . . . I would have no hesitation in estimating this picture for an auction at $35/45,000 and, therefore, would recommend a fair market value of $40,000. This figure is quite a bit higher than Naumann's and much higher than the IRS's."

Jacob's Dream, also in the Queen's exhibition catalog, had been merely "attributed" to Paolo de Matteis; that is, we were uncertain of its authorship, and some experts had suggested Corrado Giaquinto, another excellent Neapolitan artist. I asked Clovis Whitfield, an experienced London dealer specializing in Italian baroque paintings, to determine the artist and provide a valuation. His wife, Irene, who is the world's expert on Corrado Giaquinto, did not believe the *Jacob's Dream* to be by him, so Mr Whitfield discussed the work with Professor Nicola Spinosa, the world expert on de Matteis. When he confirmed it as indeed a fine work by that artist, Mr Whitfield sent me a valuation of $60,000 for the painting.

In August 1992 my attorneys in Milwaukee filed a protest with the IRS, introducing these new valuations. In September we received a letter from Mr Frank J Freimark, an appeals officer of the IRS in Milwaukee, advising us that he had been assigned to our case, and Isabel and I met with him several times to discuss the matter. Mr Freimark is a portly, bearded, friendly man who told us that he knew more about fish than paintings. He was there to help, and indeed he did try. He explained the reasons for the panel's low evaluation and listened carefully to our case, but he could go only so far. He was not even certain that he could persuade the panel to split the difference. He knew what every experienced negotiator knows, that to suggest such a course is a sign of weakness. We certainly would not have agreed to split the difference; we hoped for a refund on the grounds that Dr Naumann's appraisal had been too low. Mr Freimark could only submit all our information to the IRS Art Advisory Service, which in turn would ask the panel to reconsider.

The reconsidered opinion of April 20, 1993 however was much more hurtful than the first. I believe the panelists are overworked. They probably have to look at thousands of photographs, and their first decision could be excused through ignorance or exhaustion. After the presentation of additional material and a second appraisal by respected and knowledgeable dealers, their arguments were even more deeply flawed. In support of their reluctant increase in evaluation from $10,000 to $15,000, they compared *The Good Samaritan* to a truly mediocre work of the same subject by Lambert Jacobsz. in poor condition, which sold at Christie's in New York in October 1990 for $13,200. When he was shown the two photographs, even Mr Freimark had to agree that there is a world of difference between the unbalanced composition of the work the panel used as a comparison and the beauty of the painting at Queen's. Their additional comments about *Jacob's Dream* were even more bewildering: "Subsequent research and conclusions made four years after the valuation date have no bearing on the valuation issue as of December 1988." True, the Queen's catalog and Dr Naumann's valuation "attributed" the painting to de Matteis; it was Professor Spinosa who supplied assurance in 1992. But if I had sent the painting to either Christie's or Sotheby's for auction in 1988, they would have sent photographs to Professor Spinosa and received assurance then. This is a common practice of auction houses. Furthermore, the panelists compared my painting to a mediocre *Jacob's Dream,* not even by a Neapolitan artist, which sold at Phillips in London in April 1987 for $17,000 and increased this valuation also from $10,000 to $15,000.

Hoping to receive a more thoughtful consideration of my case, I wrote to each old master specialist on the panel, protesting the decisions. The only reply I received was from William Jordan who wrote in August 1993 that he knew nothing about the case because he had resigned from the panel the year before. His travel schedule had made it impossible for him to attend the meetings regularly.

When next we met Mr Freimark, he told us he had hoped that Mr Wiley C Grant, the staff appraiser, would vist us, but since our tax liability was now reduced from $17,000 to $13,000, the matter did not justify a trip and he refused to come. No doubt he was pleased not to have to field my criticism.

As I wrote to Mr Freimark: "The second valuation of April 1993 is quite different and much more hurtful—it truly adds insult to injury . . . The panel now has had a chance to look, for instance, at the color illustration of *The Good Samaritan* in the Queen's catalog. And the old master experts on the panel know fully well that George Wachter and Dr Naumann know as much about the values of Dutch paintings and Clovis Whitfield about Italian paintings as any member on the panel. Yet, all they did was to raise the values by only $10,000 . . . On a personal level, I must tell you that I fully understand your predicament. Before and during our meeting, you treated Isabel and me kindly. But at the end you had to say, 'There is just so much I can do.' But in your heart and in your mind, you must know that we are totally right, and if you cannot persuade the panel of that, you are wasting your own and our time. That must be as frustrating for you as it is for us."

In August I received a certified letter of deficiency to which my attorney responded with a petition to the US Tax Court, asking for a re-determination.

During a long phone conversation with Mr Freimark in September, I expressed my regret that Dr Jordan was no longer a member of the panel, because he is an authority on old masters, rather than a New York dealer. Then the thought struck me: how about asking Dr Jordan to arbitrate? I had met him only once, for a few minutes in his museum, and had had no dealings with him. He has an excellent reputation as a scholar and a helpful, good person, and I would gladly rely on his decision. Mr Freimark explained that such a procedure has been used in some cases, and I promised to submit my proposal, that Dr Jordan's fee be split 50:50 regardless of the outcome, that each party submit one position paper only, without rebuttal, and that Dr Jordan's valuation be final and not limited by the valuations claimed by me. After all, if he knew who painted *The Good Samaritan,* he would value it much higher.

Unfortunately Dr Jordan refused to serve. I was not really surprised. No doubt he is a very busy man, but he might well have been in an embarrassing position if he had wished to make a completely different valuation from that of his former associates on the panel. Further consideration brought to mind Ian Kennedy, who had long been George Wachter's counterpart at Christie's in New York until his recent resignation to become a dealer. Mr Freimark put his name forward, and we were later informed that he had accepted the request to arbitrate.

In March 1994 Mr Freimark, Isabel and I met once again, this time with two IRS attorneys who explained the mechanics of IRS Rule 124, on voluntary binding arbitration. The conditions I had suggested were fine, except that the arbitrator must be limited in his appraisals to the values claimed by me.

On October 21 Mr Kennedy submitted his valuation of $93,000 for the four paintings. This was lower than I had hoped, but over twice the panel's original valuation of $40,000. What can we learn from this? I believe the Art Advisory Panel should change its *modus operandi.* It is not right to send out a form statement such as "no public sales (of well-known artists) could be located." Even more serious is the panel's pre-occupation with trivia. Dr Naumann, George Wachter and Clovis Whitfield concentrated on the quality of the works, but were criticized because they had not supplied comprehensive auction records for comparison. The comparisons supplied by the panel were similar in size, but totally dissimilar in quality.

Except for Dr Jordan, who has resigned, the only members of the panel knowledgeable about old masters are New York dealers associated with large galleries, Colnaghi, Newhouse and Stair Sainty Matthiesen. The donor must state the original cost of the painting and the place of purchase, but this information is irrelevant to the value of the painting at the time of the gift and therefore should not be available to the panelists. Each of my four gifts was purchased years ago, very dirty, at less than $10,000, and the beauty of the works was not revealed until they had been cleaned by the best restorers I know. The purchase price has no bearing on the actual value of a painting at any given time. If I had bought the paintings from a gallery in London or New York, I would have had to pay much more, and if the panel had seen those prices, the valuations would have been much higher.

When the panel's valuation is challenged, it should respond factually, with valid comparisons, not with false innuendoes. In its second appraisal, for example, the panel suggested that the information I gave might be untrue, that in fact I might have purchased *The Good Samaritan* at a lower price at an auction in Munich. I had not. I believe that when the panel received George Wachter's fair and reasonable appraisal, it should just have accepted it, blaming overwork for its initial mistakes.

Donors should try to obtain firm attributions before donating their paintings. I relied too much on my belief that the quality of *Jacob's Dream* and *The Good Samaritan* would speak for itself. Appraising is not an exact science. The panel first valued *The Good Samaritan* at only $10,000, Ian Kennedy at $20,000, Otto Naumann at $30,000 and George Wachter at $40,000. Recently Otto Naumann told me that he now believes that it may not even be Dutch, but possibly Bolognese, close to Donato Creti. If that is correct, the valuation would have been much higher. What is most important is that Queen's has a beautiful painting, and when I reread what I wrote in the Queen's catalog, ". . . a marvel in color, surely Dutch . . ." I realize that it is possible to be convinced *and* mistaken. "Some day an art historian will have a wonderful time recognizing the artist and publishing the discovery."

The most important conclusion from this hassle however is that honest taxpayers who donate works of art need not worry. Mr Freimark, or his counterpart in other IRS offices, will treat them fairly, I am sure. To have split the difference in my case would not have been the end of the world, but I enjoyed trying to have the matter settled justly. I hope this report will be educational—to the panel and to prospective donors. I almost look forward to my next meeting with Mr Freimark.

24

Herstmonceux Castle

arly one evening in July 1992, when Isabel and I were returning by
train from London to Bexhill, I noticed an advertisement in the
London *Times*, offering for sale a castle for £5,000,000. It might
have been a bargain, so I asked Isabel whether she wanted a castle. She
glanced at the ad, and her eyes lit up when she saw that it was
Herstmonceux, which she already knew quite well. It was only a few
miles from our home in Bexhill, but no, she wasn't interested—too many
rooms to clean! "Why not look at it, just for a lark?" I suggested. Thus
it came about, after some prompting on my part, that she asked a local
real estate agent, Matthew Garcia, to find out who was handling the
sale. It turned out to be Savills of London, and a few days later Mr
Garcia and two men from Savills showed us over the castle and grounds.
Despite their beauty, they seemed so empty. They needed people to bring
them to life, and we both had the same thought almost simultaneously—
what a wonderful property it would be for Queen's University!

Herstmonceux is a moated castle, some parts of it dating back to the
15th century, but it was largely rebuilt between 1911 and 1935, with
140 rooms on three floors, and a beautiful walled garden. The 530 acre
estate had been the home of the Astronomer Royal and of the Royal
Greenwich Observatory from about 1955 until 1988 when the operations were moved to Cambridge and the Canary Islands. The telescope
buildings are intact. Best of all, it seemed to us, there was a solidly built
67,000 square foot office building just crying out to become a students'
residence. The estate had been purchased for £8,000,000 by developers
who had spent millions more to purchase additional land and to produce
plans to turn it into a five-star hotel and golf course, subject to planning
permission.

Mr Henry Richards, of Savills, told me later that in 1990 Savills and
Sotheby's had joined forces to market the estate. They produced a beautiful brochure, made presentations in Hong Kong and London and
issued press releases in Japan and America. In spite of the suggested price
of £20,000,000, more than twenty parties expressed serious interest. By
the summer of 1990 a major Japanese property company was prepared
to proceed at £25,000,000 and had deposited a substantial sum with
their London solicitors, but during the final negotiations an American
trust offered £35,000,000. Contracts with the American trust were
exchanged within a week, yet despite repeated assurances, their payment

failed to arrive, so the developers went back to the Japanese, who once again agreed to proceed at £25,000,000. Sadly, because of falling property values and the decline of the Tokyo stock market, the Japanese withdrew just days before contracts were to be exchanged in October 1990.

In the summer of 1991, the castle was offered again, now at a suggested price of £15,000,000. Again there was substantial interest, this time from a Japanese university and Tulsa University in Oklahoma, but no firm offer materialized. The developers went into receivership, and the castle then reverted to Guinness Mahon, the bank that had loaned the funds. Guinness Mahon found itself in difficulties and was acquired by the Japanese Bank of Yokohama. What a saga!

The agents who showed us the castle realized that I might be a serious buyer when I asked to see the boilers, which unfortunately were in sad shape. In the previous months many of the potential purchasers had been more interested in impressing their young lady friends than in purchasing a castle. What a bit of luck Mr Garcia had not seen our tiny home in Bexhill, otherwise he, too, might have believed I merely wanted to impress Isabel, and we might not have been shown the castle.

We returned to Milwaukee at the end of July, and on the following day I telephoned Principal David Smith at Queen's University to ask him whether he thought Queen's might like a castle in the south of England. After a long silence, his answer was polite, but there must have been disbelief. Some weeks later the Member of Parliament for Kingston, Peter Milliken, while on a visit to England, went to Herstmonceux and reported most favorably to Principal Smith. In October David Smith himself flew over and he too was as enchanted by the castle as we were.

Luckily, Jane Whistler, a good friend of Mary and David Smith and a Queen's graduate, was living in Bristol, but was very familiar with that part of Sussex. She was persuaded to become the coordinator for Queen's. She already knew many people in the area and was familiar with the intricacies of obtaining planning permissions, which would have to be secured before Queen's could consider acquiring the property. Jane was so tireless in her negotiations with government bodies, heritage committees and planning authorities, as well as the local people, that she made me think of a "Swiss army knife." She could tackle anything, yet is full of charm.

In the middle of November, Isabel and I visited Queen's to discuss the funds they would need to prepare Herstmonceux for use as an international study centre. It was not enough to find the purchase price; it would take at least another £2,000,000 to convert the facilities for students' use. At my suggestion, the Queen's solicitor drafted an agreement binding on us and our estates to provide Sigma-Aldrich shares equivalent to £6,000,000 if Queen's were successful in their bid to acquire the castle. We decided to name the figure in sterling so that Queen's would not be subject to the vagaries of currency fluctuations. I was empowered to negotiate a purchase price.

Later in November I visited Savills in London to discuss it. The first meeting lasted sixty minutes, fifty-eight of which were spent on the question uppermost in their minds: would payment actually be made if all went well? £5,000,000 was now being asked but an offer of £4,000,000 would be seriously considered. However, previous offers which had seemed serious had failed because of the buyers' inability to pay. Could I pay, they wondered? I urged them to check with my bank and with Sotheby's, just around the corner, to whom I had recently paid over £4,000,000 for a Rembrandt.

My next negotiation was with Guinness Mahon. My offer, subject only to Queen's receiving all the necessary planning permissions, was for £3,600,000. That was based on Queen's need for an additional £2,000,000 to refurbish the property and also because I like the figure 36, twice 18, the number *Chai*, life in Hebrew, for Isabel and me. This offer was rejected, but it soon became clear that this was mainly because the bank did not want to take such a substantial loss for the property in one fell swoop, a loss that would appear in their books in one financial year.

The deputy chief executive, Dr Jeffrey Cooper, who was negotiating for the bank, was obviously sympathetic to my desire to have Queen's acquire the castle, and I really liked him. Usually, when you really like a person, the liking is mutual. Near the end of our two-day negotiations I asked Dr Cooper whether he might be a relative of Phyllis Cooper, the freckled girl who would have been my first date in 1940 had I not been arrested as an "enemy alien". "No," Dr Cooper replied, "I have no relatives named Cooper. My father's name in Hamburg was Cohen, which he changed to Cooper when he came to England." No wonder we had got on so well. He was a *Landsmann!*

We eventually agreed on the price for the castle with much of the land, and in addition were given a two-year option for a farm included in the property, and two five-year options for two parcels of land which Queen's might or might not want. Some of that was land that had been acquired by the developers after they had bought the castle estate, probably to extend their prospective golf course. I was suffering from a cold on the second day of our intense negotiations, December 9, and was relieved when after my eighteenth cup of tea I was able to dictate our understanding to Dr Cooper's secretary. The bank accepted that one-page contract without change, except for the addition of one paragraph, stating that the purchase price should not be divulged. Queen's had sent me a power of attorney, so I signed for them, and Dr Cooper for the bank. I naively thought that the worst of the negotiations were over.

Back home in Milwaukee, matters proceeded smoothly. Initially, I gave Queen's 150,000 Sigma-Aldrich shares. The stock price held firm for a while despite announcements that Tom Cori and Peter Gleich had sold some stock, and Bill Schield, our stockbroker at Baird, had no problems selling 100,000 shares without depressing the market. He began selling options for the remaining 50,000 shares. He was certainly not "betting against the company," but merely trying to maximize the gift. The pound weakened, which helped, and Queen's had the funds for the purchase long before all the planning permissions were received and the contracts were finally exchanged with the bank in August 1993.

None of us foresaw how difficult it would be to get permission from all the various British planning authorities for Queen's to use Herstmonceux as an international study centre. One of the most lengthy negotiations was with the local district council, but approval by all the committees concerned finally came through on June 22, 1993. Nor had we realized what a hassle it would be once the lawyers started to draw up a detailed agreement based on the binding one-page contract of December 9. Had lawyers been present then, I doubt if we would have signed any contract on that day or even that month. The final 68-page document left all the provisions of the December 9 contract intact, except to limit confidentiality of the selling price to December 31, 1993, and it was signed in Kingston on August 24. Contracts for castles, like babies, take nine months.

In December 1992, during the week of my intense negotiation with Guinness Mahon in London, my friend, Ralph Emanuel, had taken me to a talk by Chaim Potok, the well-known Jewish writer. I had told Ralph about Herstmonceux, and as we sat down he said, "You have done so much for Queen's already, why so much more?" I was temporarily speechless, and thought of the old saying that two Jews can always agree what a third should give to charity. During his talk, Potok described how he had gone to Korea as an American soldier, become acquainted with some Koreans and—for the first time in his life—been treated just as an American, not as a Jew. The Koreans knew nothing about the Jewish problem. It had been like this with me at Queen's. For the first time in my life I was being treated completely fairly, as just another human being. Jean Royce, Art Jackson, Norman Miller, William McNeill—all went far out of their way to help me. I encountered an odd form of anti-semitism—if you can really call it that—only once. In 1944 I had been elected president of the Queen's Hillel Foundation, and we began posting notices about our meetings around the campus. Principal Wallace called me into his office and told me that this had to stop. Queen's had nothing against the Hillel Foundation, he said, but if Hillel could post notices, so could the Newman Club, and that just would not do. Not very long after that a Catholic, John Deutsch, became principal of Queen's, and a very good principal at that, I thought. Later, Catholics and Jews—including myself—became members of the University's Board of Trustees. Queen's and Canada were getting even better.

I may not have been able to convince Ralph that Herstmonceux was a wonderful gift to a great university, but Isabel and I had no doubts. As Isabel has often remarked, many Canadians tend to be almost insular, and to help thousands of Canadian students to study at Herstmonceux with British students and those, we hope, from many other parts of the world will be our dream come true. We hope that it will become a truly international centre. We expect too that Queen's will help both the local community in Herstmonceux and the university at Falmer. During our visit in December 1992, there was talk of closing the last local bank, the National Westminster in Herstmonceux, but with hundreds of students and academics, one branch may not be enough!

By the time we reached England in May 1993, it seemed virtually certain that Queen's plans for an International Study Centre at Herstmonceux would be approved. British-born Dr Maurice Yeates, previously Dean of Graduate Studies and Research at Queen's, had already been appointed its executive director. The castle grounds, which had been closed to the public for the past five years, were reopened at the end of May. The Queen's alumni in England had arranged for a dinner and ball in our honor to be held on Saturday, July 10, and for a medieval pageant and fayre to mark the official reopening of Herstmonceux on Sunday and to raise funds for student scholarships.

On that Saturday evening, Principal Smith and I spoke briefly. I outlined how Isabel's and my love for both England and Queen's had led us to make the gift and explained that this was the realization of a dream.

Our sons David and Daniel, David's wife Michelle and her parents, and Isabel's sister Marion and her daughter Margaret, over from the States and Canada, were there to share our happiness. We had a ball, literally and figuratively.

Promptly at 11 am on Sunday, the horse-drawn landau brought David and Mary Smith, Dr Agnes Benidickson, the university's chancellor, Isabel and me up to the bridge leading to the castle. Armored knights awaited us, and I was handed a medieval ceremonial sword with which to cut the ribbon. It was the first time I had ever used a sword. All sorts of fun events followed: knights in combat, morris dancing, falconry, pipe bands, croquet and cricket, tours of the telescopes, hot air balloons. We planted a Canadian maple tree and then, in the afternoon, took part in a very moving service of thanksgiving. Each minister from the area participated as did Mary Smith, herself a minister, and I also spoke briefly. It seemed appropriate for me to quote Jeremiah IX, "Let not the rich man glory in his riches," although clearly we were glorying in having helped make this event possible.

In a way, we have been able to give "their castle" back to the people of the area. In 1994 Queen's was able to take up the options for the three additional parcels so that now there are over 500 acres around the castle. People can visit once again, and the future will show what develops from our gift to the university.

It is up to Queen's. Almost everything in England costs more than in Canada, and for a year or two there will be financial strains, particularly as government grants to universities have been cut in Canada. But the castle adds a new dimension to life at Queen's, providing studies in European politics, economics, law, art and perhaps astronomy and physics aided by the telescopes. The castle is bound to become a center for meetings and conventions from all over Europe. We have been given lifetime passes to enter the castle—and we will enjoy that greatly.

Whenever I have contemplated any achievement in my life, I have marvelled how many and how diverse are the people who have made it possible, and where Herstmonceux is concerned, there were so many. I think for example of Matthew Garcia, who helped us to take the first steps; of the understanding Jeffrey Cooper; of Jane Whistler, with her keen grasp of the local problems; and of David Smith, with his infectious enthusiasm. Paradoxically, we also owe something to Tom Cori, because without my dismissal we would not have had the funds to give to Queen's. If ever there was an illustration of the old saying about every cloud having a silver lining, this is it!

The only slight cloud has been Isabel's reluctance to be in the limelight, really to have any publicity whatever. But how can you give a castle to a university and not have some publicity? If we had tried to withhold our names, reporters would have ferreted them out—easy, when so many people have to know. I am again reminded of Job: "Shall we take the good from God and not the bad?"

The one serious problem posed by such a gift is the challenge: what can we do for an encore? But with Isabel's vision, and if the Lord gives us time, we will find other great things to do with our money, which we neither want to use for ourselves nor can take with us.

Index